When Things Fall Apart
Qualitative Studies of Poverty
in the Former Soviet Union

When Things Fall Apart
Qualitative Studies of Poverty
in the Former Soviet Union

Edited by
Nora Dudwick, Elizabeth Gomart, and
Alexandre Marc, with Kathleen Kuehnast

Foreword by
Ravi Kanbur

THE WORLD BANK
Washington, D.C.

Chapter 10 reprinted, with changes, by permission of the Office of the United Nations High Commissioner on Refugees (UNHRC).

ISBN 0-8213-5067-6

Cover photo: Kathleen Kuehnast
Design: Naylor Design, Inc., Washington, DC

Library of Congress Cataloging-in-Publication Data
When things fall apart: qualitative studies of poverty in the former Soviet Union / edited by Nora Dudwick, Elizabeth Gomart, Alexandre Marc.
    p. cm.
    Includes bibliographical references and index.
    ISBN 0-8213-5067-6
1. Poverty—Former Soviet republics. 2. Former Soviet republics—Economic conditions.
I. Dudwick, Nora., 1949- II. Gomart, Elizabeth, 1967- III. Marc, Alexandre, 1956-
HC340.P6 W46 2002
339.4'6'0947—dc21

                                                                    2002024162

Contents

Foreword

There are three interrelated reasons why this book is to be welcomed: attitudinal, methodological, and political.

By attitudinal I mean that the book departs from the normal perspective of analysts in the international agencies and elsewhere, from seeing poverty in terms of dry statistics to seeing it in terms of human experience. Much of the analysis of poverty has been deeply technocratic in its orientation. There is nothing wrong with this, except when it becomes the exclusive focus. It is important to take a dispassionate view of the causes and consequences of poverty, and to gauge the broad trends through reliable statistics. But the motivation for attacking poverty has deeper wellsprings. It comes from the human connection to the experiences of others—from the instinctive feeling that, but for the grace of God, those experiences could be ours. Listening directly to the voices of the poor, unmediated by national statistical offices, is an important part of establishing this connection.

By methodological I mean that qualitative methods in poverty analysis complement the more standard quantitative techniques that international agencies have used to great effect. There is a misconception among quantitative analysts that qualitative analysis is "soft" and without rigor. Nothing could be further from the truth. As the papers in a forthcoming conference volume I am editing have established, quantitative analysis often has only the appearance of hardness.[1] And as shown both there and in this book, anthropologists and sociologists have high methodological standards, too. Moreover, this is not an either-or issue. Poverty analysis needs both quantitative and qualitative methodologies if it is to be complete and comprehensive, and each can help the other. This book demonstrates convincingly the insights that qualitative analysis can bring to standard quantitative analysis.

By political I mean relevance to policy, and this encapsulates the methodological and the attitudinal. I have often found that policymakers' suspicions of technical analysts stem from a feeling that they, the policymakers, inhabit the real world whereas the analysts do their work in some other world, one without real people. Some of the policy prescriptions that we analysts offer are dismissed, because a policymaker can see the difficulty of implementing them in a real world of real people with real feelings and real responses to the policy. The tension between the real world of policymakers and the more abstract world of analysts is a healthy one, provided each group learns from the other. This requires analysts as a community to be more aware of real people, and this book is an important contribution to that process.

The former Soviet Union is fertile territory in which to explore the inter-action between qualitative and quantitative analysis. The high expectations of the transition from central planning—ironically, a system that was driven by a seemingly rational and quantitative logic—have clearly not been met. The debate over why what happened, happened will no doubt continue. But what did happen affected real people, and this book documents their stories. In doing so, it illuminates some of the causes of poverty and some of the reasons why the transition has had such devastating effects in terms of poverty. One may hope that, in combination with more standard quantitative analysis, the qualitative analysis presented in this book can help policymakers design better the next phase of the transition.

Ravi Kanbur
T. H. Lee Professor of World Affairs and Economics
Cornell University

---

1 *Qual-Quant: Qualitative and Quantitative Poverty Appraisal: Complementarities, Tensions and the Way Forward, Proceedings of a Conference Held at Cornell University, March 15-16, 2001,* edited by Ravi Kanbur. New Delhi: Permanent Black Publishers. Forthcoming. Available online at www.people.cornell.edu/pages/sk145/papers/QQZ.pdf.

Acknowledgments

This volume has been many years in the making. The earliest study reported here was carried out in 1993; the most recent was completed in 1998. It was in 1999, however, that the editors first discussed gathering these studies into a single volume. There are many people whose contributions over this long gestation we wish to thankfully acknowledge.

First, we thank the members of the research teams that made each of the studies possible. Many of them were already trained in the social sciences or were graduate students; the remainder came from a range of disciplines and occupations: medicine, social work, teaching, journalism, law, or nongovernmental organizations. Some had worked with poor people before; others were deeply shocked by what they learned about their own country. Without their intelligence, willingness to work long hours in uncomfortable conditions, and serious commitment to the task, these studies would not have been as compelling as they are.

Several colleagues have provided feedback at different stages of the process. Deniz Kandiyoti (School of Oriental and African Studies, University of London) and Michael Woolcock (World Bank) peer-reviewed the collected chapters and provided detailed and incisive comments on each. Kathleen Kuehnast (Institute for European, Russian, and Eurasian Studies, George Washington University) provided extensive input on the volume as a whole, contributed to the introductory chapters, and, very important, inspired the title of the collection as well as those of several individual chapters. Meg Wilder provided early editorial support during the painful process of converting long reports to shorter chapters. Kim Kelley provided patient and hands-on guidance through the final publication process. And the authors are particularly indebted to Michael Treadway's sensitive and meticulous editorial input for the final stage of revisions. We are grateful for funding received to help this undertaking from the team that produced the earlier World Bank publication, *Making Transition Work for Everyone: Poverty and Inequality in Europe and Central Asia*. We would also like to thank Kevin Cleaver, former Sector Manager, Environmentally and Socially Sustainable Development, Europe and Central Asia Region (ECSSD), for his strong support throughout the long publication process, and Laura Tuck, current sector manager of ECSSD, for her strong support during the final phase of publication. The Office of the United Nations High Commissioner for Refugees (UNHCR) commissioned an earlier version of the chapter on the Crimean Tatars—and kindly granted permission for its republication.

Perhaps the final paragraph should be reserved for the people whose experiences and perspectives we have tried to capture in this volume. The people we interviewed throughout the eight countries covered in this volume responded graciously, generously, and forthrightly, providing a rich and nuanced commentary on their own lives and on the changes under way in their societies. To the extent that this volume contributes to our knowledge of poverty in the former Soviet Union, it is due in huge measure to the willingness of poor people to talk about their lives.

About the Authors

Hermine G. De Soto is a senior social scientist at the World Bank in the Social Development Unit of the Europe and Central Asia Region. She earned her doctorate in social and cultural anthropology at the University of Wisconsin in 1988. She has taught anthropology at the University of Wisconsin-Madison and held research appointments in the Women's Studies Program and Women's Studies Research Center, and at the Center for Eastern Europe, Russia and Central Asia at the University of Wisconsin-Madison. She was also a research scholar at the Humboldt-Universität zu Berlin and at the Bauhaus in Dessau, Germany. Her recent publications include the co-edited volumes *Culture and Contradiction: Dialectics of Wealth, Power, and Symbol* (1992), *The Curtain Rises: Rethinking Culture, Ideology and the State in Eastern Europe* (1993), and *Fieldwork Dilemmas: Anthropologists in Postsocialist States* (with Nora Dudwick, 2000), as well as "Reading the Fools' Mirror: Reconstituting Identity Against National and Transnational Politics" (*American Ethnologist*, 1998) and "Contested Landscapes: Reconstructing Community in Post-Socialist Saxony-Anhalt" (in Martha Lampland, Daphne Berdahl, and Matti Bunzl, eds., *Altering States: Ethnographies of Transition in Eastern Europe and the Former Soviet Union*, 2000). Since joining the World Bank in 1999, she has conducted social assessments and studies of rural development and poverty in Albania, Kazakhstan, the Kyrgyz Republic, Moldova, and Tajikistan. Current activities include developing associations for poor women and children in Tajikistan and cultural centers for the Roma, an ethnic minority group in Albania.

Nora Dudwick is a senior social scientist at the World Bank in the Social Development Unit of the Europe and Central Asia Region. She received her doctorate in anthropology from the University of Pennsylvania in 1995; her research there focused on nationalism and historical memories in independent Armenia. Since joining the World Bank in 1996, she has organized and carried out qualitative research studies of transition and poverty in Albania, Armenia, Georgia, Latvia, the former Yugoslav Republic of Macedonia, Moldova, and Ukraine, as well as studies on the social impacts of transition on rural life, education, and social structure. Recent publications include an edited volume, *Fieldwork Dilemmas: Anthropologists in Postsocialist States* (with Hermine G. De Soto, 2000) and several articles: "Political Structures in Post-Communist Armenia: Images and Realities" (in Karen Dawisha and Bruce Parrott, eds., *Conflict, Cleavage and Change in Central Asia and the Caucasus*, 1997), "Out of the Kitchen, Into the Crossfire" (in Mary Buckley, ed., *Post-Soviet Women: From Central Asia to the Baltic*, 1997), and "Independent Armenia: Paradise Regained or Lost?" (in Ian Bremmer and Raymond Taras, eds., *New Politics, New States: Building the Post-Soviet Nations*, 1997).

Elizabeth Gomart received her master's in international affairs from the Columbia University School of International and Public Affairs. She worked in Armenia for Save the Children (SCF) US in 1994 and 1995. There she conducted qualitative research for a joint USAID-SCF humanitarian strategy and community development program. Since 1996 she has worked as a social scientist for the World Bank and the Office of the United Nations High Commissioner on Refugees in Eastern Europe (Crimea). She has designed and carried out over a dozen qualitative poverty assessments, sectoral assessments (education, health, small business development), and program evaluations in the former Soviet Union (Armenia, Moldova, Tajikistan, Ukraine, and Uzbekistan) and the Caribbean (Dominica, Haiti, Saint Kitts and Nevis, and Saint Lucia). She has also conducted a qualitative participatory evaluation on client perspectives for a Washington-based social service organization. She is a member of the Washington-Baltimore Center of the A. K. Rice Institute and operates an organizational consulting practice for U.S. nonprofit and social service organizations.

Kathleen Kuehnast is a research associate at the Institute for European, Russian, and Eurasian Studies at the George Washington University. She received her doctorate in cultural anthropology from the University of Minnesota in 1997, where her research focused on the politics of gender ideologies in the transition in the Kyrgyz Republic. She has conducted poverty studies in Central Asia for the World Bank and the Asian Development Bank; these resulted in several co-authored books and various articles, including *Women and Gender Relations: The Kyrgyz Republic in Transition* (with Armin Bauer and David Green, 1998) and *A Generation at Risk: Children in the Central Asian Republics of Kazakhstan and Kyrgyzstan* (with Armin Bauer and David Green, 1997). She is the recipient of IREX, Wenner-Gren, Social Science Research Council, and other research grants and fellowships, including most recently a Mellon Foreign Area Fellowship at the Library of Congress, where she researched the topic of "Islam and the New Politics of Gender Ideologies in Central Asia." With Carol Nechemias she is co-editing a volume, *The Role of Women in the Post-Soviet Transition*, for the Kennan Institute of Advanced Russian Studies.

Alexandre Marc holds a doctorate in political economy from the Institut d'Etudes Politiques de Paris. Before joining the World Bank in 1988, he conducted research on Africa at Oxford University and performed consulting work on economic and social development for the Société d'Etudes Economiques et Sociales in Paris. At the World Bank he has worked in the Social Dimensions of Structural Adjustment Unit, assessing impacts of structural adjustment on the poor in Africa. He subsequently designed social mitigation and social investment programs in Africa, the Middle East, and Central Asia and conducted studies on the design of such programs to better reach the poor. After joining the Human Development Department of the World Bank's Europe and Central Asia (ECA) Region, he managed projects in health, education, and social protection. In 1999 he became manager of the ECA Social Development Unit. Consisting of 15 social scientists, the team focuses on local institutions, social inclusion, and conflict prevention, as well as the integration of social development concerns into World Bank programs in ECA.

Catherine Wanner is an assistant professor in the Department of History and the Religious Studies Program at The Pennsylvania State University. She received her doctorate in cultural anthropology from Columbia University in 1996. She has written articles on poverty and the role of social networks in mitigating poverty, the emergence of new forms of community in post-Soviet society, and migration and immigration. Her first book, *Burden of Dreams: History and Identity in Post-Soviet Ukraine* (1998), was based on ethnographic research into the rise of nationalism in Soviet Ukraine and on how the nationalist paradigm influenced cultural politics after the collapse of the Soviet Union. Her forthcoming book, *Communities of the Converted: Religion and Migration After the Fall of the Soviet Union*, focuses on the resettlement in the United States of refugees and recent immigrants from the former Soviet Union. She has been the recipient of grants and fellowships from the National Endowment for the Humanities, the Social Science Research Council, and Fulbright-Hays. Since 1995 she has been an independent consultant to the World Bank, conducting and overseeing research on a variety of projects relating to transition and poverty in Ukraine.

COUNTRIES OF THE FORMER SOVIET UNION

An ethnic Russian pensioner in Bishkek, Kyrgyz Republic sells her personal and household belongings in a public park.
Photo by Kathleen Kuehnast

---------------------- ✳ ----------------------

Introduction:
A Qualitative Approach to
Understanding "New" Poverty
in the Former Soviet Union

When the World Bank first became actively involved in the countries of the former Soviet Union (FSU) close to a decade ago, it embarked on a program of poverty assessments. These assessments were intended to deepen the understanding of the Bank and of the client governments of the roots and characteristics of poverty in these countries and to provide a more informed basis for designing policies and programs to improve living standards. This volume reports findings of qualitative studies of poverty in a selection of former Soviet republics, as well as some shorter studies of specific sectors, programs, and populations, all but one of which have been undertaken by the Bank since 1993. (The exception is the study of the Crimean Tatars in Ukraine in Chapter 10, which was conducted for the Office of the U.N. High Commissioner for Refugees.) The chapters cover Armenia, Georgia, the Kyrgyz Republic, Latvia, Moldova, Tajikistan, Ukraine, and Uzbekistan. The omission of the other countries of the FSU reflects only the fact that the Bank had not yet conducted large-scale qualitative poverty studies there when this volume was planned.

The fundamental nature of the changes under way in the FSU, including changes in attitudes and perceptions, called for an approach that could illuminate and enrich the data derived from quantitative poverty surveys. The

---

The original studies excerpted in this book can be accessed at www.worldbank.org/eca/poverty/ compendium.

studies undertaken in response to this need, many of which are presented in this volume, use qualitative methods such as in-depth interviews, focus group discussions, and some participatory rapid appraisal methods. Chapter 2 describes the methods used and addresses some of the methodological issues they raise.

The studies in this volume highlight certain aspects of the dynamics of poverty in the FSU and its interaction with gender, age, and ethnicity. They deepen the understanding of how poor people in these countries experience, explain, and cope with their new circumstances; the studies also identify the range of cultural and administrative barriers that hinder poor people from accessing public services and exploiting economic opportunities. Above all, they highlight important psychological dimensions of poverty in the FSU, including the collapse of values and beliefs that accompanied the increase in poverty and the resulting disorientation experienced by the poor. Finally, the studies demonstrate the continuing importance of informal support networks and the persistence of paternalistic relationships and expectations that the old regime had fostered.

When the centrally planned economies of the Soviet Union collapsed in 1991, many people both inside and outside of these countries optimistically assumed that, with the right policies, they would rapidly transform themselves into successful market economies and participatory democracies. Indeed, these dramatic political changes created new opportunities, gave voice to many, and provided the population with grounds for hope. The rapid collapse in production, however, led to a dramatic surge in poverty (see Table 1). Reversing this trend has proved extremely difficult. For large segments of the population, success in reestablishing macroeconomic stability has not translated into better living standards. It is now clear that positive change depends on success in reforming institutions, a daunting task that may take many years.

Along with the collapse in production and the spread of poverty, the gap between rich and poor has rapidly increased. Although some FSU countries have experienced positive economic growth in the last few years, it does not appear to have meaningfully reduced poverty. As the opening paragraph of a recent World Bank report on poverty notes:

> In 1998, one of every five people in the transition countries of Europe and Central Asia survived on less than US$2.15 per day. A decade ago, fewer than one out of twenty-five lived on less than US$2.15 per day. While these estimates are at best an approximation given serious data deficiencies, there is little doubt that absolute poverty has increased dramatically in the region. Moreover, the increase in poverty is much larger and more persistent than many would have expected at the start of the process. (World Bank 2000, p. 1)

Table 1. Incidence of Poverty in the Former Soviet Union, by Country

Country	Survey date	Percent of population living on	
		$2.15 a day	$4.30 a day
Tajikistan	1999	68.3	95.8
Armenia	1999	43.5	86.2
Moldova	1999	55.4	84.6
Kyrgyz Rep.	1998	49.1	84.1
Azerbaijan	1999	23.5	64.2
Georgia	1999	18.9	54.2
Russian Fed.	1998	18.8	50.3
Turkmenistan	1998	7.0	34.4
Latvia	1998	6.6	34.8
Kazakhstan	1996	5.7	30.9
Ukraine	1999	3.0	29.4
Lithuania	1999	3.1	22.5
Estonia	1998	2.1	19.3
Belarus	1999	1.0	10.4

Note: Recent survey data were not available for Uzbekistan. Private consumption data were not available for Tajikistan, Turkmenistan, or Kazakhstan. GDP per capita in current prices is used instead. Private consumption data for Azerbaijan and Lithuania are for 1998; GDP per capita (first half of 1999) is used for Ukraine. Because of errors related to survey design and implementation, poverty may be overestimated for some countries and underestimated for others.

Source: World Bank (2000).

Poverty in the FSU has unusual features that distinguish it from poverty elsewhere; these features have implications for the choice of policies and programs to alleviate it. A weaker link between poverty and lack of education than in other parts of the world, for example, reflects the relatively high level of education achieved by most Soviet citizens. Similarly, poverty and unemployment are correlated more weakly than one would expect, because much of the labor force remains employed but receives very low wages, which are often paid late or irregularly.

For many of the poor in the FSU, material standards of living, including housing and access to municipal services, remain better than in developing countries with the same level of GDP per capita. This is not surprising given the Soviet state's heavy investments in social and economic infrastructure. Today, however, the inability of poor households to contribute to maintaining this inheritance and the failure of governments to maintain infrastructure and provide services are worsening living conditions and contributing to the deterioration of valuable assets. Likewise, higher fees combined with demands for informal payments for services are serious barriers that often prevent poor people from accessing municipal and social services.

The deepening and persistence of poverty since the collapse of the Soviet Union have contributed to a profound shift in values and in people's perceptions about economic and social reality. Unlike in poor countries elsewhere in the world, poverty in the FSU struck people who had been well integrated into their society. For the most part, the newly poor had enjoyed secure employment, access to basic services, and a sense of stability. Serious shortages of consumer goods and the intrusiveness of the state in everyday life were balanced by this sense of predictability.

All these changes have taken place in the context of a sweeping restructuring of state and society. Former citizens of the Soviet Union suddenly found themselves living in new nation-states that are fundamentally redefining the identity of their populations. This reordering of state and nation has created difficulties for new minorities as well as given rise to armed conflicts, which have greatly increased poverty and distress. In the context of such ideological, political, and social disruption, the hardships of poverty in the FSU have been accompanied by symptoms of enormous social stress. These include increases in suicide, alcoholism, drug abuse, and crime and violence; the breakdown of families and the abandonment of children; and stress- and trauma-related illnesses that have contributed to heightened mortality rates. These issues appear with depressing regularity in the qualitative poverty assessments in this volume.

Finally, increased poverty and weak institutions have severely weakened social cohesion and integration, putting some groups at serious risk of exclusion. Elderly people living on their own, female heads of households, the disabled, refugees and displaced persons, and some ethnic, linguistic, and religious minorities are finding themselves gradually excluded from many informal networks of solidarity or support at a time when deteriorating public services make such support essential for survival.

The rest of this book is divided into five parts. Part One consists of chapters on methodology and key findings. Chapter 1 discusses the rationale for using qualitative methods to link the experience and perception of poverty to the behavior and attitudes of the poor and describes how researchers applied these methods in the post-Soviet context. Chapter 2 identifies some of the most dramatic impacts of impoverishment on the perceptions, attitudes, coping strategies, and social patterns that have taken place over the past decade in the countries studied.

Each of the remaining four parts of the volume is devoted to a specific region of the FSU. Part Two consists of poverty studies from the Kyrgyz Republic (Chapter 3) and Tajikistan (Chapter 4) and excerpts from a study of small businesses in the Karakalpakhstan and Khorezm regions of Uzbekistan (Chapter 5). These three countries share many features of their history and culture, but there are also significant social and economic differences among them. Tajikistan, which had been the poorest Soviet republic, is now the poorest of the FSU countries. Its population has suffered from civil war, displacement, and widespread destruction. The resource-poor Kyrgyz Republic experienced a serious collapse of GDP after independence. Its population is extremely poor, and inequality is rapidly increasing. Although richer in natural resources, Uzbekistan has been more reluctant to introduce economic reforms and continues to impose an autocratic style of government on its citizens.

Part Three includes studies on poverty and access to social services in Armenia (Chapters 6 and 7) and a study of poverty in Georgia (Chapter 8). These countries are notable for their high level of educational achievement, the entrepreneurial spirit of their populations, and their strong sense of national and cultural identity. Yet the collapse of productive and trade links with other parts of the FSU left these countries, which had been tightly integrated into the Soviet Union, in a state of severe collapse. Ongoing violent conflict and large-scale population displacement have deepened poverty in both countries.

Part Four includes two poverty studies from Ukraine (Chapters 9 and 10, the latter being a special study of Crimea's indigenous Tatar population) and one from Moldova (Chapter 11), which also contains excerpts from a study on rural reforms there. Although distinguished by vast differences in size and population, the two countries share a border as well as a similar degree of difficulty in reforming agriculture and industry. Poverty in Moldova has steadily increased since the Soviet collapse, turning it into one of the poorest countries in the region despite its rich agricultural land.

Part Five presents the case of Latvia, the richest country described in this volume. Like the other Baltic countries, Estonia and Lithuania, Latvia was less integrated into the Soviet economy, and it preserved some of the market traditions it had enjoyed before annexation to the Soviet Union during World War II. Although its reform-minded government has introduced important structural changes, deep pockets of poverty and despair persist in this relatively prosperous country.

Taken together, these chapters offer new insights into how poor people in the former Soviet Union understand and cope with the host of predicaments in which they find themselves. The authors hope that this volume will contribute to an increased appreciation of the important sociological, psychological, and existential dimensions of poverty in these countries.

Reference

World Bank. 2000. *Making Transition Work for Everyone: Poverty and Inequality in Europe and Central Asia*. Washington, D.C.

———— ✳ ————

PART ONE

BACKGROUND

A woman in the Goris district of Armenia sheaves grain from her family's farm.
Photo by Nora Dudwick

---- ✳ ----

CHAPTER 1

A Window
on Social Reality:
Qualitative Methods in
Poverty Research

Recent years have seen an increasing consensus among development specialists that poverty is a multidimensional phenomenon that is not adequately captured by measurements of income or expenditure. Broadening the concept of poverty to include vulnerability, social isolation, insecurity, and voicelessness, however, has increased the demand for a broader range of qualitative and quantitative methods, particularly in countries undergoing rapid change, where the usual concepts and categories for measuring poverty are in flux.

Since the mid-1980s the World Bank has relied primarily on its Living Standards Measurement Surveys (LSMS) and Priority Surveys to measure poverty at the household level. The LSMS provides detailed household-level information ranging from measures of consumption, income, and expenditure to the use of health and educational services. The Priority Survey is based on the same methods but uses shorter questionnaires and larger samples. In the mid-1990s, in the countries of the former Soviet Union (FSU), the Bank began implementing the LSMS to replace the Soviet-era household budget panel surveys, incorporating additional sectoral modules, which varied depending on the country.

The need to use qualitative research tools to complement the LSMS is particularly pressing in societies in transition from socialist central planning, where the rapidity of change and the dearth of information about the direction of change or the extent of local variation can seriously undermine the reliability of the usual categories and definitions that such surveys employ. This chapter identifies some of the comparative advantages and some of the limitations of qualitative and quantitative methods for poverty research; discusses relevant issues of representativity, generalizability, and validity; and finally, describes how qualitative methods were employed in the studies in this volume.

Characteristics of Qualitative Methods

Most social scientists concur that the dividing line between qualitative and quantitative research methodologies is far from rigid, and that poverty research should ideally integrate both (Carvalho and White 1997; Kandiyoti 1999). Hentschel (1999) argues that it may be more useful to analytically separate "methods" from "data," since qualitative methods (such as observation) may yield quantifiable data, such as the number of people attending a given event, and quantitative methods (such as the LSMS) may provide insights into qualitative issues, such as household relationships or political participation.

A key characteristic of qualitative methods is their focus on understanding human behavior in its social, cultural, political, and economic context. Within this framework, studies that use ethnographic and participatory methods, as well as longitudinal village studies carried out in a single community, can be more "contextual" than large-scale household surveys, even when the latter are adapted to the particular country in which they are administered. Contextual methods that take account of local perceptions, norms, and practices may be more difficult to generalize to an entire country. On the other hand, depending on the care taken in selecting sites and respondents, they can produce findings with significant implications for policy (Hentschel 1999).

Despite general agreement that understanding local perceptions and practices is important for designing sensible policies, qualitatively oriented researchers differ from quantitatively oriented researchers in how they evaluate the validity of their findings. Validity must be considered in relation to the specific objectives of qualitative research. Although most qualitative researchers avoid extreme positivist assumptions about "objective reality," they do assume a shared social understanding of reality against which the *descriptive validity* of an account can be evaluated. Whether the research is quantitative or qualitative, the validity of the account can stand or fall according to the training, competence, and integrity of the interviewers. The objective of accurately representing people's experiences and perceptions also raises the issue of *interpretive validity,* which researchers often try to address by grounding their accounts or narratives in the actual words and concepts of the people studied, and submitting their report to the community for feedback before making it public. (See Maxwell 1992 for a useful description of validity in qualitative research.)

Another frequent reservation about qualitative research concerns its *generalizability.* Much qualitative research is not intended to lead to findings that can be immediately applied to a wider population (*external generalizability*). For the most part, generalizability in qualitative research involves the use of case studies to develop a theory about how observed social processes can make sense of similar persons or situations. On the other hand, *internal generalizability*—the extent to which one can make accurate inferences from limited data, such as an interview—is very important in qualitative research (Maxwell 1992).

Perhaps the more relevant issue, however, is designing qualitative tools that can elicit data that meet the specific needs of policymakers. Designing local or regional policies, for example, generally requires greater understanding of local values and expectations and social norms and networks, all of which qualitative methods are designed to elicit. Large-scale surveys may be more appropriate for generating the kind of data necessary for policymaking at the country level. Yet even here, qualitative studies that include diverse sites and households or individuals representing a broad range of personal and social characteristics can complement quantitative research by generating hypotheses, by explaining anomalies or unexpected trends, and by illustrating how different aspects of poverty come together in concrete cases.

Because qualitative research often involves smaller samples than quantitative surveys, it generally makes use of purposive rather than probability or random sampling. Done well, purposive sampling allows the research to include sufficient variation in the phenomena under study (Maxwell 1992, p. 293); of course, done poorly, purposive sampling can introduce considerable bias into the findings. Although qualitative research sometimes makes use of probability sampling, it often focuses on analyzing the behavior of outliers to understand why they deviate from the usual pattern (Bamberger 2000, p. 10).

Both qualitative and quantitative methods are only as good as the instruments used and the interviewers who use them. Because qualitative methods are inherently flexible, and their data analysis is less systematized than that for quantitative research, their success in providing valid and useful findings depends perhaps even more heavily than that of quantitative methods on the interviewing and reporting skills of the interviewers, as well as on the analytical skills of the lead researchers.

How Do Qualitative Studies Complement Quantitative Surveys?

Qualitative and quantitative methods can complement each other in a number of ways, depending on how they are sequenced. Qualitative methods can be used to develop hypotheses, refine the design of quantitative surveys, or explain anomalies in quantitative findings. Quantitative methods can be used to determine the extent to which qualitative findings can be generalized to larger populations. Spalter-Roth (2000, p. 48) suggests that research intended to influence social policy ideally includes both *numbers*, to define the scope and patterns of a problem, and a *story*, to illustrate how the problem manifests itself in daily life and to evoke empathetic understanding.

Qualitative research can allow the individual subjects themselves to challenge and revise the categories of inquiry. The LSMS and other quantitative poverty surveys use closed-ended, prepared interview questions to which people respond by choosing among a set of limited, precoded answers. The design and objectives of such surveys preclude the possibility of interviewees contextualizing or qualifying their answers or taking issue with the way in which a question or a choice of answers is formulated. Although this type of research design may not pose significant problems in countries that have been studied for a long time, it can undermine the accuracy of data in such volatile and poorly understood regions as Eastern Europe and the FSU. Preliminary qualitative work can therefore complement quantitative survey methods by providing more context-sensitive formulations.

For example, local strategies for circumventing Soviet-era registration laws, along with adaptations to recent poverty, have affected the very composition, definition, and function of "households" in a way that can make responses to questions about household income, expenditure, and decisionmaking extremely unreliable (Kandiyoti 1999). Patterns of employment are important for devising poverty reduction strategies, but the very definition of "employment" is now at issue in these countries. Qualitative research has demonstrated that many people who are engaged in informal or private sector activities respond to questions about their employment status by describing themselves as "unemployed," not because they are hiding information, but because they equate "real" employment with state sector employment.

Qualitative methods allow subjects to introduce issues about which researchers may be unaware. In Eastern Europe and the FSU, for example, where deep and widespread poverty is a recent phenomenon, many of the newly poor feel profound humiliation and shame at a predicament once associated only with the most marginal and dysfunctional members of society. Understanding this experiential aspect of poverty has become important for analyzing why people respond to their situation the way they do. By giving interviewees the freedom to introduce new issues, qualitative methods complement the extensive data produced by surveys such as the LSMS with information on the range of innovative and unusual strategies that people use to cope with poverty.

A strength of qualitative methods is their ability to shed light on the relationships between different behaviors as well as on issues of causality, because they encourage people to explain the reasoning that goes into their own decisionmaking and strategizing. In this way qualitative methods are a practical complement to quantitative methods, in which asking "why" questions often yields responses that are too general or superficial to be useful (Kozel and Parker 2000, p. 61; Chung 2000). Qualitative methods are essential for getting at issues of process and the nitty-gritty details of *how* people pursue and achieve their goals or overcome obstacles.

Because of the relatively smaller sample size and case study methodology, qualitative approaches can encourage the delicate probing often necessary to move to the more complex reality that may underlie the informant's initial response. In the post-Soviet context, understanding why many people were reluctant to leave their state sector jobs even when their salaries were months, even years, in arrears was at first a baffling issue. In-depth interviews that probed for motivations found that people often remained at work because of nonsalary benefits, such as the social status and self-respect associated with their position, and because their work collectives continued to be an important source of information and informal social support.

Qualitative methods provide a contextualized description of attitudes and behaviors that help in understanding why and when people respond to certain events or circumstances in an unexpected way. For example, extended family networks and a strong ethos of reciprocity among relatives can obscure the reasons that some elderly people or families do not benefit from such assistance. Open-ended interviews in Armenian villages, for example, revealed that although people asserted that they would never let a member of the community starve, they were less likely to give assistance to needy elderly people who had adult children, on the grounds that it was the responsibility of the children to support their parent. Likewise, certain people—in one case, a disabled couple who had married and had children—were seen as "undeserving" of assistance and therefore were allowed to fall into deplorable conditions.

Qualitative methods can also complement quantitative survey methods by eliciting information on behaviors that violate social norms or laws (including unusual domestic arrangements, prostitution, stealing state property or using it for private business, bribe taking, smuggling, and narcotics use and sale). Obtaining such information depends in part on purposive sampling, which benefits from personal introductions or already established relations of trust between interviewee and interviewer, from careful choice of "expert" informants, and, most important, from the rapport and trust that can build up in the course of an interview that is only minimally structured, lasts several hours, and takes place in the home. Such interviews have produced significant information about different forms of corruption, including the role of "connections" in obtaining access to valued resources or information.

The Assumptions and Tools of Qualitative Methodologies

Qualitative methods rest on the assumption that reality is socially constructed through ongoing communication and negotiation within communities or groups, and therefore that every member of the community possesses important local knowledge. Because social reality and "local knowledge" are constantly evolving through this ongoing process (an example of which is how local mores evolve in response to outside influences or economic pressures), it is more realistic to assume that there will never be complete agreement within a community about "reality," but instead a range of opinions and judgments. This assumption about the nature of reality and knowledge strongly shapes qualitative methodology. Purposive sampling also allows the researcher to construct a better picture of local social relations, by selecting further respondents on the basis of a given interview.

Another important assumption underlying the studies in this volume is that perceptions are important because they influence behavior. Because the short-term, applied nature of poverty research does not allow for extended participation in and observation of host communities, qualitative poverty studies often rely on teaming outsiders, who are less prone to take local practices for granted, with insiders, who may share local concerns, understand culturally appropriate ways to approach communities and pose questions, and can interpret responses in ways that make sense to outside researchers. Local interviewers are in a good position to probe, because they are better able than outside researchers to identify responses that appear incomplete, ambiguous, contradictory, or evasive. They are also better positioned to share information about their own experiences and perceptions as a means of increasing rapport and stimulating a freer exchange of information. Insiders are also more able to judge the relative social position of a household. For example, an outsider might not even notice the brand of a television set in a home, whereas local interviewers are often able to relate the brand of an item (such as a more or less expensive or even an imported model) to the relative social status of a household in a particular community.

The most important methods employed by the studies in this volume include discussion, particularly in the form of semistructured individual, household, and "expert" interviews. The semistructured nature of the interview loosely directs the conversation to issues central to the research but allows informants opportunities to raise new issues, or even to challenge the very assumptions underlying particular questions. Even the order in which an informant addresses issues can provide useful data regarding his or her relative priorities. Household interviews provide a wealth of data on how different household members experience or cope with poverty. Moreover, observations of interactions among family members or with neighbors often provide information about the psychological or social ramifications of poverty (including lack of privacy or the presence of domestic tension) that respondents may be unwilling or even unable to discuss. They are also a rich source of data about intrahousehold and intrapersonal dynamics and the norms that govern, for example, relations between the sexes or between generations.

Whereas each qualitative interview provides a window on social reality, information from additional individuals (or groups, or households, or other units of analysis) further enriches understanding of this social reality. Thus, although qualitative researchers distinguish between "expert" informants (people assumed by virtue of their formal or informal position or job to have a broader than usual understanding of a particular issue) and ordinary individuals or households, in qualitative research every informant is implicitly considered an "expert" in describing and interpreting his or her own reality. In addition, local specialists or socially recognized experts are often able to provide a broader or more analytical, even if locally rooted, perspective on a given topic.

Qualitative interview methods encourage flexibility and allow researchers to reflect upon their observations and use their intuition to question (but not argue with) interviewees' responses and delve beneath their surface.

Focus groups, which often group people according to an important social characteristic presumed to shape their views (such as sex, age, educational level, or occupation), are useful for rapidly assessing and characterizing group-specific interests, needs, and concerns. Focus group discussions can reveal the parameters of an issue and raise new concerns. Finally, the very process of dispute and negotiation during discussions provides information about how much diversity exists (or is tolerated) within a given social group or community.

Careful observation and description of interviewees' housing, furniture, and living conditions, their clothing and general appearance, and the social interactions that take place during the interview act as an important validity check. They can significantly add to, corroborate, or in some cases cast doubt on what people say about how they are coping with different dimensions of poverty. Researchers' observations are enriched by the fact that people often respond to the qualitative interview, which resembles a spontaneous discussion rather than a question-and-answer session, as a social occasion. Interviewers in these studies were frequently offered coffee or tea and sometimes invited for meals. These provided even richer opportunities to observe the extent to which people were able to live up to basic social expectations about hospitality, or, conversely, the extent to which poverty had reduced their ability to interact socially.

How Qualitative Research Methods Were Implemented in These Studies

Open-ended interviews (with individuals, households, and local or international experts), focus group discussions, and observation were the key data-gathering methods used in the studies reported in this volume. In most cases the principal researcher prepared an interview guide based on her background knowledge of the country and regions in question. These guides outlined the areas of inquiry—perceptions of poverty, access to health and education services, the role of nongovernmental organizations (NGOs), and so forth—as well as key issues for each. After discussions with local researchers, these guides were revised and translated into the appropriate language.

Although interviewers were asked to address certain specific issues considered relevant for the particular interviewee, they were given a free hand to change the order and emphasis of questions and to decide how much detail to probe for. Interviews were particularly useful for obtaining detailed and concrete accounts of people's experience, as well as linking their behaviors to the particular strategies they devised. Since these studies focused on the relationship of perception and practice rather than on opinions, researchers were encouraged to probe on issues most relevant to respondents, and where they were likeliest to draw upon their own experiences. Given the unwillingness of many people in the FSU to share their personal experiences of poverty or the details of their coping strategies in front of their peers, the researchers found focus group discussions most useful for eliciting attitudes toward certain aspects of poverty, general experiences with social service delivery, and opinions about reforms under way. Findings from these discussions were then used to revise the interview guide, ensuring that all of the relevant issues raised were pursued in greater depth during the individual and household interviews.

Key informant interviews were carried out with local specialists with relevant professional experience or experience in working with the poor. Key informants included hospital and school directors, local religious leaders and NGO activists, journalists, economists, local officials, and in some cases entrepreneurs. Interviews with representatives of international donors and NGOs also proved useful, since the perspectives of outsiders who were knowledgeable about the local situation often shed new light on certain phenomena, or simply offered information about which local people were unaware.

All of the studies relied on purposive sampling. The aim was to focus primarily or exclusively on poor people while including a range of household types, a balanced representation of ages and of both sexes, a wide range of educational backgrounds and professions, and a representation of major ethnic, linguistic, and religious groups. For national poverty studies, sampling was also stratified according to geographic sites, which were chosen to include as much diversity as possible in environmental conditions, level of urbanization, kinds of livelihood strategies, social and cultural practices, and proximity to roads, markets, and borders, as well as particular local conditions, such as ongoing conflict or recent natural catastrophe. Although the researchers made the initial selection of sites, they usually consulted with local officials to confirm the final choice. Several studies deliberately included communities where quantitative surveys had recently been carried out, so that findings could be compared and integrated.

Researchers selected individual and household respondents by combining sources and methods, including lists of persons receiving social assistance, identification by officials or other informants, and limited use of random selection (within selected neighborhoods or buildings) to ensure the inclusion of representatives from major categories potentially relevant to the study objectives. Each research team was responsible for achieving this balance, often beginning by meeting with local town hall or social service officials, who were able to provide them with names of families known to be poor. Interviewers generally followed up by "snowball sampling": asking interviewees to suggest the names of people even poorer than they.

In countries with sizable ethnic and linguistic minorities, care was taken to ensure they were represented among the interviewers, to facilitate rapport with minority interviewees. For interviews in Georgia's South Ossetia region, for example, interviewers were recruited locally so that they would have credibility among local officials and the population. In the same study, interviewers who spoke Armenian were used to carry out interviews in regions predominantly inhabited by ethnic Armenians. Interviewers were also encouraged to write their reports in the language they felt most comfortable with.

All the studies relied extensively on the knowledge of local interviewers to guide the choice of sites, to follow appropriate protocol when approaching officials or potential interviewees, and to complement information obtained directly from interviewees with their own observations. Because most Soviet research in social issues had relied on large-scale surveys, however, it was difficult to find interviewers trained in qualitative methodologies. As a result, research teams were recruited from a variety of disciplinary backgrounds and then received classroom and field training in interviewing techniques and report writing. In many cases the outside researcher accompanied the interviewers into the field for a considerable part of the fieldwork itself and participated in daily debriefing sessions designed to think through and modify or add questions in response to findings. The studies in Armenia, for example, were carried out by ethnographers with considerable interviewing experience, although their previous focus had not been on contemporary social issues. In the other studies, interviewers included sociologists, journalists, and members of local civil society organizations, as well as teachers, doctors, and other professionals.

The authors of the studies prepared the final synthesis and analysis of the data collected, working either from individual interview reports or syntheses of interviews from each site. Working hypotheses were discussed at different stages with professionals within the country, and in most cases the final draft was submitted to them for further comments. The authors believe the studies succeed in providing an interpretive account of how a diverse group of poor people in a given country experienced and coped with poverty. The studies also highlight trends, patterns, motivations, and dynamics that account for findings or anomalies from other kinds of studies, including quantitative poverty studies, and make sense to policymakers and other clients. As with any research, the validity of the final reports rests significantly on the competence and conscientiousness of the researchers, as well as on the use of data from a variety of other sources to confirm or disconfirm hypotheses and conclusions.

References

Bamberger, Michael. 2000. "Opportunities and Challenges for Integrating Quantitative and Qualitative Methods." In Michael Bamberger, ed., *Integrating Quantitative and Qualitative Research in Development Projects.* Washington, D.C.: World Bank.

Carvalho, Soniya, and Howard White. 1997. "Combining the Quantitative and Qualitative Approaches to Poverty Measurement and Analysis: The Practice and the Potential." World Bank Technical Paper 366. Washington, D.C.

Chung, Kimberly. 2000. "Issues and Approaches in the Use of Integrated Methods." In Michael Bamberger, ed., *Integrating Quantitative and Qualitative Research in Development Projects.* Washington, D.C.: World Bank.

Hentschel, Jesko. 1999. "Contextuality and Data Collection Methods—A Framework and Application to Health Service Utilization." *Journal of Development Studies* 35(4): 64–94.

Kandiyoti, Deniz. 1999. "Poverty in Transition: An Ethnographic Critique of Household Surveys in Post-Soviet Central Asia." *Development and Change* 30: 499–524.

Kozel, Valerie, and Barbara Parker. 2000. "Integrated Approaches to Poverty Assessment in India." In Michael Bamberger, ed., *Integrating Quantitative and Qualitative Research in Development Projects.* Washington, D.C.: World Bank.

Maxwell, Joseph. 1992. "Understanding and Validity in Qualitative Research." *Harvard Educational Review* 62(3): 279–300.

Spalter-Roth, Roberta. 2000. "Gender Issues in the Use of Integrated Approaches." In Michael Bamberger, ed., *Integrating Quantitative and Qualitative Research in Development Projects.* Washington, D.C.: World Bank.

The closure of preschools and milk kitchens in Central Asia
has long-term consequences for this Kyrgyz child.
Photo by Kathleen Kuehnast

✳

CHAPTER 2

From Soviet Expectations to Post-Soviet Realities: Poverty During the Transition

T he studies in this volume cover eight countries, each with a distinctive pre-Soviet history and culture. Carried out at different times in each country during the volatile and fast-changing period between 1993 and 1998, the studies are not strictly comparable. Rather, for each country they document a particular moment in the emergence and institutionalization of poverty. Poor people throughout the world share many concerns, as recent World Bank studies of poverty demonstrate (see, for example, Narayan and others 2001, Narayan and Petesch 2002). Yet for most, poverty has long been a fact of life, and the meaning of "poverty" and "the poor" are clearly defined and articulated in their understandings. By contrast, in the former Soviet Union, except for the older generation who lived through World War II, the massive and sudden impoverishment witnessed after the collapse of the Soviet state is unprecedented. Thus, in these countries, poverty itself and the way in which people interpret it have undergone a dramatic transformation in less than a decade.

This chapter highlights three moments in this transformation. During the first years following the Soviet collapse, because of shared material conditions, practices, and ways of interpreting the social world, people throughout the former Soviet territory reacted to impoverishment in strikingly similar ways. Over time, however, differences in the ways in which these new countries have approached the task of nation and state building, differences in legacies of resources and assets, and differences in social and cultural traditions called forth increasingly differentiated individual and household responses to poverty. By the late 1990s, serious poverty, along with coping mechanisms initially thought to be temporary or deviant, had become a normal aspect of everyday life.

Responding to the Shock

Between the 1960s and the 1980s, the standard of living of Soviet citizens had steadily improved, and the remaining serious poverty remained hidden in prisons, labor camps, long-term care hospitals, and residential institutions for children, the elderly, and the disabled. During the 1980s, however, inflation, unemployment (particularly in Central Asia), continuing consumer shortages, and increased rationing of items such as sugar and butter forced Soviet citizens to rely more heavily on extensive informal networks and the shadow economy to obtain necessary goods and services. Nevertheless, the state continued to convey the strong ideological message that poverty reflected individual rather than societal failure. Poverty as a social phenomenon was depicted as a feature of capitalist rather than socialist societies.

When the economic collapse occurred, however, it spared no social group, with the exception of the top political and economic elite, who were able to convert power over resource allocation into ownership of important assets. Although the newly poor came from all walks of life, they had in common the fact that they (or at least the overwhelming majority) had been employed, housed, and socially integrated into their communities before the collapse. They also shared many ideological convictions: that the state should provide full employment, free education and health care, and a wide array of social supports, and that it should prevent the emergence of huge economic inequalities.

Accustomed to strong official and public disapproval of poverty, most respondents in the studies reported in this volume resisted describing themselves as poor, instead saying they were "living on the edge of poverty" or "just making ends meet." Even those living in the direst conditions tried to identify others who were even worse off. Or they responded to questions about who in their community was poor by asserting, "We are all poor." Occasionally, respondents acknowledged that they found it too painful to admit even to themselves that they were indeed poor.

Bewildered at finding themselves in such a shameful predicament, people groped to understand the reasons. Generally, people blamed their own poverty on the failure of the Soviet state and the corruption, indifference, and incompetence of their new leaders. At the same time, however, they often attributed the poverty of others to individual failure, such as laziness, alcoholism, having too many children to support, or having too few children to provide for their old age.

Although cynicism about labor relations had been widespread during the Soviet period—"we pretend to work and they pretend to pay us"—work had nevertheless played a central role in the lives of most Soviet citizens. Employment had provided a socially recognized position and status, and "work collectives" had served as important networks for exchanging information and favors of all kinds. Having lost jobs or positions from which their status and income derived, people who had once enjoyed respect and authority in their communities simultaneously lost material security and self-esteem.

Many respondents reported depression, even suicidal feelings, resulting from their multiple losses: loss of employment and social position; loss of confidence and self-respect; loss of opportunities to participate in social, cultural, and intellectual life; and, most profoundly, a lost sense of stability and predictability that had previously allowed them to plan their future. Striking differences emerged in the way men and women responded to impoverishment. Women, perhaps because they had multiple identities as workers, wives, and mothers, were able to adapt more successfully to the loss of formal employment than did men, whose social identity was more tightly bound to their role as worker and breadwinner. Unemployment thus contributed to a deep sense of emasculation, which intensified already-existing patterns of self-destructive behavior.

Poor men and women expressed feelings of shame and guilt for failing to fulfill ritual and social obligations, and of depression at their exclusion from social and ceremonial life. At the same time, because formal and informal socializing remained essential for cultivating support networks and exchanging information, poor people felt increasingly abandoned in their hour of need. They described the rich and the poor as increasingly inhabiting separate worlds, with the poor fighting for survival and the rich fighting to protect their wealth.

Initially, people responded to their sudden loss of income, savings, and services by building on and expanding strategies already in place during the Soviet period. When reducing consumption, pilfering from state-owned industrial or agricultural enterprises, or finding cheaper alternatives did not suffice, people sold furniture, appliances, clothing, jewelry, and cars. In some cases they sold centrally located apartments, bought cheaper housing in poorly served urban outskirts, and lived off the difference. People also borrowed extensively, in some cases becoming so indebted to professional moneylenders that they were forced either to surrender apartments they had unwisely offered as collateral or to go into hiding.

Where garden plots had once been used to supplement diets, subsistence gardening and farming became important survival strategies, even in urban areas, where people continued to work for the state sector while commuting to villages or planting small gardens next to their high-rise apartments. Rural inhabitants relied almost exclusively on their own production, both for consumption and, in the absence of cash, to exchange for manufactured goods and services.

People experimented with small, informal enterprises, including money-lending, financial speculation, petty commerce, provision of skilled services, and artisanal production. When the poor attempted to expand into formal entrepreneurial activity, however, complicated administrative procedures and the corrupt and exclusionary practices of local officials often proved insurmountable. People with more effective personal networks were better able to overcome these obstacles, while those without the right connections were pushed out of business. Similar problems confronted people employed in the emerging private sector, where lack of formal contracts made them vulnerable to harassment, summary firing, and late or partial payment.

Men, especially, revived old traditions of labor migration, and the Russian Federation became the most important destination for men working in construction as well as for highly skilled professionals. The practice of returning from organized tourist trips abroad with suitcases full of scarce, foreign-produced commodities to sell expanded rapidly into an international "shuttle trade." Women, in particular, moved into this arena, ignoring the low social estimation of commerce as "speculation." Women sought service sector jobs locally and abroad as housekeepers, nannies, and waitresses. Some engaged in prostitution locally, in new urban brothels, or abroad.

For most respondents, income poverty was worsened by the failure of the state to honor what they considered its basic responsibility: provision of low-cost or free services. A once-comprehensive social safety net and a host of subsidies shrank to minimum levels. Access even to those services that remained was often inhibited by application procedures that were complicated, inconsistent, or humiliating. For example, deteriorating public health practices, undernutrition, lack of heat, poor hygiene, and stress contributed to increased illness even as access to affordable and reliable health care radically diminished. Demands for formal and informal payments put essential medical care out of many poor people's reach. As a result, the poor increasingly resorted to self-treatment, home remedies, or faith healers, avoiding the formal health care system until illness or injury became life-threatening or chronic.

Respondents were angry and bewildered by their governments' failure to meet traditional responsibilities, and they felt that this failure violated basic tenets of social justice they had internalized during the Soviet period. Many suspected government officials of exploiting the political and economic turmoil for their own gain, at the expense of ordinary citizens. Indeed, many suspected that anyone who had managed to become rich during this period of widespread impoverishment must have done so through illicit activities. Yet most respondents believed their governments should and eventually would reassume their previous responsibilities of providing jobs, low-cost housing, and utilities and maintaining affordable prices for consumer goods.

The Normalization of Poverty

Poverty as a mass phenomenon had been seen as an aberration in the Soviet period. Ten years later, however, street children, "bag ladies," beggars, and refugee camps, as well as the poverty that manifests itself in the deterioration of dwellings and public buildings, in the spread of contagious illness, and in crowded social assistance offices, had become commonplace. If, 10 years ago, the newly poor expected that the government would eventually restore their jobs and benefits, by the end of the decade it had become clear that they could no longer depend on the government for help. A significant underclass of poor has emerged, and reduced access to good education, health care, and social services has created conditions for its perpetuation.

Increasingly excluded from the old, overlapping social networks of colleagues, friends, neighbors, and kin, the newly poor drew such support as they could from those who were equally impoverished. Others moved into clientistic relationships with the new elite, where the absence of legal recourse made them vulnerable to severe exploitation. The newly poor felt their voices no longer mattered, and they found themselves cut off from the previous last resort: appealing to Moscow for protection against local abuses of power. As a result, cynicism about the interest or ability of the government to respond to their needs, and lack of confidence in their own ability to create change has contributed to passivity and voicelessness among the poorest of the poor.

The lack of adequate social safety nets and legal protections, together with the weakening of old support networks, has made even the nonpoor vulnerable to impoverishment. Knowledge that job loss, crop failure, a health crisis, or a legal problem could easily push a struggling household over the edge has created a pervasive sense of insecurity. Particularly among the poor, insecurity and social isolation have increased the level of alcohol and drug abuse. Especially in countries such as Ukraine and Latvia, where heavy alcohol use was entwined with a host of cultural practices, alcoholism has become one of the most serious social ills, throwing many families into dire poverty and contributing to the dramatic increase in male mortality. Although alcohol has traditionally played a less significant role in Tajikistan, Uzbekistan, and the Kyrgyz Republic, in those countries a growing narcotics trade has resulted in greater drug use among the population.

Short-term responses to hardship have gradually evolved into longer-term strategies for surviving the harsh new conditions. For example, criminal organizations have transformed prostitution into large-scale trafficking of women and girls for the sex trade with Europe and the Middle East. Not only has drug use increased throughout the region, but large-scale narcotics trafficking has successfully recruited poor people, including women and youths, from impoverished mountain regions in Central Asia to produce and transport drugs. The largely institutionalized corruption of the socialist period has expanded and diversified, often taking on violent forms, and often severely restricting the ability of those who are poor and marginalized to move out of the shadow economy.

This striking reorganization of social relationships and the collapse of formal and informal institutions of inclusion have undermined the ties with neighbors and communities that once linked people to each other. Although the ideology of social justice still resonates among the poor throughout the formerly socialist countries of Europe and Central Asia, the dominant theme of these emerging market economies is one of unfettered individualism. The economic and political changes of the last decade have given new opportunities and freedoms to people in the former Soviet Union like those enjoyed in the West, but they have also brought them closer to the West in terms of social ills: increased inequities and new forms of social and economic exclusion and alienation.

References

Narayan, Deepa, Meera Shah, Patti Petesch, and Robert Chambers. 2001. *Crying out for Change* (*Voices of the Poor* series, volume 2). New York and Washington: Oxford University Press and World Bank.

Narayan, Deepa, and Patti Petesch, editors. 2002. *From Many Lands* (*Voices of the Poor* series, volume 3). New York and Washington: Oxford University Press and World Bank.

———— ✳ ————

PART TWO

THE KYRGYZ REPUBLIC, TAJIKISTAN, AND UZBEKISTAN

The *Kyrgyz Republic*, with a population of 4.8 million people, is a mountainous country with abundant water but few exportable natural resources besides gold and hydroelectric power. During the Soviet era, cultivation of sugar beets was central to the agricultural economy in the north. In the southern oblasts of Osh and Jalal-Abad, silk and tobacco were key agricultural products. With a tradition of nomadic pastoralism, the Kyrgyz were first introduced to agriculture by the Russians in the early part of the 20th century. Unlike their Uzbek and Tajik neighbors, whose cultural lives have centered around Islam since the 10th century, the Kyrgyz converted to Islam from their shamanistic beliefs only in the late 18th century. After 1991 the Kyrgyz government embraced the people's Islamic and nomadic roots but also advocated democratization and marketization. By 1993, however, impoverishment was increasingly evident. Unemployment and a lack of market opportunities for the majority (65 percent) rural population have pushed an estimated 51 percent of the population into poverty.

Tajikistan is one of the poorest countries in the world and has the lowest income per capita of any country in the former Soviet Union. Its legacy of poverty dates from the Soviet era. With a civil war raging on and off between 1992 and 1997, Tajikistan has had a difficult time in its economic recovery, and the poverty rate among its 5.9 million people currently hovers around 93 percent. A small, mountainous country with borders on Afghanistan, China, Uzbekistan, and the Kyrgyz Republic, Tajikistan has long had a significant relationship with Russia, on which it relies to help maintain security at its southern borders. But today the Russian Federation provides little economic support, and Tajikistan depends largely on exports of cotton and a few other agricultural goods, which amount to only $120 million a year. With salaries in Tajikistan averaging only about $10 a month, the outlook for the future is bleak.[1] During the Soviet era the capital city of Dushanbe was considered one of the most Europeanized and cultured centers in Central Asia, partially because of the many Russians exiled there by Stalin. Devastation by war and a dearth of economic opportunities have triggered a major emigration of non–Central Asian ethnic groups. With ongoing strife in Afghanistan, Tajikistan has experienced a surge of Afghan refugees in the last five years, which has added another burden to its fragile government. The country has also become a crossroads for drug and arms trafficking.

Uzbekistan, recognized as one of the most powerful Central Asian states, has experienced its own share of difficulties over the past decade. With a largely rural population of nearly 28 million people, the country has attempted to navigate through the transition with its abundant oil resources and dependable cotton production. By contrast with the Kyrgyz Republic, its economy is still highly centralized. The poverty rate is rising and is estimated at 35 percent. With a highly arid climate, water shortages and scarcity of arable land are becoming increasingly volatile issues, not only internally but also with its neighbors Kazakhstan, the Kyrgyz Republic, and Tajikistan. The Uzbek government has traditionally resisted outside influences, and did so even during the Soviet era. Today it is viewed as one of the more authoritarian of the post-Soviet states.

Exchange rates

Kyrgyz Republic: $1 = 17.7 som (April 1998)
Tajikistan: $1 = 754 Tajik rubles (1998)
Uzbekistan: $1 = 81.32 sum (February 1998)

A nomadic Kyrgyz mother poses with her child.
Photo by Kathleen Kuehnast

※

CHAPTER 3

Poverty Shock:
The Impact of Rapid Economic
Change on the Women of the
Kyrgyz Republic

Kathleen Kuehnast

The qualitative study reported in this chapter was conducted between August and October 1993, with the intention of identifying groups of women vulnerable to the effects of the transition in the newly independent Kyrgyz Republic. The study examined the various coping mechanisms these women employed during the early years of the transition. It was among the first qualitative studies of poverty in the former Soviet Union executed under the World Bank's direction, and the qualitative forerunner to the Kyrgyz Poverty Monitoring Survey, a quantitative study conducted in the fall of that year.

Proud of their newfound independence from the Soviet Union and seeking to be a part of the global economy, the citizens of the Kyrgyz Republic instead found themselves in 1993 confronted with erratic inflation, a breakdown of social supports and economic infrastructures, deteriorating living conditions, and a growing problem of poverty. An already difficult situation was made more serious when, in May of that year, a new national currency, the som, was introduced. Inflation soared, and shortages of the new currency left many banks without reserves to pay monthly benefits or salaries. A year later many people living in the rural regions of the country had yet to see the new currency, salaries were months in arrears, and the economic process of "market shock" had turned into the experience of "poverty shock."[1] Those first affected by the economic transition included the newly unemployed, pensioners, the disabled, households with large families, and students who had relied on government subsidies to further their education. Women were especially vulnerable to the economic uncertainties of the transition, because they found themselves without the state supports and benefits that had constituted an important social safety net. Women came unexpectedly to the realization that they were on their own: the government and even their once-dependable social networks could no longer provide the needed daily support to help them run their households, especially child and eldercare supports.

Surviving Change

The women and girls of the Kyrgyz Republic make up 51 percent of a population of 4.5 million. They are multiethnic, the majority are literate, and the average woman has at least three children. Although some have embraced the decade of change with optimism, many have found themselves in a hopeless predicament. Despite differences among them, several common features are evident: the vast majority continue to maintain a strong work ethic as well as a deep commitment and daily orientation toward assisting their immediate and extended families.

According to the women interviewed in this study, the gap has widened dramatically between their recollection of the familiar social assistance programs of the former command economy and their expectations of the yet-nascent market economy. In their own words, women expressed the view that they were the first to be affected by the economic changes, because they were typically the first to lose their jobs. They were also the first to deal with the lack of child care, because many of the government-supported kindergartens and child care centers had been closed. Because women in this society are the primary caretakers of both the young and the old, they were also the first to experience the implications of the lack of medicine and medical assistance, and the first to struggle with the daily decision of whether to buy milk or meat when their small and irregular incomes could not keep up with rapid inflation. Because women were dealing directly with the collapse of the socialist system's supports, it comes as no surprise that women were also the first to inititate self-help programs and to engage in the new nongovernmental organizations being formed to assist those in a more desperate position than themselves.

Some women found such changes in their everyday lives not only difficult but indeed insurmountable. The most common problems cited were economic in nature: lack of jobs, low salaries, terminated benefits, high prices, unfair privatization, and an inability to buy necessities. The elderly, the unemployed, mothers with many children, and young rural women were especially vulnerable. They lost not only their economic security, but also, and just as troubling to many, their self-respect and social position in society. This change in status was particularly noted by the elderly, since in both the Soviet system and Kyrgyz nomadic tradition the elderly were highly revered and cared for. Even women who had large families felt this enormous shift in societal respect, from recognition under the Soviet system for being "mother heroes" to disparagement as poverty cases. For younger women the sudden change in the education system, from one that was free for all to one fraught with hidden costs and bribes, was extremely disappointing. Recent alterations in government social policy and support were deeply unsettling for all of these women, for they recognized that their current sense of alienation could well continue for a long time.

A government official tells the interviewer frankly, "It is a very hard life for women here. When it comes to women, we have to admit that we have a problem."

The economic breakdown had an indelible impact on social norms. For example, among the Kyrgyz a strong sense of reciprocity and relationships was built upon the shared ability to provide things for one another. Economic changes had curtailed this capability in many families. With an informal economy so dependent on the capacity for gift giving, women spoke often of their shame when they were unable to offer a sheep to their relatives as a gift, and instead had to sell it at the bazaar in order to feed their family. Thus, in addition to the personal degradation of being unemployed, many women experienced a deep sense of demoralization.

A Kyrgyz woman describes the situation in her village: "Here, women are not living; they are just surviving. They have extremely low salaries. They cannot go anywhere. They cannot visit family members. The situation is breaking apart family ties that are based upon being a guest, or having a guest, which is a central feature of Kyrgyz culture."

Throughout the country, for ethnic Kyrgyz and non-Kyrgyz women alike, the ideological and material shift from a state of socialism to the new, unfamiliar market economy was troublesome. Socialism had provided free education, full employment, child care benefits, and food subsidies. Now these familiar realities had fallen away. This early stage in the transition process was precarious; the outward excitement had turned inward, and people were feeling disoriented. They recalled the past nostalgically, and even the problems and limitations of those troublesome former days looked more appealing than the uncertainties of their present predicament.

> An administrator in an unemployment office expresses the general sense of disorientation: "Imagine traveling along in a car for 70 years and suddenly the road disappears and your car crashes. You don't know where to go."

The Study

This study was designed to provide a more complete picture of those women who were most vulnerable to the effects of economic change and social disorientation under way in the Kyrgyz Republic. A small team of researchers interviewed over 600 women throughout the country; 572 women responded to a 47-question survey, and 30 participated in in-depth interviews.[2] The respondents were drawn from ethnic, regional, and age categories in proportions that reflected the variation in these categories in the country at the time. Respondents were selected through formal and informal channels, including local employment, pension fund, and social service offices; local authorities and regional governors' offices; bazaars and kiosks; collective and privatized farms; the local press;[3] mosques and Russian Orthodox churches; and interviewers' personal acquaintance with officials and other people in each oblast (administrative region).

The respondents were interviewed either in their home or at their workplace. Direct observation by the interviewers provided additional information regarding the availability of food, living conditions, and the overall health status of the respondent and her family.

> One of the interviewers, a Kyrgyz doctoral candidate in sociology, attests to the value of on-site observation: "I saw the poverty with my own eyes. The situation in the women's homes told everything. I saw what they ate, wore, and how they live. Sometimes people would say that things were fine, but when I entered their house, then they told me the truth."

In addition to individual interviews, meetings of three different focus groups consisting of women from the rural regions addressed more specific questions about unemployment and difficult living conditions. These allowed for a more free-flowing exchange of ideas, as women tended to challenge one another if they felt that their conditions were being misrepresented.

One purpose of this form of social inquiry, as described by Salmen (1992), is to amplify the voices of those for whom development is ultimately intended. Thus, throughout this chapter, the statements of individual respondents are quoted. Short vignettes offer additional perspective on the conditions of women in the country.

Unemployment

According to the survey results, the women most vulnerable to the effects of the transition in the Kyrgyz Republic fell into four categories: elderly Russian women residing in urban regions, Kyrgyz mothers with more than three children, women living in remote mountainous regions, and women who had lost jobs and social support as the result of enterprise and collective farm privatization.

Of the women interviewed, 77 percent described themselves as unemployed. Most had been laid off from their jobs within the past year; other reasons given for being unemployed included maternity leave, quitting work, and health problems. Among the unemployed, 50 percent had not applied for unemployment benefits, and 20 percent did not even know such benefits existed. Because many of the unemployed were not registered with the employment services office, maintaining an official count was difficult. Complicated bureaucratic processes and transportation problems were the primary reasons women gave for not applying for benefits. For those who did apply, the process was a discouraging one: only one in four had ever received any payment from the government.

The disappearance of jobs, especially in the service industries, was reflected in rapidly rising unemployment among women of all ages in both urban and rural regions, but especially where collective farms had been privatized and thousands of workers laid off. In urban regions very few new industries had emerged to fill the demand for jobs. Of the 77 percent of respondents who described themselves as unemployed, more than two-thirds had attempted to find another job. Most expressed considerable confusion about why they had lost their job, where they would find other work, and where they would find help. Many women (47 percent) indicated that they relied primarily on themselves, but some (25 percent) relied on their parents and other relatives for assistance. Only 18 percent of the women expected any sort of help from the government. When asked "Where have you searched for a job?" the women responded as follows:

Response	Percent
Not applied anywhere	29
Government enterprises	24
Employment services office	22
Former workplace	5
Private enterprises	2
Cooperatives and associations	2
Other	16

Unofficial unemployment appeared much more widespread in the rural regions. Many rural enterprises that had closed—kindergartens, hospitals, canteens, camps, barbershops, hairdressers, and service organizations—had primarily employed women. Some of these were seasonal positions. Even health resorts were no longer an employment option for many rural women, because their jobs were being filled by employees from the city. The rural women expressed resentment toward urban women (whom they called "migrants") who had moved to their region and taken their jobs.

The disintegration or privatization of the collective farms ended up dismantling entire community infrastructures. The collective farm system had provided comprehensive social assistance: in-kind food donations, education of children, and distribution of benefits. The economic networks that had managed these transactions had been severed, and the workers themselves, in the case of coal supply, for example, did not have the bartering power to orchestrate such trade.

A 38-year-old Kyrgyz woman from a rural area compares the past and present systems: "Right now, we don't know whom to turn to for help. Things were better when the collective farms were working. At least there was a director, and we had someone to complain to. Now it is as if the government didn't exist. The only one you can rely on is yourself."

In those areas where collective farms had not yet been privatized, people appeared to be weathering the economic crisis better. The collective farm was still able to address local problems, such as fuel or food shortages.

The unemployed rural women seemed the least informed about the economic changes under way in the country, and especially about the government services still available to them, including employment services and unemployment benefits. Many of these women had been associated with a collective farm, which had acted as a central clearinghouse for nearly all their social needs. Thus they lacked extensive social networks outside the collective farm for gleaning information about the emergent economic terrain. These women had been receiving not only their monthly salaries through the farm, but also in-kind assistance in the form of free food and fuel. Women who used to work at the collective farm indicated that privatization has meant that the few people hired were either relatives or friends of the new owner.

A government official comments, "People don't understand privatization—they think of it as what you can grab. Ignorant people now have become millionaires."

Many rural women discussed how unready they had been, psychologically and economically, for privatization of the collective farms. Their ideas about work were based on a collective model, and they pointed out that, for all intents and purposes, the largely nomadic Kyrgyz people had a collective orientation long before the Soviet collectivization. They expressed confusion about why people did not have jobs under the new system.

On the collective farm, the women explained, they had worked hard, but many of their daily concerns had been taken care of. They indicated that they preferred the collective model of livelihood over that of the market economy, where, in their opinion, only a few can work, and the owners seemed to no longer care about their workers.

A Kyrgyz sociologist explains that "The liquidation of collective farms is the reason so many rural women are unemployed. Even though there's privatization, many owners of these new farms don't know how to manage them. I talked to many people who want to return to the collective farm model. They were used to this unification of work and family life."

In the urban regions as well, female unemployment had become rampant. In Bishkek (the capital, formerly known as Frunze), where 85 percent of the registered unemployed were women, layoffs were a common occurrence. Unlike their rural counterparts, unemployed urban women seemed more likely to utilize assistance from employment services, and they sought out career consultations more than did men. More women applied for unemployment benefits in Bishkek, which may reflect the fact that access to the employment services office was easier and that services were better understood in this larger urban region. During the first six months of 1993, approximately 777 people went to the employment services office for consultations, including career testing. Of these, 625 were women. When asked, "Where have you looked for a job?" the percentage anwering "Employment services office" varied by oblast as follows:

Oblast	Percent
Bishkek	41
Talas	28
Issyk Kul	25
Jalal-Abad	22
Osh	19
Naryn	13
Chui	4

When asked, "Have you applied for unemployment benefits?" the percentage answering "no" varied by oblast as follows:

Oblast	Percent
Talas	66
Osh	64
Issyk Kul	53
Jalal-Abad	51
Naryn	49
Chui	42
Bishkek	27

Among the unemployed, the group most affected was women between the ages of 17 and 30. They often lacked experience and connections that might lead them to other jobs. They were generally discouraged, and many talked about getting involved in small business ventures, including prostitution.

A Kyrgyz graduate student in sociology observes, "The most vulnerable group, and the one that potentially will cost the government and our culture the most if we do not pay attention to it now, is our young people between 18 and 25 years of age."

Young mothers were experiencing difficulties because they were often laid off during their maternity leave. Even though, in theory, they were protected by law, several of the respondents gave pregnancy as the reason they had lost their job. Among young married women there was a new phenomenon: absent husbands. Many young women who had been laid off in the city returned to relatives in the rural regions while their husbands either stayed in the city to earn money or moved to other regions for employment. Commuting between city and countryside to maintain the family's integrity was quite difficult. Women in this predicament described their awkward dependency on parents and the difficulty of separation from their husbands.

Women were actively searching for work, significantly reducing their expenditure, and selling homemade products or household goods. Some were involved in "speculation," buying at one price and selling at a higher price at some other location. Some of the young students were engaged in prostitution. Most women were not looking to the government for help, nor were they relying on nongovernmental groups. In fact, 90 percent of the women interviewed had never heard of any women's organizations.

A multitude of new social problems had arisen as a result of women's unemployment. Particularly in urban areas, women reported a perceived increase in crimes committed by women, an increase in suicide among elderly Russian women, an increase in the number of pregnant teenagers, and the rapid development of semilegal prostitution rings. It was estimated that about 20 new prostitution businesses were operating in Bishkek in 1993. In some instances these companies resembled a small version of a collectivized enterprise. Up to 10 prostitutes lived together in an enterprise-paid apartment, received low-maintenance medical attention, shared food and other expenses, and kept approximately 50 percent of their earnings. The prostitutes were not working outside of the law, but their manager or pimp could potentially receive up to five years in jail. Considering that each company had its own policeman paid monthly by the company for protection, however, it was doubtful that many had had problems with the law.

Wandering into an apartment in urban Bishkek, two young prostitutes are surprised to find no men who want them this late evening, but only an American woman who wants to talk to them about their work. Both younger than 22 years, the two were school friends before beginning their latest line of work. Her bleached blond hair gives Gulya, a Kyrgyz, the stereotypic look of such workers of the night. But her hardened exterior, well developed after three years in the business, is easily betrayed by the candidness of her comments: "I am often afraid. I am relieved when I find it is a foreigner or even a Russian client. They are nicer. But if it is a Kyrgyz man, they are usually drunk, but what is worse is that they think so badly of me."

Her friend Elena, just six weeks on the job, adds that she does not like the work. It makes her nervous in spite of the fact that she has to keep on smiling. When asked why she chose to go into prostitution, she responds, "I was unemployed. I was laid off at the radio factory in Tokmok. I didn't work for six months and I needed the money. I tried to find work in my training as a kindergarten teacher, and also I type well. But schools are closing and there are few jobs for secretaries. I registered at the unemployment office and qualified for benefits. But after three months, these ended. Gulya told me about her work. Well, I had few choices."

Without being asked and in a confessional voice, Elena recounts her first night on the job. "I cried a lot. I thought I was so bad. I didn't consider myself a woman, a human. When I went to the hotel, I was so angry, I destroyed the room. I couldn't stand myself. But after my first night, I returned to my girlfriends as they were counting their money, and the pain went away." Elena describes the awful feeling of having to depend on her parents and their pensions when they, too, were struggling so much. "There's a saying in Russian, 'He who doesn't work must not eat.'"

Alhough unconcerned about HIV/AIDS, both are worried about other diseases. Elena interrupts to explain that their company has its own doctor, whom they are required to see every Monday morning. They cannot work without a "clean bill of health." Gulya, a seasoned prostitute at 20 years old, says that the work is harder on one's psychology than on one's body. Sometimes suicide or alcohol is the outcome if people don't know when to leave the profession. "But it's difficult to leave," she smiles. "You know, this business, it is like a narcotic."

Despite claiming to depend only on themselves, both rural and urban unemployed women repeatedly said that they turned to their relatives for help, especially in locating work. In 59 percent of cases, women first sought out family or extended family members for assistance before going to an employment services office. Women consistently expressed their trust in their relatives. As one older woman said, "It's better to work with your own family than to be employed by some stranger." When asked what it meant to work with nonrelatives, she explained that it could lead to problems. Without further elaboration, she implied that it was a shared value among Kyrgyz, since trust within a small group had been essential for survival at times during the Soviet era. In this context it was not uncommon for Kyrgyz women to tell stories about family members who had been killed under Stalin because someone they thought was a friend had accused their relative of some anticommunist activity.

In summary, unemployment for the women interviewed represented more than simply being without an income: losing one's job had many other social ramifications, such as loss of status. Women raised and educated during the Soviet period had come to value being a member of the work force. Some considered it a personal failure not to contribute to the overall productivity of the country. The demoralization that accompanied unemployment was apparent in many interviews: many women were embarrassed to discuss their unemployment, as they felt it was an indication of their own lack of ability to adapt or to find other work. Some explained how unemployment also meant the loss of access to many important socioeconomic networks. For women who had worked under the socialist system, a job was rather like a one-stop service center that distributed everything from family benefits and child care support to an apartment to live in and in-kind contributions of food and fuel. In an economy where many informal transactions took place as the result of an intricate network of cohorts helping one another out, survival in the command economy encouraged a high degree of interdependency. The loss of social networks for rural women was compounded by their lack of mobility due to increasing costs of public transportation. In addition to the loss of a community, some interviewees explained that the physical and psychological isolation was giving rise to more and more alcoholism among unemployed rural women.

Living Conditions

The rapid rate of economic reform had taken a devastating toll on many households: some respondents compared it to an earthquake—much more an abrupt shock than a smooth transition. Almost half of the respondents described their current living conditions as extremely difficult; 58 percent of this group were older than 50 years. Slightly more of them were non-Kyrgyz (47 percent) than Kyrgyz (43 percent; about half the total population are ethnic Kyrgyz). Most of the other respondents (49 percent) described their living conditions as worse than one year ago, and most of these were under the age of 40 years. Only 6 percent of the women evaluated their family living conditions as sufficient, and over half of these were under 29 years of age. From survey results and interviews, it was evident that elderly women were suffering most from the everyday deterioration of their living conditions: some elderly women indicated that they were eating only bread and tea.

The respondents unanimously stated that the first coping mechanism they used in their new economic predicament was the curtailment of unnecessary foodstuffs. During the first half of 1993, the majority also stopped buying clothing (70 percent) and household items (75 percent); some had stopped purchasing butter (20 percent), meat (14 percent), and milk products (14 percent). Many households with more than six children were buying day-old bread and giving their children tea instead of milk, which they could not afford.

Although only a small percentage of women had expected assistance from the government, 71 percent actually received some form of social benefits. However, the amount was steadily being reduced, as the lag time for receiving benefits averaged from one to four months, and such benefits accounted for very little of their usable incomes given the increase in consumer prices. When asked, "What kind of benefits do you receive?" the answers given were as follows:

Response	Percent
Child or family benefits	37
No benefits	29
Retirement pension	16
Pregnancy leave benefits	8
Disability benefits	3
Unemployment benefits	3
Veterans benefits	1
Other	4

The reduction in benefits, coupled with inflation and the introduction of the new currency, left many families without cash to buy food. When asked how they were paying for things without cash income, the rural women said that they were selling both their household belongings and food from their gardens that was originally intended as a winter cache for their family. This new behavior was particularly disturbing to older Kyrgyz women, because during the Soviet period selling one's produce at a local bazaar was seen as a form of family disgrace. It was expected in this highly gift-based society that this food would be offered as a gift to a relative or friend.

The changing economy also was affecting informal social networks. Amid the reduction in governmental assistance, 58 percent of the women surveyed indicated that they did not receive any financial or food support from family or relatives. Among those who had received help from their family, food (15 percent) was the primary means of support, although some received cash (11 percent). Very few received clothing, animals, or support in building a house. When asked about this lack of traditional, and formerly dependable, support from relatives, the women explained that everyone was struggling and that surplus food and other goods were not as available as they had been in the past. Without governmental and familial support, two systems that were key factors in their social protection network, women were left to their own resources.

Elderly urban women, especially Russians, appeared to be among the most vulnerable. In most cases, they were women. Seldom did they have more than one or two children, and in many cases their adult children had migrated to the Russian Federation. It was nearly impossible for an elderly Russian to leave, since she would lose her pension. A survey of retirees in Bishkek indicated that most of these women were coping by engaging in small-scale trade, selling off saved-up possessions and producing handicrafts or homemade food products obtained from garden plots.

In 1993 the majority of the population (62 percent) resided in the rural regions, where living conditions continued to be more difficult than for urban women. Although many families had private gardens in the fertile valleys of Chui, Ferghana, and Issyk Kul, they were not immune to the general breakdown in transportation and communications infrastructure, and large parts of these regions are mountainous. Deteriorating roads inhibited travel to employment services offices, banks, and jobs. Fuel shortages, breakdowns of buses and trucks, and difficulty in finding spare parts had seriously affected food production and distribution. In addition, few rural households had telephones; most depended on a central telephone station to call other family members.

Many rural women indicated that they lacked running water in their homes, instead relying year-round on a pump located in the street. Even more problematic than water was fuel for heating homes and schools. One nine-person family living on the northern shore of Lake Issyk Kul stated that, as a result of their farm being privatized, they had not received their annual allotment of coal. They anticipated passing the winter in their summer kitchen, because it could be heated more easily with green wood than their house. Trees in this mountainous area were few to begin with, and so there was great concern about an increase in spring mudslides because of the number of trees being felled for winter fuel.

In addition, many rural respondents described the large numbers of children who were quitting school by the age of 14, because rural schools were losing qualified teachers. Teachers were choosing to sell at the local bazaar in order to earn a better income. Older children were also being recruited to work to help bring in needed cash for the family.

A Kyrgyz family of 10 in the rural southern part of the country is housed in one room. Everyone shares the floor for sleep. The cupboards have a few cups and dishes on them, but there are no obvious signs of food stocks of any sort. The woman of the household, 37 years old, offers the interviewer some dark bread. It is old, but it is a gift that cannot be refused in Central Asia. Her twins are two months old, but they are small, more the size of a one-month-old. The woman's face is worn, almost grandmotherly. The other six children hang out around the new twins. They have not gone to school this past year, she explains, and there is little food or clothing. "My husband works in Uzbekistan," she says. "This year is more difficult than last year. There are few products and no clothes for my children. I am worried about my new twins. They are not growing very quickly. I haven't received my family benefits for five months. We are waiting. We don't know what else to do. I am busy with my twins, and so my oldest son, who is 11 years old, goes to the market and sells small produce."

Finally, her husband arrives home with a can full of apples. The children jump up and down as he hands them his pickings. He tells of his daily difficulties crossing the Uzbek border in order to work. When asked why he works in Uzbekistan and not in the Kyrgyz Republic, he says that there is work there now. He works in the fields harvesting tobacco and cotton, which is usually done by women, but now men, too, must work in the fields in order to have any work at all.

A common concern among rural women was the increase in drinking and crime among the young males. There was little entertainment available, since many of the youth clubs had shut down and most movie theaters could not afford to show films. But with surging imports of alcohol, drinking had become the major social activity. One rural coroner in the town of Cholpon Ata reported a rising number of knifings and beatings among drunk youth. Rural women reported the use of opium and marijuana among the young.

A 43-year-old Kyrgyz woman expresses her concerns: "It worries me a lot that children have started to quit school in eighth grade. Children should study in school like they used to. Without school it is difficult for teenagers—for boys—to get along. Attention especially has to be paid to filling vacancies in schools, where there aren't enough teachers in various disciplines. Also, we have to keep our children from selling cigarettes and alcohol, since there's a danger that they will try it all themselves first."

Rural women may have had the advantage of gardens or orchards on which they could depend for food production during the summer, but even rural respondents repeatedly expressed their concern about their food supplies lasting beyond the winter. Further, not all rural regions had gardens, because of the high altitude and short growing season in the mountains, which make up 90 percent of the country. Certainly these regions were experiencing more difficult conditions. In Susamir, in Chui oblast, gardens were few, and the transport that had formerly brought produce from Bishkek was becoming infrequent. Some of the women who had been employed by the collective farms had no idea where they would find coal for heating their homes this winter; the farm used to provide them with such in-kind assistance. The lack of trees at the higher altitudes made procurement of fuel for heating particularly problematic. The women expressed great concern for their children's health.

A Kyrgyz interviewer summarizes her observations: "We see the disintegration of the family: men are working in one area, and their families are living elsewhere. The relationships between people are tense because of the impoverished situation. It affects the husband-wife and the parent-child relationship. I think it is quite likely that the number of divorces will increase as the result of these social and economic problems. We have identified the symptoms. We have to get to the cause."

As the socialist infrastructures collapsed during the early 1990s, people in rural areas often expressed their worries about the deterioration of the health care and education systems. Embedded within their general concerns were more regional concerns. Kyrgyz women with many children in Naryn oblast were troubled most about the lack of medicines and growing infant mortality, whereas Russian women in Talas oblast were concerned more about educating their children in their native language without having to move to another region or another country. Women were anxious about the approaching winter, when temperatures would fall below freezing for at least five months of the year. They had no money to buy clothes or shoes for their children; the last time they had bought any children's clothes was over two years ago. Now the clothes were wearing out, and the children had outgrown the shoes. Some women doubted that their children would be able to continue their schooling with clothes and food so limited. When respondents were asked what kind of humanitarian aid would be most helpful, children's clothing was the third most frequent answer, after medicine and flour.

A Russian woman in rural Chui oblast says, "High prices worry me most of all. I really want prices to stop rising and salaries to increase. Come winter there's no coal or firewood, and children are running around without shoes or warm clothes."

Increasing Incidence of Poverty

Reflecting the dramatic fall in living standards for much of the population, most women (79 percent) said that they had observed signs of poverty in their neighborhoods. When asked to describe what they meant by poverty, most (74 percent) said it was a condition in which people could not buy food. It was easier for most women to report on a neighbor's difficult situation than to tell about their own predicament.

A larger share of non-Kyrgyz (86 percent) than of Kyrgyz respondents (74 percent) perceived poverty among the people they knew. A sharp decrease in the standard of living of the urban elderly was evident from both respondent surveys and direct observation. There was an increasing number of suicides among the elderly Russians. A priest at the Bishkek Russian Orthodox church reported that another problem among the elderly was that many families could no longer afford to bury their dead, and bodies were being left unclaimed at hospitals. Russian women were devastated by this prospect. Some in the bazaar described selling their few family heirlooms, such as silver samovars and jewelry, in order to pay in advance for their burial plot.

In Naryn oblast, government officials and the interview team concurred that this oblast was one of the most impoverished in the country, yet in evaluating their own living conditions, more women in Naryn answered that they enjoyed an "average lifestyle" (55 percent) than in the other five oblasts. This discrepancy between observed hardship and reported satisfaction could be explained by the degree to which the Kyrgyz people value optimism and maintain a discreet attitude about their own problems: 96

percent of the women interviewed in Naryn oblast were Kyrgyz, a proportion that reflects the overall population of this region but exceeds that in other oblasts.

A Kyrgyz sociologist says, "Our people are heroic people. They will never tell you that they are in a bad situation. If you ask a dying Muslim, he'll respond, 'I am getting better every day.'"

Through observation in nearly 600 respondents' homes, the research team saw the deteriorating living conditions firsthand. They found a number of women, especially among the elderly and mothers with more than five children, having great difficulty feeding their families. The poorest group was those who lived in the more remote and mountainous rural areas, where some women lacked the means to buy food and could not grow it because of the short growing season.

An unemployed Kyrgyz woman says of her household, "You can see for yourselves that we are poor. But don't say that to the other people in our village. We consider ourselves to be living like everybody else."

The issue of food shortages seemed related more to problems of distribution than to low production. Some farmers reported that their production was down because of seasonal storms and because they could not afford to hire enough farmhands. Natural disasters, such as the large earthquake that hit in 1992 and several small ones in 1993, had also added to the rapidly deteriorating living standards, especially in the south. The resulting landslides had affected transportation to the more remote areas, and dangerous mudslides were predicted for the following spring.

Local assistance for newly impoverished women and their families was minimal; such assistance was first allocated to the disabled and to the elderly. Forty-eight percent of the women interviewed expressed little or no confidence in the local government's ability to assist families in need. Even some of the most impoverished families felt that they could not depend on assistance from the government. Nor had women received support from local businesses, which as a rule only helped their own employees. The significant sums of money spent by these enterprises on philanthropic projects did not ensure a fair distribution of social aid. Some women said that they had expected help from their collective farm, but that they could not depend on it as they had the previous year. In general, they relied only on themselves, their immediate family, or relatives; but they, too, were in a similar predicament.

A Kyrgyz student interviewer notes that "The number of unemployed people is increasing every day. As a result, there are many problems; the main one is poverty. Poverty has its own consequences. It begins with the problems of feeding oneself and ends with psychological problems. We used to talk about the quality of the food. Now we talk about the quantity of it. The main foods eaten are tea and bread."

International humanitarian aid first arrived in the Kyrgyz Republic in August 1992, but women in Jalal-Abad oblast discussed how discouraged they had been when cases of outdated medicine and spoiled foods were delivered. Assistance to the earthquake victims was still needed. In some ways conditions were even worse now, because the transition was one year farther along in dismantling the Soviet infrastructure. There was little food and medicine available in these regions. In 1993, the Kyrgyz earthquake refugees, many of whom had lost their homes and villages, had congregated in Osh, and some in Jalal-Abad. They were among the poorest; they received no social assistance, since they did not have *propiska* (residence permits) to work in Osh.

Despite the wide range of opinions among respondents regarding setting up soup kitchens for those in need, the survey results spoke to the necessity of this type of aid for elderly women and single mothers. Although most people reported that they themselves would never use a soup kitchen or other forms of public support as a coping mechanism, 34 percent of the women agreed that these services should be available to the poor. The highest level of support for this sort of assistance was found among respondents in Chui oblast (56 percent) and the lowest in Issyk Kul oblast (10 percent). This difference may be due to Chui's proximity to Bishkek and thus greater familiarity with international assistance.

In general, however, the women interviewed for this study were wary of international assistance. They worried that it meant borrowing money from international banks, which would greatly burden their children's generation with debt. One regional governor refused at first to allow the interview team to work in his oblast because, as he put it, aid organizations kept coming to him for information, and so far he had not seen any benefits. After a lengthy discussion, he agreed to assist the team and ended up providing cars and drivers so that interviewers could travel to some of the more remote areas in the oblast. Nevertheless, governmental officials were in general far less patient with the interviewers than the local women were. The officials discussed the stress they were under as advocates for their country before the international organizations.

An employed Kyrgyz woman from a rural region expresses a common sentiment: "The way to escape from economic crisis lies only in the people. The people have to work. You can't wait for help from the outside. Debts won't make you wealthy again. You have to pay off your debts."

Some Early Indications of Growing Civil Society

The rapid development of nongovernmental organizations (NGOs) in the Kyrgyz Republic is a hopeful sign: by 1993 the country had over 200 registered NGOs. About 30 percent of these focused on social protection and poverty alleviation. Although many were run for and by women, most of the women interviewed in this study (as noted previously) had never heard of them, which in part reflects the fact that the NGOs were primarily located in urban centers. The interviewees doubted whether such groups could actually help with the social assistance concerns of women, but they agreed that unification of these women's groups would be one of the better ways in which to help address women's problems in the country.

According to a government official, "Women are afraid to add their own problems to the government's problems. We are trying to solve our own problems."

One of the newly developed NGOs was the Kyrgyz Congress of Women. The few interviewees who had heard of this NGO perceived it as a group organized for women who were a part of the elite. They did not see it as helping with humanitarian aid. The Congress of Women first met in May 1993 with the goal of unifying the various women's groups. Because of differences in political opinions, however, progress toward this goal had been marginal. A second meeting was held in September 1993, with representatives from Kazakhstan, to examine the common concerns of Central Asian women. The Congress of Women appeared, however, to have philosophical aims rather than practical solutions to increasing poverty and unemployment.

Another NGO, the Committee on Women (formerly the Zhensovet organization), was considered by many women as providing a working model for women helping themselves. This "at home" work program offered women a small wage in exchange for sewing clothing. The club sells the finished products at its own kiosk, and part of the proceeds go to buy more raw materials. About 16 clubs affiliated with this organization exist throughout the Kyrgyz Republic. In Bishkek 300 women and a few men participate in the sewing program. In both rural and urban regions, women brought up the need for a women's center for training and education and as a distribution center for medicine and food.

> An unemployed Kyrgyz mother of four in the town of Kochorka stresses that "Women's organizations have to be organized in villages. On every street there should be a neighborhood committee that would bring women to order."

Summary

Because many women in the Kyrgyz Republic had lost not only their jobs but also important social networks, they had to find new ways to make ends meet. For rural women, household gardens had become an important means of providing food for a family. For urban women, selling goods at the local bazaar had become commonplace. With cutbacks in governmental social supports, especially child care and elder care assistance, women were carrying the greater part of the social burden. Overall, the quality of life for most of the women participating in this study had decreased.

Women no longer viewed the increase in poverty and unemployment in their country as a temporary condition. They perceived the difficulties as resulting from the introduction of the market economy (44 percent) and the collapse of the Soviet Union (26 percent). These were rather consistently observed responses; others included the introduction of the som (9 percent), reluctance to work (5 percent), and "God's will" (4 percent).

Many of the more vulnerable women, particularly mothers with many children, women in poor health, pensioners, and unemployed women, were pessimistic about the new governmental measures intended to curb overall social expenses in order to help bring about a turnaround in the economy. Only 19 percent of those surveyed expected any assistance from government institutions, whereas 42 percent expected that things would improve only by their own personal efforts.

> A government official notes, "Women were in a better situation during Soviet times. No one is concerned with the problem of women now. Nongovernmental organizations are trying to help, but they have no money. Social difficulties are increasing daily. Women are particularly vulnerable."

Some women accused the central government (30 percent) and local authorities (13 percent) of ignoring women's problems. A few respondents also pointed out that they themselves lacked knowledge about economic issues (5 percent) and lacked qualifications (3 percent), especially compared with men. Some (22 percent) indicated that they were simply unable to adapt to present conditions.

Women repeatedly expressed an understanding that the Kyrgyz government was going through difficult changes, which meant in their eyes that they had to depend on themselves.

> An unemployed Uighur woman says, "We're poor because our government is poor. If the father is poor, how can the son be rich?"
>
> A Russian pensioner comments, "We don't know who to blame now—maybe only ourselves because we are the only ones who can save ourselves."

Although there were indications of an increasingly conservative attitude toward women in society, influenced by the growing numbers of practicing Muslims,[4] there was nonetheless a strong sense of nostalgia for what women described as "the time when things worked, when there was no unemployment, and when food was affordable." The currently depressed economy may have led them to inflate their estimation of the former system. Nevertheless, there was a strong sentiment emerging for a return to communism, especially among the generation over 40 years old.

> A 68-year-old Russian pensioner expresses her despair: "This is not a temporary situation. I am not optimistic. I was a communist for 45 years. I have no religion. When things went to the som, I couldn't afford anything anymore. I am ashamed that I have come to this place [the pension office]. They say so many things bad about the Communist Party, but everything was good then. Now look at me. I don't hold out very much hope."
>
> A 26-year-old Kyrgyz woman, unemployed but with a technical edu-

cation, argues for a return to the old regime: "If it means peace, we should really escape from the torture of the market economy and return to socialism. Capitalism heartlessly ignores the common man and has no pity for him. It turns out that the ones who can become capitalists are the most perverted and least scrupulous."

Postscript

In 1996, when the author returned to conduct another poverty study, she found that the initial enthusiasm and general support for building a democratic society and creating a market economy had been tempered by widespread disappointment. Estimates by international development banks suggested that at least half of the population was living in poverty (see Bauer, Green, and Kuehnast 1997). Among women there was a pervasive feeling of fear about the future and a sense of hopelessness. Yet in spite of their hardships, women were not passively waiting for the government to save them. They acknowledged that they would have to help themselves if they were to save their families from poverty. But with their limited resources, limited amount of time, the increasing speed of inflation, and the long lag in the receipt of government payments of salaries and benefits, women had become preoccupied with the struggle to survive.

Notes

1. "Market shock" is a term that economists have given to the process of rapid economic transformation of the Central European countries during the early 1990s. This same approach was applied to the former Soviet Union after 1991, including rapid privatization and economic liberalization.

2. The preparation and pretest of the survey in both Russian and Kyrgyz required utmost flexibility. Only minor alterations were possible once the team was in the field.

3. This research added a new category of women to the socially vulnerable, namely, prostitutes, who advertised their services in the newspaper *Evening Bishkek*.

4. Muslim affiliation was stronger in the south, where local religious leaders advocated a more conservative role for women. The social implications for women included an increase in average family size. As one female doctor from Osh explained, these changes had made women more afraid to seek abortions or birth control, even when they had more children than they could adequately feed. The growing Islamic Center was training hundreds of boys and young men.

References

Bauer, Armin, David Green, and Kathleen Kuehnast. 1997. *Women and Gender Relations: The Kyrgyz Republic in Transition.* Manila: Asian Development Bank.

Salmen, Lawrence F. 1992. *Beneficiary Assessment: An Approach Described.* Washington, D.C.: World Bank, Poverty and Social Policy Division, Technical Department, Africa Region.

This single mother is a returnee to Vose following armed conflict in that area.
Photo by Elizabeth Gomart

---

*

CHAPTER 4

Between Civil War and Land Reform: Among the Poorest of the Poor in Tajikistan

Elizabeth Gomart

I n 1996, when the fieldwork for this study was conducted, the civil war that had plagued Tajikistan since 1992 was smoldering in the mountains of Gharm, northeast of Dushanbe, and the rest of the country was at relative peace. Little was then known about the impact of the civil war or the transition from communism. Officials in Dushanbe claimed that the affected regions were stabilizing, people were rebuilding, no one was going hungry, privatization was moving along smoothly, and land was being offered to returnees from Afghanistan. Some top-level foreign diplomats even doubted that severe poverty (that is, hunger) existed in Tajikistan except among some aged Russian pensioners in Dushanbe.

The study was conducted to inform the Tajikistan Pilot Poverty Alleviation Project, whose objective was to scale up existing antipoverty programs of international nongovernmental organizations (NGOs) and set up a Social Investment Fund. The study was part of a social assessment, intended to provide information for decisionmakers regarding the design of these components. A team of local social scientists and NGO workers were trained in participatory rapid appraisal techniques to conduct the assessment in a total of nine sites in four oblasts (administrative regions)and Dushanbe, the capital of Tajikistan in May and June 1996.

The social assessment found deep poverty and enormous inequities in privatization. Most households had been hit hard by the crisis. The war had destroyed thousands of homes, cattle, and harvests and had limited access to markets. People were dealing with insecurity, dramatic inequities, and lawlessness as the winning localist groups and their leaders exploited their positions of power.

Background

The civil war had killed 25,000 people between October 1992 and May 1993 and created 600,000 refugees. Even before the war, Tajikistan had been the poorest of the former Soviet republics, with the next-to-lowest GDP per capita, the highest rate of population growth, and an extremely low standard of living. Since independence in 1991, Tajikistan had been faced with the enormous task of building a new nation-state under conditions of widespread poverty, limited natural resources, and a power struggle between old and new political entities. Localist clan rivalries had emerged out of the divide-and-rule strategy of the Russian and later the Soviet empire, and structural weaknesses linked to the breakup of the Soviet Union were underlying causes of the civil war.

At the time of the fieldwork, opposition forces occupied the eastern part of the Gharm Valley and the districts of Darwaz and Vanj, on the threshold of the Pamir Mountains in the east. According to eyewitnesses, these regions were administered by opposition loyalists and heavily militarized. The Gorno-Badakhshan Autonomous Region, in the Pamir Mountains, benefited from an alliance with the opposition leaders, which provided relative stability and security. In 1996 government forces blockaded the eastern regions by setting up 14 posts on the 100-kilometer road from Dushanbe to the city of Gharm. In the spring there was renewed fighting that extended to within a few kilometers of Dushanbe. The status of Gharm was expected to worsen as the opposition forces tried to consolidate their position in the region.

Throughout the interviews, household heads and community leaders were convinced that only peace would improve the economic situation, reduce insecurity, and bring back the rule of law. Some hoped for a neutral ruler, whereas others thought a coalition government would bring the political factions together. A precondition was to end the political meddling of outsiders in national politics, particularly from the Russian Federation, which favored the pro-communist government then in power against the increasing extremist voices of the opposition.

The study consisted of individual and group interviews conducted at nine sites in the four main geographic areas of the country: Dushanbe,

Khodjent, Khatlon, and Gorno-Badakhshan. (Khatlon lies in southwestern Tajikistan; its eastern portion, formerly known as Kuliab, is the home region of the localist subgroup currently in power.) The sites were Roshqala and Anjin in Gorno-Badakhshan, Avul Street and the bus station in Dushanbe, Varzob village northeast of Dushanbe, Shakhistan in Khodjent, and the Vakhsh and Vose districts and Kurgan Tyube town in Khatlon. Five sites were rural and four urban; the urban sites included one large town, Kurgan Tyube, and the Dushanbe, capital. Fieldwork covering Gharm was limited to interviews with travelers from Gharm at the Dushanbe bus station and central market, because the Gharm area was under control of opposition forces, heavily mined, and deemed unsafe. The team conducted group interviews, drew maps, and conducted ranking exercises with respondents they found at the bus station and the market.

Interviews with residents, local and regional officials, and key informants were conducted at each site along with at least one focus group, depending on the size of the site. The team of 11 Tajik interviewers was diverse in terms of region of origin and multidisciplinary, including sociologists, doctors, teachers, economists, and NGO workers. The team was trained in participatory rapid appraisal tools and topic guides. Part of the team spent three to five days in each community and interviewed over 200 persons from May to June 1996.

Who Are the Poor?

Local officials and residents were loath to admit to social stratification. Common answers to the question, "Who are the poor?" sought to iron out any differences: "We are all poor." Officials in particular seemed put on the defensive by and tried to avoid the term "poverty," as it was seen as reflecting badly on their leadership and policies.

By avoiding the words "poverty" and "poor" and by probing for local criteria, interviewers were able to elicit explanations from respondents of how they estimated levels of well-being. First, respondents said they assessed the household's ability to provide for its basic needs, which they defined as food, shelter, clothing and shoes, and emergency health costs. Then they looked at the household's labor resources, assets (cattle and personal property), access to other productive assets, salaried employment (and thereby regular cash income), and ties to the ruling localist clans. Often communities pointed to a few well-to-do families and described the rest as "spending their days running after a piece of bread." The main implication of this finding is that present income and asset levels were not seen as the sole indicator of household living standards; rather, in these times of severe flux, respondents valued the household's potential to produce (thanks to available labor, assets, employment, and social connections) as an indicator of reduced vulnerability and improved well-being into the future.

Social Stratification of Poverty

Poverty in Tajikistan was dramatic yet varied widely by region. In areas affected by the civil war, there was mention of dead children, raped sisters and daughters lying catatonic in back rooms, and husbands who dared come to the villages only at night for fear of being killed by neighbors. In Gharm, fields were said to be uncultivated and pastures unused because of land mines. Near Kurgan Tyube, residents complained of harassment of businesses and civilians by security forces. In Gharm both opposition and national forces harassed local businesses, extorting goods and bribes as a condition for safe passage. In eastern Khatlon the poor were systematically excluded from land privatization because of localist loyalties and confusing privatization laws. In the Pamirs, where most households depend on foreign assistance for basic food, poverty was linked to isolation, limited natural resources, and lack of available labor to work the rocky land.

In all regions the poor struggled to get food, even if only bread, on the table. Some had relied more than others on allowances and other subsidies during the Soviet period. They tended to be overly dependent on collective farm salaries, social services, and unskilled labor. In general, poor families had few or no working men, large numbers of children, little or no land, and insufficient inputs, and many were in poor health.

A family living in a small village in the Vose district of eastern Khatlon, near the city of Kuliab, has fallen into poverty as a result of the civil war. In the past they had 10 to 15 hens, a cow, and a household plot planted with vegetables. Today they have one cow and a ruined house. They have sold everything in the house, including the wood floor planks, to buy flour. The husband works at the collective farm but has not received a salary in years. Officially, he is a shareholder—a status he neither understands nor benefits from—and owns land, but he cannot work it because it is too far away. He says he receives cotton stalks, which the family sells or uses as fuel. He and his wife cannot feed their seven children, who have not gone to school in two years. In the corner of the house is a heap of drying grass from which the mother says she will make bread. Her older child takes care of cattle for relatives in exchange for bread. A few days ago, when the mother went begging with a group of women from her village, she was bitten by a dog. The wound became infected, but the family cannot afford the medicines to treat it. Her arm is visibly infected and possibly gangrenous, according to the doctor who interviewed her. There is no *tabib* (traditional healer) in the village, and the family is faced with the decision of whether to sell their only cow to buy medicine or let the illness run its course.

Households at greatest risk included those headed by women; young parents with small children; families with many young children and no grown-up sons; families headed by collective farm workers, doctors, or teachers working full-time (whose salaries were small, if paid at all); and families whose male members were incapable of demanding physical work. A large household with many men ensured access to the market, access to activities with higher income potential such as cattle sales, and seasonal mobility to other former Soviet republics.

Average families were those who, by summoning all their resources, were able simply to meet their basic daily needs. Families in this group usually had at least two working males and fewer women and children than other families. In areas such as Gorno-Badakhshan, agriculture demanded at least two males to prepare the rocky, mountainous land for cultivation. Average families had access to land for cultivation and had two or more cows, or a cow and some sheep or goats. Remittances from family members working outside the country were also important. The average family lived in fear of corruption, insecurity, and market fluctuations, which might at any time wipe out their source of livelihood.

Zaynura, a collective farm worker interviewed at the bus station in Dushanbe, is part of a household of 13 people in Gharm. This spring she cut hay, for which the collective farm gave her 10 kilograms of flour but no salary. She exchanged two goats for 50 kilograms of corn, and a lamb for 50 kilograms of wheat. She still has a cow and half a hectare of land, where she has planted wheat. She also has a household plot with 12 apple trees, where she has planted potatoes, tomatoes, cabbage, and onions. She sells half of the produce at the market and buys bread with the proceeds. She also sews dresses and pants on order. People pay her in food because cash is so scarce. She travels to Dushanbe to sell her apples and buy various small items, which she sells in Gharm. She also buys secondhand clothes for her children.

Households with savings or productive assets were seen as doing at least a bit better. In each village a handful of people had gained control of agricultural equipment through early privatization or had skills that they could use to earn income. These people were generally able to provide for their families. Remittances made an important contribution to the household budget, allowing for investment and improvements, which otherwise might have been difficult.

A tractor driver interviewed in Vakhsh owns his own tractor and charges 1,000 Tajik rubles for each hundredth of a hectare he works. His family grows and sells lemons and other fruits and vegetables, as well as small quantities of corn and wheat. With remittances from his sons working in Russia, he has been able to buy some household appliances.

In general, the well-off had links to management of local industries, local or regional government, or security forces. In many villages they were the only people to have a cement home, and they leased large amounts of

Day laborers near the village of Galadzor in eastern Khatlon work in the bean field of a large land leaseholder. *Photo by Elizabeth Gomart*

arable, irrigated land planted with cash crops. In towns and large district centers, respondents perceived that the well-off had gotten where they were through corruption, exploiting their position or connections to the localist clans in power.

In villages and towns, wealth and opportunities were clearly linked to membership in a small, localist patriarchal clan,[1] which was identified by village or neighborhood of origin and family ties. As a result, historical background was very important in understanding access to resources at a site. Localist clans controlled access to employment in industrial and political bureaucracies and distributed the benefits to a narrow group. Localism and its power dynamics were further complicated in areas that had been resettled after World War II in an effort to develop intensive agriculture in the desert valleys of southwestern Tajikistan. In western Khatlon collective farms were very large, with as many as 20,000 inhabitants. The farms were a collection of smaller settlements, each segregated by localist group, a legacy of the massive (and tragic) resettlement programs of the late 1940s, which had brought in people from mountainous Gharmi, Pamiri, and Kuliabi villages. But localist clan dynamics were still at work at many sites. In the village of Varzob near Dushanbe, at Shakhistan in Khodjent, and in the Vose and Vakhsh districts in Khatlon, local residents pointed to people who were considered outsiders even though they had lived in the area for generations. As resources became scarcer and individually owned, these outsiders were at a disadvantage when it came to land and asset privatization, transport for schooling, and being hired as wage laborers. Respondents said that members of the governing clans had helped themselves and their relatives during privatization of farm assets (equipment, inputs, cattle, and use of arable land and pastureland) and industrial assets.

On the Goib-Safar-Zoda Collective Farm, the inhabitants of the village of Galadzor, Vose district, systematically lost out during privatization. The residents explain that even though they have lived on the collective farm for four or five generations, they are originally from Hovaling (a city to the north) and usually marry people from that area. As a result, they are not relatives of the collective farm managers, who reside in the valley in Kaduchi village, and they have few linkages to local power.

Until recently, most of the village lived on collective farm salaries and subsidized food staples from the local state shops. Cattle and sheep grazed on the collective's pastures. Food production on household plots has always been very limited because there is no water supply in the village. The one water pipeline from a neighboring collective farm was cut off recently in the face of shortages. Market links are weak because of low production and distance.

Today the pastures have been given out as presidential decree land to residents of Kaduchi village.[2] The cattle need to be taken (illegally) to the next district, 20 kilometers away, for pasture. Those who cannot afford to pay the shepherd to herd their cattle to the faraway pastures let their sheep run through the fields of the large leaseholders, at the risk of having them slaughtered. The new brigade leader, who is originally from Kaduchi village, has received hundreds of hectares of land. He and the farm's accountant have leased an extraordinary amount of quality land: a total of 1,230 hectares. In contrast, the village residents have each been given a few hundredths of a hectare of vineyards 12 kilometers away. In the fall they will get to keep the wood for fuel and some of the harvest for sale. The terms of the lease are open and depend on the harvest and on one's relationship with the chief economist of the farmers' association.

The residents of Kaduchi lease the more profitable apple orchards. At different times during the year, the leaseholders provide daily jobs for the collective farm workers from Kaduchi, excluding the men in Galadzor. The state shops are closed, and the collective farm only provided a few kilograms of flour per person this year. None were available to the residents of Galadzor. The poor in the village rely on selling their cattle, bartering eggs for soap, collecting hay, stealing from the nearby fields, and begging in neighboring villages.

Meeting Basic Needs

The poor were unable to meet their basic needs for food, clothing, shelter, and fuel. Health care, education, and investment were completely out of reach, especially for the rural poor. Food was especially scarce for many poor families in the springtime, when their food reserves ran out before the first grain harvest.

Respondents throughout the country referred to the lack of flour or bread as a criterion of poverty. Bread is a staple in the Tajik diet; its availability and quality are indicative of a household's living standard. Government-subsidized bread was provided to selected apartment residents in some secondary cities and district centers. Families with access to land produced their own flour from wheat, which they milled in the village. In the spring, when reserves were depleted, families turned to corn flour, which was perceived as less digestible and could not be cooked in the same way as the traditional Tajik flat bread. Large numbers of families in Vakhsh and Vose districts milled a mixture of hay, bran, and other seeds (including cottonseed) to compensate for meager or nonexistent wheat harvests.

Lack of shelter was the most important criterion of poverty in the war-affected areas. Reconstruction of demolished homes had been slow, and multiple generations were often crowded into one room. New construction required that the family give up part of the household plot, an important loss for those dependent on subsistence farming and income from cash crops. In contrast to the rest of the country, in Shakhistan, a town untouched by the civil war, large amounts of construction materials and new constructions were visible on family plots. In eastern Khatlon poor young families lived in mud buildings, pilfering timber and roofing materials where they could.

In Galadzor a young wife and mother of a six-month-old who is not thriving explains that she and her husband are from the neighboring village of Kaduchi, part of the same collective farm. They were unable to afford cement to build a home in the valley. After their first child was born, they built a home out of clay in Galadzor because there was no room for building in Kaduchi. They bought roofing materials from a neighbor, but the wife expects that he will take them back since she is ` unable to pay. Her husband will then have to build a mud roof, which needs to be reworked after each heavy rain. When asked where they found the beams supporting the front entrance, the husband smiles and points to a remaining telephone pole.

Clothes and children's shoes were the second-largest component of household expenditure after food, according to recent surveys and household estimates. Poor families felt a real tension between the need to meet immediate food needs and the need to provide shoes for school. Shoes and clothing were also a priority issue for displaced people and refugees.

Health services were becoming fee-based in towns and closing down in rural areas, for lack of essential supplies. In one site in Gharm the local village first aid station had opened when humanitarian supplies were delivered but closed down again when they ran out. The poor had access to consultations in rural areas, where they were mostly free or low cost, but not to essential medicines for treatment. Urban clinics and hospital doctors increasingly charged informal fees. Hospital stays were very costly; the patient had to provide all the medicines, supplies, and bedding. The poor had at times been turned away from services, even in emergencies.

Increasingly, people were turning to the traditional healers, who charged fees based on ability to pay and used supplies available locally.

The Tajik Constitution guarantees free access to education, yet schools in towns were shifting to a fee-based system. Schools required parents to contribute to school repairs and pay for "additional" courses such as chemistry and English. Poor children were pressured to move to other schools or simply to quit. In cities and towns such as Dushanbe, Kurgan Tyube, and Kuliab, young boys sold small goods or pulled carts at the market to cover their own school fees and supplies. Girls, limited perhaps by gender expectations, lacked opportunities to earn even small amounts of cash.

Attendance was usually high in elementary school but decreased in secondary school. In small villages some primary schools had closed for lack of funds and teachers. Without regular bus service, children were dropping out or attending sporadically. Children lacked appropriate shoes and winter clothing. Supplies were also very scarce. Furthermore, economic priorities conflicted with school attendance on a daily basis. Children had household responsibilities: caring for cattle, caring for siblings, and helping with the cotton harvest. The lack of security also affected school attendance, as young women in Gharm stayed home for fear of being harassed or even attacked by armed men on their way to and from school. Fearful young children of Gharmi or Pamiri origin in Kurgan Tyube stayed at home rather than venture out to the next village for classes.

The value of education was often low, especially in villages. Attendance by girls 11 years and older was deemed unnecessary, even undesirable, by many parents, especially in Gharm and Kuliab, which were considered more traditional than Khodjent (which is mostly ethnic Uzbek and fairly urban), Kurgan Tyube, and Dushanbe. In contrast, in Gorno-Badakhshan education for girls was highly valued. One reason is that Gorno-Badakhshan is Ismaili Muslim, and the Aga Khan, the Ismaili religious leader, has stressed the importance of education, especially the education of girls, for many decades. Higher (secondary and university) rates for girls in Gorno-Badakhshan reached 51.4 percent in 1994 (Newell 1995). Elsewhere, when they did go to school, girls were at a disadvantage in comparison with boys when it came to obtaining textbooks and supplies.

Poverty affected the ability to celebrate life-cycle ceremonies. Under the counsel of the mullah, some communities had agreed to decrease the expense of weddings and funerals, which could bankrupt a household. Thus, at many sites, wedding ceremonies were confined to close relatives, and funerals required two feasts instead of five. In isolated villages, weddings were often held in the winter to avoid unexpected guests and keep costs down.

Livelihood Strategies

In the context of reconstruction in the war-affected areas (mainly western Khatlon), civil war in Gharm, and transition from a controlled economy, respondents reported a number of changing trends such as curbing of household consumption; diversification of income sources and changing relative importance of existing sources; increased participation of women and children in the labor force; and increased begging and stealing.

Decreased Consumption

Poor households throughout the country resorted to eating smaller quantities of poorer-quality food in order to survive. The use of lower-quality grain in place of wheat flour was widespread in war-affected, mountainous, and isolated areas. The poor commonly went without nonessential items such as new clothing. Reduced resources and increased prices also severely limited access to even emergency medical care and education, especially for girls and older children, with tragic consequences for many poor families.

Some resources were pooled to support the extended family. In many small villages, family networks included almost all the households in the village. Neighbors cooperated for their mutual benefit: women pooled milk production to make butter; they shared the income from milk sales, one providing the milk and the other selling it in the market; they worked together to clear each other's land or harvest the crop; they exchanged produce to sell in the market.

Humanitarian assistance was a major source of food for poor households, especially for recent returnees in the Kurgan Tyube area and in Gorno-Badakhshan. In war-affected areas, where people were without assets to sell, humanitarian assistance provided a much-needed stopgap in the spring until the harvest. In Gorno-Badakhshan families estimated that 85 percent of their food came from assistance.

Diversification of Income

New activities such as private production and sales emerged, and the roles of household members changed. In both rural and urban households, all family members except the youngest and the most infirm were involved in income-generating activities.

Community values in some areas had changed with regard to women and children's roles. Women had become more active in marketing and production in war-affected areas (such as western Khatlon), where there were many female-headed households. Women had traditionally worked on the household plot and on the collective farm; now many were also leaving the village to sell their produce or goods in the market—still mainly a man's arena. Women had become the main work force on collective farms and were paid miserly wages or in kind, if at all, for their work. Women milked cows and fed small animals on the household plot; they processed milk and wool.

The men worked their presidential and leased land or worked as hired laborers for large leaseholders. Only the poorest also worked on the collective farm. They were responsible for most of the tasks related to cattle, including pasturing, breeding, and sale. Many men worked elsewhere in the former Soviet Union for remittances, relying on networks established during Soviet times.

Boys took care of cattle, milked cows, and gathered hay. In the warm valleys, children took care of the silkworms, gathering mulberry branches and keeping the rooms heated for the worms to grow. Children, especially girls, also helped on the household plot and with child care instead of attending school regularly. Older children were expected to work on the larger land parcels, harvesting, guarding the crop, and storing the harvest.

Remittances

Remittances from abroad had long played an important role in reducing local unemployment, especially among young men. At the time of the study, the exodus of many young men was linked to insecurity (the draft and localist discrimination), the need to replenish assets lost in the war, and the economic crisis. Most people believed that those who had family members working in Russia were better off. Respondents in Kurgan Tyube and in Gharm estimated that 70 percent of the town's adult men worked in Russia or in the Islamic Republic of Iran.

Mr. Hasanov lives in the village of Soul in the Gharm Valley. He believes that he lives better than others in his village. His four sons are highly educated and have good positions in Russia. He estimates that 80 percent of his income comes from Russia and only 20 percent from his household plot. He has more than 15 apple trees on his land. He sells half of the harvest in the market in Dushanbe to buy staples. He also cultivates potatoes, onions, and tomatoes on his household plot for his own consumption. He uses his own car to drive to Dushanbe and provides rides to neighbors for a fee. There are two other "rich" people in the village: the director of the collective farm and a man who has established a small fruit processing factory, which employs six of his relatives.

Men usually left to work abroad in organized groups with a brigade leader who had arranged work for an agreed amount of time and pay. Each member paid a fee in addition to transport costs. The team leader was in charge of security and accommodations, ensuring that all went well while they were abroad. In Shakhistan, young men expected to earn 30,000 Tajik rubles (TR) for two months' work in Russia on a collective farm. Some had not yet been paid for the last year's work, but there were so few local opportunities to work that they were willing to take the chance again this year.

Localist clan and ethnic ties facilitated labor migration. In villages and small district centers, respondents explained that access to remittances depended on whether local residents had ethnic ties to neighboring countries such as Uzbekistan, or whether they had set up localist clan-based support networks during Soviet times with Russian cities.

In some villages remittances were rare. In Vakhsh, a war-affected district where Gharmis, Pamiris, and Kuliabis reside, respondents explained that Kuliabis had no preexisting networks for working abroad. There was also a perception that Kuliabis were protected within Tajikistan but were unsafe from retaliation for civil war activities elsewhere in the former Soviet Union.

For many Uzbeks, especially those living in northern Tajikistan, small-scale contractual work in Uzbekistan represented an important source of income. In villages in Shakhistan, which borders on Uzbekistan, water was scarce, and land cultivation could not be the main source of income. One head of household had earned 500 kilograms of wheat for his work, enough to satisfy the family's flour needs for three to five months. Opportunities were reduced now that the border between the two countries had been closed and a work permit was required. Fewer Uzbek men were working, and for shorter periods: one or two weeks in June and July. Men used to purchase wheat in Uzbekistan for half what it cost in Tajikistan. Now the border guards confiscated the goods they found. The workers had to limit the scale of their cargo, carrying the flour across the border in suitcases, sneaking into the country at night using back roads, or paying off the border guards.

No matter how important they were for the family budget in the long term, remittances could not be the sole source of income since their amount and timing were not reliable. There was no banking system to facilitate transfers; sometimes money was transported by fellow brigade members returning to the village; the money could be lost or stolen on the trip home. Immediate food and health needs sometimes burdened the remaining family members.

A young father left behind a family of three children to work in Russia for 18 months. Upon his return, he found his children going barefoot and one of his sons deaf from an untreated ear infection. His wife had not had enough cash or mobility to get the boy's infection treated in time. Meanwhile the father, unaware of his family's plight, had saved some money and bought himself some new clothes, a luxury.

Land

In rural areas the importance of land as a source of subsistence had dramatically increased. Both at the community and at the household level, respondents described their living standards with reference to the land, the harvest, trees, and agricultural assets. But access to land was not universal and did not provide a guarantee against hunger. Officially, land could be obtained as inheritable household plots, presidential decree land, inheritable land lease, or by a member of an association of leaseholders. In practice, access to land was determined by the available (male) labor in the household, by the household's membership in a specific localist clan, by the availability of nonlabor resources for cultivation, and by the quality of the land and its distance from the residence. Land privatization took the shape of land lease shareholding companies with limited ownership rights. State Farms were to be dissolved and reorganized as collective farms, but collective farms that performed poorly (or were not cultivated within one year) could be reclaimed by the farm management.

In theory, all rural residents had access to household plots of 0.01 to 0.15 hectare, but the productivity of the land varied greatly. Few if any household plots were large enough to provide the household with income and food year-round. Fruit trees provided income late in the summer, often too late to help the family through the difficult spring months. Crops that could be preserved (such as onions and potatoes) were considered particularly attractive, since they could provide income year-round. In Khatlon a main cash crop was lemons, and in Gharm, apples and pears. Income from household plot production could be substantial, depending on land quality, the type of produce, and ease of access to markets.

For a family on the Turkmenistan Collective Farm, in Vakhsh, located only 4 kilometers from the market in Kurgan Tyube, the main source of income is vegetable sales: tomatoes and cucumbers. The family estimates that in one year they make the bulk of their income just on these sales. They also have land planted with wheat, and they own cattle.

In mountainous villages, plots were usually much smaller and less effectively exploited because of lack of inputs and machinery. Water for irrigation was rarely available, and soil quality was poor, as was access to markets. Some families whose land was poor or who lacked seeds or access to markets reported that their incomes from the household plot and presidential decree land were minimal.

In Roshqala poor families rely on humanitarian assistance for an estimated 85 percent of their income. Home-grown produce represents 7 percent, cattle 5 percent, and salaries 3 percent. In Vose a pensioner reports that 15 percent of her meager income comes from her garden, 60 percent from cattle, 10 percent from her pension, and 15 percent from begging.

Poor families sold vegetables and fruits to buy flour or bread, substantially limiting their own consumption of fresh produce. These households marketed nearly all of their tomatoes, cucumbers, and herbs; better-off families consumed a larger amount. Involvement in market activity depended on security, availability of transport, and the mobility of household members.

Equipment from the collective farms was now privately owned and rented to users. Because there were few working tractors, villagers often needed to wait for days before their land could be worked or their crops harvested. In 1989, in the context of a first attempt at privatization, a handful of villagers in each settlement purchased tractors and other equipment at minimal prices. They now charged TR1,000 per hundredth of a hectare—a considerable amount for households strapped for cash—plus fuel costs for the use of a tractor or a combine. Households with equipment to rent could earn cash to cover their other inputs. In mountainous areas, where mechanized equipment could not be used, oxen now worked the land, much of which had never been worked before.

The main avenue for access to land for former collective farm workers was in the form of mandatory distributions of land through the 1995 presidential decree. The distribution of this land was proceeding much more slowly than mandated and had not begun in some villages in Gharm at the time of this study. Meanwhile some households cultivated collective farmland without a formal agreement, acknowledging the risk of forfeiting their harvest to the farm's managers. In Vakhsh respondents said that one grain harvest from a household's presidential decree land (0.15 hectare) provided enough flour for three to four months. Even in the south, where farmers could harvest two crops a year, families needed additional income to cover basic needs. Some hoped to buy seed for a second crop after the wheat was harvested—usually corn for use as cattle feed.

The village councils, which reviewed applications for land, often denied applications by female-headed households without a grown son, citing lack of manpower. So some of the most vulnerable households were rejected. Female respondents pointed out the irony of their being turned down even though most of the collective farm's work force was female. This was a major obstacle for households in sites in western Khatlon and Gharm that had few or no men, because the vast majority remained in Afghanistan to avoid retaliation for civil war activities. Young men were in hiding or had left for Russia to avoid the draft. Many women who remained had a difficult time claiming land because they had not formally registered as residents of the village when they married (this was common), and their husbands and families had died or disappeared during the war. Some female-headed households did not even apply for land; they were not used to dealing with village officials, or believed that they had no right to it.

In Vakhsh district, a female-headed household in Mopr, a village that had been entirely destroyed by the 1992 bombings, is among the poorest. The 25-year-old widow and her two surviving daughters (a third died of hunger in 1992) live in a partly rebuilt home, but the family has sold all its belongings, including pots and mattresses, to buy flour. This year she planted her 0.15-hectare household plot with wheat she had begged from neighbors. Most days she walks the 6 kilometers to Kurgan Tyube to buy produce in the central market, which she then resells at slightly higher prices to apartment dwellers, earning TR150, enough to buy two or three loaves of bread.

The disabled and pensioners faced similar issues based on the assumed lack of manpower at the household level. The land distribution in Roshqala, Vakhsh, and Vose excluded teachers and doctors who had not been collective farm workers and therefore, it was claimed, lacked agricultural knowledge, although as rural residents they had always cultivated their own household plots and were part of larger families engaged in agriculture.

In sites where there were great differences in land quality, there were also great inequities in distribution. In general, distributions favored the farm management and associated clans. In Shakhistan only 10 percent of the land distributed under the decree was irrigated and had been cultivated by the collective farm in the past, making the profitable use of most of the land nearly impossible. Most villagers were unsure whether they would cultivate the land they had received, since it would take considerable water, fertilizer, and labor to prepare it.

Another way to obtain land was through leasing. Leasing of land was meant to target rural residents of underperforming state-run farms to improve efficiency, but access was widely recognized as being reserved for the well-to-do within any farm rather than the average collective farm worker. The criterion for selection applied by the village councils was "ability to work the land," generally interpreted as having money and access to machinery. At the Sino Collective Farm, in Vose, the renters benefiting from open leases were the farm management staff and persons not formerly employed by the collective farm, such as prominent warlords. In Shakhistan, Vose, and Vakhsh, leaseholders included urban-based enterprises; although this was not allowed under the law, it was beneficial to the farm management. In practice, converting collective farms into shareholding companies often resulted in the de facto firing and expropriation of farmworkers, who lost their salaries and benefits—and received small amounts of land that they could not cultivate. Many farmers received land that was too far away and could not be guarded; and farmers had to pay for renting privatized equipment and for inputs such as seed and water.

The terms of the lease were generally set by the chief economist of the collective farm. One type of lease was reserved for irrigated land and allowed the leaseholder to select the crop. The second type was usually for one year; the crop was determined by the collective farm, and the price was often set at harvest time by the farm management. These leases were for ordinary collective farm workers.

Localist clan identity seemed to be a main determinant of resource allocation. At the Turkmenistan Collective Farm, although 80 percent of the population was Gharmi, all major management posts were held by Kuliabis except for one Uzbek—members of the winning clans in the civil war. As a result, Gharmis were the last to get to use the tractors and water for irrigation, owned less cattle and equipment, had less advantageous leases, and suffered from other inequities. Only 20 percent of the Gharmi residents had cattle, but each household in the Kuliabi village had several cows.

At the Turkmenistan Collective Farm, a Gharmi farmer was offered an undocumented one-year lease under improbable conditions: he was to work 5 hectares of land, 3 of which were to be sown with cotton, which the collective farm would purchase in full at a very low price determined by the management at the time of harvest. The year before, the farmer had been promised TR5–8 per kilogram but had received only TR3–5 per kilogram. His other 2 hectares are sown with wheat, but he must hand over half the harvest to the collective farm. Cotton requires considerable labor from the entire household at crucial times, whereas wheat requires little labor but costly inputs and the use of leased machinery. Respondents considered their work on cotton to be nearly unpaid labor, an added cost to their lease aimed primarily at wheat production. In contrast, on the same collective farm, the Kuliabi lease-holders were not required to grow cotton. They could grow a full 5 hectares of wheat and owed half of the harvest to the collective farm— a considerably lower "tax." They also own tractors or other equipment, which lowers their cost of production.

Residents of Roshqala and Anjin village in Gorno-Badakhshan, an ethnically homogeneous region operating with much autonomy from Dushanbe, perceived that land distribution (leasing and otherwise) was conducted in a fair manner, in contrast with perceptions at other sites. However, leasing agreements stipulated unrealistic norms of payment: 1.5 metric tons of wheat per hectare, whereas the farmers expected to harvest only 0.8 metric ton per hectare.

Because of the dire need for food production in the villages and the slow pace of effective privatization, farmers coped with their limited access to land and the restrictions on choice of cultivation by intercropping and cultivating pastureland. In Vose some apple orchards were intercropped with wheat, and in Shakhistan, with carrots. At the Sino Farmers' Association and in Gharm, collective farm workers were allowed to cultivate grain on former pastureland. In Roshqala some land was cleared by households without a formal agreement.

The importance of land in the transition cannot be overstated, nor can the negative impact of a slow and unjust process of land distribution that benefits only a few. Even urban residents believed they would be less vulnerable if they had land for food production. A CARE survey showed that half of them had access to land, but urban household plots were smaller than rural plots (CARE 1994).

Livestock

In the past, livestock had represented savings, and large expenses had been covered through the yearly sale of livestock in the fall. Basic staples such as flour and cattle feed had been available in the village stores at prices affordable to the common worker. By 1996, however, the closing of these state shops and the erosion in salaries had increased farmers' reliance on cattle sales for procuring these essential goods. In many poor households cattle sales represented the sole source of income in the spring, when stored grain was exhausted. Respondents explained that, from January until May, one cow could buy only one 50-kilogram bag of wheat flour, which lasts two weeks for a family of eight. The sale of cattle in some areas (such as Gharm) was very rapid, even alarming, residents said. The depletion of cattle holdings meant an end to flour purchases and dairy products, often families' only regular source of protein. In war-affected villages in Kurgan Tyube, an estimated 80 percent of households no longer owned cattle.

Cattle productivity was reduced because the land reserved for hay or pastures had been distributed for cultivation as presidential decree land or for leasing. Farmers in mountainous areas, who relied most on cattle breeding, had been squeezed out by the expansion of cultivated land. There was a drop in feed and hay production, and thus in the number of cattle that households could maintain throughout the winter. Yet cattle remained an important productive asset and source of income in mountainous or isolated villages in Shakhistan, Gharm, and Vose. Even in towns, researchers saw cows grazing in public parks and along canals. Rabbits and chickens were kept in cages on balconies of apartment buildings.

Participation in Markets

In the regional centers and other long-established towns, large markets attracted goods from the surrounding area, from Dushanbe, and from neighboring countries. Markets were an important source of income for many urban households. However, trade activities required startup capital and a product to sell (usually produced or processed at home). Insecurity limited the scale of market activities, the military draft kept young men away from public places, and there were formal and informal fees to be paid to officials.

A woman living in Dushanbe took a loan from a neighbor to start a business reselling bread. She would buy 100 loaves from the local bread factory and resell them for a small profit. Twice the loaves were taken by the police, however, and as a result she has given up her business. She sold everything she had to pay off her debt and has no other source of income.

Access to the central market was controlled by the market's management. At the central market in Kurgan Tyube, each seller paid a formal fee of TR100 a day to sell small amounts of produce, such as cucumbers from a 50-kilogram bag. The fee varied by location and according to the quantity of produce. Prices of goods were set in accordance with the prices charged by others. The sellers checked on each other and would not allow someone who undersold them to return the following day. Registration of small and medium-size enterprises entailed a round of formal and informal fees to local officials.

With the breakdown of state shop networks, smaller auxiliary markets had sprung up around the town. With only a little capital, households could purchase goods from the central market and resell them at higher prices in the smaller markets. Many of these traders used to work in factories; some were skilled workers. Teachers were also often involved in market activities, since they could take public transportation for free and had plenty of free time. Children and young girls were involved in selling; adults usually did the purchasing of goods for sale. The income from this type of activity was not sufficient in itself to cover the needs of a family but was a good supplement.

In Kurgan Tyube a young family struggles to make ends meet. The father is a university professor, and the mother a schoolteacher. Both continue to work in their professions. Every morning he goes to the market to purchase an assortment of small goods and brings them to their neighborhood. He and his son set up a stall by the roadside. The mother and son take turns at the stand during the day. She may travel back and forth to the central bazaar to replenish goods at the stall. According to the mother, two-thirds of the family's income comes from their roadside stall and only one-third from salaries, pensions, and privileges provided to teachers, mainly free transport and public utilities.

Town residents acted as intermediaries, buying produce in bulk from distant villages, buying goods early in the morning from nearby villages or from villagers at the market, and selling at the market. Those with cars or trucks and cash for fuel could travel to the villages. There was a perception that Uzbeks dominated the markets throughout the western part of the country because of their access to cheaper goods in Uzbekistan, a tradition of trading, and secure places in the market. Lack of startup capital limited the types of activity.

In Kurgan Tyube a teacher quit his teaching job to sell imported goods in the market. Last year he made TR500 a month teaching, and this year his salary had been increased to TR1,200, but this was not enough even to buy bread for his family. He now sells imported clothes and other goods, which he purchases in Termez or Tashkent, in Uzbekistan, or in Ura-Tyube, in the Khodjent region. His wife and children sell the goods at the market. He says that he can make TR40,000 to 50,000 a month selling clothes.

Shops that sold imported food and clothes remained in government hands for the most part, staffed by four or five young men to ensure security. Traders believed that local authorities had manipulated prices during privatization to make the shops inaccessible to the local population, and then purchased the goods themselves at a lower price.

Poor women produced goods such as dresses or paper bags for the market. Such value-added products had very narrow profit margins, however.

Mukhabat lives in a village near Kurgan Tyube. She came back last year with her five children from Afghanistan, but her husband stayed behind. Her sister, who lost her husband in the war, and her elderly parents also live with her. Three of her children attend school but have only pens and paper—no textbooks. This spring they mixed wheat flour with corn flour to make bread, a sign of poverty. Mukhabat grows herbs, cabbage, and carrots on her household plot for sale at the market. This year they will plant wheat on their household plot and presidential decree land. She and her sister got a sewing machine from SCF/UK last year, which they use to sew paper bags. She buys paper for TR5 a meter and sells bags for TR15–20 each at the market. From time to time she gets an order for a dress from her neighbors.

Traditional crafts were practiced in many rural homes. Many items were made to be passed on to one's children at the time of their wedding and not for sale. In Kuliab, however, a few women offered to sell some of these items without any consideration of the time spent or the cost of the inputs, because of their dire situation. In contrast, in Shakhistan women made rugs and other items for their children and were reluctant to sell them because of the low prices they commanded on the market.

In the past, access to markets for village produce had been ensured through cheap transport and government marketing networks. At the time of the study, access to markets was dictated by distance from the nearest town or district center. Market activities and cash crops abounded in villages within walking distance (10 to 15 kilometers) of a lively market. Villages near towns as well as villages with a history of producing cash crops such as lemons or onions depended on markets to lift their incomes. The impact on household budgets varied according to market access, security, distance, local production, demand for home-produced goods, costs of production and marketing, the sex of the seller, and access to transport (cart, tractor, or truck). In villages farther away, access was limited to those who controlled the collective farm machinery, which they could use to transport the produce to market. Residents of these more remote sites were less likely to exploit their presidential decree land or household plot fully. Trade in these villages was usually limited to itinerant merchants, traveling on foot, trying to sell goods door to door, or middlemen purchasing produce in bulk. In these villages household plots seemed to be used for produce that could be easily preserved and trucked (potatoes, carrots, onions, eggs, dairy products), with only a few vegetables being grown for home consumption.

Trade within villages was mostly limited to petty trade. Villagers set up small stalls at one of their street-level windows, selling mainly imported cookies and cigarettes. In a relatively well off small village outside of the center of Shakhistan, 14 of these stalls were counted. Most were operated by young women or children, suggesting a low level of activity and income. On main roads stalls offered alcohol and cigarettes and were usually run by men.

Lack of security inhibited local-level economic activities throughout Tajikistan but was most severely felt in areas where there were few men to protect their households from abuses; in western Khatlon those of Gharmi and Pamiri origin suffered from lack of security more than others.

In Kurgan Tyube a village woman headed to market to sell cucumbers is stopped at police posts on the way, and each policeman takes his

> share. An old man selling cucumbers in Kurgan Tyube comes from a village 6 kilometers away. He paid TR100 for the ride. He comes twice a week to the market with half a bag of cucumbers. A couple of times he came with a full bag, but the bag was stolen by the police, so now he only sells small amounts because he cannot afford the risk.

Purchasing goods from abroad raised issues of security for traders as they transported the goods and cash. Merchant-client relationships provided a degree of protection by enabling merchants to keep a low profile. Insecurity and corruption also affected how medium-scale traders were able to conduct their business. Women traveled abroad by air or bus to purchase clothes and appliances; respondents explained that women knew best what would sell, and they were less likely to be harassed by border guards. They usually traveled in prearranged groups. Bus trips were arranged so that bribes to border guards and police posts were included in the fee and handled by the bus driver. Groups traveling by air could bring back as much as 750 kilograms of goods per flight: 300 kilograms legally as baggage, another 300 kilograms by "reaching an agreement" with the baggage staff, and 150 kilograms as carry-on luggage. Men traveled more by road or train, where security could not be ensured. Border guards often stopped trucks of goods coming from abroad, extorting sums of up to $200. Businessmen who imported flour and sugar said that they had to dress poorly and bring in only one truck at a time to avoid being perceived as someone who could pay large bribes. They had transportation and capital, but security remained an obstacle.

Insecurity shaped the decisions of the larger entrepreneurs as well. Of 20 buses that used to travel to Gharm on a daily basis, only 4 remained in service. One respondent estimated that a truck carrying produce could expect to lose 20 percent to government or opposition forces or bandits by the time it reached Dushanbe. Sometimes trucks and automobiles were confiscated and the driver and other occupants ordered to serve the military for a few days before being released.

Stealing of harvests was widespread; only cotton was safe, since it could not be eaten or sold by individuals. Villagers complained of thefts of food by neighbors or armed gangs coming at night. They were particularly fearful for their potato and vegetable harvests, which often constituted the bulk of their expected cash income. The forced draft of men aged 15 to 45 to fight in Gharm had an important impact on available labor at the household level. Young men left home to work in Russia if they could afford to. If they were unable to leave, they stayed hidden at home to avoid the roundups.

Skilled and Unskilled Labor

Skilled workers—mechanics, shoe repairmen, and carpenters—were able to sell their skills at a higher price and with more regularity than nonskilled workers.

> A carpenter from Shakhistan near the Uzbek border says that he has orders from Uzbekistan that keep him busy once or twice a year for a few weeks at a time. He uses the money for inputs to cultivate his household plot and to breed cattle. He has not needed to sell cattle to purchase flour, an indicator that his savings are not depleted and that he is able to satisfy daily basic needs.

Unskilled labor was turning increasingly to seasonal work and odd jobs. Hired labor had increased dramatically with the advent of large leaseholders and the inability of many villagers, who were often former collective farm workers, to gain access to arable, irrigated land. Male labor was widely available, especially in villages unaffected by the civil war and without access to seasonal employment abroad or a local market (eastern Khatlon, for example). Agricultural seasonal labor could be hired for a few months at a time, and salaries were higher than those paid by the collective farm. Hired agricultural labor was noted at all sites except Roshqala, where fertile land is not plentiful enough to attract large leaseholders.

Large groups of 40 to 50 men stood around near the bazaars hoping for someone to hire them. Men from villages traveled to town in the hope of being hired for odd jobs, often waiting around all day for an offer of construction or agricultural work. Factory workers worked on weekends or during their free time, selling their specialized skills. The work was difficult, reserved for the strong and healthy, yet the earnings from sporadic employment were not reliable or sufficient to raise a household out of poverty.

Salaried Employment

For most urban households, salaried employment remained the preferred source of income even though salaries were very low and irregularly paid. Some jobs offered access to equipment, fuel, and raw materials, which could be sold or used for private production. Benefits such as housing, free utilities, a kindergarten, or a clinic attached to the factory were still associated with some salaried positions. However, many people had been compelled to leave their jobs because of staff reductions, work stoppages due to lack of raw materials, and nonpayment of salaries. Those most affected by low and unpaid salaries were teachers, health workers, and other social services workers; unskilled laborers; and workers in uncompetitive industries. In Kurgan Tyube the main factories retained only an estimated 10 to 15 percent of their employees. Unemployment could affect entire blocks or neighborhoods since workers often lived in factory housing.

The manager of the transistor factory in Kurgan Tyube explains that although the factory is not currently producing anything, he tries to retain his most qualified workers in case work begins anew. His workers have meanwhile been able to identify private sources of income. The manager allows them to use the workroom, supplies, and electricity at the factory to work on private orders. He says that those still working in the factory are doing neither better nor worse than those who have been fired. The latter have turned to the market and wage labor, yet many come to the factory regularly to ask for work.

Some factories provided opportunities for income generation: bread, oil, soap, and cotton processing. The salary could be sizable, up to TR10,000 a month at the cooking oil factory, and workers could sell the goods they had made. In Kurgan Tyube, the market had five or six stalls with men selling soap from the government factory. One man working at the oil factory explained that he needed only to work there 25 days to live well for the next two months. But not all salaried workers had such viable alternatives.

Although the factory manager says that the average salary has doubled since the previous year, workers in the textile factory, most of them female, say that they have not received a salary in six months. Sometimes they receive partial payments of TR200–500. The women explain that they are sometimes given dresses on credit to sell on the open market. If they sell them, they can make a 10 percent profit. If they do not sell them within a month, they owe the value of the dress to the factory. They continue to work to have access to thread (which they use for private orders) and to qualify for a pension. Younger workers stay to learn to sew.

Formal salaried employment had been an important source of income, even in the villages, for the majority of the population in Soviet times, even though unemployment was a chronic problem, especially among young men in rural areas. In many villages collective farm salaries had not been paid in months—not since 1994 according to some respondents. However, they continued to be paid to collective farm management, who retained their positions as the farm privatized. Payment for collective farm work was mostly in kind. In cotton-growing areas (such as western Khatlon) it could include cotton stalks to sell or use as fuel, and in non-cotton-growing areas (such as eastern Khatlon) it could include 10 kilograms of flour every six months but sometimes nothing at all. Many rural residents still considered themselves collective farm workers and were confused about the new farmers' associations, where they received no salaries, and many were unable to eke out an income from their land.

Women and unskilled workers were most affected by unemployment or underemployment, especially in villages and secondary towns. Factories had closed their branches in many villages, reducing their rural work force, which consisted mainly of women. Women and children were relegated to working on the collective farm for minimal wages.

Gathering, Begging, and Stealing

In mountain villages the gathering of medicinal herbs and wild plants for home consumption and sale was often an important supplement to income. Pensioners and children gathered these plants and sold them on the side of the road or in markets, providing a minimal source of income. In springtime, wild greens provided the first source of fresh food for isolated households. They were not an answer to poverty.

Davlota Khurbi is a pensioner from Pushieni Miena, a village in the Sino Farmers' Association. She has not received her pension in six months. To make a living, she goes to the mountains and gathers medicinal herbs and edible plants to sell in the market. The last time she went to the market, she made TR900.

In eastern and western Khatlon, Gharm, and Gorno-Badakhshan, women spoke of organizing in small groups to beg in neighboring villages for food. Researchers were surprised at how common these activities were in Vose, because it went against the common belief among the Dushanbe-based interviewers that, in eastern Khatlon, "everyone would be riding in Jeeps."

Stealing was growing in importance. In Soviet times, stealing cash crops from the collective farm for sale at the market was a way to supplement incomes. Now respondents said that it was a consequence of food insecurity and lawlessness. That spring it represented the main source of food for some families in Galadzor village in Vose. For the last two years they had had no access to land for cultivation.

Each day in the mountain village of Galadzor, bands of 10 to 12 young girls, led by an elder male guardian, steal beans and barley from the fields of the two large leaseholders. Meanwhile their parents await the loot at home, unable to earn income as hired day laborers or from the small vineyards they were given as presidential decree land. There are no buyers for the grapes, they lack inputs, and the land is generally much too far from their homes to make the round trip daily or protect the crop. A schoolteacher and a group of women from the neighboring village, armed with bags as if going to the market, were also stealing from the fields. One woman says that since her husband is unemployed and her grain stocks are exhausted, her family has been eating stolen beans and homemade yogurt. The leaseholders patrol the roads all day long on horseback or tractor, charging at the bands of children to scare them out of their fields.

According to residents of Galadzor, the farm management brought in the army at harvest time last year to protect the fields from the young thieves. The armed soldiers surrounded the village until the harvest was completed.

In Shakhistan and Gharm, thefts of fruit from the collective farm orchards had supplemented household incomes even in Soviet times. But the scale of the thefts has increased. A new large landowner in Shakhistan said that the whole of last year's harvest had been stolen by the inhabitants. The current collective farm manager had decided to lease the orchards to the residents to give them a stake in protecting the harvest. In Vakhsh, a densely populated district, stealing took place mostly at night. Entire fields had been stripped of potatoes at harvest time the last two years, forcing owners to sleep in their fields to guard their crop. Vegetables were rare on leased or presidential decree land because they required constant guarding. The poor were not the only ones who stole. Residents in Vakhsh claimed that armed men had stolen their harvests or their cattle.

Community Institutions

Foreign organizations often seek partners locally to participate in and implement their programs. Yet in Tajikistan the representativeness of local leadership was ambiguous. Soviet repression had severely weakened traditional local institutions. Although they may yet be revived to the benefit of the communities, recent history showed how they can also lead to tragedy: the resurgence of religious and community leaders in the 1980s was tied to the rising opposition to the Soviet regime and the violence and destruction of the civil war.

At the time of the study, few institutions worked effectively to support households and communities. For the most part, traditional institutions were informal (even unstructured), traditional, male dominated, and family, clan, or locality based; many were religious. Formal institutions that had their origins in Soviet times, such as the Women's Councils and the Youth League, still operated in a centralized, hierarchical, and top-down manner. Even though a few local representatives were still at their posts, they generally failed to generate local membership or participation, and representatives sometimes exaggerated their importance and activities in rural communities.

The Mosque, the Mullah, and the Elders

Religious leaders in Tajikistan occupied an important place between the local community and nationalistic politics. Their diversity in experience and in their relationship to central power had a considerable impact on people's perceptions. People living in regions affected by the civil war, such as western Khatlon, were respectful but cautious about the role of the mullahs, whom some saw as having been instrumental in leading different factions to violence. Those mullahs now involved in the civil war (in Gharm and the northeastern part of Khatlon) were considered more extremist and traditionalist. Ismaili Muslims (in Gorno-Badakhshan) and Uzbek Sunni Muslims (mainly in Khodjent) supported their own leaders and had their own traditions.

In the towns the mullah was appointed by local government officials as in Soviet times. He answered to the Committee on Religious Affairs and received a salary. In most villages the elders selected the mullah on the basis of their assessment of his religious knowledge. The village mullah was not salaried; he usually practiced a profession and received payment in kind or cash for prayers and advice. Each day the local elders met at the mosque to pray and to discuss the problems of the village. In Gorno-Badakhshan, several villages jointly elected the *khalifa,* an Ismaili religious leader who occupied a rank above that of mullah.

The mullah and the group of elders played an active role in the context of humanitarian programs by disseminating information, gaining community support, mobilizing resources, monitoring program quality and timely execution, and resolving conflicts. In rare cases the council of elders, led by the mullah, was charged with resolving community-level conflicts and collecting funds for projects that benefited the entire community; more commonly the council would resolve conflicts between spouses or households. The elders and the mullah took on more active roles in Uzbek communities in Shakhistan because, as some interviewers explained, communities there were more ethnically homogeneous, and these leaders had not been discredited by their involvement in the civil war. But some mullahs in the war-affected villages of western Khatlon also played an important role in uniting villagers behind the concept of targeting assistance to female-headed households. Their support for the concept of excluding better-off households from assistance, in an environment where many officials denied the existence of poverty and inequalities, was progressive.

The female counterpart to the mullah, the *bibikhalifa*, conducted ceremonies in the home upon invitation. She was responsible for the religious education of women. Religious rites were passed down from mother to daughter, but with the revival of religious faith, many were self-appointed. The level of respect the *bibikhalifa* received from communities varied greatly. She was not salaried and received payment in cash and in kind during the ceremonies. She might also play other roles in the community.

The *mahallah* (street or quarter) representative acted as a liaison between the city officials and the neighborhood. In cities the position was formalized. The urban *mahallah* representative registered families; organized and distributed social assistance to poor families; collected land taxes, fees for garbage collection, and contributions for weddings and funerals; and managed a common hall for ceremonies. These representatives were found in neighborhoods with private homes; apartment buildings were administered by staff of the town council. The *mahallah* representative, usually a well-respected male pensioner, was elected by the community. By tradition he also received informal payment from each household.

In villages the *mahallah* representative was selected by the villagers each year. He was usually a member of the village council as well, and he was not paid for his duties. Representatives continued to be selected in most villages countrywide except in eastern Khatlon, which was affected by the civil conflict; there the *mahallah* representatives were appointed. The representative rallied people to get involved in public works such as building canals and repairing roads. He organized assistance to families at difficult times such as funerals, kept order in the village, and defended the rights of the people before the government. In Roshqala the representative worked through a council of five people, including one woman, who was selected by the villagers for her energetic nature. She organized women's activities, kept an eye on the health of women and children, and, when necessary, organized help with support from the Khujain and the rest of the council.

Formal Organizations

Researchers encountered a variety of formal institutions during the study. Although many claimed to represent an active membership, they rarely did. The brigade leaders (from the local collective farms) and other local officials were appointed by local, regional, or national officials. They did not represent the local communities, and, especially in western Khatlon, they came from a different region with clan ties to the Kuliabi leadership. Resource allocation was decided by the collective farm management for each village; the village council was de facto subordinate to the farm management.

Formal associations still existed on paper but had little power and few resources. The Dushanbe-based head of the Women's Councils garnered attention from international agencies, but none of the sites had active representatives. They were not respected community leaders outside the large cities. In Gorno-Badakhshan the Council of Veterans of War and Labor claimed to safeguard the interests of disabled people, yet a mere eight disabled people were registered with them in the district center, including two children. Without money the council could do little. Other organizations claimed to undertake activities, but these had been suspended because of lack of funds.

Regional Differences

The regional distribution of poverty reflected in large part the inherited regional cleavages and the localist clans' struggle for power. In Soviet times, resource allocation had been mostly controlled by powerful officials, originally from the Khodjent region. After Dushanbe and Khodjent, western Khatlon and Gharm were the most well off, maintaining healthy market networks and benefiting from the development of infrastructure: roads to markets, irrigation schemes, and social services. Eastern Khatlon had the lowest salaries and least developed social infrastructure.

Power relations changed in 1992–93. At first a coalition government of pro-democracy and Islamic religious leaders represented Gharmi and Pamiri interests, but it was replaced by a Kuliabi-led government supported by the Khodjentis. Throughout the fieldwork researchers expected to see high levels of investment in the winning regions, since considerable resources had been diverted from other regions. However, benefits were narrowly targeted to small localist clans. These controlled access to resources through employment in industrial and political bureaucracies. As a result, eastern Khatlon as a whole remained poor and ill equipped for the transition.

Using the respondents' definition of poverty, one could distinguish those regions that were seen as chronically poor, Gorno-Badakhshan and eastern Khatlon especially. Other regions, such as western Khatlon and Gharm, were seen as at risk, and poor in the medium term because of the lack of men in many households, the destruction of shelter, and the depletion of assets due to the war. In these regions there was a sense of hope that, if the political situation stabilized, prosperity might return.

Khatlon. The Khatlon region was formed in 1991 by joining the regions of Kuliab and Kurgan Tyube. The two areas faced very different issues. Before the civil war Kurgan Tyube was a wealthy, heavily populated, and heavily irrigated valley in southwestern Tajikistan. In the 1930s and 1940s, as noted above, large numbers of people were forcibly resettled from mountain villages into the valley to cultivate cotton. By the 1960s the area was fully developed with appropriate social and agricultural infrastructure.

At the time of the study, to put it simply, the winners of the civil war were those who had been the losers under the Soviet regime. Now the Kuliabis were the leaders in government, excluding the Pamiris and Gharmis of Kurgan Tyube, who had been the managers in Soviet times and the heart of the opposition until Kurgan Tyube town was destroyed in 1993. Officials named to administer the city of Kurgan Tyube and the region of Western Khatlon were of Kuliabi origin.

Poverty in Khatlon was linked to war destruction, insecurity, and lawlessness, and the tension between the cotton monoculture and the need to grow more food. Most of the 500,000 people displaced by the civil war were Gharmi and Pamiri residents from Kurgan Tyube. The war had destroyed community and household assets; entire villages in the Vakhsh, Bokhtar, and Shartuz districts had been bombed and pillaged. Basic needs such as shelter and food were still unmet.

An old man originally from the Turkmenistan Collective Farm, now teaching in the city of Kurgan Tyube, recalls that in 1947, after he was forcibly moved as a youngster with his parents from Gharm, the situation in the valley was precarious. There were no homes, no water, only cotton. By the 1960s, when he was a young man, life had normalized, with good schools and hospitals and plentiful household gardens. In 1993, when he returned from a refugee camp in Afghanistan, his house had been destroyed, his cattle killed or stolen, and he was refused his old job as a teacher in the collective farm. He had to start life anew.

Many families marketed produce grown on household plots, but continued insecurity inhibited economic recovery. Police and armed gangs were major obstacles to stability. Men were returning to the region slowly, and meanwhile numerous female-headed households struggled to cope. Some farmers had startup capital for food processing or marketing, but the lack of security made business ventures unattractive. Households felt at risk physically and economically.

Cotton had brought wealth to the region in Soviet times. At the time of the study, however, cotton and grain production on many collective farms had declined. Cotton production and sales benefited the collective farm managers, not the individual farmer. The social cost of cotton cultivation was high in terms of shortened school years for children and forgone incomes for workers forced to work for miserable wages. At harvest time, from mid-September until December, schools (grades 5–8) and roads to the market were closed during the week in order to force laborers and children into the fields. Family incomes dropped. Severe salinization of the land and the water table as well as poor health from pesticide use had taken a toll on communities.

Eastern Khatlon is a region of rolling hills and plateaus that has been chronically poor and isolated. Nutritional surveys found that over 30 percent of children in the region were chronically malnourished (CARE, 1994). The region specialized in cotton production on the plateaus and cattle raising in the hills. The two sites visited in Vose were extremely poor. Although the region had been only indirectly affected by the war, the depletion of personal assets was alarming. There were few opportunities to replace lost incomes from agricultural salaries with market activities or remittances. Eastern Khatlon did not have a tradition of planting crops to supplement incomes, perhaps because of the lack of irrigation, distances to major markets, and conservative perceptions of market relations. Nor could households rely on remittances from young men sent to work elsewhere in the former Soviet Union. Gender roles were notably more conservative in this region than in western Khatlon: women remained village bound, and girls were often pulled out of school when they reached 11 years of age.

Gorno-Badakhshan. With only small amounts of arable land, the very mountainous and sparsely populated region of Gorno-Badakhshan lacked alternatives to compensate for lost salaries and failing cottage industries for income generation. At the core of the food problem was the difficult issue of limited land resources, exacerbated by the lack of equipment and seed, since households had not cultivated in the past. One family estimated that it had taken two brothers two years of hard physical labor to prepare 0.3 hectare of land before wheat could be planted. They had also had to dig their own irrigation canal.

In Soviet times, industries had been limited to crafts and cottage industries (processing mainly wool, leather, and wood). At the time of the study these activities had ceased, and the raw materials piled high without markets. The region's strong commitment to education for both boys and girls remained the main asset. The region was unable to meet its own basic needs in terms of fuel and food. Widespread deforestation affected the valleys where the population was concentrated. Food needs were met in large part through humanitarian assistance. Yet although poverty was deep, households benefited from strong community networks. The Aga Khan Foundation was committed to supporting the local population.[3] Families said they went hungry in winter, however, when the distributions were delayed or had to be cancelled.

Certain districts had suffered from the war in neighboring Gharm. There was instability in Darwaz and Vanj, where the opposition was strongest, and an inflow of displaced people fleeing the conflict areas because of renewed fighting. There were few outside middlemen in Khorog or the other district centers because of the limited market and limited wealth. The road from Dushanbe to Khorog was closed most of the time because of fighting in the town of Tavildara, in Gharm. The road to Osh, in the Kyrgyz Republic, which is also a main opium route, was dangerous because of the many police and customs checkpoints.

Gharm Valley. In 1996 ongoing fighting between opposition and government forces, corruption of police at roadblocks, harassment of travelers by armed forces, and a de facto blockade were strangling the once-productive region of Gharm. With reduced access to markets, the population sought to survive on limited land resources. However, the state of conflict in the area created an environment where informal and illegal land acquisition benefited the powerful. In some districts, leaseholders used hundreds of hectares of land, crowding out small farmers. According to reports, presidential decree land had not been distributed in some villages in Gharm district. Deforestation had accelerated because of the need for heating fuel. The livestock market, which had been a major source of income for the region, was closed. The residents explained that there were no more cows to sell: all had been stolen, killed, or sold to buy flour. The few people who still had cattle feared that the army would take them if they ventured to market. To make things worse, the pastures around five villages in the district had been mined. Both men and cattle had been killed by the mines, and so no one was using the pastures any longer.

The war had caused direct damage, destroying homes, cattle, and water systems, in addition to the mining of fields and pastures. In Gharm center, 380 of the 800 homes were destroyed in the fighting. Tavildara was also said to have been destroyed by helicopter bombing in the spring of 1996. Social services in many villages had been suspended. Insecurity limited residents' mobility. Young women feared harassment from armed forces or retaliation from extremists trying to enforce strict Muslim traditions. Farmers kept their cattle and machinery out of sight and out of the fields to avoid having them stolen by the army. Insecurity, harassment, and the forced draft of young men had prompted a labor drain as Gharmi men fled to work elsewhere in the former Soviet Union, and trained workers fled to the capital, to Khodjent, or to Russia.

Dushanbe and the Western Districts. Poverty in the western districts and Dushanbe was linked to a decline in salaries, the industrial slowdown, erosion of the social safety net, and a breakdown in social services. The western districts and Dushanbe were linked through a network of enterprises, which employed villagers from these districts. In addition, the Tursunzade aluminum plant west of Dushanbe had brought considerable wealth but also serious health problems to the population. In 1996 most factories operated at lower capacity and employed fewer people than before.

The assessments in Dushanbe and other towns showed that the standard of living there had dropped for the majority. Markets, industries, bureaucracies, and strong informal networks provided opportunities for households to meet their most basic needs. Families who were unable to cope included those headed by disabled members, single-generation families with many children, Russian pensioners, and other persons incapable of working. They relied inordinately on the weak government social safety net or access to an ineffective family support network.

Khodjent. Khodjent had been and remained the richest region in Tajikistan. It benefited from 70 percent of Soviet investments in agriculture and industry in the country. The lowest levels of subsistence farming were found in this region, where the average household marketed close to 48 percent of production (Birkenes 1995, SCF/US 1996). Its fertile land in the Ferghana Valley enjoyed access to other Central Asian markets, but there were pockets of poverty in this otherwise relatively prosperous region. There were isolated and undeveloped towns and villages in the mountains, especially facing Dushanbe, around the prosperous town of Pendjikent, and in the district of Mountainous Mascho.

Since the civil war the situation had changed. During the assessment, unemployment was particularly visible and was due in part to the industrial slowdown. It was felt in the cities as well as in district centers and villages with industrial branches. The closing of the border by Uzbekistan and the requirement that men obtain a permit to work there had reduced another source of household income. Many men said that they could only work abroad for a couple of weeks at a time because of these new restrictions.

Land was being distributed very slowly in Khodjent. Only 3,000 hectares were being leased privately by May 1996. Presidential decree land was distributed to residents in Shakhistan in June 1996, five months after the deadline. Land issues were compounded by the shortage of water. Tensions with Uzbekistan and the Kyrgyz Republic were likely to continue along with the demand for irrigation water for the newly cultivated land.

Each geographic region faced challenges of its own, and the level of well-being varied greatly between them. At one end of the spectrum, Khodjent stood apart as isolated from the impact of the war until recently and reliant on still open and thriving markets. Some residents prospered in Dushanbe and the districts west of the capital, benefiting from proximity to markets in the capital, fertile land in the valleys, and links to powerful warlords. At the other end of the spectrum, western Khatlon had only just begun reconstruction and repatriation of Gharmi and Pamiri residents. Eastern Khatlon remained isolated and poor. Gorno-Badakhshan was in a dire situation, relying for its survival on food and fuel assistance provided by the Aga Khan.

Conclusion

In the period of relative peace during which this study was conducted, the lack of information (and the extent of misinformation) in the capital about the situation in the regions was striking. Even as some in Dushanbe questioned the incidence of severe poverty throughout the country, the dynamic of poverty was fully evident just a few kilometers outside the capital, where farmers and other common workers struggled to survive. Privatization had stripped the poor majority of both land and salaries, and the relatively well off made meager profits at the central markets while others lived on unreliable remittances from relatives in Russia or elsewhere. Meanwhile a few warlords and their localist clans profited inordinately from privatization, opportunities for trade, and enormous amounts of poorly targeted humanitarian assistance. Political antagonisms and regional-clan networks pitilessly excluded those outside the clan system. For the respondents, the combination of violence and official harassment contributed to a general sense of insecurity, which inhibited reconstruction and growth. In the eyes of the local interviewers who conducted the study, the lack of a broader sense of community beyond personal and clan interests, and the resulting injustices and inequities, were clear signs that their country was not recovering but only in a hiatus between violent outbursts.

Notes

1. Localist clans in Tajikistan unite patrilinear family networks of the same local origin or "locality." A family's locality is the village or villages from which it claims to originate. Thus residents of a village in the eastern Khatlon region, for example, can be of different localities if they originally came from different places, even if these are within the same geographic or administrative region. The term "Kuliabi," widely used to describe the dominant ethnic group, is too broad to convey exactly who holds power: the powerful Kuliabi clans are an alliance of clans from specific localities in what is now eastern Khatlon and exclude other residents of the region. At the family level, a family's network extends around the male head of the household, including his parents, his siblings, and their descendants. The parents of his wife are also included in this network, but her siblings are secondary. A man usually lives in the same compound (or village) as his parents and male siblings. His sisters live with their husbands' families.

2. A presidential decree of October 1995 directed collective farm managers to distribute to all rural households up to 0.15 hectare of arable land, and 0.5 hectare of mountainous (pasture) land.

3. The Pamiri districts of Gorno-Badakhshan are primarily Ismaili Muslim, whereas the rest of Tajikistan, including the districts of Vanj and Darwaz, which border on the Pamirs, is Shiite Muslim. Although religious education was suppressed during Soviet times, and few Pamiris know even the basics of Ismaili Islam, the Aga Khan is widely revered among them.

References

Birkenes, Robert. 1995. "Tajikistan: Survey of Household and Bazaar Economies. SCF/US, Dushanbe, Tajikistan. Save the Children Foundation US. January 1996.

CARE and CDC. 1994. "Rapid Food Security and Nutrition Assessment: Tajikistan, August 1994. Dushanbe, Tajikistan.

Newell, Andrew. 1995. "Social Security, Education, and Health Care in Tajikistan." Draft Consultancy Report. World Bank, Washington, D.C. Processed.

Villagers gather at the local
market in Khorezm.
Photo by Elizabeth Gomart

---------------------------------- ✳ ----------------------------------

CHAPTER 5

Standing
on a Knife's Edge:
Doing Business in
Uzbekistan

Elizabeth Gomart

The economic cost of an incomplete and corrupt transition is often hard to capture. In Uzbekistan the gradual approach adopted in the transition to a free market economy resulted in a blizzard of decrees, laws, and regulations seeking to control and manipulate the development of an independent private sector. In 80 in-depth interviews, small entrepreneurs and officials in the Khorezm and Karakalpakhstan regions of the country in May 1997 described in detail how excessive regulation and rampant corruption had forced them into illegality and informality. The private sector, they explained over and over in these interviews, was kept small and informal, teetering on the edge of profitability and constantly vulnerable to harassment by officials.

Excessive regulation had reduced the profitability of trade and services, raising operating costs by forbidding common practices such as barter and cash payments (with few exceptions, all payments had to be made through bank transfers) and limiting access to foreign currency. Meanwhile access to other productive sectors continued to be barred to investors as they struggled with the small amount of bank financing available and diminished sources of self-financing. By providing incentives for the private sector to remain informal and even to deformalize in some cases, the regulations rendered the private sector increasingly vulnerable to legal prosecution. Unfriendly banking and tax regulations made compliance too complex and costly. As one entrepreneur put it, "We stand on a knife's edge, always vulnerable to being closed down by officials." The current environment allowed the government bureaucracy, along with its business partners, to exploit privileged positions, translating administrative control of scarce resources, lack of legislative clarity, and relative judicial immunity into gains from economic rents, business investments, and professional promotion. The resulting business climate hindered the development of a strong, formal, taxpaying business sector. These findings support the need for the government to revisit some of these punitive regulations and provide support to businesses moving into new sectors.

Background

The private sector is not a new phenomenon in Uzbekistan. By the late 1980s it had become an indispensable and growing branch of the Soviet planned economy in sectors where the government was most inefficient, such as the distribution of goods and services tailored to local demand. New businesses grew out of small-scale trade, local services, crafts, construction, and labor-intensive agriculture. At the time of this study, private businesses retained many of the "second economy" traits of their forebears: most of their links were with partners elsewhere in the former Soviet Union, they focused on services and trade, they routinely used consignment and barter rather than cash, and the majority worked informally, routinely broke contradictory laws, and paid off or otherwise ensured the protection or interest of government officials.

The strongest private sector entrepreneurs were often those who had experience in cooperative and private business during the Soviet period, when they were able to accumulate personal assets early on (before the currency devaluation), acquire knowledge of markets throughout the former Soviet Union, and establish business networks. They also had strong personal or business links to local officials. A second tier of enterprises included those that had grown out of other sectors, moving from unregistered or licensed self-employment to more formal trade or service activities.

Barriers to Growth

Until 1996 the private sector expanded enthusiastically into the import-export trading sector, where a small investment could produce quick returns and generate valuable liquidity. The costs of the resulting flood of foreign goods into Uzbekistan were the corresponding lack of development of local production in some sectors and, because of the use of cash or barter, reduced government revenue. In addition, the government was unable to control the declining market value of the local currency, the sum, as evidenced by inflation at home and a sagging exchange rate. To remedy these negative effects, in 1996 the government adopted a policy of import substitution: it imposed stiff tariffs on imported consumer goods and commodities and made the import of production equipment a national priority; it tightened the banking sector's grip on cash and foreign currency; it limited financing mostly to manufacturing and production activities; and it practically eliminated the common entrepreneur's (legal) access to foreign currency.

Given the private sector's concentration in trade rather than production or processing, and given its reliance on trade income for self-financing, this sudden change in policy had an inordinately negative impact on the bulk of small businesses. According to small business owners, resources were not available to support their move away from trade into production or processing. A successful trader who had acquired experience and partners during Soviet times explained, as did many others, that he lacked the knowledge necessary to launch into activities other than trade: "Beyond our current partners, it's a dark forest." Equipment was still held by government-controlled or newly privatized enterprises that were unable to rationalize production because of the new currency controls, which impeded imports, and because of the conditions imposed under the country's privatization scheme. In Karakalpakhstan few entrepreneurs were involved in processing of agricultural goods and raw materials. In Khorezm entrepreneurs were starting up processing activities with equipment obtained from Turkmenistan or purchased from privatizing firms at home. However, local officials (with their own business interests) were able to easily control these new production firms, which they often saw as competitors. For example, local authorities ordered private rice mills in Khorezm to close in the spring and summer months until the "rice plan" was filled, to induce farmers to sell their rice to the government at below-market prices.

Delays in Privatization

The private sector could have been assisted in its expansion into production activities if the government sector had relinquished control of productive assets through privatization. Yet uncertainties and ambiguities about ownership rights slowed the privatization process. In Uzbekistan privatization distinguished among ownership, control, and management of assets. Thus privatized enterprises were privately managed but lacked full control, and ownership rights were rescindable. By 1996 a first phase of privatization of small shops, craft workshops, services, and other small-scale enterprises had taken place, and a second phase involving medium-size enterprises was under way.

Respondents considered an enterprise privatized once it was 100 percent in private hands and registered as a private enterprise, as distinct from a collective or a joint-stock company where the government had de facto control over decisionmaking. In contrast, the government considered an enterprise privatized when 25 percent of its stock was held by the employees. In reality, such an enterprise continued to respond to procurement and production plans from the regional "mother" enterprise until it was entirely privately held. For example, the director of a joint-stock company that was 49 percent privatized said that he received all his orders—whom to buy from and whom to sell to—from the central government in Tashkent. He reported regularly to Tashkent about his activities. One benefit was that the ministry had the authority to buy and sell foreign currency, allowing the company continued access to foreign exchange.

In the experience of the interviewees, ownership rights acquired through privatization were alienable and conditional. The government committee on privatization had taken back property on a number of occasions without due process and without reimbursing the new owners for the price of acquisition or any improvements.

The free development of the private sector was also limited by conditions imposed on privatized enterprises. The new owners had no doubt that these conditions were real and binding, but privatization officials repeatedly denied even their existence. Privatized firms had to continue to provide the same goods or services, for three to five years after privatization, at a level at least equal to that of the last year of state operation. A wide array of enterprises described similar conditionalities in both Karakalpakhstan and Khorezm. Another condition was to retain the same number of employees on the payroll after privatization as before. In Nukus, a city in Karakalpakhstan, respondents said that this policy was not official. However, firing employees was seen as a sure way to attract the ire of the local government. Local private pharmacies were required to sell a list of medicines at government prices. As a result, these medicines were simply not stocked. Bread and basic food stores in Urgench, a city in Khorezm, were privatized under the condition that the new owners sell only bread for five years, that they buy flour and bread from the government factory, and that they sell government bread in the morning and their own bread only in the afternoon.

Genuine privatization of land had not taken place in 1997. "Long-term land distribution" entitled farmers to land use rights for a minimum of 10 years, but control and management were restricted by conditionalities set by local officials. The land remained the property of the state, which could take back the land if the farmer failed to meet production and land conservation standards. This gave the state wide authority to take back land in a region that was severely environmentally degraded. The amount and quality of land received were determined by local and regional authorities, and thus by political and social forces rather than market forces. Moreover, land leasing or long-term use was not open to everyone. The process of obtaining land was also controlled by local officials: a number of respondents said that they had been approached by local officials who offered them land, not the other way around.

A private farmer explains that he was approached by the local mayor (*hokim*) to receive land because he is a respected religious figure. He says that the *hokim* is more likely to provide opportunities to people of his own social status. According to the new farmer, "The rich help the rich and God helps the rich." Because he has authority in the community, he will be able to get water on time and other forms of assistance from the director of the government-owned collective farm. He explains that he discusses crop choice with the local authorities. If he were adamant about planting a certain crop against the wishes of the local officials, he might be allowed to do so, but their crucial help would be withheld— no more water, inputs, or machinery. This would be risky: "We are all dependent on each other, links in a chain." The *hokim* requires all lease-holders to plant cotton on their land and to plant a certain percentage under plastic, which increases planting time and costs exponentially. Prices are set by the local processing firms or the local authorities. The farmer concludes, "I am not the master of [my] land."

The requirement that these newly privatized firms continue to produce the same goods as before failed to reflect the realities of post-Soviet trade. To meet the requirement, many enterprises needed raw materials and other inputs that were no longer available at affordable prices on the local market. Others were limited by low local demand for the low-quality products they were obliged to produce. Some entrepreneurs viewed these newly privatized firms as long-term investments and were already planning three to five years ahead, when the onerous conditions would expire. Others planned to start up more profitable activities in the same locale, subsidizing unprofitable activities with profits from the new activities.

In response to the sluggishness of these newly privatized firms, shackled to unprofitable activities, the government re-created a number of regional and republic-level procurement and distribution entities, referred to as "concerns" or associations. Membership was officially voluntary, but newly privatized enterprises came under pressure to join because privatization contracts were three-way contracts signed by the concern or association, the government privatization committee, and the new owners. The official role of these entities was to provide access to essential inputs and markets. But they provided no essential support or additional expertise to the enterprises themselves. From the point of view of entrepreneurs, they simply acted as an additional intermediary between the market and the enterprises, limiting their choice of partners, dictating prices, and further isolating them from their clients.

Lack of Finance

New enterprises were eager to access new technology for processing and production. However, the effectiveness of local financial institutions in providing access to capital was repeatedly questioned. The government set aside 50 percent of privatization proceeds to support the private sector through an institution called the Business Fund. Foreign donors also made large amounts available for loans to the private sector. The eligible activities were local manufacturing, construction (including manufacturing of materials), agricultural production and processing, and services such as tourism. The application process was complex, requiring numerous signatures and approvals from different government offices, which could take up to six months. In addition, enterprises were often selected to receive loans not by financial experts but by local government officials, representatives of the Ministry of Foreign Economic Relations, or the Chamber of Commerce, leading to accusations of corruption. Mistrust of market forces also prompted local officials to put forward a short list of proposals based on their economic priorities. Applicants found the selection process random and distrusted it.

Commercial banks did not extend credit to the common entrepreneur. Small traders had their own bank, but in Karakalpakhstan it was no longer providing loans but instead was concentrating its efforts on recovering loans already in default. Other sectoral banks were set up to meet the demand of their own shareholders—established government firms—and lacked incentives to lend to new startups, according to respondents. Some private businessmen said they held shares in local banks where they used to work, which gave them access to advantageous credit conditions.

The only remaining options for financing startups were therefore high-interest short-term loans (reserved for production activities) and self-financing. Yet short-term (two months to a year) loans at annual interest rates of 40 to 50 percent were not a realistic way of financing businesses, since production activities did not generate rapid returns. Collateral requirements of 120 percent of the value of the loan, or requirements that a guarantor be designated, also proved to be obstacles to small businesses, who saw these as aimed expressly at themselves, whereas large government entities could use their state-owned assets. Many entrepreneurs said that they had circumvented the banks and gone directly to those entities with liquidity to secure an informal loan. When respondents did receive bank loans for production purposes, they said they applied the loan toward trade activities in order to repay the loan quickly and, in some cases, generate capital to pursue their production activities. Officials and entrepreneurs wondered if such investments in production actually ever took place, given the lack of local evidence of a growing production and manufacturing sector.

Because access to loans was difficult, entrepreneurs found ways to self-finance. Trade has served as an essential source of startup, working, and investment capital for small and medium-size enterprises alike. Trade was conducted alongside other activities (such as services, manufacturing, and processing) in order to generate liquidity and provide a buffer against fluctuations in revenues and expenses of these other activities. These sources of liquidity had diminished with the limitations on cash transactions, currency convertibility, and higher import tariffs. Another approach was to trick the system and make informal loans to friends and partners. A number of entrepreneurs said that they lent money to close partners by writing up fictitious contracts for goods or services and then paying 50 percent of the value of the contract up front, as legally required. A group of entrepreneurs said that they had set up a kind of revolving credit fund in this manner.

Trade Regulations

From the point of view of small businesses, currency convertibility licensing, import and export duties, and restrictions on barter and consignment served to keep private sector competitors out of markets controlled by the government sector. To trade internationally, a private enterprise had to register with the Ministry of Foreign Economic Relations. This process was costly (some respondents put the price at $50,000) and time consuming. Control over currency convertibility, which has been tight since November 1996, has created a difficult situation for small and large traders alike. Nationally, the number of licenses issued had been reduced from 1,400 per year to 85. Only a few licenses were being provided in each region. By May

1997 only two enterprises in Khorezm had long-term licenses, and another four had received one-time approvals. These were mainly large, joint-stock companies, not small or fully privatized businesses.

Larger state-owned firms in Tashkent and Ferghana had obtained convertibility licenses and were benefiting from the restrictions. The requirement that traders pay hard currency for foreign goods kept small private businesses out of the international market. Small traders said that they were now obliged to do business through these large firms, who acted as importing intermediaries, increasing the cost of goods and reducing the small traders' profits. The licenses, combined with the prohibitions against barter and consignment, had effectively made traders and producers more vulnerable, since they could no longer contract with foreign partners directly. Many said that they had lost deals to larger companies because they could not meet the convertibility requirements. Others said that they were producing at only a fraction of their capacity and had to periodically stop production until they could arrange a new deal with foreign partners. These new regulations had eroded networks with foreign partners, who already perceived Uzbek businesses as too unreliable and too small scale. Foreign currency restrictions had pushed many importers and producers who relied on imported raw materials, spare parts, and other inputs into illegality.

A producer in Karakalpakhstan says, "I am a crook. There is no other way for me to continue working. I cannot negotiate openly with factory managers [in the Russian Federation] because I do not have convertibility. I have to work through friends. The managers [in Russia] write up a fictitious contract with my partners in Kazakhstan. When the goods arrive in Kazakhstan, I pick them up in my private car. I pay in kind or in cash."

The restrictions had created a black market in foreign currency, visible in every open market. However, local supply was limited. One entrepreneur estimated that the total daily supply of dollars in Nukus did not exceed $2,000 to $3,000, too little for financing of productive activities other than small trade.

Traders sought out alternatives to foreign currency deals. Historically, barter and consignment had been legal in Soviet times, and although they were made illegal in 1996, they remained the principal modes of payment for enterprises that were short on cash and working capital because of banking regulations and lack of access to foreign currency. A barter deal might involve several partners. For example, one entrepreneur in Khorezm paid for lumber with processed agricultural produce and then traded the lumber to a third person who provided him with parts for his processing firm. A bank could approve a consignment deal only if the recipient had 100 percent of the value of the contract in his or her account, which defeated the purpose of obtaining goods on consignment. Prepayment requirements of a minimum of 15 percent further limited trade. One limited solution was for the entrepreneur to generate foreign exchange through trade. For example, a pharmacist exported rice to Russia and used the foreign exchange to buy pharmaceuticals to import to Uzbekistan.

Trade restrictions included a prohibition on exporting certain agricultural products from one oblast (administrative region) to another within Uzbekistan, beyond a quota of a few kilograms per person. Farmers in Nukus said that these internal barriers impeded their trade in local agricultural products. Food products such as rice, meat, and meat products could not be freely "exported" from Karakalpakhstan or Khorezm to Tashkent, where they would fetch a higher price. Regional import and export duties forced up the price of imported goods, protecting the market for centrally located government producers and maintaining the monopoly of government-controlled processing enterprises, which remained the only bulk buyers of local production. Export and import tariffs on foreign trade also made it unprofitable for local producers to trade in certain products legally. These tariffs likewise functioned to maintain the predominance of central, state-owned enterprises, which were able to "export" regionally without limit and import from abroad.

Informalization of the Private Sector

Complex, impractical, and costly legislation contributed to weakening the private sector. Regulations increased the cost of business, created black markets, and generated opportunities for rent seeking by bureaucrats in a position to negotiate how laws would be interpreted and implemented locally.

Limitations on Cash Withdrawals

All registered small private enterprises were required to open a bank account and deposit cash receipts daily. By law, a legal entity could only make a payment contract with another legal entity and had to operate through bank transfers. Although the National Bank officially denied it, the regional and commercial banks enforced limits on withdrawals set by the National Bank. Productive enterprises that deposited cash each day could withdraw from zero percent (trade and construction enterprises) to 7 percent (restaurants) of the deposited daily amounts for cash purchases. These cash restrictions had become tighter over the last two years. Since January 1997 no cash could be drawn from accounts for any reason other than salaries, travel per diems, and other staff-related expenses.

These cash limitations translated into a cash scarcity. The enterprise lost control of cash once it had entered the banking system. A high value was placed on cash (called *nal*, a shortened version of the Russian word for cash, *nalitchnie*) compared with noncash (*bez nal*). The discount was linked to the expected taxes to be paid on products. As a result, there was a high discount rate for prices in cash over prices in noncash. Thread, for example, that cost 50 sum in cash on the market cost 150 sum by bank transfer. Construction materials cost 70 to 75 percent more by bank transfer than in cash.[1] Even state-owned enterprises listed different prices for cars imported from the Republic of Korea: $15,600 in cash or $21,800 by bank transfer. Registered enterprises that went by the banking rules could not compete with self-employed traders, who were not required to work through a bank account. Cash placed in the bank lost its value.

A pharmacist explains the cost of working through the formal banking system, "I get paid by the patient in cash at the market price, but then I need to procure the same medicines by bank transfer [at the higher price]."

Cash could be bought (*obnalichit'*, Russian for "to turn into cash") with noncash at a rate of 100 noncash sum to 40 to 75 cash sum, depending on the supply situation of a particular good. Enterprises wrote up fictional contracts in which only cash and bank transfers were exchanged and no goods or services. But there were limitations to this method: some entrepreneurs said that only large amounts were exchanged in this manner: above 200,000 sum in noncash. Some entrepreneurs also said that these illegal activities were inherently risky, and two said that they had never received the promised cash after having transferred noncash.

As a result, entrepreneurs avoided the banking system. One construction company owner exclaimed, wide-eyed, "Never hand over cash to the bank! It's too valuable." He estimated that he hands over a minimum of cash to the bank, approximately 5 percent of receipts. Cash was essential to purchase goods at a reasonable price as well as to obtain scarce goods from informal sources. A bookstore owner explained that, without cash, he could no longer afford to ship books from Tashkent to restock his store; the price had almost doubled in just one year, because he used to be able to pay in cash but now had to pay the noncash premium. In addition, he explained, many books could only be obtained abroad—a source now closed by the currency requirements—or as stolen goods through informal channels from state-owned publishers, but again only for cash. The best scenario for entrepreneurs was when they could purchase goods by bank transfer that could be easily sold for cash, because they could control the goods and the cash in hand, but not money in the bank.

The banks tried to anticipate how much cash each enterprise would need to hand over each day (its "cash plan") in order to enforce the mandatory daily cash deposits. However, these cash plans were informally "negotiable" with the local bank tellers. As a result, the official cash plan was a fraction of daily receipts. In Urgench, for example, the cash plan for an enterprise comprising a hotel, restaurant, and beverage store was 150,000 sum per month. According to the manager, the hotel alone provided 225,000 sum per month in cash. An ice cream store in Khorezm had cash receipts of 52,000 sum per day, yet its cash plan was only 25,000 sum. Because the owner purchased all materials through the regional association, there was no reason (such as the need to make "essential purchases" in cash on the market) why the store should have been allowed to retain any cash under these regulations.

Taxation

The tax system was difficult to navigate, and there were strong incentives for legally registered small businesses to evade taxes. Although the local tax officials recommended that businesses hire a lawyer and an accountant, none of the small businesses interviewed had taken on such an expense. Not only profits but also expenses such as the salary fund fell prey to high tax rates.[2] Banks acted as an arm of the tax agency, reporting incomes and transactions without the account owner's knowledge. To avoid taxation, entrepreneurs said that registered firms preferred cash or barter payments. They declared lower than actual prices on their sales to avoid reporting profits, and a minimum salary to reduce tax liability for the enterprise and the employees. A tailor explained, "I list 400 sum in my official accounts as the price I charge, but the real price for clients is 1,000 sum." Unreported additional payments to workers were made in cash or in kind to supplement low official salaries. Some enterprises set up parallel accounting systems: one for the accountant and the tax department, and one for the partners and management to review the performance of the business. Others simply avoided registering as a business and operated under a self-employment license.

A shop owner in Nukus has registered her four employees under four different self-employment licenses, to avoid having to register as a private enterprise. The four employees receive a salary from the shop owner, who procures goods for sale and sets prices. In this way she reduces her tax burden to well below 10 percent of revenue and avoids the banking restrictions.

Some small enterprises avoided registering or licensing altogether. There were many such businesses operating on the local markets. They engaged in small-scale trade (selling imported goods) or sold their own production (such as baked goods). These small entrepreneurs often claimed that they could not afford to pay the flat fee for registration. However, after some probing, interviewers repeatedly found that they earned more than enough to cover the registration fees and perhaps were more put off by the process than by the cost. Some enterprises were large enough to be well known at the community level but somehow avoided registration. Even though they came to the attention of the interviewers, they were too frightened to agree to be interviewed. Other, larger enterprises registered only part of their activities: a registered tanning factory invested profits in Astrakhan sheep, which were not registered as assets; the valuable skins were tanned and sold off the record. Some manufacturers also managed to register as farmers or as nonprofit organizations (by housing the local soccer team, for example) in order to qualify for lower taxes.

Customs

Import and export trade was commonly tainted by informal or illegal activities. Bribes were provided to speed up the process even if all papers were in order. Registration was time consuming and costly, especially if the commodities required quality testing. However, the amount of the bribe was far less than the cost of legal registration. Buying off the customs officers was therefore an acceptable cost of doing business. The amount depended on the personal relationship between the importer and the customs agent.

An importer of luxury goods says that, instead of paying 50 percent duty on the goods he imports, he paid 5,000 sum per suitcase at first, then cut a deal with the customs agent—exchanging favors—and now pays 2,000 sum per suitcase.

Other Regulations

Some regulations, such as health and work safety regulations, were applied unevenly and seen by entrepreneurs as a means of keeping small businesses vulnerable and needing to pay for protection from prosecution. Inspections could happen weekly, with inspectors claiming to work for obscure agencies, checking compliance and requesting bribes in exchange for leniency. For health inspections, the law required that doctors come once a month to take samples and test for cleanliness where food was prepared or sold. Instead, in the case of a cafe in Nukus, the cafe manager would go to the health inspection department and drop off documents to be signed, placing money in the booklet. He would come back the next day and pick up the signed documents.

In Urgench a man selling candy in the street says that sanitation officials visited him and required that he obtain quality certificates from his suppliers, or that they be tested locally at a cost of 2,500 sum per product. When he refused, saying the former was impossible and that he could not afford the latter, the officials confiscated 15,700 sum worth of goods. He concludes that he remains at the mercy of these officials.

Other regulations required the use of two safes: one for documents, the other for cash. Another pegged salary increases to increases in production, and a third required the use of the local language in signage. These regulations contributed to placing enterprises at the mercy of local officials.

Vested Interests

Government officials had an interest in maintaining the private sector's dependence on them. They translated their administrative control of resources and information into economic profit through rent seeking and their own business investments.

Rent Seeking

The enforcement and interpretation of regulations were negotiable at the local level. Officials sometimes used contradictory or confusing rules and regulations to extract additional payments for documentation or legal privileges.

Entrepreneurs could negotiate leniency for noncompliance or illegal activities by paying regular, repeated bribes to the agents charged with enforcement. With no one to whom to appeal, and given their general vulnerability to prosecution, small businesses were often subject to harassment and theft by government officials, tax inspectors, and others. One entrepreneur reported that the tax inspectors would always find problems with a tax report unless they received payment in the form of construction materials. At the market in Urgench, a tax inspector was observed taking a belt from the display of a clothing retailer without so much as a word of explanation. A local furniture producer had made 12 chairs for a customer when a local official dropped in and took 7 of the chairs for himself, without paying.

Profitable businesses were able to operate thanks to a "roof," that is, a high-level government official who provided them with protection from prosecution and harassment from other officials as much as possible. These officials offered their services in exchange for a 10 to 20 percent share of the profits. Without this protection, entrepreneurs said, they would be constantly harassed by all sorts of local officials and inspectors looking for their share of the profits and helping themselves to the products.

A restaurant owner says that, thanks to a relative who works in the police department, she can avoid harassment by low-level officials. Should any occur, her relative can create all kinds of problems for the officials involved, forcing them to exchange favors by relinquishing their claims on her business in exchange for the policeman's leniency on their account.

A large clothing retailer explains matter of factly that she cannot operate without protection: "We are not novices. We know our business. Anyway, we have clients [in these government offices]. Today, if you don't have loyal people in key places, you can't take a single step in business." This loyalty comes at the cost of 10,000 sum a month to the tax inspector and the police chief. This retailer chose to register her business under her mother's name, because officials would not dare to bargain too hard and constantly renegotiate their terms with an older woman.

With property rights in the countryside even more tenuous, a farmer explains, "If someone from the collective farm management comes to ask for something [meat or milk], I cannot refuse, because the land belongs to them. They could take it back at any time."

Large one-time payments were sometimes required to facilitate even legal administrative procedures such as registering a firm, obtaining review of an application for credit, converting foreign currency, and obtaining access to government-controlled goods and contracts.

Credit applications were also subject to bribery. The cost of a loan was a bribe of 10 percent of the value of the loan in cash. The bribe was provided in advance to "motivate" the bureaucrat to support an application. If the application failed, the bribe was usually returned. Additional bribes and gifts were also provided to further grease the process, for example, to keep the bank from monitoring how the entrepreneur used the loan. Cash transactions were also affected. One entrepreneur said that it usually cost him 10 percent of the amount he wanted to "motivate" the cashier to give him cash from his own account for paying salaries, a legal transaction.

One-time payments were provided to purchase government-controlled goods held in "funds" such as feed, flour, and dry milk. Even timely access to water required large bribes. A construction firm seeking to secure contracts with government-controlled enterprises commonly paid the enterprise's top managers 10 percent of the value of the contract.

In addition to bribes already received, local officials sometimes demanded that entrepreneurs support certain social services (such as a kindergarten or roads) or community activities (such as a soccer club). There was much confusion about whether these requests were for contributions required by law or random requests.

Business Investments

Government officials were not permitted by law to head their own private enterprises. In reality, official positions and networks were exploited routinely. To get around the legal restrictions, entrepreneurs working in government agencies or government-controlled companies named a relative, often their wife or a younger relative whom they felt confident they could control, as the formal head of the enterprise.

One entrepreneur tells the following story: "The local mayor called me and asked that we work together. He told me to open a firm, but unofficially he would be the boss. The town was rebuilding for a centennial celebration. The mayor provided our enterprise with a large amount of work on the town's reconstruction. The municipality was the enterprise's only client. The company took on so many projects that it could not procure materials quickly enough. The mayor again intervened, forcing other construction companies in the town to set aside materials for the enterprise to use, so we could continue to work. The companies gave us cement and other materials. They were paid for these materials, but only much later, once the projects were completed. The mayor solved the problem of credit by obtaining a loan of 4 million sum. The enterprise used 3.6 million. The other 10 percent went to red tape, the customary bribe. Of course, things changed after the mayor left his post. The company no longer exists."

The practice of officials having their businesses registered under a relative's name and siphoning off public funds to their firms seemed widespread, or at least entrepreneurs believed it to be. Perhaps an indicator of how commonplace this practice was is that local entrepreneurs would not believe that this researcher was working only for a salary and was not scouting out business opportunities.

Alliances with government officials could take different forms. A number of manufacturing entrepreneurs had informal ties to government and state-owned enterprises that guaranteed privileged access to inputs, privatized equipment, credit, and so on. In exchange, the entrepreneurs offered their personal automobiles for official use, provided lodging and salaries to a soccer team, or performed other services.

Defending Government Interests

Officials in government bureaucracies and government-controlled firms stood to lose from the growth of an effective, independent private sector. The local mayor received a bonus based on growth in the government-controlled sector in his region. Growth in the private sector was not tracked. Restrictions on credit and convertibility benefited the government-controlled firms by excluding small, private businesses. Restricted access to raw materials, equipment, and foreign suppliers and markets benefited Tashkent-based, government-controlled monopsonies at the expense of the small trader. Local authorities seemed to be protecting government interests by creating obstacles to enterprises renting or upgrading a locale, or by expanding and using governmental inspections to harass businesses.

This obstructive stance was most harshly felt in the countryside, where collective farm directors still controlled access to assets (equipment and land), essential inputs (seed, feed, and water), and access to markets through the state-owned processing facilities, which set prices.

A private farmer explains, "The collective farm obstructs private farmers. In the past two years, there has been no shortage of water. Yet the collective farm will let the water flow to the lake rather than give it to private farmers. I've been to see the mayor repeatedly, who then goes to talk to the collective farm director. The director then promises water, but there is no result. We never got water."

Conclusions

These findings for Karakalpakhstan and Khorezm are likely to hold true for the other regions of Uzbekistan because of the national nature of the relevant legislation. However, because these two regions are relatively isolated from Tashkent, the impact of the legislation—which tends to benefit well-connected enterprises located at the center—may be stronger. In addition, the relative lack of investment in Karakalpakhstan is now an obstacle to its development, with a narrow range of networks and experience accumulated from previous times and few assets available through privatization.

This study has shown how the government's intent to control the gradual growth of the independent private sector has created a burdensome legal and political framework and a perverse incentive structure. The results were limited and thwarted growth for those enterprises without government connections, services, and bribes, and increased inequities within communities. Another consequence was a sense of vulnerability and instability on the part of those enterprises forced into illegality. Their fate rested on corrupt officials who could demand enough goods or bribes to endanger their profitability and put them out of business. The government needed to make changes in the incentive structure at the level of local bureaucracies to encourage transparency and universal enforcement of laws and regulations. One recommendation made by the local entrepreneurs was to set up a commission of entrepreneurs, government officials, and legal experts to monitor the impact of regulations and provide feedback to the central authorities. However, these recommendations may be to no avail without a clear and unambiguous commitment of the government to support the development of the private sector.

Notes

1. This discount rate had fallen from a high of 100 to 150 percent in the fall of 1996. One explanation for the decrease in the discount rate was the computerization of the bank transfer system, which now allows for prompt payments.

2. The new tax code to be put into force in January 1998 was meant to address some of these taxation issues.

--------- ✳ ---------

PART THREE

ARMENIA AND GEORGIA

Armenia is a small (29,800 square kilometers), landlocked country, 90 percent of which lies 1,000 meters or more above sea level. This largely Orthodox Christian country, with its ancient language and culture, is unique in the region for its large diaspora: Armenians living elsewhere in the former Soviet Union and abroad have been an important resource during the postindependence period. The vast majority of Armenia's population, now estimated at around 3 million, is ethnic Armenian, with Russians, Yezidi Kurds, and other minorities making up less than 2 percent of the population. The country lies in the southern Caucasus, where it borders Azerbaijan in the east, Georgia in the north, the Islamic Republic of Iran in the southeast, and Turkey in the west. When Armenia became independent, it was already contending with the consequences of the devastating December 1988 earthquake, which killed more than 20,000 people and left 40,000 homeless. It also became involved in a military conflict with its neighbor Azerbaijan over the status of the largely Armenian-populated enclave of Nagorno-Karabakh, which was seeking independence from Azerbaijan. From 1992 to 1994 Armenia suffered additional blows: a catastrophic decline in production, hyperinflation, blockaded borders with Azerbaijan and Turkey due to the Nagorno-Karabakh conflict, severe shortages of electricity and heating fuel, and drastic cuts in salaries, pensions, and social assistance. By 1996 surveys were finding that more than half of the population were poor. Since then, although conditions have improved for some, chronic poverty has increased, and Armenian society has become extremely stratified, with a gap between rich and poor (as measured by a Gini coefficient of 0.6) comparable to that of the United States or Brazil.

Georgia is a country of 4.9 million people located between the Caucasus Mountains and the Black Sea. Its ethnically, religiously, and linguistically diverse population is 70 percent Georgian, with significant minorities of Armenians (8.1 percent), Russians (6.3 percent), Azeris (5.7 percent), Ossetians (3 percent), Abkhazians, Greeks, Jews, and others. In Soviet times Georgia was known for its wealth, agricultural abundance, spectacular resorts, rich architectural legacy, and entrepreneurial population. After the breakup of the Soviet Union, Georgia became embroiled in major armed conflicts, as the regions of Abkhazia and South Ossetia sought independence, and a civil war, fought along regional lines, deposed President Zviad Gamsakhurdia. The conflicts displaced 200,000 people and impoverished large segments of the population. By 1996 the country had achieved relative political stability under its new president, Eduard Shevardnadze. Yet since 1999, despite economic growth, the country has been among the poorest in the region, with increased chronic poverty and vulnerability.

Exchange rates

Armenia: $1 = 400 drams in 1995
           = 410 drams in August 1996
           = 500 drams in December 1997 and August 1998

Georgia: $1 = 1.2 lari (1 lari = 100 tetri) in 1995

A young woman widowed during the recent conflict in Nagorno-Karabakh raises her children in a war-damaged house near the Azerbaijani border.
Photo by Nora Dudwick

--- ✳ ---

CHAPTER 6

When the Lights Went Out:
Poverty in Armenia

Nora Dudwick

A rmenia's economic decline after the collapse of the Soviet Union was worsened by a tragic combination of political conflict and natural disaster. A dispute between Armenia and Azerbaijan over the Nagorno-Karabakh region (a predominantly Armenian enclave within Azerbaijan) resulted in interethnic violence, a two-way flood of refugees between the two republics, and a blockade of Armenia's transportation routes through Azerbaijan and Turkey. Destruction from a severe earthquake in the northwest part of the country in 1988, the resulting closure of the Metsamor nuclear power plant, and the disruption of the Soviet economy caused widespread unemployment. The population, including half a million earthquake victims living in temporary housing, shivered through three harsh winters with only a few hours of electricity a day and a constantly interrupted supply of cooking gas. As the war dragged on and the blockade continued, many of Armenia's most able and talented citizens left the country, among them highly educated urban refugees from Azerbaijan.

By July 1993 as many as 1 million workers out of a labor force of 1.7 million were either formally unemployed or on involuntary leave without pay (Scott 1994). People received their diminished salaries late; factory workers were sometimes paid in goods rather than cash. Yet people continued to work—to preserve their routine, from a sense of duty, or to socialize with colleagues. Work also had practical benefits: some positions gave access to bribes, information, humanitarian aid, or professional contacts and potential contracts.

Subsistence agriculture became an important survival strategy for many. Armenia's radical land privatization program broke up the republic's state and collective farms. By the end of 1992 Armenia had 280,000 independent farmers. Many had never worked in agriculture before, while the more experienced farmers complained that they could not afford to farm given the high price of inputs. Skilled workers and professionals—including refugees—treated farming as a subsistence strategy until they could find "employment" again (by which they typically meant employment in the state sector) or leave Armenia (World Bank 1994; Holt 1995).

Armenians greeted independence with fervor, but they still shared common Soviet values of egalitarianism and the belief that citizens were entitled to education, a job, and a host of subsidies and benefits. Growing economic differentiation, the abrupt withdrawal of these social entitlements, and unemployment have left all but the new elite bewildered and nostalgic for an idealized, predictable, and secure Soviet past.

Soviet rule had fragmented Armenian society and created deep distrust between people. Armenians therefore lacked the experience of working cooperatively to pursue shared interests. The extended family remained the primary indigenous social unit capable of effective cooperation, and Armenians' response to the current economic crisis consisted largely of individual and family coping strategies and a reliance on strong local and transnational kinship networks.

This chapter presents the experiences and views of a sampling of the Armenian people regarding their predicament. It was part of a comprehensive poverty assessment carried out by the World Bank (World Bank 1996). The research team was made up of ethnographers and graduate students from Yerevan State University and the Armenian Academy of Sciences. Between October 1994 and March 1995, researchers conducted semistructured interviews with individuals from approximately 700 poor and low-income households identified through social assistance office lists of "vulnerable" households and snowball sampling methods (see Chapter 2). Researchers also interviewed health care workers, psychologists, teachers, aid workers from local and international nongovernmental organizations (NGOs), and village, district, and city officials.

To understand the relationship between local identities and traditions, specific regional problems, and coping strategies, researchers chose for examination a subset of regions that represented the range of local economies, including those that had suffered the impact of war and dislocation and the consequences of the 1988 earthquake. Sites included the districts of Akhurian, Spitak, Tashir, and Vardenis in the north; the districts of Vaik and Goris in the south; and the capital city of Yerevan.

Ethnographic Background

Despite its small area and population, Armenia is a geographically, socially, and culturally diverse country. Present-day Armenia consists of communities that speak different (although mutually comprehensible) dialects and have different customs; those from a given community prefer to marry within that community. Before 1988, Azerbaijanis made up the single largest minority. They were overwhelmingly rural, practicing agriculture and husbandry. Remaining minorities include the Yezidi Kurds, Russians, and Greeks. With the economic crisis as well as increasing nationalism, the last two groups are gradually emigrating.

Shattered by the impact of World War I, the Turkish invasion, and a massive influx of sick and penniless refugees, Armenia offered little resistance to Sovietization in the 1920s. Many Armenians had occupied important positions under tsarist rule, and the tradition of Russian-Armenian bilingualism and generally positive relations with Russia continues today, despite a restrictive law favoring the Armenian language, which has driven many Russian speakers out of the country.

Armenia became industrialized and urbanized after World War II, and two-thirds of the population were living in towns at the time of independence. Yerevan grew dramatically in the 1970s, with a large influx of migrants from rural areas. Although most villages had electric power, the countryside remained significantly less developed than the cities, and most urban Armenians regarded the rural population ambivalently, as bearers of the "pure" national tradition, but also as backward and ignorant.

Despite these regional differences and a strong urban-rural split, Armenians share many values. Perhaps the most important of these is family stability and reciprocity. Family relations are maintained with the "internal diaspora" of Armenians living in the other former Soviet republics, as well as with Armenians abroad. Throughout the Soviet era, contact with their diaspora gave Armenians at least some window on the outside world, and today it provides a lifeline for those seeking work outside Armenia.

Who Are the Poor?

Whether a household identifies itself or is identified by others as poor depends not only on how people prioritize and try to satisfy their physiological needs, but also on social and cultural expectations. The typical Armenian family before this study was undertaken, with four people living in two rooms, lacking a car and a washing machine, would have considered itself quite comfortable: salaries sufficed to pay for food, clothing, holidays, and gifts, and people enjoyed access to heavily subsidized housing, social benefits, medical care, and education. Widespread poverty is so recent that Armenians themselves are only beginning to develop explanations for it.

Dimensions of Poverty

When the respondents in this study compared present and past standards of living, they were prone to label themselves poor. As one respondent put it, "There are people who live worse than I do, but there are also those who live better. For some I am poor, for others not, but compared with my own former situation, I am a beggar." In the northwest, most people considered the earthquake to be the threshold event: before the earthquake they had lived in stone houses or solid apartments, surrounded by possessions inherited or acquired over a lifetime. For refugees from Azerbaijan, "before" was a different place and time, when they lived in the neighboring republic as part of a prosperous, well-integrated, largely urban community of professionals and skilled workers. For many workers, "before" was that period when Armenia was a Soviet republic and they received salaries and generous subsidies.

When people compared themselves with those around them, however, they were reluctant to use the label "poor." Armenians like to characterize themselves as a particularly hard-working and industrious people. Poverty, as revealed by old, patched clothing, a poorly furnished home, or meager hospitality, traditionally signified a lack of moral and social worth. In group discussions, people freely acknowledged their shared impoverishment, but during private conversations people were at pains to point out that other families had even greater difficulties.

Criteria of Poverty

When judging whether a given family was poor or not poor, respondents considered the most important criterion to be whether it could provide for its own minimal sustenance: "That person is poor who for 20 days out of the month eats boiled potatoes without butter, drinks tea without sugar, and doesn't have enough money to buy subsidized bread." Bread has symbolic significance for Armenians beyond its nutritional value. When they cannot obtain bread, they feel dissatisfied and hungry. When bread was subsidized, people often stood in line for hours to buy it, despite raw winter weather, and when forced to substitute other staples such as potatoes, they felt as if they did not have enough to eat.

Aside from hunger, people listed problems with heating their homes (especially in the northern mountainous areas), problems with maintaining minimal hygienic standards, and the loss of status and sense of social worth. In the earthquake region, the lack of a permanent stone home or solid apartment was a sign of poverty. People living in shipping containers or even new wooden houses viewed their homes as temporary. Those who had already lived six years in the metal containers, which are difficult to heat and corroding from dampness, were overwhelmed with a sense of impermanence in their lives.

Increasing Economic Stratification

Households in the middle of the income distribution stigmatized extreme poverty, except among the elderly or the disabled, as the result of moral inadequacy. Even these families, however, suffered from the daily fear of future hunger. Although they preferred to define themselves as "impoverished" rather than "poor," they nevertheless viewed the tiny but visible minority of newly rich with suspicion. Many middle-income and poor households believed that one could become rich only if one had relatives in important positions, or wealth and power from previous party or government posts. Jobs with the police force and social service offices were considered particularly lucrative because of the income to be gained from bribes. As one informant in Akhurian district put it, "The police support their families just by showing their shadow."

Poor rural families were most likely to blame land privatization and the corruption of local authorities for their plight. They complained that privatization had been carried out unfairly, and that they had received the most unproductive, rockiest plots of land and had been cheated out of cattle. Many attributed their problems to inflation, which had drastically depleted their savings and shrunk the value of their wages. They considered independence and unresponsive government to blame for the decline in the general standard of living, and they criticized the central and local authorities for passivity and indifference: "People now place their hopes in God, since the government is no longer involved in such matters." Those in the earthquake zone were least likely to attribute poverty to individual failings and most likely to attribute poverty to the earthquake. Already accustomed to receiving aid, they tended to take it for granted and to stress their poverty and helplessness. Refugees ascribed their difficulties to the fact they had been forced to leave their homes and possessions behind and now faced prejudice in Armenia. Despite their awareness of the larger economic context and reasons for their predicament, Armenians often internalized their inability to improve their economic circumstances and feared the judgment of their neighbors.

Changing Family Relationships

The family carries great importance in Armenian society. Without a respected, well-connected family, people feel socially and economically unprotected and vulnerable. Armenians have always considered the family rather than the state to be the most reliable form of social insurance, but its ability to perform this role depends in part on the respect in which it is held in the community. Respect is tied up with local notions of family honor: men must earn enough to support their wives and children and maintain the family's position in the community through public demonstrations of prosperity. Women are expected to behave modestly and play a subordinate role in the family economy.

The inability of many men to earn a living wage, and women's new activism in the economic arena as traders, put considerable pressure on family relationships. Parents who were interviewed expressed concern that their children would not find spouses from well-placed, prosperous, or respected families if it were known they came from a poor family. The resulting tensions disrupted traditional patriarchal and hierarchical relationships in the family, even resulting in divorce. This was a deeply upsetting development for Armenians, who pride themselves on family stability and having one of the lowest divorce rates among the post-Soviet republics.

The economic crisis had made it more difficult to form new families, and the number of marriages had declined. In regions where large numbers of young men had gone to Russia and other republics to work or avoid the draft, unmarried women far outnumbered available men. Men were marrying later because they could not support a family. In Tsovak village in Vardenis district, approximately 50 men over the age of 25 remained unmarried. In normal times most village boys would have been married by this age. At the same time, girls tended to marry younger, partly because their parents no longer considered a higher education important, and partly to extend relations of reciprocity to in-laws. Parents now considered the financial standing of the prospective spouse more carefully. A refugee couple in Vaik, for example, reported that their daughter was only 17 and wanted to enroll in the university, but they were encouraging her marriage to a 32-year-old Vaik man working in Moscow because he could support her and perhaps help the family.

Poverty and Reciprocity

Increasing economic differentiation combined with general hardship was weakening kinship ties and reducing reciprocity. Informants commented that rich families helped their poorest relatives only in the direst emergencies. The reduction of mutual assistance, even within the nuclear family, was more marked among young people. For example, an unemployed construction worker, living with his wife, their daughter, her two children, and an unmarried son, reported that his son was involved in trade. The son periodically provided the family gifts or food but often disappeared, leaving his family without support. Although he claimed to be in debt, he dressed better, ate at restaurants, and seemed to live better than the rest of the family.

Armenians in rural and urban communities insisted that they would "never let anyone starve." Nevertheless, elderly pensioners with adult children or close relatives in other towns often received little help from neighbors, who felt that pensioners were the moral responsibility of their own children. Some elderly people said they preferred to die rather than receive help from indifferent relatives. Poverty was acute among elderly people, especially among women living alone, and among refugees. Many refugees had been separated from their relatives, friends, and neighbors when they came to Armenia.

Violetta, a childless widow from Baku, Azerbaijan, was born in 1923. She lives in a small, neat house in a village with a large refugee population. Well liked by her neighbors, she often helps them with her knowledge of folk medicine and her skill in mending quilts and mattresses. At the time of the interview, she is upset because there was a small fire in her house during the night. She frequently weeps during the interview.

"My husband died a long time ago. We didn't have any children. In Baku I worked for 40 years as a railroad guard. My sister was killed in Sumgait [an industrial town in Azerbaijan and the site of anti-Armenian violence in February and March 1988]. Her children went to Russia, but I don't know exactly where. We came to Yerevan, and from there a bus brought us here. [After privatization] I gave my land to my neighbor. We agreed that he would work it and give me two sacks [100 kilograms] of wheat flour. Autumn came and I went to him, but he kept delaying. I went 10 days without bread. Probably my neighbors gave him a hint, for he finally took pity on me and sent me two sacks of barley flour. It was impossible to eat it, but what could I do? I don't want to live like this. I go into the street, and children yell, 'There goes the beggar!' The children evidently pick this up from the adults.

"I have one very kind neighbor, Ashot. He helps me with everything. He planted my garden, gathered the harvest, and gave it to me. But he wants to emigrate. How will I live without him? I have asked Ashot and the village chairman to help me move to an old peoples' home. They say, 'Auntie Violetta, why should you go to such a place?' Son, I help many people. I sew blankets for them, mattresses. They have even come to see me from Vaik. One day I got up and there was nothing to eat. It's unbearable to wait, to hope that someone will bring something. . . . I left a note in my house so that no one would be blamed for my death, and I decided to throw myself off the cliff. On the road, I ran into the chairman of the neighboring village. I couldn't help myself—I started to cry. He calmed me down, for which I am grateful, and convinced me to return home. I am not complaining about people. Ashot supports me, but soon even he will leave. Son, they say there's an old people's home in Yerevan. Tell them, ask them to take me. I can't live this way. In an old people's home, no one will blame me for being old. I don't want to accept help from others."

Poverty and Social Life

General impoverishment had reduced the number and scale of social and ceremonial events, which had once brought people together and maintained solidarity between kin and neighbor. Now people rarely celebrated birthdays, formerly marked by a sumptuous "open house," or the birth of a new child. "So someone's born, let him live without fuss. What good is all that now?"

The number of wedding celebrations had diminished because fewer marriages were occurring and because families no longer celebrated marriages. "Bride-stealing," a form of elopement in which the groom and his friends "kidnap" the bride, had increased so that families could avoid the expense of a wedding. Several young couples compared their own modest weddings, attended by 20 or so close relatives, with those of older siblings in the early

1980s, when hundreds took part. People now avoided celebrations so they would not insult others by not inviting them, or, conversely, so they would not put them into the embarrassing position of refusing to attend because they could not afford to buy a gift.

Funerals remained the one event that still united communities. Family members felt great pressure to show their worth by properly honoring the memory of the deceased with a large funeral meal. Although everyone who came made a contribution of cash or food, an unexpected death could still mean financial catastrophe for a poor or middle-income family, forcing it into debt.

The casual socializing once characteristic of Armenian society had been sharply curtailed. People used to call on each other at any time of day or evening and expected to be received with a snack or meal. Now people hesitated to visit each other for fear of putting their hosts under pressure to provide hospitality they could not afford. Visits between villages or in towns and cities were further deterred by the price of transportation.

Confined to their own homes, unable to afford newspapers or watch television, people felt increasingly alienated and isolated from each other and society as a whole. Because people were no longer able to gather to compare and discuss their reactions to current events, they were unable to form "public opinion" or exert social control over their government. People in rural regions were especially isolated because of deterioration in the telephone system and public transportation. Lack of social intercourse retarded the development of civil society. This may be one of the less obvious but most dangerous long-term effects of poverty on post-Soviet Armenian society.

Coping Strategies

Armenians have developed a multitude of strategies for coping with their impoverishment, ranging from simply eating less expensive foods and using home treatments rather than consulting doctors, to working on contract outside Armenia and sending money to their families. Although some strategies differed in kind and scope between rural and urban areas, they can be broken down into four major categories (following the scheme adopted by Howell 1994).

Reductive Strategies

Middle-income and poor families had changed their diet and reduced their purchases. They spent the greater part of their income on food, fuel for heating and cooking, and electricity. Whenever possible they substituted cheaper goods or services for more expensive ones.

Diet. Most informants had reduced their meat consumption. In urban areas the poorest informants lived on a meager diet of potatoes, grain, legumes, bread, and tea, with additional foods provided by humanitarian organizations. One poor urban couple now gave their children bread spread with a paste of powdered milk and water instead of butter. In rural areas people consumed only what they produced: potatoes had become an important staple, along with cabbage and locally grown apples, pears, and vegetables. Families with one or two cows were able to supply their own dairy needs. In some villages visited for this study, however, as many as one-quarter of households lacked livestock.

Heating. During the winter, families closed off all but one room, where they set up a wood-burning stove. Many people purchased wood; others purchased kerosene heaters and kerosene or received these through humanitarian aid organizations. In Akhurian district people used both coal and wood. People also cut down trees on abandoned land, collected fallen branches, and used anything that burned. In rural areas people burned dried bushes or dung, formerly used to fertilize fields. Many felt that using dung was primitive and complained about the smell. Relatives moved in with each other for the winter to conserve on heating expenses. Sometimes space limitations prevented families from relocating as a unit in winter, and they were forced to separate, with the wife and children returning to her parents, and the husband living with his.

Transportation. The price of transportation relative to cash incomes had become so high that people in rural areas were often forced to walk long distances, even in winter. In rural areas people rode horses or donkeys or used them to haul goods. In Spitak people used dogs to pull sleds. In Yerevan the subway remained the most reliable and cheapest form of transportation for those living and working along its one line. After the price rose from 5 to 20 drams in April 1995, however, daily ridership decreased 15 to 20 percent. Many people in Yerevan were unable to pay to ride the new minibuses, which served more routes but charged higher fares than municipal buses, and stayed at home if they could not walk to their destination. Some professionals had resigned their positions because their transportation costs exceeded their salaries.

Depletive Strategies

Most families had already exhausted their savings. Many had lost their savings when the introduction of the Armenian dram in November 1993 led to rapid inflation, which also caused the real value of salaries to plummet. Prices had finally stabilized in May 1994.

Selling Assets. For those whose savings had been wiped out, selling assets became an extremely widespread means of coping with extraordinary expenses. As one respondent reported, "After the earthquake, we sold our car. We put the money in the savings bank, and we ended up with 25 drams!" Refugees who had been able to sell apartments and possessions reported that the proceeds were by now almost gone. Sale of private assets was most common in villages or towns connected with or dependent on government enterprises. People sold assets to buy heating fuel, pay for medical treatment, purchase clothes for their children, pay tutors to teach their children English or help them pass university entrance exams, pay for weddings, bribe military authorities to exempt their sons from service, raise money to leave Armenia, and even to buy sweets for their children for New Year's. Assets sold include automobiles, furniture, washing machines, refrigerators, televisions, cut crystal wine glasses and vases (a part of every self-respecting Armenian household), and the gold jewelry women had received at their betrothal or wedding or were saving for their daughter's dowry.

Sometimes people traded personal clothing for food products. In Yerevan several middle-aged women periodically took the bus to a nearby village, where a T-shirt, for example, might be exchanged for 4 kilograms of onions and 1 kilogram of cheese. A woman in Akhurian district exchanged two gold rings for 10 sacks of flour. In rural areas many families had sold a cow or sheep each time a family emergency arose, or to buy grain and other staples before winter. For families with only two or three cattle, the sale of even one made them significantly less able to cope with the next bad harvest or unforeseen medical expense. Many had already sold all their assets. Others reported that the worst of the crisis had passed and that they were no longer selling possessions in order to survive.

Buying and Selling Apartments. A Yerevan sociologist noted the tendency for the newly rich to move into Yerevan's center, as the newly poor sold their apartments in order to live more cheaply at the outskirts of town. A pensioner living on her own willed her apartment to a distant relative in exchange for his help with the weekly shopping and picking up the 20 liters of kerosene she received as humanitarian aid. Another elderly pensioner sold her apartment for cash, with the agreement that she could live in it until her death.

Two years ago, Rosa, the single mother of a six-year-old son, sold the conveniently located two-room apartment where she had grown up for a one-room apartment in a poor, badly serviced, and distant suburb. Rosa had been adopted. After the death of her adoptive parents, relations with their relatives had ceased. The father of Rosa's son was a refugee from Baku, who had established a new family and took no responsibility for his son. Rosa, trained as a pediatrician, was unwilling to insist on bribes from her patients. When she was finally forced to sell the apartment in which she had grown up, she had to part from neighbors she had known since childhood. She also changed jobs, since she could not afford bus fare from her new apartment to her old job. On several occasions she has visited former neighbors to ask for a small loan. Her neighbors have commented on the ragged and hungry appearance of her son. Rosa is now searching for a job that will pay her a better salary.

Maintaining Strategies

Most respondents believed that people in rural regions lived better than those in the cities. As far as provision of basic necessities such as food and heating was concerned, this appeared to be the case. Most rural residents were able to produce their own food, although agriculture rarely provided a profit. Yet gardening was also an important subsistence strategy for those people living in towns who had received garden plots. Fishing was an important source of income near Lake Sevan in Vardenis district, where it had long been monopolized by those Armenians who had migrated to this region in 1828–31. Later migrants, such as refugees from Azerbaijan, complained that they were completely excluded from this lucrative practice.

Urban-Rural Migration. There was a slight trend for families to move from the cities and towns into villages. In several rural districts, local families had moved into formerly Azerbaijani villages or bought houses from emigrating refugee families. Some 30 to 40 young urban families had moved to Shurnught village on the Azerbaijani border. A number of families from the town of Vardenis had returned to fishing villages on Lake Sevan. In most cases people moved into villages where they had relatives and through whom they had obtained land.

Agriculture and Husbandry. Most informants complained about the high cost of farming. Many fed themselves from fruits and vegetables grown from their gardens but left most of their arable land unplanted, because they lacked money for seed, fertilizer, pesticide, and fuel. In the mountainous north, wealthy families preferred to invest in business, and very poor families could not afford to farm.

Many people complained that they had not received enough land to farm at a profit. Allotments varied a great deal in terms of size and quality. In Tashir district, refugees living in Dzyunashogh and Dashtadur villages had received large, productive plots, but locals in Metsavan had received rocky, unproductive ones. Sometimes collective farm leaders had acquired extra plots by registering them under the names of relatives or acquaintances.

During livestock privatization, many people had chosen not to apply for cattle or did not receive the cattle they had applied for. Some collective farm leaders had convinced people (especially older people living alone) that they would be unable to pay the proposed milk procurement tax.

A 72-year-old refugee woman recalls, "They gave us land, but I refused to take cattle and now I'm sorry. They told me, 'We can give you a cow, but you won't be able to take care of it.' I thought that being from the city, I wouldn't know what to do with it, so I refused it. They evidently expected that—after all, they could have explained to me, convinced me, or promised to help me at first."

In Akhurian district many families had failed to receive the two cows and three sheep they expected, which could have resolved their food worries. Instead some families had received 10 to 15 cows and others none.

A resident of Akhurian district tells interviewers, "During privatization, those people who had a patron received five or six cows, but the rest didn't get anything. The whole collective farm was plundered, and the chairman, together with the district leaders, themselves took the remaining 100 head of cattle to Turkey and sold them for [the equivalent of] $2 a kilogram."

Farmers also complained about the high price of renting farm machinery and paying equipment operators. In many cases farm machinery was either sold to the operators or remained in the yards of the operators, who treated it as their private property. Lack of affordable fuel, especially to run the farm equipment, remained a serious obstacle to farming. Farmers resented the high prices charged by the "gasoline mafia" and complained, "How is it that a private businessman can bring in diesel and gasoline, but the government can't?"

Now imported from Turkey through Georgia, pesticide cost between 5,000 and 20,000 drams a liter. Because of its high price, as well as lack of cooperation among landholders, farmers were unable to make a concerted and simultaneous effort with their neighbors to combat pests. As one farmer put it, "Now the mice taste the grain before the combine does."

Barter in a Cash-Starved Economy. The only cash available to most people in rural areas came from salaries and pensions. Farmers could not afford fuel to transport their produce to the cities. Because local produce markets did not exist, farmers acquired goods through barter, exchanging food and animal products for fuel, sugar, cooking oil, soap, liquor, and clothing. Most trade occurred in and between villages. Villagers complained that traders were able to dictate the terms.

> A young father in a village in Goris district describes the situation: "The villagers don't have grain. They keep some cattle for exchange, but no one brings grain. My children need warm stockings, but a week ago a car came from Iran loaded with cigarettes and sweets. For cigarettes I had to give him 2 kilos of dried cherries. What could I do? He only brought imported cigarettes and only wanted to exchange them for dried cherries."

Reciprocity. Exchange of goods, services, and money between relatives used to play an important role in Armenian society. In the more prosperous Soviet past, people could call on their relatives for large cash loans. People now complained that kinship ties had weakened and that even relatives would not lend cash: "Our relatives can barely support themselves, so how can they help us?" Exchanges of food and labor remained frequent. Frequently, sons or sons-in-law came to their parents' village during the agricultural season. Many town residents survived on food regularly supplied by close relatives in the villages.

Remittances. Remittances from relatives abroad were a critical source of income for many families. People were reluctant to reveal precisely how much they received, possibly for fear of jeopardizing eligibility for humanitarian assistance or exciting envy from neighbors, but for many people remittances made the difference between survival and starvation. In Gndevaz village in Vaik district, the village chairman estimated that 15 to 20 percent of village households received help from relatives in Russia. A retired Gndevaz couple, for example, felt they would survive the coming winter only because one of their sons had found work in St. Petersburg and had sent them $300. Although the "external diaspora" (Armenians living outside the former Soviet Union) contributed considerable funds, the steadiest source of personal remittances appeared to be family members working in Russia and other former Soviet republics.

Looting. In areas bordering parts of Azerbaijan occupied by Armenian forces, looting served as a strategy of enrichment, but the benefits were temporary: Armenians seized cattle, building materials, fuel, farm machinery, grain, other foods and wine, furniture, carpets, wood, and medicines. People who had cars and could afford fuel were able to collect the most booty. The occupied territories in Azerbaijan were thoroughly plundered, although some families had moved into these areas to use the available pasture for raising livestock.

Regenerative Strategies

Many Armenians hoped that the state would assume its former role as major employer. Nevertheless, over the previous three years Armenians had adapted to their new circumstances by devising new ways to make money.

Seasonal Labor Migration. Labor migration to Russia had become the single most important way of earning a cash income. It was particularly widespread in northern Armenia, where the earthquake had destroyed much of the industrial infrastructure and agriculture has never played a major economic role. The majority of labor migrants found work as artisans or skilled construction workers. They generally traveled by invitation to construction sites in Russia in groups of 4 to 10 relatives, friends, or fellow villagers. Sometimes they risked travel to regions where they had only heard about the possibility of work. Most worked in construction, especially road building. Since 1992 many fathers had taken sons who had completed eighth grade, in order to "teach them independence" and avoid their being drafted into the new Armenian army.

Labor migration often left women in a difficult economic position. Narine, a 43-year-old kindergarten teacher with three children, told interviewers her husband was working in Irkutsk as a builder. She had not received any news from him in seven months. Her only cash income was her salary of 900 drams. "If it hadn't been for help from the village," she said, "the children would have died of hunger." While they waited for their husbands to send back their earnings, women in rural communities sometimes earned small amounts doing housework for their neighbors.

Labor migration splintered families. Sometimes men abandoned their families in Armenia, or sons married in Russia and refused to return. Some men had established second families where they were working in Russia. The Armenian wives tended to swallow their pain and humiliation, knowing that they and their children were dependent on the earnings from Russia.

Often families had to sell assets or borrow money at interest to raise funds for the journey. Returning was also a problem. Of the 800 men who had left Metsavan for Russia, half were unable to return after a season because they lacked money for the trip. In Svrants, a poor and isolated village in Goris district, the village chairman reported that many families had left for other Armenian towns and cities before 1990, and some had continued on to Russia. Since privatization, no family had left. They lacked the money to leave, and they were unwilling to risk selling their cattle to raise the money.

Lack of an effective banking or postal system made sending money back to Armenia difficult, even dangerous. Family members working outside Armenia either had to bring the money themselves or wait until they found a trusted acquaintance who was traveling to Yerevan. Once in Yerevan, the problem remained of getting the money or gifts to the family's town or village. On several occasions, when Armenian men organized a celebration to mark the end of their season's contract and their departure for home, local racketeers orchestrated brawls and stole their earnings. In some cases Armenian men were severely beaten during robberies; 10 men from the village of Metsavan were killed.

Petty Trade and Commerce. Petty traders bought and sold goods locally or sold goods supplied by others. Some rented market stalls by the day; others paid the local "market mafias" to rent a permanent place in the market. People who set up sidewalk tables or kiosks generally had to pay the city for a license as well as regular bribes to local police. Sellers who worked on commission might earn as much as $10 a day. Sellers tended to work individually, although they would occasionally pool their goods, so that each person would sell a particular item such as shoes or sweaters in a greater range of sizes and styles. Both men and women engaged in retail trade, although women predominated inside closed markets and shops, whereas men and school-age boys worked at sidewalk tables.

In towns and even in villages, some families bought candy, cigarettes, soap, and other small items to resell. In Goris every third or fourth house appeared to operate a tiny shop from a window sill or front room. Such petty trade helped many of the poorest to supplement their pensions. On city streets, and near markets or subway entrances, people resold bread purchased at subsidized prices, earning several hundred drams a day. "People get involved in commerce only to earn a piece of bread," one respondent said, "not to get rich."

Women and Trade. Women proved unusually active in trade. With many young men in hiding to escape the draft, women could travel more openly. In cases where husbands and brothers were working abroad and unable to send money home, many women were left without money to support themselves and their children. Unmarried, widowed, and divorced women predominated among the traders, as well as women whose husbands were unemployed.

Nelli, a chemistry teacher by profession, is divorced and lives with her 14-year-old daughter. In 1989 she took a course in bookkeeping and began working in a cooperative in addition to teaching. After the cooperative closed in 1991, Nelli resigned her teaching job to engage in trading full-time. Taking a loan from acquaintances, she made a business trip to Romania with several other traders. This first trip was profitable, the second trip less so. She therefore switched to Poland, but this trip proved financially disastrous. Nelli was forced to sell her gold jewelry to pay back her loan so that she could maintain her reputation with her creditors. Because of her losses in Poland, Nelli stopped trading abroad and started trading in the market. At the same time, she and her daughter worked in her garden, thanks to which they were able to feed themselves.

In the fall of 1993 Nelli began taking business trips again, this time mainly to Turkey. When necessary, she borrows money for her trips at a percentage. Nelli actively studies the Armenian market, trying to predict the seasons and holidays when people are likely to buy gifts. She also maintains a permanent place at the market. She has taken advantage of the fact her brother lives in a large, relatively prosperous village just outside Yerevan and has successfully sold her goods there. Despite occasional unsuccessful trips, including one in which $3,000 was stolen from her, she now manages to adequately support herself and her daughter.

Border Trade. Considerable trade took place across the Iranian and Georgian borders. Metal traveled from Armenia to the Islamic Republic of Iran, and gasoline came into Armenia from Georgia, to be traded for dollars or farm produce. At Sadakhlo, just across the border in Georgia, the benefits of commerce overrode ideological or ethnic differences among Armenian, Azerbaijani, and Georgian traders. Most informants characterized trading at Sadakhlo as very profitable but dangerous. A lively trade also took place in Armenian border towns and villages where Russian army troops were stationed.

Moneylending and Money Changing. In urban communities many men earned a living buying and selling rubles, drams, and dollars. There were usually one or two "professional" moneylenders in each small town. People in villages also borrowed small amounts of money to get through a difficult period or to raise capital for an enterprise or for trading. People were frequently unable to repay these loans and were forced to sell assets to pay their debts.

Anna, 53, is a retired, widowed schoolteacher with three adult children. Recently her sister took Anna's son to Poland on a business trip. He borrowed money at a percentage but lost money on the trip and went into debt. A friend then offered him a job in St. Petersburg. He borrowed money for the trip, but once in St. Petersburg he lost money through a racket. Anna's daughter traveled to St. Petersburg to bring him more money, but this was stolen en route. Her son's creditors are now demanding their money. They have already seized some furniture, which they threaten to sell if they do not receive their money in two months. Anna and her two other children have moved in with her late husband's brother in order to hide from their creditors. Anna is afraid to return to her apartment to get the food she conserved for the winter, and reluctant to sell the small family garden, located 10 miles away, because gardening remains the family's only reliable source of subsistence. Anna's daughter, who just graduated from the Medical Institute, recently refused a job offer as a public health worker, calculating that working on the garden would pay a return greater than the proffered salary of 1,500 drams. The family of Anna's brother-in-law is also poor. The wife and adult son are unemployed, and the family survives on the potatoes and cabbage the husband grows on unused land at a university facility, where he works as a gardener.

Small Enterprises. After 1988 many people attempted to open small businesses and engage in production. Numerous obstacles, however, had forced most of these businesses to close or move. In Azatan village a new textile enterprise, employing 60 to 70 people, had closed, as had a resistor factory, which had employed 100, and several food processing plants. Attempts to operate carpet weaving, stone working, woodworking, sewing, and meat processing enterprises in rural regions had also failed. In Vaik district several entrepreneurs established jewelry-making businesses to take advantage of rich local resources of semiprecious stones. One such business in Zaritap village employed 15 workers, paying them 10 times the average salary, but the business was failing because of an intermittent supply of electricity, problems in obtaining licenses and certificates, and marketing difficulties.

Of those businesses that had opened in 1993–94 and were surviving at the time of the study, the great majority involved trade rather than production. Informants complained that the only businesses that were thriving were those whose owners had connections with officials in the police force or the Ministry of Internal Affairs. Others were overwhelmed by problems obtaining capital and credit and harassed by tax officials.

Many rural residents proposed ideas for enterprises that they felt would help their community. Arevik, a village in the earthquake zone, produces an abundant wheat harvest and specializes in the production of *lavash*, a flat, tortilla-like bread baked in underground clay ovens. The village already supplied 80 percent of the market in the city of Gyumri. Unfortunately, it lacked a mill, and farmers had to transport their wheat at considerable cost. Villagers felt that a mill would relieve them financially. They could establish bread-baking and pasta-making enterprises, supply the region with high-quality grain products, and provide local employment.

Many families had started small family enterprises, making and selling homemade items. The artisans sometimes traded their wares for food products. People came from many surrounding villages to trade food products for pots made by an elderly woman in Jadjur, who fired the pots in her underground clay oven. Artisans also sold their products to shops, or for cash at open-air markets such as Yerevan's Vernissage. Successful operations were often very small scale, family-based enterprises. Most people operated these small businesses out of their own homes and avoided registering them, to avoid taxes and bureaucratic harassment. Many were marginal operations, their success dependent on various "connections" to secure electricity, equipment, and supplies, as well as on a combination of enterprise and skill.

Marina, 50, and her husband Albert, 55, are a married couple with three children. They live with their youngest son, Ashot, 21, in a three-room apartment. Their other daughter and son are both married and live separately with their families. Neither Marina nor Albert received a higher education. Albert used to work as a conductor on the Yerevan-Moscow train but has been unemployed since 1990. Marina worked at a candy factory until being laid off two years ago.

Recently Marina decided to put her considerable baking skills to work by baking pastries in her home for sale. Through personal connections, Ashot illegally hooked up their apartment to an electricity source. Marina purchased a homemade stove and oven. Through personal acquaintances, she is able to buy flour, butter, and sugar at the market for wholesale prices, which are 10 to 20 percent lower than retail prices.

At first, Marina baked piroshkis stuffed with potatoes. The basic ingredients—flour, oil, and potato puree—were inexpensive, and she could bake six piroshkis at a time on the stove. They were cheap, easy to make, and tasty. For the first two months, Marina sold them for 30 drams apiece to a salesperson working at the market next to her apartment. The salesperson resold the piroshkis for 40 to 50 drams apiece.

Marina baked 100 to 150 piroshkis a day and made a profit of about 100 percent. Gradually, competitors appeared, selling piroshkis that were smaller and poorer in quality but sold for 5 to 10 drams less. Marina switched to *khachapuris* (a pastry stuffed with cheese and topped with egg). These required more expensive ingredients and were more complicated to prepare, but there were no competitors. At 70 drams apiece, Marina found it harder to market them. At first she gave them to acquaintances and relatives to distribute at their workplaces, including hospitals, clinics, and department stores. Because the quality was high, a demand developed. Marina began receiving orders for special events such as birthdays and weddings. Although the business was profitable, sometimes she was unable to fulfill orders when a break occurred in the electricity supply.

Eventually, a shop agreed to buy 20 to 30 *khachapuris* on a daily basis. A neighbor of Marina undertook to market the *khachapuris* to other shops, kiosks, and sidewalk stands. Through her work, Marina is able to cover basic family expenses.

Rural Wage Labor. People in rural areas had begun to hire themselves out as wage labor to richer farmers. Often men preferred working in distant villages, considering it shameful to work for hire. In several villages in Tashir district, refugees who were professionals or skilled workers and preferred to work in Russia had received large, productive plots. They hired peasants from Metsavan, who had received rocky, unproductive plots, to farm their land in their absence. But Armenians were ambivalent about this new development.

In Khoznavar village, on the Azerbaijani border, a wealthy farmer explains that he hired a married couple the previous year. "They looked after my cattle and their own. I worked their land, gave them the whole harvest, and paid them a salary. They never complained. But village people began to tease them; they called them wage laborers who worked for a 'lord.' When the couple worked for me, they had four cows. Now they only have two left, and they have not yet managed to plant their land. But they will not come back to work for me, even though I still need workers." Expressing the village perspective, a young school-teacher comments, "He may have become a big farmer, but we are not his serfs!"

Begging. The sight of elderly or disabled people begging alms at church was not unknown in Soviet Armenia, but by the time of the study it had turned into a new, sometimes quite successful, survival strategy. In Gyumri several dozen beggars congregated at the large open markets, often coming from their own villages, where they were ashamed to beg. Street musicians have become a frequent sight in Yerevan; sometimes the performers were well-trained musicians who passed the hat to supplement other incomes.

Artur, 46, is married, with a 14-year-old son and a 17-year-old daughter. He teaches Russian and English at a school just outside Yerevan. His wife teaches music. A guitarist and singer, Artur performs on the street in winter, or when the school closes to allow children to help relatives with agricultural work. Although his family lives in Yerevan, Artur stays at the school during the week, sleeping in his office, because he cannot afford the daily bus fare to and from Yerevan. According to Artur, the education authorities are considering reimbursing teachers for their transportation costs, but they have not yet made a final decision.

Last year, the school gave Artur a plot of land on which he was able to grow enough fruit and vegetables to supply his family's winter needs. However, he finds the labor very difficult. Before that, he had tried to engage in business and trade. He sold newspapers but soon realized that this was not for him. From street performances he can earn up to 1,000 drams a day. Sometimes he receives invitations to sing at weddings or other social events. Since he started singing in public, his family has lived much better. But he is ashamed of this work and refrains from performing if he learns beforehand that his children will be in the city center.

Prostitution. Prostitutes had become more visible in cities and towns, and known brothels operated in Gyumri and Yerevan. In rural settings local Armenians often accused refugee women of engaging in prostitution. This may have been true in some cases, given the difficult economic circumstances and the refugees' lack of extended family networks. In other cases, however, the accusations reflected a clash of urban and rural mores. Armenian village morality strictly regulates women's behavior, condemns sexual relationships outside marriage, and is quick to label women as prostitutes for violating local norms. In Yerevan prostitution increasingly catered to the many Iranians who regularly came there on business. The rise in prostitution, together with male migrant labor, quite likely contributed to the reported rise of venereal diseases in Armenian cities. Family members, even husbands, sometimes turned a blind eye to their wives' prostitution, because the income was essential to the family.

Theft. In rural regions informants complained that theft of cattle and feed had become common. In both urban and rural areas, people reported theft of winter food stocks. People in towns reported a rise in pickpocketing. The appropriation of equipment and raw materials from state enterprises was practiced by private cooperatives, which sometimes operated on factory premises. State resources such as building materials and machine parts also provided a small income to those who sold them in the market. Stealing electricity was not uncommon during Soviet times, when people boasted of knowing over a hundred ways to avoid paying for it. In the past three years, with many households receiving only a few hours of electricity each day, often during the night, or going without electricity for weeks at a time, people had devised numerous ways to obtain it illegally.

Enlistment in the Russian Army. In northern districts it was common for young men to join the Russian army stationed in the region. By agreement, 50 percent of the troops had to be Armenian citizens. Serving in the Russian army allowed them to stay in Armenia yet avoid service in the Armenian army.

International Organizations. In Yerevan, Gyumri, and to a lesser extent in other towns where NGOs and embassies had opened offices, many people worked as office managers and staff, translators, or computer consultants, as well as drivers, cooks, or housekeepers, earning up to several hundred dollars a month. Many women earned $30 to $50 a month as housekeepers for the expatriate community. For women trained as music teachers, engineers, or accountants, this work was a source of shame that they often kept secret.

Coping Strategies among Intellectuals

The fate of Armenia's intellectual and cultural elite has important ramifications for the future intellectual and cultural development of Armenia as a whole. This elite includes the scientists and scholars affiliated with the Academy of Sciences and institutes of higher education, as well as writers, artists, and performers.

Many of the cultural and intellectual elite had been forced to abandon their professions, because they were no longer able to live on their salaries. Of the 8,000 researchers working for the Academy of Sciences, approximately two-thirds had left their jobs. Some had found positions teaching at the many new private institutes of higher education. Others had gone to Russia or entered into contracts with foreign universities or firms in Europe, the Middle East, and the United States. Several years ago many Armenians had sworn they would never "abandon the homeland." At the time of this study, a majority of young people interviewed saw leaving Armenia as their only hope of surviving.

Many teachers and professors earned money by tutoring students to pass the university entrance exams. Students paid tutors from $150 up to $1,000 for a November-July academic year. A Yerevan scientist reported that his mother, a retired schoolteacher now tutoring four pupils, had unexpectedly become the economic mainstay of his seven-member family.

Some intellectuals had found new professions or even entered commerce, but unemployment remained a serious problem. Used to the high status of their professions, some highly educated people were reluctant to accept work they considered beneath them. They were unwilling to engage in business because they considered it demeaning, or because they feared dealing with the criminal underworld.

Health and Health Care

While the government of Armenia debated how to restructure the health system, practitioners and consumers were already privatizing medical care. Paying for medical treatment had become ubiquitous. Except for vaccinations, preventive medicine was virtually nonexistent. Interviewers were struck by the prevailing pessimism.

Most people no longer felt they could afford to see a doctor except in the direst emergencies. The head doctor of Vaik district thought only 2 or 3 percent of district residents in need of treatment actually sought it. Many towns lacked specialists.

Throughout Armenia interviewers observed a very uneven distribution of medical personnel. Nurses had little authority. Their main functions were administering shots and distributing household medicines, but they were unable to do either because village pharmacies were empty. Most medicine coming into Armenia was distributed by donors to hospitals, but all informants reported having to pay for medication, often at prohibitively high prices.

Most people complained that hospitals were difficult to get into, poorly equipped, and gave poor service. In northern districts some hospitals even closed for the winter. People preferred to call emergency services because they charged less than doctors and often had supplies of medicine unobtainable at pharmacies. Increasing numbers of people preferred to consult folk healers, rely on home remedies or medicinal herbs, or resort to various magical rites.

For the most part, rural practitioners tended to demand payment in line with what their patients could afford, and they often accepted payment in food products. The closer to the town center, however, the more real the problem of cash payments became. People were often forced to sell assets to pay for treatment. The problems were especially acute for female refugees, who lacked the kinship network through which they might have been able to exert influence or obtain favors from medical practitioners.

Many people could not afford transportation to the clinic or hospital. In many villages emergency services and ambulances had ceased to function; patients relied on neighbors or relatives to donate gasoline or provide a vehicle. Access was a problem in the earthquake zone despite the network of diagnostic and treatment centers built by international organizations. Families of children who had lost limbs during the earthquake and received prostheses complained that all four Armenian prosthetic centers were located in Yerevan. They found it difficult to travel to Yerevan and could not afford to stay unless they had relatives there. Children outgrew prostheses and needed frequent refitting. Lack of access therefore posed serious problems for the disabled population.

Home deliveries had increased in recent years, partly because they were cheaper than hospital births. Sometimes women gave birth at home because they had been unable to arrange transportation in time to the nearest hospital, or because roads were closed by snow. Women also feared that doctors would order unnecessary cesareans to make money. Even straightforward hospital deliveries were expensive. Parents had to pay routine hospital costs, including daily tips to hospital staff, as well as a large sum to the doctor. The total might come to several hundred dollars. Many newborns were underweight, and many women claimed they were unable to nurse. Although international organizations supplied formula, many women were unable to get from their villages to the district center where it was available and were reportedly feeding their babies cow milk diluted with water.

Official statistics did not necessarily reflect the current level of poor health in Armenia, because many people did not consult doctors. In many cases it was difficult to separate elements of stress, cold, and poor nutrition. This was especially true for the earthquake zone, where, after six years, many people still lived in temporary metal cargo containers. Still unemployed and homeless, many had lost faith in the future. Fighting, alcoholism, stress-related diseases, and suicides had risen in Gyumri and the earthquake zone.

Likewise, although people with access to gardens were usually able to maintain reasonable nutrition, town and urban populations remained at risk. In cities it was not uncommon for children to come hungry to school or faint in the classroom; sometimes people lost consciousness on buses. Many of the symptoms people complained about, including deteriorating vision or loss of teeth, could be related to lack of vitamins. Botulism had increased, since people were often unable to can food properly for lack of fuel.

In many homes, lack of running water, electricity, and heating fuel made bathing very difficult. People living on the top floors of high-rise apartment blocks often had to haul their water, since water pumps did not work. Armenians found their difficulties in maintaining usual standards of hygiene deeply demoralizing and felt they were "losing their human appearance."

Education

Armenian parents expressed deep concern over the reduced quality of education, and they feared for their children's future. In November 1994 an unprecedented teachers' strike for better conditions and higher salaries sought to draw the government's attention to the crisis in education. Lacking widespread support and a grassroots organization, however, the strike soon petered out, and teachers continued to leave their jobs.

Perhaps the most serious problem affecting the education system was the outflow of qualified teachers. Some 10 to 20 percent of the 60,000 teaching positions in the country were vacant as of March 1995. Some teachers had been replaced with less qualified staff, and the burden of work on those remaining had steadily increased. Most of the teachers who had left or planned to do so explained that they could no longer afford to work as teachers; they were leaving to devote their full time to other occupations, including subsistence agriculture. In Vaik district officials told angry teachers that there was no money in the budget to pay them. A village chairman turned down a request by local teachers to be excused from paying their taxes, claiming he lacked authority to waive the tax, but he acknowledged that teachers were under great social pressure in the village to continue teaching.

Some village schools were no longer able to provide teachers in a full range of subjects. Refugees in Vardenis reported that their local school was using teachers from the neighboring village. The teachers came several times a week by foot; on the remaining days the school remained closed. In many communities qualified teachers had been replaced by university students, recent graduates of private cooperative universities, or pensioners. Many schools lacked specialists, especially in Russian and English.[1] School clubs, choirs, theater groups, and orchestras no longer existed.

For most teachers, low salaries signified a loss of respect. Especially in rural regions, schoolteachers were representatives of the intelligentsia and highly respected. Teachers who came from Yerevan enjoyed additional prestige because of their knowledge about the workings of "the center." Now teachers were forced to supplement their low salaries through trade or agriculture, which they found quite demeaning.

Male teachers had always been a minority, but they had greater authority and prestige than women. Most of the men still teaching were pensioners. A young man in Khoznavar village told interviewers he had left his teaching position even though he loved his work, because he needed to earn money in order to marry. Women teachers experienced the declining salaries and prestige of their profession as an especially hard blow.

The government network of special residential schools had suffered particularly from the decline of state support. Many schools remained open thanks only to gifts of food, clothing, and equipment from the diaspora and from religious and other humanitarian aid organizations. In addition to providing education and training, residential schools had increasingly taken over the burden of providing for children when parents were unable to do so. The director of a Yerevan residential school for mentally handicapped children explained that some parents from outside the city could not even afford the transportation costs to pick their children up when the school closed for the winter. Instead some teachers took children home with them. The school attempted to provide vocational training but lacked the resources to do so. Its shoemaking workshop was down to its last jar of recycled rusty nails. Classrooms, bedrooms, and even the "sick room," where two sick children huddled under wool blankets, were clean but stingingly cold. Clothed in donated secondhand clothing, the children, during interviews, unanimously voiced their preference for the school over home, for a single reason: they received more to eat at school.

Truancy

Teachers felt they could no longer provide an example that good education guarantees a decent living. Parents and teachers worried about the increasing number of pupils dropping out before finishing eighth grade. In the southern districts of Vaik and Goris, informants knew families with three or four children who kept their children home from school for lack of clothing. A teacher in Jermuk reported that some of her pupils had attended school in winter wearing cloth bedroom slippers instead of boots. In Akhurian district 45 pupils failed to start school in 1994 because they lacked adequate clothing. Sometimes children from one family took turns attending school in order to share one set of warm clothing or pair of shoes.

In rural areas parents increasingly needed their children to help with farm work during the school day. Some boys had left school to accompany older men on seasonal work outside Armenia. Some teenage boys spent weeks away from school at a time, taking care of livestock. In the cities school-age boys could be seen selling goods at the market or at sidewalk tables. Even pupils planning to attend university felt they were no longer able to prepare adequately at school. Ambitious parents increasingly pulled their ninth- and tenth-grade children out of school to study full-time with tutors. In such cases they paid teachers not to record their children's absences so that they could receive their diplomas. Teachers complied because lowered attendance would jeopardize their own positions.

Schools had become inhospitable and dreary. Children had to share textbooks in class and could not take them home in the evening. Many parents could not even afford notebooks for their children, but had to recycle those from the previous year. In the earthquake zone many children still attended school in temporary buildings. In border villages near Azerbaijan, many school buildings had been severely damaged during the bombardments. The school in Khoznavar had lost most of the glass from its windows (now covered with plastic) and part of a wall. Schools were cold and barren, without equipment or decoration; electricity and water functioned very sporadically, making it impossible for staff to cook hot meals or even to prepare and serve the powdered milk distributed by humanitarian aid organizations. In the year this study was conducted, distribution of kerosene allowed some schools to remain open throughout the winter. In some cases teachers and parents also supplied kerosene or wood.

Higher Education

Although Yerevan State University remained ostensibly free to better students, parents paid large sums to ensure high marks for their children on each of the entrance examinations. Access to the university was thus gradually becoming limited to children of prosperous or well-connected families.

For young people in rural areas, access to higher education had become more difficult. Even if they were admitted to a university in the city, their parents were often unable to provide for their living expenses. Some students had enrolled at an institute of higher education but were forced to return home because they could not afford to live apart from their families. In most of the villages studied, the number of high school graduates coming to Yerevan or other cities for higher education had dropped from three or four to one or none. Some students registered at Yerevan State University but only came to Yerevan for their exams.

A number of private "cooperative" universities had been founded and continued to function, although they were not yet accredited by the Ministry of Higher Education. According to a lecturer, the government had an interest in keeping these cooperative universities open, since they paid taxes. Many boasted highly qualified faculty hired from the state university and the Academy of Sciences. Instructors felt that the students at the cooperative universities were not as well prepared as those attending government-run institutions. Moreover, students often dictated conditions. Professors were unwilling to fail students, since their salaries depended on attendance.

Cooperative universities had sprung up in towns and even some villages, along with new branches of Yerevan State University. Although the fees at private universities were considerably lower than the bribes required to enter the government university, parents sacrificed to send their sons to state institutions of higher education, because enrollment there allowed them to defer military service. As a result, the cooperative universities had a predominantly female student body.

Overall, however, institutions of higher education had suffered from declining enrollment as well as the loss of qualified faculty. Subjects such as agriculture had lost popularity. A technical education in engineering, mathematics, chemistry, or physics had once been in demand by local industries, particularly in Gyumri, but these industries had been destroyed or were no longer functioning at capacity. Law, which was always lucrative, and foreign languages and economics, because they opened up possibilities for work abroad, had taken their place.

Older Armenians recalled a time when bright village children were able to attend the best institutions in the republic and continue graduate work in Moscow, Leningrad, or Novosibirsk. Many members of the old intellectual and cultural elite had grown up in villages. Today poor families worried about the move toward paid education, which they feared they would not be able to afford. At the same time, education was losing its allure, since a diploma could no longer guarantee a minimum living wage. If these trends continue, education, especially quality higher education, will become a privilege of the new elite.

Aid and Assistance

The government provided a range of pensions, benefits, and stipends to pensioners, the disabled, students, single mothers, and children. The real value of these forms of assistance had drastically decreased, however. For many the small pensions represented their only cash income. The government operated homes for the elderly, special residential schools, and orphanages. Many of these institutions were only able to function because they received food, clothing, and other forms of assistance from NGOs.

The free cafeterias that operated in Yerevan, Gyumri, and a few other towns were a completely new form of institutional assistance. As of March 1995, 12 such cafeterias operated in Yerevan, each providing a daily meal to 100 to 200 pensioners, disabled persons, large families, and the unemployed. For many they provided the only meal of the day. District executive committees had primary supervisory responsibility but lacked sufficient resources to maintain the cafeterias over the long term. The Armenian General Benevolent Union operated four free kitchens. Shortages of funds had forced some free cafeterias to close temporarily, and in some cases permanently. In many cases official social service lists determined eligibility for free meals, but an NGO operating a free cafeteria reported that the official lists were so inaccurate that it had taken its own survey. The free cafeteria in Goris had come to serve a social function, especially for elderly women. While the men gathered at the House of Veterans or the chess club, elderly women tended to remain isolated in their own apartments. Although some of the needy were still too ashamed to come to the cafeteria, others gathered in an adjacent square hours before it opened, just to socialize.

Lack of Information

Obtaining timely and correct information about government and private aid distribution was an endemic problem. In villages few people had access to newspapers, radios only worked when people received electricity, and most televisions were out of commission for lack of parts. In larger cities, buildings and even districts went without electricity for weeks at a time. As a result, people sometimes missed news of aid being distributed or were uncertain how and where to apply for it. When people did hear about aid distributions, and the announcement clearly stated which groups were eligible, they would still apply to the executive committee because they wanted to hear the information for themselves.

In Yerevan, most aid was distributed by the Ministry of Labor and Social Services. Especially in the district offices, personnel were often rude and indifferent to less educated, working-class applicants. Unable to present their problem in the proper bureaucratic terminology, these applicants often found themselves shunted from one office to another in the ministry, or even sent to other ministries. In winter this posed a special problem for the elderly and the disabled who could not afford bus fare.

Mistrust of Authorities

People in rural areas suspected that local officials distributed aid according to their own agendas rather than according to official program rules. Local officials were sometimes unfriendly toward direct NGO distribution of assistance; some NGOs reported that local officials had harassed local organizations. The director of the local Goris office of an NGO that ran a low-fee pharmacy reported considerable tensions with district authorities, who felt that they themselves should control all local aid.

Problems Obtaining Aid

People were not always able to provide the documents necessary to prove their eligibility for aid. Authorities frequently required repeated visits with ever more documents, sometimes holding up pensions for seven or eight months. People often had to pay bribes to receive their pensions. Because people frequently changed households or moved from district to district, especially during the winter, they had difficulty finding out where to apply and what documents to show.

Sometimes local officials confiscated documents for nonpayment of taxes, thereby preventing the document holder from demonstrating eligibility for assistance. Some parents were denied pensions because they were hiding draft-age sons. Many refugees from villages in Azerbaijan occupied by Armenian forces were unable to receive government aid allocated to refugees. The Armenian government refused to categorize them as refugees, hoping to encourage their return home.

Local Philanthropy

Some villages now had rich "patrons," usually a villager who had worked abroad, often in Russia. Some of their gifts were directed at schools, for example to construct a kindergarten in Gyumri or to aid a village school in Shirakamut. Some local philanthropists paid wages to local workers for the construction of monuments. One distributed about 2 million drams to needy villagers to rent farm machinery and buy heating fuel and potatoes. A Spitak city council deputy solicited food from local businesses and organized a free kitchen for needy pensioners. The kitchen now received NGO assistance and served 200 pensioners.

Church Aid

For decades the Armenian Apostolic Church had attempted to maintain its religious function while avoiding government repression. During that period it had lost most of its social function. The church still enjoyed considerable respect as a national symbol, yet few people saw it as a source of material or even spiritual assistance. Some placed no more trust in church officials than they did in government officials.

The Catholic Church in Rome sent assistance to the northern districts where Armenian Catholics are concentrated. Four nuns from the Vatican worked in a school in Arevik village and distributed aid to needy families.

Because the Catholic Church and diaspora Armenian churches sometimes distributed aid through local governments, most people assumed the latter were the source of the aid.

Some Armenians gravitated toward proselytizing Protestant religions, which they termed "sects," but many people accused the Pentecostals, Jehovah's Witnesses, Baptists, and other religious groups new to Armenia of using aid to recruit believers, especially among the elderly or the isolated. Converts encountered considerable animosity in their communities, based on accusations that these "sects" threatened Armenian traditions. Some government and Armenian church officials shared this hostility.

Popular Perceptions of NGO Assistance

Most aid recipients believed that aid distributed by local authorities had originated with the government or the Armenian Red Cross, the latter because deliveries were often made in vehicles with a prominent Red Cross logo. This belief simply reinforced the popular conviction that the government could and should take care of them. People were most aware of and expressed positive feelings about NGOs that used expatriate staff to personally supervise aid distribution.[2] Most aid recipients were convinced that Armenian NGO employees directed aid to their own families and friends, sold some of the aid, or, even if the employees themselves were honest, gave in to pressure from local mafias to divert aid.

Many international organizations were not familiar with local traditions and conditions, and recipients did not always carry out the programs as intended. A school food program was designed to supply schoolchildren with a daily glass of milk and a high-protein biscuit, but in some schools the teachers gave the children four or five biscuits at a time, or all 45 biscuits at once, so that the children would not feel "humiliated" by the offer of a single biscuit. In schools where there was no running water, staff were unable to prepare the powdered milk and instead simply gave children the powder to take home.

Targeted Aid

In all communities, "targeted aid" was an issue fraught with controversy. In Jermuk, where researchers observed the distribution of humanitarian assistance, a written notice listing eligible groups had been taped to the front door. Nevertheless, several ineligible applicants brought their personal documents to prove they were pensioners or that their spouses were "invalids." Most of the ineligible applicants disregarded the official letter and distribution list, although written in Armenian, feeling that they, too, deserved assistance.

In Jermuk and many other communities, refugees were particular objects of resentment. Their lack of proficiency in Armenian, their different ways, and, in rural settings, their urban habits set them apart from the local population, who viewed them as "Turkified." Many local Armenians considered themselves just as needy as the refugees and were angry that even well-to-do refugees received regular food parcels while poor nonrefugees went hungry.

Refugees, for their part, acknowledged that the food aid had been absolutely indispensable. Yet they still felt at a disadvantage in comparison with their neighbors, who in their view were better supplied by their network of relatives in the villages. Even the assistance they received hardly compensated for the isolated life they now led, or for the loss of family, friends, possessions, and familiar surroundings.

Similar tensions were noted in Gyumri among the disabled population, who felt isolated and excluded from Armenian society. Armenian families tend to regard birth defects and mental or physical handicaps as shameful. Most often they hide family members who have been handicapped from birth so that they will not reduce the marriage prospects of the "normal" children. Especially before the earthquake, Armenians were unaccustomed to seeing people with any sort of deformity and were often repulsed at the sight. Since the earthquake, however, considerable aid had gone to the disabled. For example, in the so-called Austrian Quarter consisting of housing funded from Austrian donations, the disabled, along with their able-bodied relatives or guardians, occupied 100 apartments designed to accommodate wheelchairs and well supplied with electricity and cooking gas. Each disabled person had a "patron" in Europe who supplied him or her with money and clothing and sometimes even funded holidays. Although the disabled people who received such aid were materially taken care of, they felt ghettoized and isolated. No special transport linked the Austrian Quarter to Gyumri. The disabled were confined to their neighborhood, where there was a special school, a small church, a clinic, and a small shop. They still considered themselves poor because they had not earned what they had been given and did not see any prospect of employment or integration into the larger society.

Meanwhile others in the earthquake zone who had lost close family members, and remained extremely ill housed and needy, felt they had suffered just as much as those who had been disabled. This resentment meant that disabled people often suffered from name-calling and hostility when they ventured from their immediate surroundings into Gyumri.

Changes in Armenian Society

It is impossible to view impoverishment in Armenia apart from the dramatic political, economic, and social changes that have taken place since 1988. Government no longer has the resources to guarantee employment or maintain previous levels of education and medical care. Yet the majority of people interviewed for this study implicitly or explicitly expected the government to eventually reassert its old role in providing employment and organizing agriculture. Self-help groups or indigenous structures of power had not yet emerged, especially in rural areas. Most people relied on their own efforts or cooperated with related households to ensure their immediate survival. In the absence of clear laws and a tradition of enforcement, connections to those in local positions of authority had taken on new importance.

Impact of the War

The war in Nagorno-Karabakh had slowed development in Armenia in various ways. It had resulted in the blockade levied by Azerbaijan and Turkey. A number of young draft-age men had left the country to avoid being drafted into the army. Bombardment by Azerbaijan had destroyed private homes, schools, and public buildings in the border areas. War needs in Nagorno-Karabakh had diverted fuel and medical supplies needed in Armenia itself. Some people suspected profiteers of creating provocations to maintain high prices.

Armenian occupation of territory lying between Armenia and Nagorno-Karabakh now allowed Armenian farmers to plant and harvest in relative security, but the people living along the eastern Armenian border still felt insecure. The war had taken a psychological toll: many had fled their villages in panic during the bombardments, and some had moved away permanently. Especially among refugees, many of whom had barely escaped Azerbaijan with their lives, fear and trauma remained acute.

Women

Impoverishment tended to lower the status of women in the family. In Armenian families, women have always taken primary responsibility for housework and child care, even though many had higher education and a majority worked outside the home, contributing significantly to household income.

With mass unemployment, women could no longer contribute cash to the household economy. Yet their labor had increased as they added gardening, husbandry, and food preparation to their daily tasks. In the words of one interviewer, women in the countryside had become little better than "household slaves." Especially where the husband supported the family, women were afraid to risk any sort of disagreement or conflict because they were so completely dependent on his income.

Women were rarely prepared to be the primary economic support for their family. Women who had never worked outside the home, or who had left work after the birth of their children, were at a serious disadvantage in finding new employment. They now formed a majority of those registering as unemployed. Family tensions frequently resulted when men were unable to work and their wives were forced to take an active role in supporting the family. Husbands and neighbors sometimes looked askance at a woman's success, especially if she was involved in foreign trade. Divorced women, single mothers, and never-married women have always had low status in Armenian society and risked being branded as prostitutes when they took on an active economic role.

Children and the Elderly

The very old and the young also constituted groups at risk. Certainly, elderly persons living alone or with an elderly spouse, a handicapped adult child, or a small grandchild were among the poorest people interviewed. Elderly people without close relatives were at risk because their pensions were rapidly exhausted, and most had already sold their assets. When they fell ill, they had no resources for paying doctors or buying medicine. Although families favored young children with the best food, children remained vulnerable to undernutrition, stunting, and rickets. Children as a group were also at risk from the deteriorating educational system and declining access to good higher education.

Refugees

With the general economic decline, refugees remained ill housed and had not been fully absorbed into Armenian society. Although Armenian-speaking refugees from rural Azerbaijan adapted to their new rural settings with relative ease, those from urban backgrounds had much greater difficulty. In stable, long-settled regions such as Vardenis district, refugees complained of being excluded from local government.

Despite their grievances, refugees had yet to form organizations to represent their interests. Even within a single village, refugees formed a heterogeneous group. Having come from different cities or towns in Azerbaijan, they had yet to form the strong ties of reciprocity that still characterized local kinship networks, and most viewed their new status as peasant farmers in Armenia as temporary. Those of working age were doing their best to leave Armenia for Russia, the other Slavic republics, or the West.

Conclusion

Since 1988, Armenians have been dealt a series of blows: war, blockade, earthquake, dislocation, and energy crises. Even families who are able to provide for their material needs are confronted at every turn with drastic changes in their daily lives. Ties of kinship reciprocity between rural and urban regions and across state borders have helped most Armenians survive severe impoverishment. But hardship and emigration have also fragmented extended families. Networks of reciprocity have retracted to include only the closest relatives. Frequent socializing has diminished because people can no longer afford hospitality and hesitate to impose this burden on each other or to appear hungry or needy themselves. Labor migration has separated families, sometimes permanently. Although a new elite has emerged, most Armenians look with increasing nostalgia to the past, when strong Soviet authority maintained ethnic peace and prosperity.

Armenians are now living through a critical transition period. They continue to demonstrate fortitude and ingenuity in their struggle to improve their lives. Despite inexperience and setbacks, they still place strong hopes in the construction of a legal system that can protect their personal liberties and facilitate development of a viable free market system. At the same time, it will be important to ensure that the weakest groups in Armenian society do not turn into a permanently disenfranchised underclass.

Notes

1. Russian language teachers had lost their jobs several years before, and many may have emigrated, as a result of the postindependence language and education law that had resulted in closure of schools that used Russian as the main teaching language.

2. When the author accompanied the staff of MED-AIR, a Swiss-based NGO, through several "container neighborhoods," many people proudly invited us to

see the pit latrines that MED-AIR had built for them, or simply praised MED-AIR as honest. MED-AIR had also very creatively addressed the information problem in Gyumri by posting announcements of aid distribution in bread shops and on the sides of trolleys.

References

Holt, Sharon. 1995. "Using Land as a System of Social Protection: An Analysis of Rural Poverty in Armenia in the Aftermath of Land Privatization." Armenia Poverty Assessment Paper 3. Washington, D.C.: World Bank.

Howell, Jude. 1994. "Coping with the Transition: Household Coping Strategies in Kyrgyzstan." Save the Children UK (December). Processed.

Scott, Wolf. 1994. "Emergency and Beyond: A Situation Analysis of Children and Women in Armenia." Geneva: UNICEF.

World Bank. 1994. *Armenia: Agriculture and Food Sector Review.* Washington, D.C. (June 10).

World Bank. 1996. *Armenia: Confronting Poverty Issues.* Report No. 15693-AM. Washington, D.C. (June 10).

A single mother is head of this household in rural Armenia.
Photo by Elizabeth Gomart

---------------------------------- ✳ ----------------------------------

CHAPTER 7

No Way Back: Social Exclusion Among the Poorest in Armenia

Elizabeth Gomart

In 1997 an assessment focusing on the poorest of the poor in Armenia followed up on the qualitative work conducted in 1994–95 and reported in the previous chapter. The situation had by then improved considerably in some ways. Electricity shortages had been eliminated, schools had reopened and remained open in the winter thanks to international assistance, a long-lasting ceasefire with neighboring Azerbaijan had allowed Armenians to return to Nagorno-Karabakh, and a level of normality had been restored to the border areas. Yet the improvements failed to benefit all Armenians, as the society had become one of the most socially inequitable in the world.

This qualitative study was undertaken in December 1997 to complement the description in the Armenian State Department of Statistics' (SDS) Household Budget Survey, undertaken the year before, of extreme poverty in Armenia. The aim was to improve targeting and protection of the poorest and to provide information at a crucial time in the design of policies and programs. The qualitative research provided exploratory leads for the team analyzing the quantitative data from the SDS survey. It assessed assumptions, explained correlations, and provided more analytical depth and detail.

Fieldwork consisted of in-depth interviews with 110 of the poorest households (defined as those unable to adapt to the transition and meet even their most basic need, namely, food) and with key informants such as local officials, professionals, social workers, and staff of international and national NGOs. Snowball sampling was used, relying on key informants in the community and local criteria of poverty. Five urban and 13 rural sites were selected from the northern, southern, and western parts of the country, the eastern conflict area, the earthquake zone, and the industrialized center including Yerevan, the capital. Sites were selected for their high incidence of poverty as identified through the SDS survey.

The Face of Extreme Poverty

What prevents a household from lifting itself out of poverty? In Armenia a number of factors made the poorest vulnerable: they had fallen through the social safety net because they did not fit the criteria for receiving assistance, and they were excluded from opportunities such as trade and work abroad, which required mobility and good health. Their limited access to social services exacerbated their current situation and predisposed their children to poverty today and in adult life. The current coping and adaptive mechanisms of many of the poorest households—dependence on formal and informal support networks, menial jobs with low or unpaid salaries, and odd jobs—had been unreliable. The 1995 World Bank Poverty Assessment and the SDS survey had described a growing contingent of destitute people in Armenia. In absolute terms the poorest were unable to meet their most basic needs in terms of food (adequate calories), warmth (fuel and clothing), and basic hygiene (water and soap). In very crude terms, people in the poorest households were hungry, cold, dirty, and sick.

Although poverty had not been unheard of in Soviet times, the vast majority of the population in those days were able to meet basic needs. A notable drop in living standards affecting most Armenians began in the late 1980s and continued with the 1988 earthquake, independence in 1991, and the conflict with Azerbaijan over the enclave of Nagorno-Karabakh that followed. Housing, services, and factories in the earthquake region were destroyed. Inflation soared. The end of trade links with other Soviet republics intensified shortages. Bread and flour shortages, due to the government's inability to import sufficient quantities to supply the subsidized bread program, were an emotional issue. Factories that had relied on fuel or other inputs from Azerbaijan were closed. Hidden and open unemployment began to rise, and people began selling off assets.

The worst years, 1992 to 1994, marked the peak of the struggle over Nagorno-Karabakh and the resulting blockade imposed by Azerbaijan and Turkey. Services and industry collapsed throughout the country, leading inexorably to more unemployment and sharply lower real wages for those still employed. In the winter of 1993–94 schools were closed for lack of fuel. Electricity was rationed, with most households receiving only two to four hours a day. In early 1995 bread prices were gradually liberalized, and their rise limited households' access to a staple of the Armenian diet.

At the time of the research, macroeconomic figures showed a turnaround in living standards for the overall population. After a plunge in GDP of 70 percent over the previous three years, the economy was growing at a rate of 3 to 6 percent a year. Overall living conditions had improved: almost all households (an estimated 98.7 percent) had access to electricity, and the vast majority (88 percent) had piped water, according to the SDS survey. Schools had reopened and government services were functioning. However, respondents felt that growth had not benefited all households equally, and the SDS survey confirmed strong inequities.

Food and Nutrition

To identify the poorest households, researchers looked for those that were hungry, and found them at all research sites. The SDS survey defined poverty as the inability to meet minimal food and nonfood needs, and extreme poverty as the inability to meet basic caloric needs. By these criteria over half of the Armenian population (54.7 percent) were poor, and more than a quarter (27.7 percent) were extremely poor. Long-term food shortages leading to stunting (based on height-for-age norms) affected 16 percent of children, yet there were no observed cases of acute malnutrition, as estimated on the basis of weight-for-height norms (Children's Aid Direct 1996).

Poor households were limited to a monotonous diet and poor-quality produce. Even those in rural areas could consume only what they or their relatives could grow themselves. Seasonal hunger or fear of hunger was common in the late winter and early spring. Many adults reported having lost weight over the previous five years. Mothers said that their children suffered from nutrition-related health problems such as chronic respiratory infections or fainting spells. In an extreme case (reported further below), one rural mother whose husband was absent said that because she could not produce breast milk, and alternative infant foods were unavailable, only two of her seven children had survived infancy.

The extent of food deprivation varied within the family. Nonworking parents (mostly women) said they were most likely to go without food, allowing those who were working (mostly men) and young children to eat first. Respondents often said that they provided food to the children of poor families rather than to the parents. For adults, meals were often provided in lieu of payment for work. Cases of extreme food deprivation were mostly found in urban areas such as Charentzavan, where industries had closed and residents did not have links to the surrounding villages. Most rural poor were able to obtain at least some food through land cultivation or local informal networks. The urban poor were much more dependent on unreliable incomes.

Hunger in many rural households had been held at bay through the sale of cattle and subsistence agriculture, but a growing number had become impoverished since privatization. Some rural families had depleted their assets in order to finance land cultivation and had been unable to replenish them. The SDS survey also showed destitution among rural residents. Rural families without good-quality land, sufficient labor to work the land, and the ability to afford inputs and market goods were at risk of hunger.

An elderly couple in Koti, a formerly well-off village in the conflict area on the border with Azerbaijan, finds itself going hungry. They live in an old, crumbling home. The wife has no shoes. They own land and pay taxes on it (withheld from the wife's already small pension), but they have never cultivated the land and do not know where it is located. They have a son in the Russian Federation and a married daughter living in Ijevan, a town 60 kilometers away. Their daughter comes to visit once a year and brings food and clothing. Their food stocks for the winter consist of a pile of dried greens and two bags of wheat gathered from other people's fields after the harvest. An old can of oil provided by the Red Cross sits on the windowsill. Half the day's soup, consisting mostly of water, dried herbs, and four small potatoes, is set aside for the evening. A loaf of bread made from flour from the Red Cross will be rationed by the couple to last for two weeks.

Many of the poorest households had reduced the number of meals to two or one a day. Rationing of food was also widespread among respondents. One household had a regimen of two potatoes per meal per person for the rest of the winter. Another household had developed an intricate system of rationing bread (see below). People "tricked" their stomachs with warm "tea" without tea leaves or sugar or drank thin soups of boiled water and dried herbs.

A household in Charentzavan is composed of a bedridden grandfather, a grandmother, their daughter-in-law, and her three school-aged children. The father is in jail awaiting trial for selling a motor he claims to have found in a field. The grandfather stores bread in a bag above his bed. Every three days his daughter-in-law hands him two loaves of bread, and he cuts each loaf into 10 equal pieces using a ruler. The two loaves must last the household three days. Each of the three adults receives one piece a day, and each of the children is allowed two pieces. The grandfather keeps track of who has had how many pieces, because the children tend to forget they have already eaten and ask for more. The family also rations the walnut-sized potatoes they bought at 60 drams a kilogram: 1 kilogram a day for six persons. Over the summer they gathered wheat and beans from harvested fields in nearby villages. There is little seasonal variation in their household diet. Once this summer the mother was able to buy an apple for each child. Consumption of other food products varies with the income-generating opportunities that can be found that day.

There were seasonal fluctuations in food availability. The majority of the poorest households expected to run out of food by the late winter or early spring and feared going hungry. Food stocks, savings, and cash incomes were insufficient to smooth consumption throughout the year. Traditionally, food was stored in the summer when prices were low to help the household through the winter months when prices were high, income-generating opportunities were even more scarce, and mobility was reduced. The poorest households had insufficient stored food because they had no sugar, fuel, or jar tops for canning, no home-grown fruits and vegetables, and no money to purchase these items. In rural areas seasonal hunger was sometimes averted by eating the seed stock, a clear sign of vulnerability.

The diet of the poorest households consisted mainly of potatoes and bread. Rice and macaroni were sometimes available depending on the flow of income and assistance, as were vegetables in small quantities: cabbage, carrots, onions, tomatoes, peppers, and greens. The poor could not afford to purchase meat and milk products (butter); urban households had to rely on their relatives in the countryside. In the southern mountains and pasturelands, cheese was a staple even among poor households. The quality of the produce was an issue. Many households showed the interviewers small potatoes the size of walnuts; some were blackened and smelled so bad that the children preferred to go hungry rather than eat them. Entire villages in the Gugark and Sunik regions had poor-quality potatoes for lack of water, fertilizers, and pesticides. Illness, emigration, or death of a relative had a ripple effect on food intake throughout the extended family. Cash or in-kind infusions from salaries, pensions, a day's wage, sale of assets, or humanitarian assistance occasionally allowed other products—oil, macaroni, rice, sausage—to be added to the diet.

Households defined poverty as the absence of bread. Bread, like rice in many Asian cultures, is an essential product on the Armenian table. Respondents claimed that they continued to be hungry when other foods were available but there was no bread. The poorest households struggled to meet this cultural dietary standard. Wheat was milled and baked or, when fuel was low, ground into a meal to make a water-based porridge. Parents sometimes mixed other grains into the meal to economize on wheat. The poorest households sometimes saw dramatic fluctuations in the quantity and quality of food. Lack of inputs and insufficient land often limited crops to one staple, either wheat or potatoes.

Electricity: Light, Heating, and Cooking

The poorest households struggled to balance food and electricity expenses. Reforms in the energy sector had increased tariffs 10-fold since 1994. Poor households were often unable to cover electricity costs, and episodes without electricity were considered a good indicator of poverty. Nonpayment was due to acute fluctuations in household income. Many households had gone for weeks and months on end without electricity. A few had sold the electric meter to buy bread, and they could not afford to replace it or pay the flat price for electricity without a meter. To benefit from the lowest price for electricity under the stepped pricing system (15 drams per kilowatt-hour for the first 100 kilowatts per month), use was limited to one light bulb (or the equivalent) for three hours a day. This limited consumption to lighting the one bulb and television viewing. Households sought alternatives for heating and cooking—a wood stove and a supply of firewood or other combustibles, or a kerosene stove (obtained through humanitarian assistance)—or did their cooking and washing at relatives' homes.

According to both the SDS survey and the responses to this study, access to electricity was a greater problem in cities, where alternative fuels were more costly and difficult to find. The poorest urban households reported higher electricity expenses than the poorest rural households, and urban households were more likely to have forgone electricity. The qualitative study was conducted when the stepped pricing system was already in place, and most urban households—when they reported expenses—paid between 1,000 and 2,000 drams a month. Inability to cover energy costs resulted in electricity cutoffs, inadequate heating, limited meal preparation and food processing for storage and income generation, and health problems such as respiratory infections and chronic illnesses.

The stepped pricing system was not an effective system for all households, since many could not control their electricity use as easily as others. A household's composition affected its energy needs. Schoolchildren needed light to do homework; infants' clothes needed to be washed frequently in boiling water. Some respondents who had experienced being trapped under rubble in the aftermath of the 1988 earthquake said that they would rather go hungry than have to endure the anxiety of darkness.

Shelter

In many of the poorest households, poverty was evident in the lack of repairs: leaking roofs, plastic sheeting on broken windows, wallpaper peeling off blackened walls. Some homes had been cannibalized: door frames, window frames, and wood floors had been used as firewood or sold to cover immediate needs.

Receiving a permanent home in the city of Spitak has been a mixed blessing for a very poor household headed by a wheelchair-bound victim of the 1988 earthquake. The family lives in the 'Uzbek' neighborhood a few kilometers from the city center, far from shops, health services, the local soup kitchen, and government offices. The stone house has two stories, but the second floor is not equipped for wheelchair access, nor can the toilets be accessed by wheelchair. The Uzbek architects who built the neighborhood after the earthquake did not adapt their design to the local climate: the kitchen faces south, and the living room faces north and is always cold. This year the household has not received any kerosene from humanitarian assistance, even though this style of home is reputed to be difficult to heat. In 1996 the household received $100 from the town council for firewood and kerosene.[1]

Crowding was an issue among some of the poorest households. Poor families explained that they were unable to spread out in independent housing units because they relied on a shared income or had taken in needy relatives. Multiple generations and multiple family units regrouped to live as one household.

Clothing

The poorest households rarely purchased clothing, but instead generally obtained it secondhand from relatives and neighbors. Whereas some adults wore old but clean clothing, others were dressed in rags. The problem was most severe in winter. Clothes are an important status symbol in Armenia, and poor clothing was most problematic for school-aged children as they outgrew shoes and overcoats. A number of families kept their children out of school for up to a year because they could not afford proper clothing and school supplies. In Karkop village a teenage boy had dropped out of school because he lacked appropriate shoes. His father suggested that he use the money he earned gathering aluminum to buy a pair of shoes, but the teenager said he would rather spend his money on food. Some children shared a single pair of winter boots, taking turns wearing them to school.

Education

Education is highly valued among Armenians. The last few years have seen a shift to a system based on formal and informal payment for quality services. The main issue remained access to quality education for the poorest students (see Appendix A for a 1996 education sector social assessment). There were schools in the cities and in the vast majority of villages. Enrollment was close to 99 percent through age 14, the last year of mandatory education, according to the SDS survey. Even in the noncompulsory grades the majority of children were enrolled. In the ninth and tenth grades enrollment rates among the very poor were a little lower than for the total population, but the enrollment figures understated the problems of unofficial dropouts and chronic absenteeism.

There was an emerging difference between the sexes with regard to education. Often girls completed the ninth and tenth grades while their brothers dropped out. Education was no longer seen as providing a means to support a family, but it was still valued as a status symbol for women.

A village parent explains that the family cannot afford to send two children to school: "We allowed my son to drop out [after eighth grade]. Anyway he won't need [education] in his life. It's more important for my daughter. For her, education is essential. And also my son is free to help me."

The poorest children were notably less well equipped than others for school. They went to classes hungry and with inadequate clothing: sandals in winter and no overcoats. They had few of the required textbooks. Most families were able to afford the rental fee for textbooks where renting was an option. Obtaining a quality education meant paying for private lessons (provided by the same teachers who taught for free in the schools), buying textbooks when these could not be rented, and ensuring (through bribes, presents, or good clothes) enrollment in a prestigious school or class. The poorest reported that they kept educational expenses low by avoiding these extra costs. The quality of education was considerably worse in rural areas, where there were few qualified teachers and children were half as likely to take private classes, a prerequisite for entering prestigious high schools and institutes of higher education. School supplies were also more difficult to procure in rural areas.

Enrollments in higher education had dropped significantly, even though some universities and special technical schools offered free but highly competitive entry. It was widely reported that grades for entrance exams into institutions of higher education could be bought in both the free and the paid systems. Only two of the interviewed households had children in higher education or special secondary schools. Poor parents covered educational costs by borrowing money, accepting gifts of clothing from neighbors and relatives, selling produce or other belongings, or using the child's income from work over the summer.

Hygiene

Personal hygiene was difficult for the poor because of poor water supply and lack of cash for soap. Only 78 percent of rural households had running water, according to the SDS survey; the figure for urban households was 94 percent. Many of the villages visited did not have water within the village limits. In Karkop, in the north of Armenia, villagers had to travel up to 5 kilometers to fetch drinking water. In Koti, Akhtanak, and Lernapat, water was for sale from trucks. In Akhtanak lines for water lasted all day long, with family members taking turns in line. Some urban apartments in Yerevan, Yeghegnadzor, and Chambarak still did not have regular water supply; water was provided only once every few days or only on the bottom floor of a multistory apartment building.

Some families had obtained soap through humanitarian assistance or had learned to make soap from lard and ashes, but others complained of going for weeks, sometimes months, without soap. A young mother in Ararat village, waving her blackened hands, complained of not having washed her four-month-old with soap since he was born. She could not afford detergent to wash his diapers and clothes; she could only rinse them. The high cost of electricity and other fuel to heat water limited the ability to bathe in winter. A woman in Yerevan washed only once a month because of lack of heating fuel and soap. In many households bed linens and clothing went unwashed for prolonged periods to save on cleaning supplies.

Health

The main obstacle to health care was the cost of care rather than physical access to facilities, a finding supported by other recent studies (see Appendix A for a 1996 health sector social assessment). The cost of care included the cost of medicines, consultations, tests, and other services as well as informal payments used to guarantee quality care and secure costly medical interventions.[2] Respondents often reported that they were in poor health, but they were unlikely to seek treatment from formal medical institutions. They avoided laboratory or other diagnostic tests, took medicines instead of undergoing costly operations, opted for local rather than central and more expensive facilities, or took an incomplete course of treatment. Health emergencies led to the rapid depletion of the meager assets of the poorest households. A household became more vulnerable when its savings buffer was reduced and health expenses pushed it further into poverty, forcing members to forgo food and electricity in order to deal with the crisis. Many families reported dire conditions during health emergencies.

A teacher in Yerevan and her unemployed husband, formerly an engineer, report that they consumed only boiled water for one week while their daughter was in the hospital. The mother's salary and their income from the sale of assets went to cover medical costs. They paid off their debt with $50 from an acquaintance living in the United States.

A couple in Charentzavan recall that the worst period for them in the last seven years was when their eight-month-old infant fell fatally ill. They sold their remaining assets and their electricity was cut off. Since that time they have not been able to redress their situation.

Humanitarian assistance sometimes played an important role in providing health care for the poorest families. Local charities and health professionals sometimes supplied free drugs or vaccinated children born at home, but this assistance disproportionately benefited the nonpoor.

Poverty had a direct impact on the health of family members, especially children. Mothers complained that their children suffered from chronic pneumonia or other respiratory infections. Doctors had linked the children's poor health status to poor nutrition, some parents said. But how were they to improve their children's nutrition when they were already paying more for medicines?

A mother in Artik village says that she has had seven pregnancies in the last five years, but only two of the children survived their first year. She lost three babies between the ages of two and four months to starvation (she could not produce enough breast milk) and respiratory infections. The other two pregnancies resulted in stillbirths. When one of her children fell ill last April, she asked for infant formula, but the doctor said there was none available. The household is landless and has no cattle. The woman's husband returned the land he had received from privatization after two years of negative returns. He is gone most of the year, serving in the independent force guarding the border area. She receives his salary of 10,000 drams a month. In 1997 he worked five months but had only been paid for three as of late November. She has no family in the village whom she can ask for help, and his parents do not offer any material assistance. The family has not had electricity since June 1997 or firewood for the last four years. She collects dung from the village streets to use as fuel, a sign of destitution according to fellow villagers.

The need for information and access to affordable family planning methods was evident among the poorest families. Many of the newborn babies in these very poor households were born because the parents could not afford an abortion, still the main method of birth control. A few respondents openly acknowledged using needles to try to force a miscarriage (in Yerevan) or agreeing to sell their newborn to the obstetrician (in Charentzavan), although in the end the transaction was not completed. Other parents placed newborns and older children whom they could not feed or clothe in government boarding schools or orphanages.

A number of rural households had switched to giving birth at home because of lack of emergency transport and because maternity hospitals were costly and had poor and unsanitary conditions. Some home births were assisted by a nurse. In two cases where the mother had given birth in the hospital and was unable to pay, the doctors refused to release the mother and child from the hospital while they tried to extract money from relatives. Children born at home were not systematically vaccinated.

Just as poverty led to poor health, so, too, health problems often led to family impoverishment through the depletion of assets to cover health expenses, indebtedness, and temporary or permanent loss of the ability to work. The SDS survey showed that the very poor relied more on the sale of assets and less on assistance from relatives and friends to cover health costs.

Other Expenses

Even the poorest households spent valuable cash on cigarettes, coffee, and alcohol. Women rarely smoked, but men devoted a considerable share of their monthly wages and daily earnings to cigarettes. Many men reported smoking approximately two packs of cigarettes a day, at a cost of 120 to 200 drams. A husband in Yerevan who supported 11 people brought home only 1,300 of the 2,000 drams he earned each day. He spent the rest on snacks and cigarettes. Another husband in Karkop village spent 120 drams a day on cigarettes: 3,600 drams out of his monthly salary of 8,000 drams. These figures were typical. This diversion of cash for cigarettes was often a cause of marital disputes. There was no mention or understanding of the long-term consequences of smoking in terms of health costs and forgone labor.

Women commonly bought a pack of coffee in order to provide a cup to guests. Often neighbors appeared with coffee and a coffee grinder after respondents who were out of coffee knocked on their common wall. Alcohol use remained understated; alcoholism in Armenia has not reached the scale attained in other former Soviet republics. When alcoholism was present, the effects included lost income and diversion of income away from basic needs. Some of the most destitute and isolated households were headed by an alcoholic parent.

Why Are the Poorest Unable to Cope?

The coping mechanisms of destitute households were limited and insufficient to draw them out of their extreme poverty. The poorest shared an inability to benefit from the widespread income-generating activities available in the country: trade, agriculture, and remittances. Instead, they reduced consumption, increased their dependence and indebtedness, and sold off assets and personal belongings.

The Labor Market

At the household level, the lack of well-paid local employment opportunities was seen as the main cause of poverty. Unemployment was high in Armenia. Officially, at the end of 1996, 10.1 percent of the labor force was registered as unemployed. The SDS survey put actual unemployment at 28.3 percent of the labor force and 45.8 percent for those between 17 and 25 years of age. In the informal sector and in the formal private sector, and for those seeking work abroad, employment and income-generating activities required startup capital, bribes for employment, and social ties.

For some, pride, lack of education, or being female limited opportunities for taking jobs. Trade and self-employment were stigmatized. Some respondents who held positions in government institutes said they were unable to quit because they would lose their status and sense of self-worth as an intellectual, even though they might make more money. Some respondents had turned down jobs that they considered beneath them. Young women were often discouraged from working as waitresses because it was considered improper, and young people were discouraged from engaging in trade because it was seen as a risky, dangerous business.

A highly educated Yerevan couple with two teenage children both work in government institutions. The wife is a librarian and the husband a mathematician at the Academy of Sciences. They earn 5,200 drams and 7,300 drams a month, respectively. The daughter studies at the institute and receives a stipend of 2,100 drams. They lost all their savings to the currency conversion.

Why do they live mostly on their salaries? The wife explains that she has thought of giving private classes in Armenian language and literature but that she lacks connections. She does not have a name in the field, and students usually choose to take private classes with well-known university teachers. Her poor health prevents her from working too much, but in the end she believes her "mentality is in the way"—she feels helpless. She says that her husband needs his job for intellectual stimulation. He would feel he is nothing without his job. As for her daughter, she considers that there is no appropriate work for her—the family lacks the ties and the money to get her a good job.

She asked her professional association for help but was turned down because, they said, so many people are in her situation.

The family cannot afford to buy enough food on their salaries. They go to the market asking sellers for the cheapest, half-rotten produce. They are treated as beggars and ignored. They feel so ashamed after this experience that they have lost hope and want to die, the mother says. Sometimes they barter a kitchen utensil for food when they have no money. Her unmarried sister, who works at the Geophysics Institute, is their emergency source of income. So when her children are hungry, she sends them to her sister, who feels guilty and feeds them. Last time, she gave them money for sweets and the children bought 10 eggs instead. She avoids other relatives and friends because she has nothing to offer them—no sweets or coffee.

The son recently transferred to a boarding school, where he feels that there is less discrimination against the poor than in the neighborhood school. The teachers are not as good, but they pay equal attention to all the children, and he is fed there twice a day. He can also prepare for his classes in school with textbooks there instead of having to buy his own.

Access to formal employment was seen as being limited to the relatives and friends of the owners and managers of enterprises. Most respondents explained that one was "invited" to take a job, and it was useless to look for a position unless one had a relationship with enterprise owners or managers. The most sought-after jobs—those where economic rents could be extracted or products obtained—often required a bribe to the hiring manager. A position as a hairdresser or an auto mechanic required a bribe of $100. This tradition of paying for certain positions dated back to the Soviet period and affected jobs in the services sector, where the employee's salary could be supplemented by a tip many times higher than the official price of the service.

Even if the head of household had work, salaries were irregular and payment was often delayed. Work was often part-time or irregular even in formal enterprises, and wages were low—too low to support a family, even when several adults were employed.[3] In some cases employees were paid in kind.

A cleaner in a factory reports that she was paid in coffee grinders. She was unable to sell them locally because the market was flooded by other workers also trying to sell them, so she sent them with a friend who barters agricultural goods for consumer goods in other regions of Armenia.

The poor who worked in the formal sector occupied subordinate rather than managerial positions. They were factory guards, janitors, street cleaners, teachers, and teachers' aides. Engineers, academics, factory workers, and agricultural mechanics (tractor drivers) were also among the poorest households but were less likely to be working full-time. Hospital workers and other workers who benefited in ways other than from their salary were conspicuously missing from the sample.

Even though salaries went unpaid for months on end, workers were reluctant to give up their jobs. Formal employment was highly valued as a source of status and of future income. Because the work did not take up the whole day, there was time for additional income-generating activities. It was widely believed that quitting a job where salaries had been withheld for months on end was like gambling: payment might be forthcoming at any time, and to quit would be to renounce wages due for work already completed. Thus the longer the employee worked without payment, the higher the stakes of quitting. There was also an expectation that the employee was saving a place for when the economy improved and the enterprise started working at full capacity once again.

Unskilled labor required physical strength, free time, and social connections: people expected that employers would seek them out and offer them a job. Men were hired to support agricultural, domestic, and trade activities: plowing, planting, harvesting, carrying, towing, loading and unloading, chopping wood, repairing or setting up heating systems, and building. Women were hired to assist with domestic chores: cleaning shops, sidewalks, or apartments; preparing food; or picking berries and herbs. Craft production was uncommon, there was little demand for services because of the lack of cash, and agricultural processing activities were limited.

Opportunities were sporadic, and the poor were idle many days out of the month. The physical nature of the available jobs made them unsuitable for the many households without able-bodied men. Local unskilled labor for men was commonly paid at the rate of 1,000 to 2,000 drams a day, enough to buy bread or other staples for the day and some extra to store for the winter. Respondents were often paid in kind or given meals in lieu of pay. They worked as hired labor for three or four days a month, or two to three days a week in good times. The SDS survey confirmed this humble level of earnings from self-employment among the very poor.

Incomes from informal employment were subject to seasonal fluctuation. More odd jobs were available in the spring and summer when there were fields to work, cattle to bring to pasture, homes to repair, and trade activities to support. In the fall there was harvesting and cutting wood. In the winter there was almost nothing to do.

A village woman says that she worked a full month this summer gathering 100 kilograms of medicinal herbs under the hot sun. She was paid a total of 8,000 drams by a buyer who came to the village.

Informal employment was risky: there was no job security from one day to the next and no effective legal recourse in case of injury or nonpayment. A common complaint was that wages were not paid or were a fraction of what had been promised. In other cases respondents had taken jobs without clarifying how much they would be paid before completing the task. A few respondents had been disabled, temporarily or permanently, by work-related accidents and had not been able to afford care. One injured worker said that his employer had promised him treatment but failed to provide it.

Trade was one of the main income-generating activities and one of the main coping mechanisms in the transition. Those urban households (and rural households without good-quality land) who did not trade were often the poorest in the community. Among those who were not presently trading, some had tried but failed to make a profit, had become indebted, or had lost major assets in the process. Others were reluctant to wager their limited assets or their health to undertake a risky, highly competitive activity. Another obstacle was the lack of startup capital: small-scale trade in clothes and produce required $50 to $100, according to respondents from a trading village near Sadakhlo, the main market for consumer products just across the border with Georgia. Other reasons for avoiding trading were pregnancy, child care responsibilities, health problems, and the low prestige of trade.

Sometimes the poorest were involved in trade only sporadically, to cover specific needs as they arose. There were few very small traders selling fruit on the side of the road or in the local markets. Most rural producers went through middlemen because they lacked the capital and mobility to reach the market. Owners of sheep and cows might sell milk and cheese. Many were limited to bartering, since intermediaries often brought produce from another region to exchange for local produce.

Work abroad, especially in Russia, was one of the main means of subsistence for poor Armenian families. An estimated 20 percent of the population had left Armenia over the last five years because of the poor economic and social situation.[4] In this study the poorest households were commonly those whose breadwinners were unable to make the trip to Russia or were unable to earn enough money once in Russia to support their families back home. These included female-headed households who might maintain telephone contact with their husbands in Russia but had not received any financial support for years.

Families often sold their most valuable assets (their furniture or their home) and even productive assets (cattle, a car, or a truck) to raise the money to work abroad, depleting their savings buffer. Working abroad was subject to several requirements: capital for travel and initial expenses; social ties in the city of choice; some assurance that there would be work; good health, because labor in Russia was mostly physical; and support for meeting family responsibilities, such as arranging for the care of elderly parents, wives, and children left behind.

Sending money home was itself a challenge, given the lack of a banking network that could effectively transfer money earned abroad. Families at home lived on savings, the sale of assets, home production, and credit from local stores and the electric company until an acquaintance, a fellow villager, or, preferably, the worker himself could return with the wages earned. For the sojourn abroad to be a success, the worker needed to cover the cost of the return ticket; any debts incurred to take the trip (at a rate of interest of up to 20 percent a month); any debts incurred by the family during his absence for food, electricity, and land inputs; needs postponed during his absence (such as clothing or health costs); cash for the household to live on for the coming months (to purchase firewood and food); and savings that could be converted into productive assets such as cattle.

Land

Large numbers of rural residents owned and worked land for subsistence. They grew food staples—potatoes and wheat—for household consumption rather than higher-value crops to be sold. This explained the limited attempts to rationalize cultivation.

Landless rural households were likely to be very poor, since home production was the main source of income for the majority of rural households. In theory, the land privatization implemented between 1992 and 1994 had distributed government land to all rural households registered in the village. However, some households still did not have land. According to the SDS survey, only 65.8 percent of very poor rural households had land, compared with 82.7 percent of the poor and 90 percent of the nonpoor.

The qualitative study identified a number of causes of landlessness: very little or no land was available to privatize in some locations; the household had turned down the land because the members worked in village- or town-based industries and had no agricultural experience at the time of privatization; the household labor force was insufficient or unhealthy (consisting, for example, of a single parent with children or other dependents, or disabled persons, or pensioners); and fear of land taxes and water fees. In some cases the household returned the land to the municipality because it was unfit for cultivation (salinized or eroded) or because the household had been unable to cover its costs after several seasons of farming and did not want the tax liability. Some households missed out on privatization because the men came back too late from Russia and had not turned in the applications on time, or because the household had arrived as refugees after privatization had occurred. In some cases entire villages had no land to cultivate. Industrial villages (administratively counted as towns) had no arable land to distribute. Land was privatized or distributed where there was a collective farm on the territory of the village or town. In large villages in industrial regions (such as Kotaik), some households had turned down land in the belief that the industries would continue to be their main source of income.

Land ownership was not always sufficient to raise a household out of extreme poverty. Many destitute households were unable to cultivate more than a small part of their land because they could not afford to pay for equipment costs (tractor fees, fuel costs, and the like) or water, let alone other inputs. As a result, productivity was very low.[5] One qualitative indicator of low productivity was the need to buy flour in wheat-growing regions. The head of the village council in Vaik region estimated that 50 of the 190 households bought bread.

In Ararat village, a matriarch, her two grown sons, and their families are limited to planting hay because the quality of their land is so poor. Whereas others get three harvests in a season, they get only one because they cannot afford to irrigate after each dry spell. They gathered enough hay to cover half the land taxes and water fees for one irrigation.

The family has trouble with cash expenses. Since the death of two milk cows in 1995, they have had to rely on irregular salaries (4,000 drams a month) and pensions (2,300 drams a month) for cash. Most of this money goes to pay off debts at the bread shop and for electricity. They have not been able to buy oil or soap for three months. They have no potatoes, and they grow only tomatoes on their household plot. Each adult tries to work for others in exchange for vegetables (cucumbers, carrots, and peppers), which they preserve for the winter, but work is scarce from November until March. When they have enough cash to buy macaroni, they cook it with water (in lieu of the traditional oil preparation) and a can of vegetables.

The two brothers gather and sell aluminum scrap using their motorcycle. They can earn 1,500 drams a day on good days selling the aluminum. Having run out of heating materials, however, they are cutting up the motorcycle's tires to burn in the stove. Over the last three to four years the mother has sold all her gold jewelry to cover food costs. Last spring they ran out of food and sold the bricks from their unused animal shed. They will rely on this stock of materials to cover food costs this winter, too. They have been told that the village council is withholding their family benefits until they pay their land tax.

Productivity for poor households who could not afford inputs fluctuated dramatically with the weather. Some households said that they had harvested less than they had planted. Others said their harvest was so poor that they would be compelled to plant a smaller area than they had the year before. A smaller harvest could have a domino effect if the household was unable to compensate through other income sources. The poor household found itself forced to choose between maintaining consumption levels and saving enough seed stock to plant the following year.

Productivity had decreased dramatically because of mineral depletion and salinization. The poor made crop choices based on the cost of inputs. Potatoes required mechanized equipment to till the soil and harvest the crop, and some access to water. Wheat and other grains cost more for equipment rental and other inputs, although wheat required less water. The most commonly reported impediment to effective cultivation was lack of irrigation due to poor water supply or high cost. As a result, households were leaving their land uncultivated or seeing productivity drop. The village council of Akhtanak, near the Georgian border, estimated that 80 percent of the villagers were not cultivating their land for lack of water. In Koti, on the border with Azerbaijan, the land used to be of superior quality; since the war, however, the Azerbaijanis had cut off the only source of irrigation water. Declining use of inputs had resulted in lower-quality produce, which was difficult to sell to intermediaries and market buyers.

In Lernapat village, Lori region, in the earthquake zone a family has 4,000 square meters of land, half of which is not irrigated. They planted two bags of wheat and harvested four bags on their nonirrigated land. They planted six bags of potatoes and harvested four bags on their irrigated plot. The previous year they had harvested eight bags of wheat and were able to bake bread until July. This year they expect they will need to buy bread in March. The potatoes are of poor quality, black and small. They exchanged 8 kilograms of potatoes for 2 kilograms of sugar.

Their main source of cash is child allowances—6,000 drams a month for their three children—but they had just received their September allowances in December. Each year they sell assets to cover cash debts for electricity and rental of agricultural equipment.

A month ago, the family went two weeks without food. They had run out of money and were unable to mill their wheat into flour. They fed the three children hot water. Sometimes a neighbor brought over a plate of macaroni, which the mother would then spoon-feed to the children. Once a neighbor brought over a loaf of bread, which they cut up into small pieces and ate over two days. Finally, they sold an old rug and bought food. Neighbors provided them with money to buy shoes and food for their children last year. Their relatives live in town in Gyumri and come to see them two or three times a year, bringing food and old clothes. The wife's brother left for Russia and brings 10 pieces of *lavash* (traditional Armenian bread) when he comes to visit. The husband's brother also works in Russia, and when business is good, he brings clothes, sweets, and money to their family.

The poor said that cultivating the land was not profitable and could result in debts that had to be financed by other income-generating activities. The 1995 Farm Survey pointed to a high level of borrowing to cover cultivation costs. Seasonal indebtedness was a way of life, since expenses were incurred in the spring when winter reserves had been depleted and before the harvest could be sold the following fall. Families merely subsisted on the food they had harvested, while financing cultivation with income from the sale of meat (calves), dairy products, nuts, and fruits; remittances from family members in Russia; and other off-farm activities. For some households, however, this other income was insufficient.

A household estimates the annual cost of cultivating wheat on its 3 hectares of land in Zar village, in the Abovian region, at 100,000 to 150,000 drams, including equipment rental, diesel fuel, seed, fertilizers, transportation of the harvest, and hulling. The household also pays 3,000 to 4,000 drams to irrigate three or four times a season. The land tax is 10,000 drams. The household's outstanding debt for 1997 is 10,000 drams.

In Panik village, Artik region, a family pays 80,000 drams for equipment and diesel fuel to plant and harvest wheat and oats on 1 hectare of land. This includes 12,000 drams for tilling, 12,000 drams for costs associated with planting, and 1,500 drams to transport the harvest.

Elderly households and female-headed households with child care responsibilities lacked the time or the physical strength to cultivate their land. In Ltsen, Sisian region, the village council representative explained that 20 of the 875 households were very poor because they lacked labor capable of working land that was very dry and required a lot of strength to cultivate. Land was sometimes left uncultivated in the conflict area when it was considered dangerously close to the border with Azerbaijan. Farmers feared sniper shots and shelling. In Koti 1,000 out of 1,700 hectares of arable land was not cultivated because it was located on the border.

Although land could officially be sold or leased, some households chose to return the land they were allocated during privatization or had refused it to begin with, and none of the households reported selling their land: Land leases were also rare: only three poor households who were unable to cultivate their land reported leasing it. One pensioner rented out her land in exchange for 10 percent of the harvest. Another did the same but received nothing because the harvest was so poor. A third was relying on in-kind payments ranging from 5 to 50 percent of the output. Households who had chosen to return their land shrugged off questions, explaining that they did not expect the lease to more than cover the land tax. Indeed, the average leasing price of 1 hectare of land was in the range of the land tax: around 18,000 drams per hectare. In an economy where cash to pay taxes was scarce and productivity was low and unreliable, many households viewed land ownership as a liability. Land ownership also prevented residents from being registered as unemployed; in one case a respondent had been turned away from a factory job because the manager gave priority to urban residents without land.

Depletion of Assets

Traditionally, assets and personal belongings were amassed during good times or brought by the young bride as dowry to allow the household to survive bad times by selling off these items. In the last seven years, assets had served as the main store of savings, since cash savings had been lost to the currency reforms and continued to be eroded by inflation. The poorest relied inordinately on the sale of property and valuables to cover large, one-time costs (such as bribes and health costs) as well as daily consumption needs (electric bills, food, school supplies). Assets provided the necessary startup capital to engage in productive activities such as trade, to send a husband or son to Russia, or to keep the household's workers healthy. Some of the poorest households had sold their consumer goods, or these were in disrepair. Households in cities had sold even their most personal belongings: gold, the family car, furniture, bedding, pillows, shoes, even gold teeth. In Yerevan an open-air market dealt in used personal items, from underwear to kettles. For rural households cattle were an important productive asset: villagers could forgo home consumption and sell milk and cheese. Cattle were commonly sold each fall to avoid feed costs over the winter. The proceeds were used to pay for heating, school-related expenses, and agricultural debts.

Increased Dependence

In Armenian society, relatives and neighbors are expected to provide material and psychological support to each other. This close support network helps to buffer households in times of need. These traditional networks are regulated by a set of social rules that identify the responsible helper, the level of reciprocity required, and the expected scale and type of assistance.

Many of the families interviewed relied on relatives for 80 to 100 percent of their daily food consumption, clothes, and fuel. For most of the households interviewed, however, this assistance was insufficient to raise the household out of extreme poverty. Dependence was seen as a sign of extreme poverty, not of relief from it. The level of poverty, even absolute destitution, did not determine the timing of assistance. It was given only after the needs of the donor household had been satisfied, and only if the needy household met certain conditions. In most cases support was initiated by the donor, and the result was that many of the poor went unnoticed and neglected.

Assistance within a family was strongest between parents and their children. A grown child's duty was to care for his or her parents, and parents in turn looked after their grown children. The youngest son was expected to care for his parents. If a man was absent from a family, his parents and brothers were expected to take on his role as provider and help his wife and children. Respondents said that assistance was prioritized along male kinship lines. Sisters, daughters, and daughters-in-law exerted little control over the household income and were less effective in providing assistance to needy relatives. They were outsiders in the patriarchal household. One impoverished female respondent was surprised at the suggestion that her sister's husband, who lived in the same village, might help her: "Why would a complete stranger help me?" There were stark contrasts in living standards even between sisters who lived close to each other (see below). Brothers and male cousins were expected to help their close relatives, and mothers often provided long-term assistance to their children's households.

Assistance was mostly described as sporadic or crisis-driven.[6] Neighbors helped with domestic chores or provided psychological rather than material support, such as inviting a single pensioner to come and spend an evening in a warm room with a light or sharing a pack of coffee. Relatives, neighbors, and friends provided food or cash, which usually required repayment in cash, kind, or labor. People sometimes provided their poorer relatives with products on credit for them to sell on consignment. Many households worked for their neighbors or relatives in exchange for cash or in-kind payment. Many respondents felt that such assistance left them indebted to the donor. A mother explained that the reason she got so much assistance was that she was very humble and never refused to do chores for neighbors who helped her. One worker said that she did the work to keep up social ties, to maintain others' respect even though her children were hungry. Some found this inhibiting, however. An alcoholic father in Spitak scoffed and said that he usually refused assistance from those who might expect him to work in return, because he did not want to become anyone's slave.

A husband and wife in the industrial town of Charentzavan, both physically disabled, live across the street from the wife's sister. The sister's husband provides the couple with sunflower seeds to sell in payment for standing all day selling goods he brings back from Sadakhlo and produce from surrounding villages.

The household is in a dire situation. The two adults make approximately 500 drams a day, which they spend on a pack of spaghetti and two loaves of bread. But this is not enough. They are now eating the food they acquired on consignment. There is no sugar and no oil in the house. Small boiled potatoes are on the menu for lunch. Their diet rarely changes over the year. They can never afford to buy fruit, and they are physically unable to collect herbs and wild berries in the spring and summer. They have sold most of their belongings, even their pillows, to buy food and pay off debts. The local shopkeepers no longer provide them with food on credit. The electricity was cut off for eight months in 1996 because they could not afford to buy a meter. They expect it to be cut off again this week because they have not paid their bill for months. There is no other heating or cooking fuel for the winter.

In contrast, the sister lives in a warm, comfortable apartment decorated with attention to detail. Her two children are plump and rosy-cheeked. Fried potatoes, spaghetti, rice, and canned vegetables are stored for the winter. Her husband is often absent, working in Russia and trading.

Access to assistance through the informal support network was based on a moral distinction between "deserving" and "undeserving" poor. Deserving households were the disabled, single pensioners, orphans, and divorced, widowed, or single mothers. Households with males capable of working were not usually entitled to assistance except on a crisis basis. Assistance from neighbors, shopkeepers, and relatives was more readily available when the household was deserving. A household could become temporarily deserving when the breadwinner was absent or temporarily incapable of work, but once the crisis was past, assistance ceased abruptly and entirely.

When a household was seen to be responsible for its own poverty, it was generally ignored, according to respondents, no matter how desperate its situation. Families with an adult alcoholic were pointed out as the poorest, but they were scorned by relatives and excluded from government and informal support networks. The alcoholic husband was often unable to hold a job because of his drinking, and many spent any cash they earned and even sold in-kind payments to buy alcohol. The families were often hungry, dirty, and living in absolutely horrifying conditions. Where the homes had not had the regular upkeep usually performed by husbands, the walls were blackened by years of smoke, plaster was falling off, furniture was falling to pieces, and there was general disorder. Disabled parents were blamed for having worsened their situation by choosing to have children.

A household with four children and two work-capable adults living in Spitak has a history of being unable to rise out of poverty. The husband returned the night before from an unsuccessful nine-month stay in Russia. He had been unemployed in Spitak, and he failed to find enough work in Russia. He has never tried trade—his wife explains that he does not have the right "character" for trade. He is too kind and likely to give goods away instead of selling them, because people need them and cannot afford to pay. The family has no assets left, only bad debts. They live in a shack that they built themselves with wood planks.

The husband is an orphan, raised with his cousin who lives next door. His cousin's family berates him for being unable to earn a living. His wife refuses to ask them for help. During the husband's absence, the family accumulated debts from stores and the electric company. Now that he is back, creditors have been appearing at his door all morning. His friend who lent him money for the trip sits in a corner. The electricity has been cut off in the hope of collecting on unpaid debt.

The family relies to a large extent on food provided by the wife's mother, who lives in a village with the wife's brother. She expects that when her mother dies, assistance will cease. A neighbor provides cow's milk each morning for the newborn. In exchange, the wife does all the neighbor's chores and shows humility and gratitude.

The wife, who was pregnant throughout the summer, was unable to cultivate their small plot of land. They have no food stored for the winter. With three young children and a newborn, she was unable to stand in line for hours to register for humanitarian assistance. The administrators refused to include her as they went door to door to register the disabled in her neighborhood.

Social norms limited asking for help and required waiting until relatives and neighbors noticed the situation. Asking was equated with begging and was especially looked down upon if there were work-capable males in the household or male relatives nearby.

A young village mother who has lost three infants in five years to malnutrition says, "I would rather die than ask for help every day from my neighbors. They bring me something—bread, a glass of flour, milk—approximately once a week. They respect me for suffering through these conditions quietly."

Single pensioners were loath to ask for help from households with children, saying children's needs were paramount. Adults with grown sons were also uneasy about asking for help from neighbors or other relatives. In contrast, daughters felt at ease asking their mothers for help.

Other informal systems supported poor families. Food and bread shops provided credit, and the local electric company tolerated some delays. Households commonly pledged their child allowances, unpaid salaries, pensions, and future remittances to secure credit. However, once creditors believed that the households could no longer pay, they withheld credit. Many of the poorest households no longer had access to credit because their sources of income had dried up.

Government transfers—child allowances, disability pensions, old age pensions, and unemployment stipends—represented an important source of income for the poorest, but they were too small to lift households out of poverty. They were unreliable, often paid months after they were due. Administrative hurdles made it difficult to acquire the status of disabled, and both cultural and fiscal constraints understated real unemployment. Assistance was guided toward vulnerable groups, not the work-capable poor, and excluded landowners regardless of income. Sometimes transfers were denied for nonpayment of land tax or pension tax, or taxes were deducted directly from the allowances. Many families counted on allowances to cover the electric bill, buy food staples, pay off accumulated debts, and retain the ability to borrow in the future.

Meeting government requirements for assistance was difficult and costly. Documenting disability required a medical consultation, diagnostic tests, and certification from the regional health commission and was subject to transport costs and bribes, especially if the documented level of disability provided a pension and other privileges. Unemployment benefits were provided to the registered unemployed who had previously had formal employment, and then only if the household was landless with none of its members formally employed (or on forced unpaid leave). Only one household member could receive benefits a year, and benefits were limited to five months the first year and three months the second. Refugees were defined as those who had left Azerbaijan between 1988 and 1991. Those displaced from former Armenian territory held by Azerbaijan or who had fled Nagorno-Karabakh were not considered refugees.

An application for disability status by a severely mentally ill man and his family has been rejected by the local health commission. The man's parents are unable to persuade him to get into the car to bring him to the health commission in the region's administrative center. He panics at any pressure from his parents, whenever they try to touch him, let alone confine him in a car. He has not allowed his mother to wash him for two years, since she took him home from the psychiatric hospital in Yerevan. She believes that his visceral fear of contact is due to a traumatic experience he had in the hospital where he was severely beaten and, his parents believe, raped. His parents offered to rent a car for health commission members to come to their home to assess his case.

The commission refused, insisting that the man is physically well and therefore capable of working.

Paros, the formal government welfare targeting system, used a formula to identify vulnerable groups based on age, handicap, and status: divorced, widowed, orphan, or refugee. If there were work-capable adults in the household, it was not eligible for assistance. The Paros system lacked the flexibility to reflect the current situation where a majority of the Armenian population was poor. (For a beneficiary assessment of Paros in 1998, see Appendix B.)

None of the households interviewed was aware that Paros used a formula to calculate eligibility. They did not have the information to know when they had been excluded improperly. This seriously limited their ability to seek recourse and administrative accountability. Some opted not to register when they might have qualified for assistance. Almost all urban households registered, but in some villages registration levels were dismally low. In a village in Kotaik region, for example, only 12 of 357 households were registered with Paros. In some villages the village council had organized to fill out the passports of selected residents and take them to the social protection office in town.

A few households were unable to register even after standing in line for days. This was most problematic for pregnant women, women with child care responsibilities, and people with health problems. Rural residents had to register in towns, and problems arose when their papers were not in order and they had to get additional documentation from home or municipal offices.

Two divorced brothers living together in Yerevan were not registered for Paros. Liudvic, 63 years old, has been bedridden since a tragic accident last year. He cannot move without assistance. Robert, 59 years old, has not held a permanent position since 1991. He had been receiving a pension of 2,000 drams for a nervous illness, but the pension ceased earlier this year. He said the small amount was not worth the time or aggravation of clarifying the situation. Now both brothers live primarily on what neighbors bring (cigarettes and leftovers), but no one provides assistance on a daily basis. Their sister comes by once or twice a month with fruit preserves and canned food. Robert begs for leftover produce at the market. They sell personal items, such as Liudvic's shoes for 3,500 drams, and Robert goes through the trash in search of bottles that can be turned in for 5 to 10 drams each. He can collect approximately 20 bottles a day. Both brothers have been on the edge of starvation since the accident. They have not had electricity for a year. They expect their sister to bring kerosene this year to heat the room.

Robert refuses to reregister with Paros. He is not familiar with social services because Liudvic used to deal with administrative issues before the accident. He is put off by the process of registering and cynical about the small scale of assistance. Liudvic would like to be registered but cannot do it himself. He hopes the assistance would be sufficient to guarantee a minimum of food.

As of December 1997 the Paros formula was seldom used to distribute assistance. NGOs used the Paros lists to select out pensioners or other vulnerable groups but rarely to target families with a certain score. The information in the Paros booklets was commonly inaccurate with regard to incomes, pensions, status of household members, and household composition. The Paros registration system would now require households to update their information annually.

Conflicting interpretation of documentation requirements impeded accurate registration, especially with regard to medical disability, refugee status, unemployment, and separated mothers. A representative of the Ministry of Social Protection explained that households should submit documentation that reflects the actual situation. This would allow a family that was not officially divorced to register as divorced or single, if the housing maintenance company (known by its Russian acronym ZhEK) was satisfied that the husband had been absent for a substantial period. This was a common occurrence when men left for Russia and were never heard from again. However, this policy was difficult to enforce and control because the ZhEK does not report to the Ministry of Social Protection.

Local social protection offices prioritized among vulnerable households by including some of them in humanitarian assistance lists. They chose households without work-capable males that had children, disabled parents with children, or single pensioners. This excluded other vulnerable households. In Charentzavan the local government handed out bread to 32 households, excluding a couple of disabled parents with two children, yet including a disabled grandfather living with his son, daughter, and three grandchildren.

Residential schools, orphanages, and schools for the physically and mentally challenged had received humanitarian assistance in the last few years through the diaspora and international organizations, but this was not an attractive alternative for the majority of poor parents, even those living in very poor conditions. Among respondents, parents who used the government boarding schools were likely to have grown up in institutions themselves. They saw the institutions as a means of getting basic assistance rather than special education. Parents used the institutions to improve the situation of the household or the child. Typically the child was from a first marriage and was rejected by the new husband, or was illegitimate. Sometimes there was family violence or sexual abuse by a parent, or there was alcoholism or overcrowding.

Parents said that the institutions provided material care that they could not provide themselves. The food was more than what the child would get at home, even if it was mostly beans and bread. The institutions were often heated, clothes and shoes were sometimes provided, and a nurse provided basic medical care. Drawbacks for the parents included the cost of picking the children up on weekends, the mixing of "normal" and handicapped children in the same school, and the hardship of separation from their children. Some took their child out of the institution because of excessive transportation time and costs or worries related to physical and sexual abuse by other children. Accountability and protection of children's rights were serious concerns.

A former street child tells of the strict discipline at the boarding school he attended, including beatings and children being locked up for hours in a cold, dark closet. (Although he uses the words for "hitting" and "beating," he says that he was never hurt so badly that there were broken bones.) The main reasons for punishment were "hooliganism," which he is ashamed to describe explicitly and will only say included smoking and running away. Kids ran away all the time (a few cases each month), he says, because they wanted to see their parents. There seemed to be great psychological pressure on the children to value their lives in the institution and to devalue and forget what they had left behind. There was no effort to keep ties with relatives intact, but rather the contrary. In a society where social and economic well-being depends greatly on family ties, this is very troubling.

There seemed to be a lack of effective supervision. The same child complains of beatings from other children over food parcels sent by parents. He even mentions rape by older boys. "It's normal in a place where there are no girls," he explains. When asked if he believes that the responsible adults knew of these problems, he answers that he believes they did.

There was a need to support needy families and especially children in difficult family circumstances (orphans, children in stepfamilies, handicapped children), but institutions did not always protect the child. The process of accessing health care services and obtaining disability status, a requirement for obtaining financial transfers from the state, was not adapted to serving the needs of mentally and physically challenged persons.

Although humanitarian assistance played an important role in supporting households, it remained poorly targeted. As much as 70 percent of humanitarian assistance was going to nonpoor households. The Red Cross targeted all households in the border area. In Spitak kerosene was distributed in the winter of 1997–98 to all households living in *domiks*, even though this type of housing was known to be a poor indicator of poverty.[7] Local charity groups and churches provided assistance for large families and pensioners. When the poor did receive assistance, it was often an essential component of the family's income. Twenty of the 1,030 households in the village of Koti relied exclusively on humanitarian assistance.

Gathering and Begging

Some of the poorest households collected leftover food. Poor rural households (especially the landless and those unable to cultivate their land) commonly gathered leftover wheat or potatoes from harvested fields. Urban residents foraged in the trash piles that lay in the courtyards of buildings, in their neighbors' trash bins, and in the streets. They looked for glass bottles or scrap metal to turn in for cash. Respondents said that this was a difficult activity, and it was degrading to be seen looking through trash. The daily earnings were humble and there was a lot of competition, requiring an early morning start. They brought home items that they might use or sell: old clothes, worn shoes, a jar of animal fat, cigarette butts, and unfinished bottles of alcohol. Urban residents went to the market at the end of the day to gather the damaged or spoiled vegetables and fruit that remained unsold. Begging for cash was mostly limited to Yerevan. In large villages and cities, a few went door to door asking for bread, but few apart from older women and children begged in the streets.

Who Are the Poorest?

It is difficult to point to a set of objective characteristics that effectively included the poorest and excluded the well off. However, it would be erroneous to conclude that poverty in Armenia was random. The concept of social exclusion provides social scientists and policymakers with a means of analyzing poverty data. It compels us to look at information to identify patterns that explain poverty at the household level.

Poverty in Armenia was found to be dynamic. The vast majority of households had experienced at least a temporary spell of poverty in the last five years. In addition, there was considerable evidence that households repeatedly moved into and out of poverty. The cycles were due to income and expenditure fluctuations from poor harvests, unpaid salaries or pensions, seasonal variations in income-generating activities, recent loss of employment, or a crisis in the extended family. Stored goods (food and fuel), assets, and savings might be depleted, but they could be replenished through work abroad. Loss of labor might be temporary: a family member in jail, a son in the army, a pregnant or lactating mother, or mental or physical illness. Fluctuations in well-being were linked not only to economic factors such as employment and income generation but also to personal networks, societal ties, and basic services. The main difference between the transiently and the chronically destitute was that the former had retained crucial links to society and continued to be able to tap into opportunities.

The poorest households often had weak connections to their kinship network. Their isolation was social, geographic, physical, and psychological. They often were in poor health or had some handicap that limited their mobility, employability, and conviviality. They lacked assets, had inherited poverty, and were inactive or underemployed. They were households in crisis.

The traditional social network determined access to goods and services. In Armenian society ties between sisters are weak, as are ties between a married woman and her parents. Single mothers rejected by their mother-in-law were also vulnerable. Relocated townspeople lacked ties to surrounding villages. Orphans, even adult orphans, had no close relatives to ask for help, and female pensioners living alone were at risk. Single-person households were very rare in Armenia and were generally perceived as extremely vulnerable. The very visible state of singleness generally mobilized family networks to support these persons. The most extreme cases of poverty occurred when the support networks were unreliable or insufficient. Indeed, there were examples of young single men in Spitak and Yerevan taking their own lives because, according to neighbors, they had lost all hope of being able to support themselves. Without kinship ties, young men were unlikely to marry. Single pensioners in villages—unable to cultivate their land, without close relatives nearby, and living solely on their pension—were often in terrible straits.

Her neighbors say that a woman of 52 years died of hunger earlier this year in the village of Karkop because both kinship and social ties had failed to support her in a regular manner. Neighbors had brought bread to her once a week. With three grown sons (living in Yerevan and Russia), she was ashamed to ask for help.

In the cases surveyed, the loss of kinship connection was due to personal differences, distance, lack of direct ties to parents or male providers (brothers or brothers-in-law), or moral issues such as alcoholism. Some street children and children selling flowers in Yerevan shared the common characteristic that their mothers were separated or divorced and had been rejected for moral or economic reasons by the husband's family.

The phenomenon of street children in Armenian cities was symbolic of the weakening of the informal and governmental support system. According to the Ministry of Internal Affairs, the Children's Acceptance and Distribution Units had picked up 100 children in 1995, 350 in 1996, and 325 in 1997. Some were returned to their families, but an increasing number were placed in government institutions. Officials were concerned that these children were involved in criminal activities such as stealing and prostitution, or that a "protector" was withholding a set percentage of the children's earnings from begging and other activities, defining where they worked, and protecting that space from others. The children and parents denied this, however.

The term "street children" was commonly used to describe children living, working, or begging on the streets. Some children lived at home and worked to supplement the household budget. The mother of a young boy selling flowers said that he could earn more money than she could selling sunflower seeds nearby. Another mother claimed she did not know that her children played music on the streets for money. A preschool-aged child lived independently from his mother and used the money he earned to buy his own food. Another child, under six years old when observed living on the streets, said that he used to catch up with his mother and sister sporadically and then return to his life with other street children.

These children had troubled backgrounds. Family histories included alcoholism and physical abuse. Most households were isolated and extremely poor. In many cases they were headed by a single female caregiver. One young mother was cast out with her children by her in-laws after her husband was jailed; another had been married to a violent alcoholic who had been jailed repeatedly. The children said that living on the streets gave them freedom they did not have at home. They escaped abuse and hunger and earned enough money to buy candy bars and sandwiches. The policy of returning the children to their parents and primary caretakers was not working: the children eventually returned to the streets. Institutions had limited capacity, and the teachers were not trained to deal with such children. One official agreed that physical abuse of children in institutions was likely to be a widespread problem. For street children who had been placed in institutions, the main improvement has been material. One child noted the improved hygiene, better diet, clean sheets, and housing. He also noted that his life now had a structure it used to lack. Health services were minimal, and the diet was monotonous but more reliable than what he had had in the street. The drawbacks of institutions from the children's point of view were isolation from their parents, physical abuse from other children, and harsh discipline.

Physical and geographic isolation eroded kinship networks, limited access to work and income-generating opportunities, and complicated access to social services. Isolation from markets was linked to rural poverty. The SDS survey showed that altitude, a proxy for isolation, was linked to both the depth and the incidence of poverty. Isolation was compounded by the efforts of the poor, especially work-capable, educated households, to hide their poverty. There was a stigma attached to poverty, and the work-capable were more likely to hide their situation than were those who fit the socially acceptable characteristics of vulnerable groups. Adults said they took pride in not asking for help and that they were respected for it. Shame and the fear of loss of social status prevented the skilled and the better educated from accepting work and trade opportunities that were seen as demeaning.

Employment required physical mobility and good health. Discrimination limited employment and social activities for those in poor health. With labor in oversupply, the strongest, healthiest workers were hired first, even when the handicapped were capable. The handicapped and the ill were less able to reciprocate in kinship relations, and this limited their ability to participate and benefit from assistance. Marriage opportunities were also diminished. Poor health exacerbated physical isolation. Lack of mobility due to handicap or old age limited the visibility of the household. In some cases illness had a ripple effect within the extended family as resources were redirected to meet the crisis and other households were no longer supported.

Without assets, households had no buffer against emergencies. In the cities and towns, the poor had sold their most precious belongings to cover recurrent needs and emergency expenses. Among rural households, landlessness was a good indicator of poverty, although an estimated 74 percent of the rural poor (including both the poor and the very poor) had land. The tax on land transactions limited the use of land as an asset that could be rented or sold by increasing the liability of land ownership and the cost of selling land.

Poverty bred poverty in a society where access to basic goods and services was increasingly determined by wealth and social connections. Market forces had officially replaced universal access guaranteed by the safety net and government subsidies, and the poor were left out of the increasingly horizontal social networks that had provided access to goods and services in the past. Many respondents had been relatively poor in Soviet times. They had only a basic or technical education and had held low-paying jobs as cleaners, guards, and street or courtyard sweepers. They had lived on subsidized bread and only sometimes eggs and meat, but they had had heat and electricity. They had grown their own food on a household plot without having to deal with taxes or water fees, and they had enjoyed access to medical care and higher education. Now they had fewer assets or personal belongings to sell as a way to buffer against emergencies or initiate new income-generating activities.

A striking characteristic of the poor in Armenia was the extent of their inactivity. Households had very few providers and many dependents: children, elderly, handicapped, and inactive adults who were unemployed, underemployed, discouraged, sick, and on leave. The unemployed were isolated from social networks, and unemployed males were stigmatized. Among the employed, wages were insufficient and often irregular. Many were underemployed because enterprises and factories had unpredictable workloads, or because they were on forced leave.[8] Even permanent jobs often required the worker's presence for only a few hours a day. Odd jobs were poorly paid, infrequent, and unreliable. Very large households, such as those with three generations or multiple families, were often pointed out as very poor, having taken in related households who could not support themselves. Some of these large households had been dependent in Soviet times and unable to move into separate apartments or build individual homes. A large number of dependents strained the breadwinners' ability to provide adequately for all.[9]

Many of the poor explained their inability to provide for themselves as a failure to adapt to the new economic order. They were unable to relinquish their government positions because they were afraid to lose the intellectual stimulation and social status. A number of respondents explained their inability to trade by saying it was a personality issue. One needs to be ready to make a profit off one's neighbor, and one cannot be warmhearted or kind, they said. Opportunities for employment were often sex and age specific.

Households with a family member in prison or a son in the army incurred large expenses and spent a lot of time traveling to where their son was serving to provide food, medicines, and moral support. Poor households were likely to suffer at least temporarily from lost labor and increased expenses. A son in the army reduced household labor and income and increased expenses, which included the traditional send-off feast, expected monthly visits, and medical costs if the son was injured or sick.

Conclusion

The most important strategies for lifting households out of extreme poverty were found to be trade, remittances, cultivation of land, and use of social support networks. The pro-growth policies adopted in Armenia focused on increasing consumption and had not translated into sufficient local investments and economic restructuring to promote the development of local employment opportunities. In parallel, there was a movement to reduce government subsidies for water and electricity and services for education and health.

Some groups within Armenian society were unable to meet their own basic needs because of geographic and social isolation, lack of mobility, lack of assets and capital, or poor health. Kinship networks and other traditional support networks were less and less effective in supporting the poorest households. As a result, a growing proportion had exhausted their resources and were living day to day, hungry, cold, anxious, and often hopeless.

Poverty was widespread in the urban population. The researchers had expected rural poverty to increase at a slower pace, but the cycles of poverty could be deeper than in urban areas. The middle class had left the villages, leaving behind only the poorest and the wealthy. Isolation would take a toll on the population in the long term as the villages lost their young, educated, and nonpoor residents. The burden rested on the new generation of children born in poverty who were growing up malnourished, poorly educated, and without access to quality education or medical care.

Notes

1. Respondents sometimes expressed monetary values in dollars or rubles rather than drams, reflecting the use of multiple currencies within the region.

2. The SDS survey put the average cost of care at hospitals at close to $380 for completed treatment for those who reported paying for care. The nonpoor were five times more likely to report hospital payments than the poor, and their reported expenses were many times higher. The 1996 Social Assessment of the Education and Health Sectors estimated the average cost of a polyclinic visit at $8 and that of a hospital visit at $70.

3. Even in private sector enterprises the average monthly wage of 20,000 drams was insufficient to raise a family of four above the poverty line. Average government wages were even lower.

4. Emigration was believed to be concentrated among young families and the middle class, but without an updated census the evidence is anecdotal. An international NGO implementing a distribution program in the town of Vanadzor found that close to 30 percent of the population was absent. In Ger-Ger, a village of 780 inhabitants (190 households) in the Sunik region, an estimated 120 men had left for Russia and other countries. Forty-five of them had left with their families. The estimate that 20 percent of the Armenian population has emigrated comes from work by local researchers for the United Nations Development Programme's *Armenia Human Development Report 1997*.

5. Analysis by the SDS cites declining overall productivity. The country produced an average of 2.8 metric tons of grain per hectare in 1988 but only 1.8 metric tons per hectare in 1996. However, potato yields increased from 9.8 metric tons per hectare in 1988 to 12.9 metric tons per hectare in 1996.

6. Even in times of crisis, such as a health crisis, the poorest received the least assistance through the informal network. The very poor were able to cover only 13.7 percent of health costs with help from relatives and friends; the poor covered a slightly larger 19.1 percent of health costs, and the nonpoor 17.1 percent, according to the SDS survey.

7. *Domik* (from the Russian *dom*, or "house," plus the Armenian diminutive -*ik*) is the name given to the large converted shipping containers provided as temporary housing to those made homeless by the earthquake.

8. Workers employed by government and state-owned enterprises were at greatest risk of poverty among the employed. Those on forced unpaid leave but who remained officially employed were in a worse situation than the unemployed, according to the SDS survey.

9. The SDS survey found a strong correlation between extreme poverty and the number of dependents. Of all households with eight or more persons, 40.2 percent were extremely poor, and 23.4 percent were poor.

References

Armenia State Department of Statistics. 1998. "Analysis of Household Survey Data." Yerevan. Processed.

Children's Aid Direct. 1996. *Report on Nutritional Screening (An Approach to Targeted Food Distribution). Martuni, Artik, Goris and Abovian, September-December 1996.* Prepared for the European Community Humanitarian Office (ECHO). Processed.

Gomart, E. 1996. "Social Assessment of the Education and Health Sectors in Armenia." World Bank, Washington, D.C. Processed.

World Bank. 1996. "Armenia: Preliminary Results of the 'Small Farm Survey.'" Washington, D.C. Processed.

World Bank. 1998. "Analysis of State Department of Statistics' Household Survey." Washington, D.C. Processed.

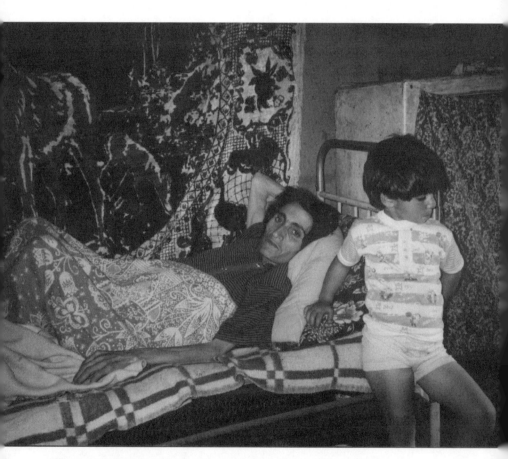

This woman in Gyumri cannot afford the surgery needed to treat her stomach cancer.
Photo by Elizabeth Gomart

APPENDIX A

Losing Ground:
The Education and Health Sectors in Armenia

Armenians pride themselves on their human resources. Soviet policies pro-
moted higher education, full enrollment, and 10 years of compulsory education for all. Health indicators benefited from high levels of education and
easy access to services. In the past few years of economic hardship, however, services have deteriorated, and parents without well-paying jobs find it
difficult to pay for essential services. Most children have suffered to some
degree from the decline in incomes and the related impact on their health
and education needs (Gomart 1996).

A qualitative and quantitative social assessment of the education and
health sectors was conducted from July to August 1996. Two questionnaires, one for education and one for health, designed by the American
University of Yerevan were administered in four of the country's administrative regions and in Yerevan. In parallel, the author conducted a qualitative study in three of Armenia's regions and in Yerevan. A team of local
ethnographers, sociologists, and physicians facilitated 24 focus group discussions (12 for each of two sectors) as well as open-ended interviews with
pupils, parents, teachers, school directors, and officials. Because the assessment was conducted during the summer months, when schools were
closed, the schools could not be observed directly. In November 1996 a
day-long seminar brought together the main institutional stakeholders—
social service providers and local, regional, and national policymakers and
administrators—to discuss the findings. Specific reform options were discussed in small workshop settings, and the resulting recommendations
were discussed in eight more focus groups to obtain feedback from the
population.

The Education Sector

Education has been highly valued in Armenia for centuries. Already in the Middle Ages the ideal man was one of many talents who could read, fight, and play music. The transition threatened to change that for some children, for whom education either was no longer affordable or was seen as unnecessary. The assessment both offered a valuable picture of what was happening to children in schools and generated recommendations from parents about ways to support them in accessing education, including the creation of a now-successful book rental scheme.

The number of years of schooling to which students had access had been reduced. At the time of the research, all children had the right to 10 years of free education, but only eight grades were compulsory. Schools weeded out poor performers after the eighth grade, but there were few alternatives (such as trade schools) to general education. Parents were afraid that if their children were not allowed to stay in school, they would turn to petty crime before they were eligible to enter the army or marry.

Attendance was problematic. Slightly more urban pupils (accounting for 54 percent of nonattendance) were not attending school than rural pupils, and most of these urban nonattendees were outside of Yerevan (by a 5:1 margin). Two-thirds of nonattendance was among boys and only a third among girls. Most of the nonattendance affected older students (after eighth grade). The most frequently stated reason for nonattendance was not wanting to attend (27 percent). For boys a main reason was working to help the family, and among girls a main reason was marriage. But children were not only dropping out in the ninth and tenth grades. Some children were never registered, or registered late or attended school irregularly.

Absenteeism among those attending school affected more than a third of pupils in the survey. The bulk of the absences (90 percent) lasted between 10 and 30 days. Again, absences affected more urban than rural residents and were more common in cities other than Yerevan. Two-thirds of the absences were for health reasons, and another 17 percent were related to the poor physical condition of schools. Many schools had been closing in the winter for lack of fuel, especially in cities. Parents in villages were asked to contribute fuel. A growing problem was absences for economic reasons: parents could not meet costs (6 percent), or children were working to help the family (6 percent). The latter response was given only by urban residents. Some village children missed school to help with the harvest or weekly bread baking. Finally, some children (mainly urban residents) simply "did not want to attend" (10 percent), pointing to the drop in value of education or other problems at school.

Transportation was not an issue for most children. Local schools were easily accessible in towns and villages: 95 percent of the sample had a school through tenth grade within their neighborhood or village. However, older children in small villages where there was no school through tenth grade often had to complete higher grades elsewhere and ran into problems with transportation costs and schedules.

The greatest challenge for parents was the cost of schooling. Nearly half of the parents surveyed had difficulty meeting the costs of their children's education. The mean annual cost of education per child was 88,000 drams. These costs included clothing and shoes, textbooks, additional classes, school fees, and informal payments.

One of the greatest concerns for parents in focus groups was the cost of new textbooks for a changing curriculum. In villages, only one in four pupils had books, and there were fewer pupils at the same level to share. The deadline for subscriptions was early summer, but parents in rural areas did not have cash before the harvest was sold in late fall or early winter, and children often had to wait for books. To meet the deadline, some farmers bartered or sold crops early in the summer or fall when prices were low.

One farmer explains, "Actually, we have no income from August until September. As a result, we need to barter goods and use them as money. Last year I harvested my potatoes in mid-August and took them to Ghapan to sell. I bought some necessary things for the children to go to school in September. So we suffered financially because the potatoes would have brought in more had we sold them later. We usually barter potatoes and wheat for coats. But we don't have anything for bartering right now."

To cope with the high cost of textbooks, children shared books with other pupils or simply went without. Parents stressed that the lack of books had an impact on their children's performance and thus on their academic future. In the focus groups, parents supported the introduction of a book rental scheme at a cost of 400 drams a year—far below the mean amount spent on textbooks (4,200 drams) for those households reporting textbook expenditures.

One father reports his family's experience: "Last year, my son was in sixth grade. He did not have all the books he needed. For that reason, he did not do well. At the end of the school year, the school director called me. I was told that my son was to be expelled. I talked with my son. He said that he could not study because he had no books. I was to blame because I was the one who should have bought him the books. But I had no money to buy them."

Parents talked about the psychological trauma of wearing old clothes, and of children being so ashamed of their appearance that they refused to go to school. The qualitative study underlined the importance of clothing and shoes, which denoted social status and made up over 40 percent of total school expenses. These costs increased in the higher grades.

Additional expenses—formal and informal—were essential to ensure success. For some families there was the cost of additional lessons to compensate for the declining quality of public education and prepare for university entrance exams. Although 64 percent of households did not spend money on additional classes, the mean expense for those who did was 26,681 drams. More urban and more female pupils reported these expenditures than rural or male pupils.

School fees such as school repair fees and fuel contributions were an added expense, and one that the poor especially resented. Only 35 percent of households reported payment of school fees, but these fees were substantial for those who did have to pay them: a mean expense of 2,776 drams.

Students routinely paid bribes to ensure top grades on oral exams, facilitate acceptance into prestigious schools, or reverse dismissal decisions due to poor discipline or performance. In Yerevan some school directors experimented with segregating below-average, average, and good students into separate classes. Within a few weeks, classes had been restructured along socioeconomic lines: the poor students were pushed out in favor of wealthier students who bought their way into the better classes. Money was widely recognized as the key to a higher education: "If you have a rich uncle, you can be a minister, a professor, or even a doctor."

A full 47 percent of parents felt they could not cover their children's school needs. The picture worsens to 50 percent among parents with three or more children. To cover school costs, households relied on current income (75 percent), sale of personal property (over 33 percent), assistance from relatives (25 percent), savings (20 percent), and borrowed money (16 percent; sums exceed 100 because many parents used more than one of these resources).

Although teachers were believed to know their pupils' situation, there was no evidence that they used that information to target assistance to the poor. In fact, the poorest were not targeted for assistance except in isolated cases. School administrators explained that assistance was generally targeted to good performers. In Gyumri a school director found a parent and a local businessman willing to provide stipends to three poor students who were also good performers. Teachers showed little tolerance of students who did not have all their books or supplies, sending them home from class on some occasions. Peer pressure and ostracism also contributed to making schools a hostile environment for the poorest.

There were no special accommodations for children with disabilities. On the contrary, because bias against physical and mental disability is quite deep in Armenia, children born with disabilities were often hidden from the community or sent away to state boarding institutions to preserve the family's status and their siblings' chances to marry. However, according to the survey, 50 percent of parents were willing to consider mainstreaming of children with disabilities. More research is needed specifically among parents of the disabled.

Education was considered most important for children who were performing well and showed promise. The value of education varied between the sexes. For girls, complete secondary and especially higher education served as a surrogate dowry: an educated bride brought status to the family of the groom. Girls were encouraged to study so that they would make good mothers, capable of overseeing their children's homework and making intelligent decisions. For boys, who were expected to become the main wage earners of their families, the value of education was more closely linked to expected earnings, which were more uncertain and seen as less directly linked to educational attainment.

Parents deplored the high cost and declining quality of education. Many seemed resigned to the belief that their children would not learn more than basic reading and writing skills. With decreased access to higher education and the relatively high current incomes enjoyed by low-skilled workers such as traders, primary and secondary education was losing much of its perceived importance.

A parent assesses the costs and payoff of her child's education: "Because I have no money, I cannot support my son's studies at the institute. There would be food, transportation, and lodging expenses—not to mention bribes, of which even a first-grader is aware. What would these expenses be for? So he can earn a salary of 10,000 drams? Now my son is keeping cows for 10,000 drams. Education is not the future."

One of parents' main concerns was low teacher motivation. Teachers were perceived to be less accountable and less dedicated because of their low salaries. Some made ends meet by giving private lessons; this raised suspicions among parents that the teachers reserved the real learning, attention, and good grades for the students who paid for these lessons. Other teachers engaged in farming or trading on the side to generate income, neglecting their teaching duties. Specialized teachers were leaving the field of teaching altogether.

Parental involvement in education was relatively high, according to a number of indicators. Parents, especially mothers, followed the children's schoolwork. Close to 70 percent of parents went to school at least once a month in the previous year. The main reason for going to school was to check on the child's progress or resolve disciplinary issues. Parent council meetings (held in at least half of the schools) were called by the school to resolve textbook problems, discuss student progress, and request funds and labor to address heating and maintenance issues.

A renewed commitment to education could be a great asset for the country. Armenians had been part of the scientific and technical elite of the former Soviet Union. The survey found the main concerns to be the high cost of education, availability of textbooks, remoteness of teachers, and lack of specialists. Recommendations included more financial support from the government; low-priced, school-centered distribution of textbooks (including rental); increased teachers' salaries; mandatory and free education through tenth grade; improved teaching materials; free or low-cost uniforms; and rescheduled public transportation to reduce tardiness among rural students.

The Health Sector

In 1996 the health ministry was in the process of implementing dramatic reforms. Government health spending had decreased as a percentage of total expenditure and in real terms. Costs had been shifted to patients in the form of formal and informal payments for services, pharmaceuticals, and other supplies. The health care system focused on curative inpatient care rather than preventive and outpatient care.

At the time of the survey there were three broad types of health facilities inherited from the Soviet system: hospitals for specialist and inpatient care and diagnostic services, clinics for outpatient care (these amounted to quasi-primary and secondary care facilities), and first-aid stations in the villages. The assessment highlighted a number of important trends. Most important, even as the system was considering a formal shift to a fee-based system, health services were already de facto fee-based, provided for an informal fee determined by the doctor. This new state of affairs, combined with the decline in availability of free or cheap essential inputs such as medicines, had contributed to a general decline in accessibility of quality health services, especially for poor and average-income families.

Another observed trend was greater use of neighborhood and village-level clinics (polyclinics): 37 percent of those who sought care used these facilities, compared with 19 percent who sought care at hospitals. This level of use of the clinics provided an opportunity for reforms to focus on these establishments to develop a system of primary care facilities. Patients used clinics for primary care visits initiated by the patient (52 percent), immunizations (27 percent), follow-up visits initiated by the caregiver (15 percent), and to receive humanitarian assistance (6 percent). Patients—especially those outside of Yerevan—went to hospitals not only for inpatient care or tests, but also for consultations with a specialist.

Most respondents (59 percent) who said they had been ill in the last 30 days were not diagnosed, let alone treated, at a formal health facility. Instead they chose either not to seek a diagnosis (20 percent) or to self-diagnose (28 percent) or to obtain a diagnosis from a doctor friend or acquaintance (10 percent) or from a folk healer (1 percent). Rural residents reported the highest rate of nondiagnosis. According to the focus groups, one reason may have been seasonal: rural residents waited for agricultural work to be completed before they sought treatment. Villagers were the only respondents to report diagnosis by a village nurse (12 percent). In the focus groups, patients said they sought diagnoses from multiple sources because they mistrusted doctors, whom they saw as motivated by profit. Patients also believed that diagnostic equipment and skills were poor, leading to erroneous diagnoses.

Among those who were ill, close to half chose to forgo treatment. The main reasons were the cost of care—including transportation costs, especially for village residents—and the patient's preference for self-treatment.

In many households the decision whether to seek treatment seemed to be made at the household rather than the individual level, as other priorities took precedence within a limited household budget. Focus group participants explained that disagreements about whether to seek care often gave rise to sharp family conflicts. Generally, emergency care prevailed over maintenance, dental problems, follow-up visits, and prenatal care. Prenatal care was often neglected, and there had been an increase in births at home or in ill-equipped village hospitals. The vast majority of health visits took place at the first-aid station and clinic level, where services were cheaper. Children's health needs prevailed over adult needs or education.

Physical access to health facilities was generally good. A majority of respondents lived within a 30-minute walk of the nearest facility. However, the existence of facilities did not guarantee access to services. Rural residents complained about the difficulty and cost of transporting patients to cities where they could access diagnosis and treatment skills, services, and supplies not available at the local facilities.

One of the most contentious topics was that of payment for health services. There was a consistency in informal prices within facilities and within a given site, suggesting a level of formality to these "informal prices." According to the survey, cost of treatment was the main determinant of access.

Prices varied greatly by type of facility. The mean cost of a polyclinic visit was $8, whereas the mean cost of hospital care was $77. According to the focus groups, there was a two-tiered system whereby prices for the same services were higher and more customary at the hospital than at the clinics. In the hospital's maternity ward, an interviewee explained, "You have to pay everyone, from the sanitation worker, to the nurses, the doctors, for the medicines, the equipment, registration, the guard, et cetera." At the first-aid stations, nurses and doctors were rarely paid. Prices varied by location. They were higher in city hospitals than in the district centers and lower in the village hospitals and clinics, where formal and informal payments were less common. At urban clinics or hospitals, payment was required to cover supplies or laboratory costs. Some prices for services (for example, for dental care) were remarkably uniform throughout the country, whereas others (abortions and deliveries, for example) varied greatly.

Although informal payments for medical care are not new to Armenia, what was new was that the health care providers set the fee, and patients were asked to pay before treatment. This arrangement was gradually replacing the traditional practice of "thanking" the doctor after a successful treatment with a gift chosen by the patient. Many respondents were confused about whether prices were formal or informal, and this limited their ability to protect their rights.

Even though payments were commonplace, direct discussion of payment between patient and doctor remained taboo. Prices were communicated by "everyone wearing a white coat except the doctor," focus group participants explained. A relative or friend would act as intermediary or protector (*ivandater* in Armenian), ensuring that the patient received appropriate treatment, conducting the negotiation with the doctor, and making the actual payment transaction.

Increasingly, respondents said that care was limited to those who had sufficient current income and assets to cover treatment. Patients who could not pay beforehand, or who had no one present to vouch for their ability to pay, were turned away from hospitals or made to wait for hours until a price could be negotiated. Patients felt that their ability to meet health costs had significantly decreased because of the drop in households' real incomes, savings, and assets they could sell to cover emergency needs. As a result, the principal source of financing of health needs was the sale of personal property (44 percent of respondents) such as jewelry, apartment, cars, or furniture. Rural residents also relied on income from their harvest and the sale of livestock. Assistance from relatives abroad was another source of financing. Focus group participants said that they relied very little on loans because they feared not being able to repay. As a result, loan amounts were limited to expected income from employment or future sales of assets.

One of the main concerns was access to medicines. Patients were often unable to afford or even find prescribed medicines. The proportion of patients who said they were highly satisfied or satisfied with their access to medicines varied by location: it was 42 percent in Yerevan but 38 percent in other cities and 35 percent in villages. Even in Yerevan finding medicines could be a time-consuming and tedious task. Many sellers of pharmaceuticals were neither pharmacists nor health professionals.

Medicines were especially scarce in villages, where the first-aid facilities were mostly empty. In those villages where a selection of medicines was periodically available through humanitarian assistance, residents were not always aware of what was supplied. Free medicines guaranteed by the new regulations for select vulnerable groups were rarely available.

A World War II veteran in Yerevan explains that he had a prescription for medicines. He chose to obtain the medicine he needed from the pharmacy next to the Ministry of Health. "I did not want to pass as a hooligan, so I dropped in to the Ministry of Health and clarified whether I could get the medicine free with a prescription. They said yes. So I asked, 'If they don't give it to me, can I take it by force?' They said, 'If you can, take it.' So I went to the pharmacy and asked to see the box of medicines to verify the expiration date. I took the medicines and said that I was leaving with them. They wanted to stop me. I told them, 'I am not a hooligan. If you want, let's go together to the Ministry of Health, and we can ask there. If I am not correct, they can take me to the police.' No one came after me."

Patients reduced the cost of health care by avoiding treatment or dropping out before it was completed. They also consulted friends, relatives, or acquaintances who were doctors, who could provide easier access to low-cost or free care where others would charge enormous sums. Rural residents sometimes turned to folk healers when the formal health system was too expensive or unsuccessful. Folk healers were consulted to set broken bones, perform abortions, treat infertility and impotence, treat burns, and help with home births. However, the formal medical system remained the most trusted choice.

Respondents were satisfied with the health services they received in terms of waiting time, providers' attitude toward patients, and medical expertise. They were less satisfied with the physical condition of the facility and the availability of medicines. Focus groups suggested an antagonistic relationship with doctors and conflicts over requests for money for treatment or supplies. Patients mistrusted the diagnoses and treatment they received because doctors seemed to be motivated by profit. If payment had to be made, they would prefer to pay after treatment was succesfully completed. They were (rightly) concerned about the physical cleanliness of facilities and the lack of heat and clean, running water.

Patients explained that satisfactory treatment by health professionals was contingent on payment. As one recalled, "I am pleased with the medical personnel. But if I had not just given them money and presents, I would not have received adequate care. I became aware of that when no one came to care for me the first three days in the hospital. My neighbor in the ward hinted that I needed to pay for someone to pay attention to me."

Most respondents to the survey and in the focus groups identified the main problems of the health care system as the high cost of treatment, the high cost and poor availability of medicines, the lack of accountability of doctors, and the poorer access to health care for the rural population. Rural patients had the highest rates of nondiagnosis and were more likely to consult a nurse rather than a doctor. They had less access to medicines and higher costs because of transportation difficulties. As a result, community priorities differ along rural-urban lines. Rural participants said that their priorities for local community care are establishing a stock of pharmaceuticals, dental care, female doctor and midwife, and first aid skills. Urban residents focused on their need to access higher-cost specialist and tertiary care services.

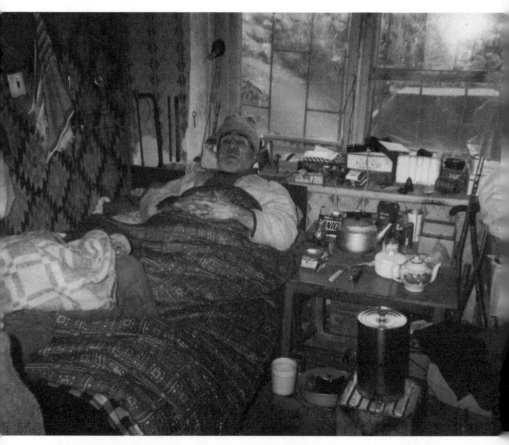

A bed-ridden grandfather guards the family bread by hanging it beside his bed for safekeeping.
Photo by Elizabeth Gomart

Trying to Reach the Poor:
The Paros Social Assistance Program

Since the earthquake in 1988, Armenia has been the second-largest per capita recipient of humanitarian assistance from the United States. Once the situation had stabilized somewhat in 1995 with the normalization of the electrical supply, the Armenian government, with the support of the U.S. Agency for International Development and the World Bank, sought to improve its methods for targeting humanitarian assistance and social benefits. In 1994–95 and again in 1997, the majority of the population were encouraged to register their household to receive a "Paros passport," or family booklet listing members and their social status. Although the intent of improving targeting was sound, the effort itself was fraught with cultural assumptions and a positivist bias toward the infallibility of machines and mathematical formulas.

Under the supervision of the author, a research team of ethnographers from Yerevan State University carried out a beneficiary assessment of the Paros system in 1998. They conducted 26 focus group discussions in four rural and two urban sites in Aragatzotn, Lori, and Geghargunik and four sites in Yerevan to discuss the beneficiaries' experience of the Paros system and the registration process. They also conducted individual interviews with beneficiaries, local officials, social workers and their supervisors, local non-governmental organizations, and donor agencies who had used the Paros system, to document the interface between institutions and their beneficiaries. The study showed how Paros had succeeded to a large extent in reducing opportunities for nepotism by placing decisions in the hands of a central agency in Yerevan, away from local interests. However, Paros had failed to make use of the flexibility inherent in its own rules and regulations to seek out and include the poor. These weaknesses were even more apparent among minority groups (such as Armenia's Kurdish population), refugees, and some residents of temporary housing. As a result, Paros was good at excluding the rich, but not as good at including the poor.

Main Findings

The Paros system relied on collected documentation related to household composition, the age and marital status of members, income from pensions and salaries, presence of dependents (handicapped, children, or elderly), ownership of land and cattle, residence (in the earthquake zone, the conflict zone, or other), and type of housing. Local offices were responsible for collecting the data. Lists of poor households were generated at the central level by the Mergelian Institute (Yerevan Institute for Computer Research and Development) and forwarded back to the local territorial offices.

In 1994 lists were compiled based on verbal representations of household composition and the status of household members. These lists were input into a central database at the Mergelian Institute, which developed a formula to identify relative poverty levels using a number of weighted variables representing demographic characteristics and relative vulnerability, based on discussions with social workers and Ministry of Social Welfare officials. In 1997 the households were reregistered in order to update information and improve the quality of household data in the central database. The information was used to compute household scores for the distribution of electricity coupons and food assistance. In the fall of 1998 the Ministry of Social Security planned to use the Paros scoring system to distribute cash transfers to between 200,000 and 250,000 households.

The Proxy Means Test

The proxy means test was a rational targeting method. The formula introduced more complexity than the traditional criterion of vulnerable groups, and the test was independent of political, family, and acquaintance networks—important in a country with a history of perceived and real abuses in the context of humanitarian assistance distributions. Yet a large degree of subjectivity was introduced and some impartiality lost when social workers exercised their right to eliminate up to 5 percent of the households on the lists and distribute up to 15 percent of the assistance through additional lists using socially accepted but untested criteria. There was little feedback to the social workers regarding these additional lists, and there were few guidelines regarding how these could best target the poor.

Voluntary Registration Process

The number of registered households had decreased considerably since 1994, primarily because of emigration and regrouping of households, according to social workers and beneficiaries. The required documents for reregistration included new Armenian passports for each adult; a birth certificate (and photocopy) for each minor; a workbook and employment office document showing unemployment status; a statement of the size of any pension received; a document from the municipality, village council, or tax department stating land, cattle, and equipment holdings; and a documentation of divorce or handicap where relevant.

The process of reregistration was quite efficient. At its peak in the late summer and fall of 1997, social workers set up temporary offices in neighborhood shops, schools, or village council buildings. There were long lines, but the amount of time spent and the cost were considerably reduced for the majority. Most households found the process simple. In some cases, however, the reregistration process was neither timely nor orderly. These cases mainly affected village residents. One reason was lack of decentralization (in the case of villages in Vartenis district); another was late outreach (in the case of some ethnic Kurd villages and other villages in Talin district of mixed ethnicity), where the process occurred well after the November 15, 1997, cutoff date for receiving electricity coupons. This resulted in considerable underregistration in these villages.

Access to Registration

The main concern about the Paros system was whether it succeeded in including the poorest and excluding the well off. In theory, any and all households should have been able to register, and the formula would determine relative vulnerability. In practice, there were a number of social, bureaucratic, and financial obstacles to reregistration. Traditional gender roles and household hierarchies kept certain households from registering: for example, the traditional subjugation of daughters-in-law to their husband's mother kept some newly single mothers from registering. A history of receiving humanitarian assistance affected perceptions of eligibility. Rural residents registered at a lower rate because of lack of information about the national social safety net and historically low levels of humanitarian assistance (except in the conflict zone, the earthquake zone, and among some refugee populations), thus leading to a perception that the process would not be worth the effort. Working poor households did not register because they lacked the demographic traits of poverty that historically have driven (and still drive today) the government's definition of vulnerability.

The cost of processing a registration (informal processing fees, documentation, transportation costs, municipal debts) and inadequate availability of information were also barriers to registration. Although reregistration was officially free, there were costs associated with procuring the documentation (including duplicates) required for registration: it cost a few hundred drams to document receipt of a salary or pension, 20,000 drams to document handicapped status, and 30,000 drams to document divorced status. The cost increased with the number of members in the household, since all members needed to show documentation. Households living in contested housing had difficulty documenting residence. This included those illegally squatting on municipal land or facing eviction due to nonpayment of taxes and utility bills; the latter was a common occurrence in certain urban neighborhoods. Unofficial costs (bribes) were commonly reported only in villages, where the lack of information made it easier for social workers to require registration "fees."

Household Data Collection and Processing

Respondents were frustrated because documentation alone could not reveal the level of their need. In many cases the poorest had not formalized (and therefore could not document) divorces, handicap, or residence. Household composition was very difficult to document. One member had to present the passports of adults and birth certificates of minors. If a family member was absent from the household, the documented number of working adults in the household was reduced, and the relative dependency ratio increased, along with the score. At a time when a large proportion of working-age men were working at least seasonally in Russia and sending remittances home to support their families, being absent was more often a sign of relative security than of vulnerability.

Income data from rural areas were very difficult to document. Lack of standardization of documentation requirements (for income from land, cattle, and equipment received at privatization, for example, or household composition) weakened the capacity to rank households based on identical criteria at the national level. Thus the system provided incentives for social workers and households to falsify information so as to include needy households and exclude those they believed were not "deserving" of assistance. Some parents registered land and other assets in the names of one or more of their children, even if they worked the land in common and benefited from it, so that parents and other siblings could claim landlessness.

The Paros Formula

The formula was not well understood by social workers or beneficiaries, and this had both positive and negative consequences. It retained a moralistic character, privileging traditionally vulnerable groups and excluding the working poor. Efforts were being made to exclude well-off households (through the use of single criteria such as car ownership), but there were no parallel efforts to include the poorest. Recent poverty studies offered information that could be used to improve the formula.

A family in Aparan village consisting of two adults, six children, and an elderly grandmother was excluded, with a score of zero, because the head of the household owns a truck, which he received when the company he worked for was privatized. The mother complained to the director of the local Paros territorial office (an acquaintance of hers) and lodged a complaint with the director, who sits on the appeals commission. She went to Yerevan and asked a highly educated relative to write a letter to the Minister of Social Security requesting an exception. Meanwhile the director of the local office requested a document from the local police to show that the truck was not in working order. The document was provided to the appeals commission, which granted an exception. However, none of the officials went to observe the family's living conditions or verify the condition of the truck. The case is still pending with the Mergelian Institute, but the household was added to the "additional list" by the local office.

The woman in the above case used her connections well; another family just as needy and similarly excluded might have had weaker connections or less determination. The family was indeed needy: their electricity had been cut off, they lived in a two-room apartment, and there was only one provider for eight dependents. Thus the case underlines the need for less systematic exclusion of households based on a single criterion and a more accessible appeals process.

Parallel Targeting Methods

Additional lists had been drawn up to distribute unclaimed assistance. In theory, these lists could introduce valuable flexibility by including the poorest who did not fit the demographic criteria of the Paros formula. In practice, they were an opportunity for social workers to, at best, perpetuate traditional and simplistic notions of vulnerable groups and, at worst, to create or strengthen patron-client relations. Most social workers had no firsthand knowledge of the households they served, since the vast majority avoided home visits and had little respect for local knowledge.

Role of Government

Among social workers and community members alike, there was a weak commitment to identifying the poor and to serving the poorest, because of the inherited Soviet ideology that blamed the poor for their own situation. The beneficiaries said that the role of government was to support those incapable of working and to provide work, not a handout, to those who could work.

Beneficiary Satisfaction

Clients were quick to criticize the Paros system. They mistrusted a system they did not understand. In one sense, however, this could be seen as a success, if independence from local influence is considered a criterion of success. Beneficiaries perceived a loss of voice. The system had become more rigid and lacked accountability and a credible appeals process. It was seen as a way for the government to avoid accountability for the bad economic situation by giving minimal handouts. Given the other international and government programs, the criticism was not unexpected. Even the positive aspects of the program—its low cost and ease of registration—were not taken into account, reflecting perhaps an overall cynicism toward government assistance efforts.

Conclusions

The Paros formula and system were an improvement on the Soviet-style targeting system based on vulnerable groups. However, to create an effective system that would accomplish more than just excluding the wealthy and providing handouts to only some of the poor, some important changes needed to be made. Some of the recommendations made by the research team were to:

- Seek out the poorest households who may be excluded by the system or unable to register

- Rely on trained and dedicated social workers

- Assess relative need based on home visits

- Create a more comprehensive package of assistance, and

- Clarify the appeals process and accountability through quality control of data entry and monitoring of distributions.

A family near Tbilisi cooks flatbread in a
traditional outdoor oven.
Photo by Nora Dudwick

---------------------------------- ✳ ----------------------------------

CHAPTER 8

No Guests at Our Table: Social Fragmentation in Georgia

Nora Dudwick

Georgia's history, social structure, and geographical characteristics have created problems and opportunities that differ from those of other post-Soviet states. Despite the country's relatively small size, Georgia's steep mountain ranges have led, over many centuries, to the development of economically, linguistically, and culturally diverse regions. Together with the administrative legacy of the Soviet Union, which defined levels of administrative autonomy according to ethnicity, this diversity provided ready-made fault lines for separatist struggles in the former autonomous regions of Abkhazia and South Ossetia, as well as civil conflict throughout the country. These conflicts led to the displacement of several hundred thousand persons, many of whom lost their homes, household possessions, and savings.

Georgia is home to a host of nationalities, some of them concentrated in ethnic enclaves. There are Georgian Muslims in Ajara; ethnic Armenians on the Armenian border, in Tbilisi, and dispersed throughout the republic; ethnic Azeris on the Azerbaijani border and in Kvemo Kartli, Kakheti, and Tbilisi; as well as Ossetians, Kurds, Greeks, Jews, Russians, and other minorities. Even among ethnic Georgians there are distinct traditions, histories, and dialects. Although active government efforts have reduced ethnic tensions exacerbated by "the radical messianic rhetoric and intense nationalist partisanship" (Jones 1996, p. 2) of the first post-Soviet president, Zviad Gamsakhurdia, the potential for conflict remains, especially in underdeveloped regions where minorities attribute official neglect to ethnic discrimination.

Today, political and economic changes have transformed the everyday social world of Georgians. In a country once known for its flourishing second economy and exuberant displays of personal wealth, most ordinary people during the Soviet era enjoyed a secure, if modest, lifestyle. Since independence, however, the gap between rich and poor has visibly increased.

Methods and Sites

Field research for this qualitative study, designed to contribute to a study of income distribution and poverty in Georgia,[1] was carried out between September and December 1996 by teams of interviewers who spent one to two weeks in each of the regions. The qualitative study was based on 600 household interviews conducted in nine regions across Georgia. In every community, interviewers also spoke with local officials, doctors, teachers, and others who could offer a different perspective or an overview of the local situation. Interviews were conducted in the respondent's preferred language (Georgian, Russian, Armenian, Azeri Turkish, or Ossetian). A member of a local nongovernmental organization (NGO) working with street children was recruited to interview the children, and an interviewer who herself had been displaced from Abkhazia focused on interviews with internally displaced persons (IDPs). Sites were chosen to include coastal plains and highland areas as well as different climatic settings, urban and rural communities, different ethnic communities, and particular population groups such as street children and IDPs. They included the capital city of Tbilisi and the following regions: Kakheti (Signaghi, Gurjaani, and Kvareli districts), Kvemo Kartli (Marneuli district), Mtianeti (Kazbegi district), Samtskhe-Javakheti (Akhalkalaki and Akhaltsikhe districts), Ajara (Batumi, Keda, Shuahevi, and Khulo districts), Samegrelo (Zugdidi and Jvara districts), Imereti (Tkibuli and Tskhaltubo districts), and South Ossetia (Tskhinval and Java districts).

The Dimensions of Poverty in Georgia

Georgians can only assess their present situation relative to what they have known. Many have reacted to their rapid impoverishment with despair, hopelessness, or anger. The very poorest respondents focused on their daily problems in securing minimal physical sustenance. Struggling households worried about adequate nutrition, essential home repairs, heat for the winter, and warm clothing for their schoolchildren.

Material Dimensions

Hunger. Both urban and rural families reported frequently going without food for several days at a time. Many poor parents went hungry in order to feed their children. Because the elderly found it difficult to provide food for themselves, they by definition were often considered poor. Hunger tended to be worse in urban areas.

In rural areas periods of hunger occurred in early spring, when people had consumed their stock of food from the previous year's harvest. Families lacking able-bodied adults to cultivate the land often ran out of food earlier in the winter. Households that did farm and raise animals complained of poor nutrition and lack of variety. In Kazbegi district, where most families were able to feed themselves, respondents could not afford fruits or vegetables. In Marneuli district poor respondents with livestock preferred to sell dairy products rather than consume them, and subsisted on produce from their garden. In highland districts such as Kazbegi, Kakheti, or Khulo, having one or more cows was considered to make a life-or-death difference. People often referred to their cow as the family "breadwinner" and put it quite simply: "Wealth is measured by the absence or presence of cattle."

Fuel Shortages. In the last few years, Georgians in both rural and urban areas had experienced frequent electricity cuts, and most municipal heating systems had stopped supplying households with hot water, heating fuel, and cooking gas. In winter most people conserved heating fuel by moving into one room and using alternative fuels and strategies to survive. Often the poorest neighborhoods suffered the most.

Only a few communities and districts continued to receive natural gas supplies. The highland region of Kazbegi is so sparsely forested that people there could not survive the harsh winters without gas. In most urban regions people used kerosene heaters and lamps when electricity was not available. Wood had become the most important alternative to gas and electricity for both urban and rural families living in their own homes. People coped with the high price of wood by substituting anything that burns, including dung.

Medical Expenses. Most respondents felt that the health of family members had significantly worsened, but few were able to afford the prevailing high prices for treatment and medicine. Respondents were unanimously negative about current health sector reforms. Even when official fees were not beyond their means, respondents felt impelled, by fear of neglect or bad treatment, to make additional informal payments to doctors, nurses, and any other medical personnel with whom they came in contact. In addition, services that respondents had considered basic during Soviet times, such as ambulance service and home visits, were no longer offered. Even vaccinations were out of reach.

Housing. Georgians consider their home to be a visible sign of their well-being; they associate poverty with poor, deteriorating, or temporary housing. Damaged, seriously deteriorated, even dangerous housing was a serious issue for poor families throughout Georgia. Even among residents who owned their own homes, housing conditions ranged from bad to dangerous.

In Tbilisi, Marina and Boris own their apartment but comment, "It could hardly be called normal when at night pieces of plaster fall on one's head, during rain the ceiling leaks, your legs sink through holes in the rotten floor, and the faucet leaks 24 hours a day."

Even where housing was available, poor families' homes were devoid of furniture and appliances, which had been sold to cover daily expenses. Respondents complained about overcrowding, which was steadily worsening as young people married and had children but could not afford to move out of the parental home, and as youth returned home because of unemployment. Many homes had been destroyed by civil conflict, fire, or natural catastrophe. The privatization of apartments gave people a piece of property to use as collateral to obtain loans for business, but many who had borrowed money either lost their apartments outright or were forced to sell them to repay loans or to cover expenses related to medical emergencies.

Zhanna, a mother with two children, borrowed the equivalent in lari of $2,000 at 5 percent interest, which soon became a debt of $3,000. To repay it, she sold her household property, and finally her apartment for the equivalent of $1,500. In her own words, she has become "a stray dog whimpering at the closed door of relatives in the hope that someone might open the door."

Water and Sanitation. Water was a problem for many poor households. Water had to be carried when water systems stopped functioning, and households were exposed to the health risk from contaminated water supplies and the humiliating difficulties of maintaining adequate personal hygiene. In 1989 only 40 percent of rural households had piped water, and thereafter the situation worsened because of lack of maintenance and overloading of existing infrastructure. In South Ossetia a 1988 typhoid epidemic connected to a contaminated water supply led to angry demonstrations against local authorities. Pipes carrying water to villages surrounding Tskhinval have been damaged by war and earthquake. Respondents estimated that a third of the city water system needed repair. Djandari village in Marneuli district has lacked potable water for five years. Some inhabitants used water from the nearby Algeti River, although it was known to be contaminated; others obtained water from the swimming pool on a nearby military base.

Social and Psychological Dimensions

Clothing. Families unable to satisfy basic needs for food and shelter complained that they had been unable to buy clothing for the last five or six years. In some cases children missed school because they lacked coats and boots. During an interview in Marneuli district, conducted on a rainy October day, the respondent's grandsons remained in bed because they lacked warm clothing or socks. Children who wore old, patched clothing to school were often cruelly taunted. Some Tbilisi youths admitted to avoiding university classes because they were humiliated at the daily prospect of appearing dirty and poorly groomed. Teachers also suffered because of their appearance, feeling that their moral authority in the classroom depended on their ability to maintain a good appearance in front of their pupils. A 44-year-old Tbilisi teacher reported her humiliation when one of her eight-year-old pupils asked her why she dressed like the street beggar he had seen depicted in a television film.

Cultural and Social Isolation. For members of the intelligentsia a depressing aspect of poverty was their inability to enjoy cultural events, formerly heavily subsidized. Professionals could no longer purchase the journals or books necessary for their profession. Information from television was politically one-sided, and people found themselves becoming increasingly isolated from the intellectual and cultural mainstream. Villagers were even more isolated. Musicians and theater troupes no longer toured rural areas.

Some villages did not even receive television broadcasts, because local relay stations had broken down and localities could not afford to repair them. In many district centers, current national newspapers rarely appeared; from Kazbegi to Marneuli, local papers had not appeared for months. In Signaghi district people received neither Georgian television nor Georgian radio, although villagers in border regions received television broadcasts from Azerbaijan, Armenia, and Turkey. In many outlying villages and even towns, telephones were a rarity. Even when they did not work, people were expected to pay for the service. When they refused, local officials responded, "After all, electricity sometimes comes on at night, and then the phone works."

Status and Shame. In Georgia, as in other Caucasian societies, lavish rituals of display, hospitality, and generosity were a critically important mechanism by which families maintained both self-respect and social standing in the community. Thus most respondents felt deeply humiliated because they could not afford to dress themselves and their children properly, take care of their homes, buy gifts on appropriate social occasions, or accept or offer hospitality (such as coffee and sweets) according to basic standards. Among Caucasian peoples, Ossetians and Georgians have been described as having a "cult of death." Funerals take on extraordinary importance as occasions for social solidarity, a time when the family of the deceased displays its pride and prosperity, and when neighbors and kin demonstrate their support through tangible gifts to help offset the very considerable expenses of a traditional funeral. Having lost their savings, many elderly found themselves caught between the fear of burdening their family while they lived, and burdening them with funeral costs when they died. Their survivors had to choose between maintaining family honor by arranging a traditional funeral and meeting their own basic material needs.

Recently, Nodar's mother died. Just after he had arranged for her funeral, his neighbor's mother also died. The neighbor arranged for her own mother's funeral to take place the same day but begged Nodar to organize his family's funeral procession and burial earlier. The reason for her request was that because she could not pay the amount required for a coffin (the equivalent of $200), she had simply rented one for the showing of the body. Her mother was to be buried wrapped only in cellophane, and the neighbor was ashamed that neighbors coming to the funeral of Nodar's mother would observe the contrast.

Explaining Poverty

Poor Georgians expressed nostalgia for the Soviet period, when they were guaranteed employment and regular salaries and enjoyed a feeling of financial security. Although few people articulated a desire to return to a planned economy, most thought the government should provide jobs, possibly by attracting Western investment. They pointed to the current high unemployment, low wages, small and late pensions, hyperinflation (and consequent loss of bank savings), and failure of commercial banks as the main reasons for their poverty. In conflict areas and among IDPs, loss of homes and property was the leading explanation of poverty. Many also blamed personal problems such as illness, old age, parental responsibilities, business failure, and inability to adapt to the market economy.

Effects of the Transition

Many Georgians accused central and regional authorities of indifference, dishonesty, lack of professionalism, and passivity. At worst, they considered these officials "mafiosi," greedily exploiting the poor; at best, they saw them as failing to attract foreign investment and create workplaces. They criticized the rapid transition to the market economy. Many rural families achieved little more than subsistence farming and felt the government should help them pay for inputs and establish markets where they could sell their produce.

The contraction of state sector employment adversely affected not only urban dwellers, but also small-town residents who commuted to state jobs. Many families in district centers such as Marneuli lacked land and could no longer commute to construction jobs in Tbilisi or Rustavi. Towns that depended on a single industry were very hard hit. In Tkibuli, a coal mining town, 80 percent of the population were without work, a third of the remaining 5,800 employees of the local coal mines were on indefinite leave without pay, and those still working had just received salaries and pensions after a six-month delay.

Many people had not yet really grasped the fundamental nature of the social and economic transition. They viewed the collapse of state enterprises and the contraction of public sector work as temporary, hoping that leaders would again undertake what they saw as the fundamental responsibility of the state and government: creating jobs and guaranteeing decent salaries.

Loss of Savings

Hyperinflation rates that reached 300 percent a month in 1993 had destroyed many people's life savings, eroding their financial buffer and making them more vulnerable to impoverishment. As one man put it, before hyperinflation he had enough money to buy a car; now his savings would buy four loaves of bread. Many people felt the government should repay them the money they had lost. Entitlements in the form of old-age pensions, disability payments, and child allowances had shrunk in value. The collapse of the pension system had come to signify for many people the government's complete indifference to its citizens.

Ascribing Responsibility

Factors such as youth, good educational preparation, and an extensive network of well-off friends and relatives were behind many entrepreneurial successes. Would-be entrepreneurs who lacked prosperous relatives or friends willing to lend money without interest paid up to 40 percent annual interest on their borrowings. In some reported cases the debt accumulated, but the business failed. Respondents described several people who had contemplated or actually attempted suicide when debt left their family literally homeless.

For many Georgians, the fact that the Georgian economy collapsed after the actual political breakup of the Soviet Union led them to attribute their pauperization to the demise of the Soviet state (complicated by civil conflict) rather than its inherent economic weaknesses. They continued to associate the Soviet Union with economic stability, and they blamed the Georgian government and its officials for their indifference and unwillingness to assume their responsibilities.

Surviving Economically

In the wake of mass closures of state-run enterprises in cities, towns, and rural areas, Georgians had found myriad ways to survive. The difficulty some people were having in adapting to these strategies showed the persistence of Soviet values.

A Changing Labor Market

Soviet ideology had made an important distinction between "state" and "private" in many domains, particularly that of work. Money earned through state sector jobs was respectable and public; money or goods earned in the so-called second (private) economy were questionable, even "dirty." The second economy had flourished in Georgia and other parts of the Soviet Union, but individuals used their official affiliations as a cover when their actual wealth derived from bribes or other forms of corruption.

Public Sector. Many labeled themselves "unemployed" if they had lost state sector employment, even if they now worked from dawn to dusk in the informal sector. Among the unemployed were those who had lost work when local enterprises closed or social services reduced their staff; former housewives who now sought work; and young people who had only found seasonal work. By the same token, peasants, even when fully occupied on the land, also considered themselves unemployed.

Despite the low salaries, people clung to state sector employment and feared downsizing.

Marina turned down a private sector job paying 50 lari a month to retain her state sector job, which pays only 15 lari. She explains that her present job is more stable and prestigious, she likes her work collective, and she believes conditions will improve.

Many people combined state sector employment with informal sources of income. As a state sector employee argued, "They have no right to demand more work from us if they can't pay us enough to minimally support our families."

Teachers interpreted the current demand for recertification as an excuse to fire them, and they tried to make themselves indispensable by organizing after-school clubs without asking for compensation. Others worked on evenings and weekends, knowing that they could easily be replaced if they refused.

Private Sector. Private sector employment paid better but was very insecure. Employees regularly received their salary late or went on forced unpaid leave, depending on the enterprise's ability to win contracts and collect receivables. Employees had no guaranteed rights to pensions, maternal or sick leave, yearly holidays, or other basic benefits. Women were particularly vulnerable.

Gocha has a well-paid job in the port of Batumi and makes 70 lari a month plus bonuses. "But it's enough to get sick," he says, "and somebody else will immediately take my place."

> Nino reports that her employer is searching for an excuse to fire her in order to avoid paying maternity leave. After Eteri's husband died, her employer started making sexual advances toward her; when she resisted, he fired her.

Searching for Work. State-run job placement institutions were not effective in finding employment, and advertisements by employers remained rare; most job seekers relied instead on their network of friends and acquaintances. School dropouts, university graduates, the elderly, and the disabled found it particularly difficult to obtain work, and the shift from Russian to Georgian as the language of state had made administrators and teachers who had not mastered formal, business Georgian unemployable.

The most important strategy for finding either public or private employment was to use one's connections and pay a bribe. Respondents paid bribes even to obtain poorly paid public sector work.

> A job teaching school in Tbilisi for 15 lari a month requires a bribe of 150 lari. Irina got her bookkeeping job in a government ministry through her acquaintance there; Alla got her job in a leather enterprise when her mother retired in order to give Alla her job.

Self-Employment and the Informal Sector

Georgians practiced a variety of income-generating strategies, which provided an important, and in some cases a major, source of family income. Most tended to involve petty commerce or services rather than production and required little startup capital. When capital was required, entrepreneurs usually acquired it from the sale of personal assets, from interest-free loans from relatives or close acquaintances, or from moneylenders at high interest rates.

Trade. Many Georgians equated the market economy with the right to engage in petty trade. The nature of the goods traded varied geographically and according to local ethnic affiliations. In the district centers many bought and sold clothing. Families in Marneuli district used their ethnic, linguistic, and kinship ties to Azerbaijan, Turkey, and the Islamic Republic of Iran to import consumer items from these regions to sell locally. In Javakheti Armenian residents organized seasonal sales of produce, taking apples from the district to sell in Armenia, and purchasing grapes in Armenia to sell at home. New international borders had created conditions favorable for particular kinds of trade and new trade routes. Certain villages along the Azerbaijani border had grown prosperous from trade in gasoline, kerosene, and oil. On the Russian border there were markets for agricultural produce and livestock from all over Georgia. These new markets had stimulated the development of trucking and freight handling businesses.

Women and the Shuttle Trade. Women had come to play an important role in trade, even traveling abroad without their husbands and absenting themselves from their families, behavior once considered unseemly. Their concern for the daily welfare of their children and family was a strong incentive to move into such unprestigious activities as street trade. Some women traveled in small groups by bus, train, or air to the Russian Federation, Turkey, Hungary, Poland, and other Eastern European countries as often as once a month. Others traded inside Georgia. The wives of unemployed miners in Tkibuli came to Tbilisi, where they shared small rented rooms, to trade in produce. Female traders had to overcome problems with police and organized crime. A respondent in Javakheti reported a 20 percent profit; others mentioned earning 100 lari a month in profits.

Skilled Labor. Skilled workers and artisans, such as plumbers, carpenters, drivers, and mechanics, were relatively successful at finding jobs, for which they got paid in cash or kind. Many worked independently on a contract basis. An electrician in the Ajara region had worked for a state factory that produced pipes; he and several former co-workers now worked as a private team within the factory. When the factory received orders, they signed a contract for a specific task, and each worker earned 100 lari a month. Some people had acquired new skills. One woman earned up to 150 lari a month baking piroshkis at home, where she could also watch over her nine-year-old son.

Domestic Labor. Although women felt very vulnerable in the job market, they were often able to find low-paying jobs cooking, cleaning, and providing child care for the newly rich. Some residents of high-rise apartments paid a woman to keep the stairwell clean. Elderly women could earn 2 or 3 lari doing laundry for neighbors. One woman cleaned the local school in an Ajaran village three times a week; she used the money to pay for bus fare to Batumi, where she earned 10 lari a day cleaning homes. Some women considered working for rich neighbors to be prestigious, perhaps because it brought them into contact with the rich and powerful.

Renting Rooms. In resort areas, near markets, and in university communities, renting out storage space, beds, rooms, and apartments was for some an important source of income. Renting out rooms during the summer season was always a good source of profit in Ajara. Families often moved in with their relatives or neighbors for a month or two so they could rent their own apartment to summer tourists. Students and foreigners in Tbilisi often shared a single room with one or two friends for 50 lari a month, and traders coming to market cities rented rooms for days, even months, at a time.

The Foreign Community. The growing expatriate community of diplomats, aid workers, and staff of international organizations itself created employment. A staff member of the European Community Humanitarian Office estimated that every expatriate created work for about three local people, as interpreters, office managers and staff, drivers, cooks, nannies, and cleaners. The foreigners provided a clientele for hotels, apartments, restaurants, and other services. Working for foreigners or foreign organizations was well paid, prestigious, and, like any other lucrative work in Georgia, obtained through personal connections.

Obstacles to Starting an Enterprise

Both formal and informal business activities involved considerable obstacles. Small businesses especially could not cope with high rents, taxes, fees, and bribes demanded by the sanitary inspectors, fire inspectors, customs officers, and traffic police, not to mention extortion from organized crime. Entrepreneurs said it was essential to have a protector (*krysha*, or "roof" in Russian), to have good relations with powerful figures in the police force, and to publicize the fact of this relationship, to protect oneself against unforeseen "accidents."

Starting a business was said to involve the equivalent of at least $500 in bribes, not to mention the same in startup capital to cover even the rent of a small kiosk for street sales of ice cream or popcorn. In some cases entrepreneurs found it cheaper to pay the tax inspector 20 lari a month under the table than to pay the required registration fee (equivalent to $50) to the state. Some respondents began by borrowing $500 from their relatives, to establish themselves at the local market. But often they were driven out by the unofficial "taxes."

Ketino, who borrowed the equivalent of $500 to open a clothing store, did not expect that she would have to pay $100 to local racketeers, another amount (which she refused to specify) to police to "guard" her premises, plus miscellaneous expenses. Having also underestimated the amount of competition she would encounter, she ended up owing the equivalent of $5,000, including interest. She had to sell her possessions and furniture to pay back this debt.

With the privatization of farm enterprises, many men owned privatized enterprise cars or agricultural transport vehicles. They had begun to rent out their services, most often to transport goods between Georgia and Armenia, Russia, and Turkey. Often, however, the need to pay fines to automobile inspectors on the road provided a big disincentive. To avoid the fines, which ranged from 80 to 300 lari, for example, trucks had to stop to be washed virtually every 10 kilometers. Drivers on newly privatized routes also operated on a very slim margin. A bus driver in Ajara, for example, paid 65 percent of his revenue to rent his bus. He also paid for parts and fuel; maintenance added up to about 300 lari a month. His monthly net income averaged 70 to 80 lari.

A Gldani businessman expanded a successful business into Russia, sending a large shipment of tea to Vladikavkaz. When it was stolen, however, his partners demanded he either return the tea or pay for it. He had to sell the family furniture, car, and apartment. At this point his wife also lost her job. He was on the verge of suicide, which only concern for the future of his children finally prevented. His wife and children now move from relative to relative, while he searches for work in Moscow.

The lack of a clear legal framework caused disaster for other would-be entrepreneurs.

Zaal, together with his son and daughter-in-law, sold their furniture, car, and house and moved into the *saray* (small storage shed) in their yard. They combined earnings with a friend of Zaal's to renovate a small factory and started to produce cooking oil. They allege that this friend absconded with their joint earnings and then sold the factory. Now the new owner and Zaal are embroiled in a court case. In the process Zaal suffered a heart attack. He remains in the hospital, because his condition does not allow him to return to the primitive conditions of the *saray.* His daughter-in-law suffered a miscarriage and still has not recovered. The court case has not progressed, because those neighbors who know the full story are afraid to become involved for fear of retribution.

Respondents in Gldani, one of the poorest districts in Tbilisi, reported that this kind of story was not atypical: many families had ended up there after having lost all their possessions because of business debts, and had sold their apartments in better sections of the city to purchase tiny apartments in this district.

Subsistence Strategies

Many poor people coped with the lack of cash through a combination of subsistence gardening and bartering garden produce for other items and services. In both rural and urban areas, people survived and coped with sudden, unexpected expenses by selling assets, borrowing, and trading services.

Cutting Back. Reducing or avoiding expenditure was the most effective and widely practiced means of survival for all poor families. This involved buying less food and saving on medical expenses by using home remedies, buying medications in the market, or ignoring illness and forgoing treatment. Poor families shared winter clothing and abstained from social occasions and even schooling to save face and expenses. Their home repairs were makeshift: cardboard and plastic in broken windows, or buckets under leaky roofs. They tended not to pay for utilities, and as a result their electricity and telephone service were often disconnected. They had difficulties with transportation and often walked long distances, even in very bad weather, to avoid paying bus fare.

Gardening. In villages, in district centers, and even in large towns, residents had garden plots where they grew greens, potatoes, cabbage, tomatoes, eggplant, beans, carrots, and rape, selling what they could not eat. If they could afford animal feed, families kept livestock and sold the dairy products. People unable to work their own land sometimes let others use it in exchange for part of the harvest. In Kazbegi everyone had a plot for potatoes. If they were not able to work the land themselves, they would "lend" it in return for part of the harvest and hire others to mow or hay. In South Ossetia people sometimes leased out their gardens; one such exchange involved the equivalent of $100 plus a share of cheese, apples, and nuts.

Some city residents also engaged in gardening and limited animal husbandry, although lack of feed over the winter limited this practice, and people on the outskirts of cities often raised pigs. If they had land in a village, some city residents would return there, since state salaries were low and transportation was expensive. Some urban residents were able to barter their skills for agricultural inputs: the services of a tractor and driver in exchange for tutoring the tractor driver's son, for example.

Selling Assets. People tended to sell possessions in three stages, beginning with personal property such as jewelry received as wedding gifts, linen, clothing, or fine crystal; then furniture, appliances, and cars; and finally their homes. Sometimes Tbilisi women exchanged used clothing, costume jewelry, or perfume for produce at the wholesale market. For respondents with nothing left to sell, their own blood provided the final source of income. In Tbilisi 400 grams of blood netted 12 lari. Most of the respondents had sold their privatization vouchers, except for a few who had invested in the local bank or bread enterprise. They understood that the vouchers would not make them property owners, and few believed they would ever receive dividends.

Borrowing to Survive. People borrowed to invest, to start enterprises, to cover extraordinary expenses, and to get by from one day to the next. The most common daily expense was for bread. In poor villages such as Sukhlis, in Javakheti, despite the extensive mutual assistance characteristic of such communities, some 50 to 60 families were said to be living only on borrowed money.

Narcotics and Prostitution. Prostitution was believed to have increased in every region, and especially in the cities. Indeed, one of the interviewers reported that he had recently been solicited several times in central Tbilisi, once by a young teenager and another time by an older woman, who offered to supply a girl of any age in return for foreign currency. A major commercial thoroughfare in Tbilisi had become the venue of several new clubs, which reportedly attracted the newly rich along with narcotics users and prostitutes.

Respondents expressed considerable concern about narcotics. In some villages near Tbilisi, people were said to be growing (and using) opium poppies. In Ajara mothers expressed fear that their children would become involved in selling drugs on the street. In one village a young man had organized district youths, including girls, to sell drugs for him; eventually some of the youths were arrested and sentenced, but the organizer escaped imprisonment. Selling narcotics was mentioned as a source of income in a number of interviews; respondents in this study, by the very nature of the sample, were those who had been unsuccessful. Their imprisonment was often the source of further impoverishment for their families.

Theft and Extortion. Rural respondents reported widespread theft of livestock and barnyard animals, crops, and household items. In urban areas people complained of street robbery as well as burglary. They often failed to report the crime because they feared police involvement. Another form of theft was petty extortion by those who had any sort of power.

Labor Migration

Many Georgians resorted to working abroad. The majority of migrants were able-bodied men, although sometimes families migrated together, selling their household possessions and their apartment to raise money for the trip. Most of the migrants chose to go to cities in Russia, where wages were relatively high. Migrant labor was the major source of income for poor Armenian villages in Javakheti, which sent every able-bodied man and even schoolboys. Individuals and small brigades of younger men left Samegrelo in the autumn to return the following summer. Even before *perestroika* there had been active migration out of this region; now every family had a member who had left for Russia. Greece was an important destination for residents of Batumi, Tbilisi, and Marneuli.

Remittances were literally a lifesaver for many families. A Tbilisi respondent got 150 deutsche marks each month from a relative working in Germany, and another received $150 several times a year from relatives in the United States. Others received money from relatives in Moscow and Israel.

Labor migration had become extraordinarily important in South Ossetia, which had experienced high unemployment even during the Soviet period. About half the people had left, mostly for North Ossetia, in Russia. Those who engaged in buying and selling there often used Vladikavkaz as a base, since they could rely on relatives already living there to house them, store their goods and vehicles, and generally assist them. The migrants experienced many difficulties adapting to highly russified Vladikavkaz, and some reputedly had become involved in criminal activities.

The absence of men took its toll on those left behind. Some elderly parents were left alone. In agricultural regions wives took on the heavy burden of farm work and became dependent on their relatives while they waited for remittances. Family members remaining in Georgia could become liable for debts. When a Marneuli man went to Tver, in Russia, and disappeared with $2,000 he had borrowed to buy trade goods, he left behind a large household of 13 people, who sold their only cow, five sheep, and other household goods to repay his debt.

Agriculture

Privatization. Land reform had begun in 1992 with a decree that a reserve of 850,000 hectares of land (200,000 hectares of which was already in use as household plots) would be distributed to individuals. The recipients did not receive full ownership rights, however: they could pass the land on to their children but could not sell it. As of mid-1996, 49 percent of cultivated land had been distributed; the rest remained in state and collective farms, most of which had ceased production (World Bank 1996).

There was considerable confusion and suspicion among farmers about the way the distribution had taken place. Some poor farmers expressed the fear that they would end up as landless wage slaves, working for an emerging class of large private landowners. Thus far, two or three farms in each village had started hiring workers. In Signaghi district, where land distribution had begun in 1992, farmers claimed that people with influence (those who worked for the police and courts, school directors, directors of shops, and other "big businessmen") had received the best land: orchards, vineyards, and fertile fields. Many families complained that the land they had received was of lower quality: unirrigated, saline, and less fertile, or distant from their homes, making it difficult to work and the harvest difficult to guard.

People had little recourse if they felt deceived. Many households in Sukhlis claimed that they had received no land whereas others had received large lots, but they felt it would be useless to submit complaints and did not even know where to submit them. Farmers had not yet received title to their land, some because they were unable to pay the 80 lari demanded. They were fearful that they would lose their land if they had not received title by the deadline. Some felt that the residents of these predominantly Armenian villages were slow to get title because of ethnic discrimination.

In Kazbegi most people had small garden plots and subsisted on potatoes. Most people also had cattle. They complained that when they inquired about the distribution of hay meadows, the local officials put them off, claiming to be waiting for the new law to clarify procedures. In the village of Djuta, residents divided the hay meadows into parcels, and each year they cast lots to determine which parcel each family would receive.

The cost of access to equipment and inputs limited farm profits. In Signaghi district the chairman of a former collective farm ended up with most of the heavy farm machinery, which he now rented out. Many small farmers could not afford to rent equipment and left part of their land unworked. In Tkibuli district, a mountainous area with poor soil, most farming was done with draft animals, rented for 10 lari a day.

Some farmers worked for local agribusinesses, which sometimes lent them farm equipment to use on their own land. Thus, near Zugdidi, households grew corn on small plots for themselves and their animals and worked for the new agribusiness in the village of Zeda Etseri. The managers worked their employees' plots without charge. In the village of Akhalcopeli, villagers had to pay 50 lari to have their land worked. Farmers who worked for the local tea enterprise and were owed back wages demanded that the fee for plowing and sowing their land be paid out of what the enterprise owed them.

Land distribution had taken on an ethnic coloration in some regions. A number of Ossetians still living in rural Georgia felt they had received less than their share. In Marneuli district large plantations of vineyards, tobacco, and potatoes ended up in the hands of private owners or renters. Many of the new owners were Svans (a Georgian ethnic subgroup), resettled six to eight years before as part of a "Georgification" policy after an earthquake destroyed their homes in Svaneti. The local Azeri population held the Svans responsible for letting the vines die and the harvests decline; they accused the Svans of inexperience with local forms of agriculture and of neglect.

Privatization had not occurred in some areas. In Ajara collective farms leased land to farmers, who paid according to their harvest and kept the rest to sell. In South Ossetia some large families had simply taken over the use of pastures, although this had aroused some opposition. The South Ossetian government had distributed garden plots to city residents and IDPs as well as rural inhabitants, but respondents claimed that those in charge of the distribution had kept the best for themselves and their relatives.

Subsistence Farming. Former collective farm workers supported their households through a combination of subsistence farming, sale of farm produce, and off-farm employment with local agribusinesses or wealthy neighbors. Their harvests had shrunk drastically because they no longer had access to farm equipment and could not afford good seed, fertilizer, and pesticides. Farmers employed a number of strategies to cope with the new conditions. In regions such as Kakheti, cash poverty had forced farmers to turn to producing wheat for their own consumption, but the harvests were not adequate to supply the region. Grape cultivation was labor-intensive, wine enterprises often paid late, and prices had fallen, leading many farmers to switch to fruit and vegetables for consumption and sale. Although families often raised a cow, a few sheep, and poultry, recently even the poultry had become difficult to maintain because of the high price of feed.

In Javakheti agricultural conditions differed significantly from one village to the next. In poor villages such as Gulikam and Kartikam, with their poor, stony soil more suitable for forage than for agriculture, most people raised potatoes for their own subsistence but survived mainly on remittances. About 30 to 40 men in each village worked on the collective farm, which paid them in animal feed. This enabled families to keep one or two cows and sell surplus dairy products in the district center.

The village of Sukhlis had better land, and some families were able to make enough money to buy minitractors and install irrigation pipes with the help of their neighbors. Without functioning farm machinery, agriculture required more heavy manual labor, and harvests were poorer. Farmers complained that by the time they drove their produce from South Georgia to Tbilisi, adding in the cost of fuel and payments to the traffic police, they ended up with only 100 to 150 lari in profit.

Farmers in Khulo, a highland district of Ajara, practiced agriculture and some husbandry. Villagers came to the Batumi market to trade cheese, dairy products, and eggs for soap, washing powder, sugar, flour, notebooks, and pens. Alternatively, traders came to lowland and highland villages with manufactured wares, sometimes from Turkey, the Islamic Republic of Iran, and Poland, to trade for citrus fruit or potatoes. Villagers felt that these traders were taking advantage of their inability to market their own produce.

In Samegrelo, poor land and small harvests meant that farmers could scarcely feed their own families, much less produce surpluses to sell. Although demand existed in Zugdidi, and even in the district centers, most farmers could not afford the transportation costs. As a result, they tended to barter their goods in village markets. Although some engaged in a limited trade for cash, it remained on a small scale.

Marketing. Lowland districts of Ajara are rich in citrus orchards, which had once supplied the whole Soviet Union and created great local wealth. Today farmers sold to middlemen who promised to pay them after they had sold the fruit. Poor respondents lacked the resources to organize marketing, in part because of the breakdown in subsidized transportation. Some were afraid to get involved in shipping fruit, which they claimed the local mafia controlled. Others were uncertain how to market it in Tbilisi: Where could they stay? How would they store their fruit? Some allowed more capable acquaintances to handle the marketing in exchange for a small amount of the profit.

Wage Labor. People living in towns as well as rural residents who ended up without land found seasonal employment on the remaining state or collective farms, or with independent farmers. Many performed backbreaking physical labor for as little as $2 a day or payment in kind. Some traveled long distances and spent several weeks or months at this work. Unemployed coal miners from Tkibuli worked seasonally on collective farms in Marneuli district, receiving 54 lari a month. Despite the low wages, there was still competition for the work. The subtropical areas around Zugdidi were once among the richest in Georgia. State tea collectives provided employment for many. Although the nearby tea plantation had not been cultivated or fertilized for at least five years, a German firm had recently leased a tea enterprise, offering pickers 10 tetri per kilogram of leaves, or about 2 lari a day. Respondents termed this "slave wages" and spoke of "medieval working conditions." Nevertheless, for some people this was their only cash income. One respondent worked the whole summer with his wife, earning a total of 270 lari.

Conclusions

Public sector employment, once the main source of stable and respectable incomes, now paid meager salaries and could not guarantee timely payment, and enterprises continued to lay off employees. The private sector offered better pay but no security in terms of job conditions or worker benefits. Self-employment was risky, not only because of the inherent risk of failure, but also because it entangled the entrepreneur in a web of official and private corruption. Labor migration offered greater monetary rewards but also posed considerable physical and financial risks. Agriculture, especially for farmers with poor-quality land and no machinery, involved much heavier labor than ever before and no guarantees in the face of crop failure.

Social Benefits and Humanitarian Assistance

Most people were angry about the low level of pensions and benefits they now received from the state. They expressed great confusion about other sources of assistance and skepticism about the fairness of its distribution.

State Assistance

For some of the poorest respondents, their old-age pension (8.5 lari) or child allowance (2.5 lari) was the only cash they saw in a month. When these meager amounts were delayed, sometimes by as much as six months, it meant serious hardship. Given the new rules and regulations, many people did not know what assistance they were entitled to by law, nor did they always know whether the source of aid they received was the government or a private organization. People received information about different forms of assistance from friends, acquaintances, or television, but never from official sources. They no longer knew where to seek information or appeal for restitution.

Some people felt they had been deliberately deceived or misled by state agencies. An elderly pensioner had been forced to seek legal advice to find out that he was eligible to receive both his salary and his pension. Some respondents who sought a required certificate from the housing authorities were unable to receive assistance from the social assistance office until they had paid off all their debts for communal services. Whenever people sought out information, they had to wait in endless lines, sometimes returning for several days in a row, and were treated in an insulting and humiliating manner.

For some potential recipients the assistance was not worth the associated costs. One mother of disabled children said she could not afford the transportation to go twice a month to the social assistance office and then to the post office to collect 8 lari in disability pensions for her children and an additional 5 lari as a single mother.

Nino, who lives in Kazbegi, could not pay to have her heart condition treated; it has become steadily worse. Now she cannot obtain a certificate of disability, a prerequisite for receiving disability payments. She cannot afford the trip to Tbilisi to the medical commission, nor does she have enough money to pay for the first examination: 20 lari plus 5 lari for the necessary forms.

Even after people had established their entitlements, they still encountered difficulties. They waited in long lines to receive pensions that postal workers used to deliver to their homes. Some had signed over the rights to aid to someone else who was willing to wait. A respondent commented that the indifference and arrogance of officials went so far that a bank manager had forced people to wait in the street for hours in bad weather to receive their pensions, because the noise they made disturbed him.

Humanitarian Assistance

Most recipients felt that foreigners should have directly distributed all aid. Even though many people acknowledged that the aid had been of real assistance, they were distressed to see it being sold in the markets. Families who had not received aid were convinced that others had obtained it through personal connections or bribes. Many respondents felt there was large-scale collusion between aid distributors and corrupt businesses. In Tbilisi the neighbor of a Red Cross worker who regularly stored Red Cross shipments of supplies in his apartment witnessed middlemen purchasing these goods directly from the apartment to resell to private businesses. Hospitals came under particular attack for their regular practice of selling medications given to them by international aid organizations. Indeed, several officials of international donor organizations believed that free medicines made up the inventory of the many newly established private pharmacies that have sprung up throughout Tbilisi.

A few humanitarian organizations were praised for their regular aid: these included the Red Cross, Doctors without Borders, and a few local organizations. Georgians expressed mixed sentiments toward the role of religious organizations. In Ajara a respondent earned a monthly salary of 80 lari for proselytizing for the Jehovah's Witnesses. An Azerbaijani family finally decided to accept aid from the group despite initial reluctance to accept a pacifist faith—what if members were called to serve in the Georgian army? They resolved this dilemma by deciding that the "less important" family members—the mother and sister—would use the aid.

The International Orthodox Churches Charities ran soup kitchens in Tbilisi and other cities; most users were elderly or disabled. In Tbilisi the kitchens served up to 1,000 people a day, running on donations from local businesses and volunteer labor. They also distributed flour, sunflower seed oil, split peas, and medicines in South Georgia, where inhabitants noted that although local Armenian and Georgian priests had organized the distribution, they did not reject any minority, including Jews, Greeks, and Russians.

Although the amounts people received in state benefits had sharply declined, these benefits were the sole regular source of cash for the very poor, such as elderly persons living by themselves and families with disabled members. The payments were often received late, and respondents were disturbed by the attitudes they encountered among public officials. Although some people considered the idea of accepting humanitarian assistance humiliating, many nevertheless had found the aid very important.

Health Care

The evolving public-private system of medical care included state provision of basic services for certain population groups, but there was little information or transparency and much opportunity for rent seeking. Health professionals were underpaid, and the system was underfinanced and underregulated. Deteriorating public health standards and inability to pay for medical treatment had produced a rise in physical illness and psychological distress among the poor. Most respondents avoided doctors and hospitals until their illness had turned into a serious emergency. They blamed the health reform—what an international aid worker referred to as "a new man-made disaster"—for much of their misery.

Declining Access

Although official fees were introduced under the new health reform, many poor could not manage the official prices. District doctors "unofficially demand twice as much," according to one respondent, and ignored those patients who failed to pay continuously during their hospitalization. Few people understood their entitlements under the new health reform, and doctors and hospitals frequently ignored them. When patients in outlying villages called emergency services, ambulances often did not come, either because they had no fuel or because the roads were so bad. When patients themselves came to the hospital, those who could not pay the fees risked being turned away. Poor families often could not even afford the 7 lari for a doctor's appointment, 9 lari for laboratory tests, and 11 lari for an ambulance—fees reported from Ajara. Medicines were also expensive, which meant that illness in a family could seriously threaten its survival. A family from Makhindzhauri, in Ajara, reported that 80 percent of their family income was spent on treatment for their disabled son.

Chronic illnesses with their heavy requirements of medication and doctor visits could be a serious drain on family budgets. Diabetes proved a catastrophe for families unable to afford regular periodic checkups. In some districts respondents reported that local hospitals no longer had supplies of insulin.

Zviad is dying of diabetes-related gangrene. One leg has been amputated, but the gangrene has spread to the other, and the family has not managed to raise money for a new operation. They were forced to sell most of their household property for the first operation, which cost $500 for a two-week hospital stay. Zviad frequently goes into a coma, and they must call on specialists. His daughter, Nino, has nephritis but can no longer afford to follow the special diet she was prescribed. A friend who is a biochemist performed some tests on her and found that the condition is worsening. But Nino cannot afford 100 lari for a proper examination.

Hospital personnel, criticized as poorly trained and indifferent, complained that they themselves had not received payment for many months. As incomes had decreased and fees increased, the number of hospital patients had fallen, as had the morale of hospital workers, who felt humiliated by patients' assumption that all the new fees went directly into their pockets.

Deteriorating Health

People now found medical care out of their reach. Poor nutrition and extreme overcrowding had contributed to a marked rise in tuberculosis in South Ossetia, Ajara, and other districts. In Soviet times tubercular patients had been treated free of charge, usually at special sanatoria. Today some patients paid as much as 150 lari. Even when treatment was free, the medicine cost 200 lari or more. Tuberculosis was a particular problem for IDPs, who lived in cold, overcrowded quarters, where there was often no water and a single toilet served many households.

Provision of vaccinations deteriorated sharply in 1991 and 1992, although NGOs provided free, complete coverage in South Ossetia. One interviewer noted that only half the households she spoke with had vaccinated their children. Following a diphtheria epidemic, people were to receive shots free of charge, but in fact many were asked to pay. As a result, coverage was far from complete. Cases of rabies were rising with the number of abandoned dogs.

Contamination of the water supply, or residents' recourse to river water, was blamed for numerous stomach infections, hepatitis, and other infectious diseases in South Ossetia, Marneuli, and other areas. In Samegrelo the low iodine content of water was showing up in more cases of goiter, especially among children. Families complained that cold, unheated homes, insufficient warm clothing, and poor nutrition were causing bronchitis, asthma (reportedly a serious problem in Ajara's damp climate), and lung infections, especially among children.

Stress-related conditions had also increased. Many respondents characterized themselves as anxious about the present, fearful of the future, and ready to explode. Smoking and heavy drinking had increased. Men and women complained of stress-related stomach complaints and depression: some had attempted suicide, in some cases after losing investments. Many men had begun drinking as a result of prolonged unemployment. Women confessed that frequent household arguments resulted in their being beaten. Others admitted to beating their children when they could not control their own anxiety and frustration.

A female respondent in Tbilisi describes her husband's routine: "He gets up in the morning, he looks at me, he asks, 'Is there any dinner?' I say there isn't any. He starts drinking."

Childhood illnesses and injuries had dramatically increased. Doctors from a Batumi children's clinic claimed that the incidence of childhood asthma had increased fourfold in the past six years. Birth defects and injuries among infants and older children, including dislocated hips or limbs, eye problems requiring corrective surgery, injuries, and burns, were no longer treated. Children had taken on adult tasks such as chopping wood, gathering fuel, and cooking on dangerous kerosene heaters, and they frequently injured and burned themselves. Parents in rural districts, especially when they were intimidated by the city or did not speak Georgian, hesitated to seek medical treatment. They did not know where to take their children, and they were afraid they could not afford treatment. Disabled children who could have benefited from special education and physical therapy were kept at home, where they remained untreated and sometimes neglected.

Maternal Health

Childbirth had become so expensive that it often forced poor families into debt. Women expressed fear of pregnancy but could not afford contraceptives. According to a representative of an international organization, the medical system had been laggard in providing contraceptives, partly because abortions were so profitable. Doctor-supervised pregnancy and assisted childbirth had become expensive options. Women reported that they tried to avoid sexual relations with their husbands, and this caused frequent arguments.

In Zugdidi district, Ira, a pensioner, lives with her married daughter and three grandchildren. Ira's 8.5-lari monthly pension is the family's only cash income. Her third grandchild is 10 days old but still does not have a name. The baby's 22-year-old mother wanted an abortion but could not find the 15 to 20 lari to pay for it. Of course, she did not have the 200 to 250 lari necessary to have the child in the maternity hospital, but

> fortunately her neighbor is a nurse and helped deliver the baby. The mother has no milk to feed the child. The family is hoping to find someone who will adopt the child so that he does not die of hunger and cold.

Women often avoided consulting gynecologists for fear they would claim to diagnose a pregnancy, just in order to make an additional $60 for performing an abortion. Few families could afford the $100 to $400 for a hospital delivery. Increasing numbers of women were resorting to giving birth at home because of the cost of hospital delivery, but also because maternity hospitals were cold and dirty, infested with cockroaches and other vermin.

> A young mother in Marneuli gave birth in the home of her husband's parents, where she had gone to live after marriage. His mother opposed calling a doctor because of the expense, and the child died. For her second child, she returned to her own parents, who paid an experienced neighbor 100,000 rubles (about $20) to deliver the child.

With new regulations and little information, even services that ought to have been provided for free were not.

> In Ajara an IDP living in a collection center gave birth there. She was unable to pay for a doctor, and so no one examined the baby. He soon got a lung infection and died two weeks later. His mother was unaware that hospitals were required to treat infants under a year of age free of charge.

Many mothers worried that they were so poorly nourished that they could not nurse their babies. Others were reluctant to take their babies home because conditions there were so bad. Not surprisingly, maternity hospitals reported a rise in babies abandoned at the hospital.

Coping with Costs

Poor people coped with most medical complaints by simply ignoring them. Alternatively, they attempted free or low-cost treatments: home remedies, massage, and consultation with local "healers." They set priorities, such as providing food first for their children, and then for themselves, and only if there was money left over would they spend it on their own medical treatment.

Nino, in Samegrelo, has terrible gallstone attacks. But she prefers to use any available cash to pay for bimonthly doctor visits (at 30 lari each) for her son, who has a neurological illness and suffers frequent convulsions, rather than apply it to the $500 her own surgery would cost.

With so many children suffering from illness, it is not surprising that pensioners were being neglected. One respondent, a 74-year-old woman, could hardly see or hear, but could not afford $300 for a simple cataract operation or a hearing aid. An elderly man sat at home in pain because his family could not afford a hernia operation. A son regretted that he could not pay the 20 lari needed to diagnose what appeared to be a cyst on his mother's thyroid gland, but he could not afford an operation for her in any case.

The need to raise money for medical or surgical treatment forced many families to sell important household assets, even their homes. Thus a sudden illness could impoverish even prosperous families. Families often had to decide between two equally costly options: treat a severe illness or pay for a funeral.

When Timur's father became ill, his family could not afford to have him moved to the hospital. The cost of his funeral turned out to be almost as expensive as hospital treatment, however. The family paid 30 lari for the death certificate, 100 lari to have the body prepared, 300 lari for the coffin, 150 lari to register for burial and dig the grave, and 300 lari for a modest wake.

Conclusions

Poor households felt that medical care had become inaccessible. Even when doctors consented to examine them for a modest fee, people were unable to pay for laboratory analyses, further treatment, or medicines, much less the high costs of surgery and hospital care. As a result, they did without treatment or, where possible, incurred debts to cover emergency care. Meanwhile poverty had taken a toll on the population's health. People expressed a marked sense of indifference to their own health and even the health of their children.

Children and Youth

The children of Georgia have proved particularly vulnerable to the transition. Their health has suffered from poor nutrition, unheated homes, insufficient winter clothing, and accidents as they take over the tasks of adults. Their education has suffered, and many have left school entirely to help their parents earn money. Children of IDPs showed many behavioral and psychological disturbances stemming from war and displacement. Although the majority of poor families gave priority to their children's needs, some parents have been unable to cope, and the social institutions that used to help families are no longer up to the task. Abandonment of infants and children, together with neglect and abuse, has also increased.

Stories of baby selling were rife. A Tbilisi respondent had heard of a woman who had sold one child for $500 to support her remaining children. Another had witnessed a 25-year-old woman in the market near Tbilisi's central train station, offering her child for sale. The woman had reportedly appealed to onlookers, saying, "The child will die of hunger—take him even if you don't pay."

Street Children

The new street children in Tbilisi represented every ethnic group.[2] Some had run away from their families, sometimes after divorce. Others had run away from boarding schools for "difficult children." Once run like prisons, the schools now let the children come and go as they pleased. Some children had families who were simply unable to provide care. And some—as young as five years of age—spent most of their time on the streets, begging, pilfering, and in some cases working.

A small study carried out by Child and Environment, an NGO, estimated that street children in Tbilisi numbered from 1,000 to 1,200 at any given time. About 20 percent came from other regions, and some were IDPs. Street children were generally in bad physical and psychological condition when they came to the attention of authorities. Many had serious bronchitis, pleuritis, and other infections from prolonged exposure to the cold and lack of warm clothing; many others had scabies, sexually transmitted diseases, tuberculosis, or wounds from injuries and burns, often from operating electric appliances and kerosene heaters in small apartments without adult supervision. Only about half had received vaccinations. Although doctors sometimes treated these children for free, their unstable living situations made it difficult to complete their treatments. The children tended to be frightened, aggressive, and unapproachable.

Some street children actually lived with their families and even helped support them with their labor. Many of the families were poorly educated and had a history of criminal involvement and a host of personal and psychological problems, but during the Soviet period they had been able to scrape by on an array of subsidies and other social supports. Some families had left their villages to engage in trade or business; others found they could make as much begging in Tbilisi as they could through subsistence farming. Some young parents had abandoned their children to elderly grandparents who received old-age pensions but not child subsidies. Many of the single mothers of street children had lost work because of illness or had been laid off. Most of the families rented apartments or rooms that were practically unlivable, in old districts or slums, for 20 to 25 lari a month. One family of five lived in a single room with two beds. Many of the unsupervised children begged their food on the streets and became involved in prostitution, stealing, or glue sniffing.

Some children were completely homeless. They slept in underground passages, elevators, or abandoned kiosks. One group of children, aged 6 to 14, slept in the public toilet near Tbilisi's central market, close to the gathering spot of prostitutes and alcoholics. Others paid 50 tetri a night to sleep in railroad cars at the train station. In winter they slept in the buildings housing communal boilers until the apartment residents drove them away. These were the most difficult and troubled of the street children, well on their way to becoming fully criminalized.

Sometimes people offered homeless children 6 or 7 lari a day, along with shelter, to work in cafes, restaurants, and gas stations. Some children even worked for street photographers, earning up to 10 lari a day. Often these children performed hard physical work. Children as young as nine years old worked in the markets, sometimes at night, carrying and loading goods, for 5 lari a day.

Children begged, with or without their parents, often in pairs or groups organized by an adult. Generally, child beggars were more successful than adults. They begged near churches—where they could earn up to 40 lari on a holiday—and near underpasses, subway stations, markets, and city squares. Often people running restaurants or bakeries gave them food, or they stole it. Likewise, children were often given clothing or bought it themselves. Some children tried to injure themselves by falling under cars so that they could then extort money from the driver.

Neither schools nor social service agencies have dealt effectively with the problem of street children. The social assistance agency maintained that they were the responsibility of the Ministry of Education, which runs boarding schools; the Ministry of Education in turn considered the children the responsibility of the Ministry of the Interior (the police). As of October 1996, the police had delivered 500 children to the Tbilisi child collector, some more than once. The building was in terrible condition, but the Red Cross and the United Methodist Committee on Relief provided food aid. Up to 50 children at a time stayed at the child collector, usually for one or two months, before being sent back to their families or to orphanages.

Education

By all accounts, public education has been steadily deteriorating throughout Georgia, and especially for children of the poor. For young people in the villages, the lack of educational or employment opportunities and the decline of village social and cultural life contributed to depression, criminality, and increased alcoholism.

Costs. Official and unofficial fees were one of the greatest concerns of poor families interviewed for this study. Schooling was free through the first nine grades, but the new school reform had introduced a fee for the 10th and 11th grades, which differed from region to region. In Samegrelo the fee was 7 to 10 lari, although some schools waived the fee for the best students. Parents were also frequently required to contribute wood or money to heat the school, plus monthly sums such as 5 lari for school renovation, to pay the school guards, or to "top up" the teachers' salaries. In Tbilisi some teachers got an extra 15 lari a month from parents. In some Javakheti villages, education continued mainly thanks to parents, who supported the school, supplied heating fuel, and contributed to the teachers' salaries. Throughout Georgia the impact of these multiple fees was that increasing numbers of children were leaving school when they completed the ninth grade, if not before.

School supplies were expensive for poor families. In some districts first graders received free books, and some residents of Tbilisi sent old textbooks to relatives in villages. In a few lucky villages, local enterprises sponsored schools.

Children had to travel increasing distances to stay in school. Many schools had been closed for lack of maintenance, to accommodate IDPs, or as a result of war or weather damage, and transportation services had deteriorated. In Ajara and Kazbegi some villages had only primary schools, and transportation links with other villages had broken down.

Attrition. Both preschool and school attendance had dropped sharply. Few poor village parents could send their children to kindergarten. Children left school to help their parents or to look after younger siblings, or because they lacked appropriate school clothing and supplies. Some children had simply never started school. In every village and town in Marneuli district, there were families who had taken their children out of school. In Ajara respondents reported that poorly dressed children refused to attend school because other children laughed at their ragged clothing. Parents also felt that teachers increasingly favored rich children.

Many children and young people had lost interest in education. Children over four years old knew the prices of everyday goods and could readily convert lari to dollars and back. Some children, having already started to earn money, no longer saw the point of school. As a 10-year-old businessman asked, "Why should I study? I know how to add and count, I can count money, rip people off, and cheat on weighing. Nobody is paying me to study, but I make 15 to 20 lari a month from trade." According to his grandmother, he had started to buy his own clothing.

Declining Status of Teachers. Because many men had left teaching to search for better-paying jobs, 95 percent of village teachers were now women, and many were nearing pension age. Teachers received 12 to 14 lari a month, two to three months late. Although salaries in Marneuli were recently doubled, to 21 lari, teaching loads were increased to 18 hours. Before 1994, 3,000 teachers had worked in the district. By the time of the study, 2,100 had left their jobs, either to leave the country or to work in trade. Even those who remained had to combine teaching with farming. Parents felt that the quality of education, particularly in middle schools, had declined, and teachers felt that their work had become a form of "drudgery" and was no longer respected. For women in particular, loss of a teaching job signified diminished status, even within one's own family.

Higher Education. Numerous private institutions of higher learning now competed with the state universities. Commercial colleges and private universities, offering degrees in management, business, banking, and international affairs, had opened in Batumi, Zugdidi, Tskhinval, and district centers throughout Georgia. In some, IDPs were granted 50 percent discounts, but many poor students could not even afford this. Even when parents managed to raise money to send their children to a private institution, they were often forced to leave when the fees increased.

The new private institutions experienced problems with materials: Russian textbooks were too expensive, and Georgian textbooks were not yet available. At the same time, the quality of public higher education had deteriorated. In Tskhinval faculty members had left for Russia, the university library had not received any new books for six years, and the student stipend had decreased to 700 lari a month. Education was losing its value for students, who felt that education now required money rather than intelligence or diligence. "With money," one student said, "even a moron can enroll in medical school."

Rural regions such as Javakheti used to send many of their young people for higher education; they later returned home or to district centers to work as agronomists, teachers, and accountants. Now few could complete their higher education, especially in the most prestigious state university departments such as law, which demanded up to $15,000 to secure admission, since they led to a lucrative profession.

Institutions. Parents who were incapable of feeding their children could request to send them to a boarding school or orphanage, although most institutions in Georgia were no longer able to guarantee even minimally adequate living conditions for the orphaned, disabled, ill, or "troubled" children they housed. These children had multiple disadvantages. They lived in conditions characterized by an appalling lack of hygiene, with cold rooms, inadequate food, and often poor care. Homes for the mentally handicapped have been described as the worst. Children without families, or with incomplete or marginal families, were additionally vulnerable because they lacked the informal ties and relationships so essential to survival during hard times (Scott and Tarkhan-Mouravi 1995, p. 25).

Conclusions

If human resources are the key to economic prosperity, then young people who are healthy and educationally well prepared will be best positioned to take advantages of opportunities in the new market economy. The Georgian population was among the best educated of the Soviet republics. Today, in contrast, the drop in family incomes, together with reduction of state support and the introduction of fees, means that poor children and youth are systematically excluded from opportunities that will allow them to compete on an equal basis with others.

Internally Displaced Persons

Background: Conflict and Displacement

Between 1991 and 1996, when research for this study began, 350,000 people had fled their homes as a result of armed conflict in the regions of South Ossetia and Abkhazia. Approximately 100,000 Ossetians left Georgia for North Ossetia and other parts of Russia. As of 1995 over half of an estimated 250,000 IDPs were living in collective centers such as hostels, hospitals, schools, and other public buildings, in overcrowded and unhygienic conditions, unemployed, alienated from local populations, depressed, and bitter. In Tbilisi, those who speak with a Megrelian or Svanetian accent (the Megrelians, like the Svans, are an ethnic Georgian subgroup) are immediately marked and excite urban prejudices, which link them to the increasing criminality in the city. As visible recipients of regular humanitarian assistance, they have also elicited resentment among a local population that considers itself just as badly off.

The government of Georgia has not hastened to assimilate the IDPs, because by doing so it would lose one of its arguments for retaining hegemony over Abkhazia. Many IDPs also resist assimilation and insist they will eventually return to Abkhazia; others have come to believe this will not happen in the next five or ten years. Although local registration has been formally abolished and a *propiska* (residency permit) is no longer required for work, according to the new constitution, respondents reported that it sometimes proved necessary if one wished to buy a home. Many IDPs are reluctant to register, however, since by doing so they would give up government subsidies linked to their status and endanger their right to move back to Abkhazia in the future. IDPs thus remain in an ambiguous situation, unwilling—and not encouraged—to integrate, yet unable to return home.

Living Conditions

In Batumi, IDPs from Sukhumi, the capital of Abkhazia, live in the Medea Hotel, where between four and seven people crowd into a single room of 13 square meters, without, of course, a kitchen or a bathroom. There are actually rooms to spare, but the hotel administrators claim they are reserving them for "guests of honor." A female occupant of the Medea sleeps doubled up on the floor of the small entryway to her family's room. She says she "hasn't slept like a human being in a bed since

1993." Their neighbor has been forced by overcrowding to sleep in the
hotel corridor, so as not infect his wife, son, daughter-in-law, and their
three children with his tuberculosis.

Although many IDPs had worked as professionals—doctors, engineers,
and professors—in Abkhazia, they found themselves, according to respondents, even more excluded from these fields than the local population. And
those who had fled without any possessions had virtually nothing to sell.
Their most important means of survival was humanitarian assistance, which
came from international donors such as the United Nations Development
Programme and from NGOs, although coverage has been very uneven, with
less going to East Georgia or to Ajara than to other areas.

The government of Georgia, through the Committee on Refugees, also
provided regular, if very modest, support to IDPs. In many regions IDPs
were entitled to free or discounted transportation, although in some
regions this right had been discontinued. In Tskhaltubo, for example, the
12,000 IDPs living in former sanatoria no longer received transportation
discounts, because city transportation had been privatized. Despite their
legal entitlement to their modest monthly payments, actually receiving
them was often difficult. IDPs in Tbilisi reported that money came to the
savings bank only once a month. Because there was never enough to go
around, people started lining up early in the morning. Sometimes the
crush became so fierce that people were injured; a young female respondent had broken her hand. The IDPs felt angry and humiliated, since they
considered the money official compensation for the property they had had
to abandon in Abkhazia.

Given the preeminent role of personal connections in finding employment, it is not surprising that the rate of unemployment and, consequent-
ly, the incidence of depression were particularly high among IDPs.
A respondent living in the Medea Hotel mentioned a young man who
had committed suicide after failing to find employment. Most IDPs lacked
access to garden plots and felt humiliated by suffering hunger and being
labeled as beggars.

In Tbilisi many IDPs traded in produce in the city markets and on the
street. The local population, however, accused them of taking over the market, buying local produce cheaply and then establishing a single price
among themselves. IDPs felt they were often taken for Megrelian traders,
who have a similar regional accent and are locally viewed with suspicion as
swindlers. One IDP complained, "They call us speculators and accuse us of
causing all their problems!"

The Place of IDPs in Georgian Society

The overwhelming majority of IDPs interviewed for this study expressed a deep sense of insecurity—"as if we are sitting on a suitcase"—and isolation from the communities in which they found themselves. They were depressed about their circumstances and hopeless about the future. Although some had managed to assimilate, either because they had relatives to put them up when they arrived, or because they had found jobs or married local people, most IDPs felt strong ties to each other, even in collection centers where they had come from several different regions. But they felt rejected by the local population, who constantly conveyed the message that "You're not one of us."

Displacement had grave consequences for the children of IDPs. A large number simply did not attend school; many showed considerable psychological disturbances and behavior problems. One couple in Tkibuli reported that their child had refused to return to school after being labeled a "refugee beggar." The overcrowding also influenced marriage patterns for young people. Some IDPs tried to marry off their daughters at an early age, just to secure their future. IDPs who married and remained living in collection centers, however, said they tried not to conceive children. It is possible that their children are among the rising number of newborns abandoned at maternity hospitals because the parents cannot imagine bringing them to live at the center.

Like the IDPs from Abkhazia, those in South Ossetia also suffered from severe overcrowding, especially in the part of the region where earthquake damage was still in evidence. Some lived in the buildings of a tourist complex, but in small rooms never intended for long-term use by families. Elsewhere people were housed in temporary wagons. Despite their material difficulties, however, the situation for the Ossetian IDPs living in South Ossetia was psychologically somewhat more bearable than that of IDPs from Abkhazia, because the local authorities had not placed so many barriers in the way of their assimilation into local society. The children exhibited their distress most vividly, with the same problems of school performance and behavior noted among IDPs from Abkhazia.

Social Integration and Disintegration

Ethnic Diversity

Georgia's regional and ethnic diversity provides ready-made fault lines during periods of political, economic, and social conflict. After the breakup of the Soviet Union, the status of South Ossetia and Abkhazia was challenged, resulting in armed conflict and massive destruction in Abkhazia and violent conflict between Ossetians and Georgians throughout Georgia. Tensions have ebbed and flowed in the border areas, particularly with Armenians in Javakheti, and less so around Marneuli, with its predominantly Azeri population.

Linguistic nationalization has a continuing impact on ethnic relations. Although a significantly smaller percentage of ethnic Georgians than of Armenians in Armenia or Azeris in Azerbaijan spoke Russian during the Soviet period, Russian remained the language of the state bureaucracy and of a significant portion of higher education. Zviad Gamsakhurdia, through his nationalist rhetoric about the role of "guests" (ethnic minorities) in Georgia, not only unsettled these minorities but also created problems for the Russian-speaking population, including Russians and other Slavs, non-Sephardic Jews, Armenians, and Georgians from ethnically mixed families or who had been educated in Russian schools. The prejudice against Russioan speakers had diminished, although Russian speakers reported problems finding jobs.

During this study the prevailing attitude was one of exhaustion with conflict. People had been driven from their homes or left to live in damaged structures. Families had been destroyed through the death or crippling of breadwinners. Communities of IDPs were seen as competing for scarce resources or contributing to increasing crime. Although most respondents specifically exonerated their neighbors, many respondents had experienced exclusion and discrimination, which they warned could increase tensions locally.

In many rural communities, particular subethnic groups maintained relationships of solidarity. In Kazbegi the Mokhevi and the Khevsuri are distinct groups who make up whole villages, often derived from a single extended family whose members maintain a close network of mutual support. One respondent noted that, when she moved back to her relatives' village, her distant relations started her family out with two piglets and some poultry and provided them regularly with dairy products. In fact, people tended to apply only to town or regional officials who were relatives, which indicates the extent to which political and kinship relations are intertwined, even merged, in small communities.

Borders. With the creation of an independent Georgian state, international borders divided ethnic communities that straddled both sides. In this respect Georgia's ethnic diversity could prove a strength, as Azeris and Armenians, for example, facilitated the exchange of goods and services through their cross-border ties with Azerbaijan and Armenia, respectively, as well as with kin in Russia. By the same token, the emigration of Georgian Jews to Israel has created cultural and commercial links between Israel and Georgia.

Because of Georgia's mountainous topography and deep snows, landslides and avalanches close some roads at least five months of the year, forcing residents of highland border areas such as Kazbegi to look to Russia (in particular, North Ossetia) as the closest place to market their goods. It was cheaper to go from the town of Kazbegi to Vladikavkaz in Russia than to Tbilisi. People have moved to Kazbegi from Tbilisi, if they have some connections and the possibility of raising some cattle, or from the North Caucasus, fleeing instability and war.

In southern Georgia, the borders with Azerbaijan and Armenia were not yet clearly defined. Ties of kinship and ethnicity and practical issues such as language have long influenced where families send their children for higher education or for marriage. This will increase with the inevitable linguistic nationalization: local populations who do not master Georgian will leave for regions where they fit in linguistically. At the same time, as already noted, border populations enjoy an advantage for commerce.

Ethnic Georgian and Armenian relations became particularly strained during the Gamsakhurdia period. In Akhaltsikhe, the center of the Samtskhe-Javakheti region with a mixed Armenian-Georgian population, Armenians accused Georgians of pushing them out of the labor market, especially in public sector jobs in banks, post offices, and other functioning enterprises. In the predominantly Armenian district of Akhalkalaki, there were fewer openings in public sector work. Armenians felt that their exclusion was the result of prejudice, as well as the fact that most of them do not speak Georgian. (The functional language used to be Russian, and Georgian was not even required in school.) Relations were calmer at the time of this study, partly thanks to efforts by national and local government. Armenians were aware that their Georgian neighbors were also suffering economically, and that local Georgians, too, were often bypassed for important posts in favor of Georgians from the center.

The Azeri minority in Marneuli has preserved linguistic and other cultural affiliations with Azerbaijan. Many speak Azeri at home, with Russian as a second language. Many have ties of kinship, friendship, and business with the population of Azerbaijan. A large part of the population lives by agriculture, either practicing subsistence gardening or working on the remaining collective farms or on their own small plots, and actively marketing surpluses in Marneuli's four markets, elsewhere in Georgia, or in Azerbaijan. The district stood out in this study in several particulars: the greater level of fear of and alienation from local authorities (although they, too, were ethnic Azeris); the lower level of educational attainment and participation in the education system; and the markedly subordinate and vulnerable position of girls and women in many households, rendered worse by poverty and hardship.

Conflict Zones. IDPs from Abkhazia who remained in collection centers tended to form closed communities, which maintained distant, even hostile relations with local populations. Unable to establish roots because they lacked permanent housing, stable jobs, land, and essential connections to local centers of power, they felt psychologically oppressed by the suspicion and resentment of the host community. A great number expressed the strong desire to return to their homes. Others wanted to go to Russia. Perhaps most dangerous for Georgia was the insistence of some IDPs that force must be used to guarantee their return.

Local populations living near the border of Abkhazia with the Samegrelo region complained about the behavior of the CIS (that is, Russian) peacekeepers who guarded the 24-kilometer border along both banks of the Inguri River. They accused the guards of stealing their poultry, pigs, and cows, extorting money from people cutting wood, and demanding food, drink, and cigarettes. Although some incidents had been discussed in the press, and people had appealed to their mayor and to the United Nations, they had not received a response. Meanwhile the border remained porous. Georgians from Gali, which borders Samegrelo, slipped over the border to cultivate their fields, trying to avoid both militia and land mines. Georgians and Abkhazians brought food to sell at the Zugdidi markets. Others gave letters and packages to the peacekeepers, who, for a sum, would carry such items back and forth between Georgia and Abkhazia.

South Ossetia, which has suffered extensive damage from war and earthquake, presents a dismal picture when one arrives from Tbilisi. One cannot use Georgian currency in the local markets—only rubles are in circulation—and the clock is set an hour earlier than in Tbilisi, to synchronize with Moscow. Most South Ossetians had not been to Tbilisi or other parts of Georgia in many years, and they expressed great curiosity about what was going on there, as well as a fearful ambivalence about closer ties. Respondents said that both Georgians and Azerbaijanis came to the border areas and even to city markets to trade, without encountering any problems.

Many Ossetian families have remained in Georgia in Ossetian or mixed villages. In Kakhetia, during the Gamsakhurdia period when paramilitary troops were active in the region, residents of ethnically mixed Ossetian families were robbed of cattle and physically threatened. Many left for North Ossetia at that time; a few have since returned and have received land in the privatization. Most of them excused their neighbors, who they said were not involved in the violence, but nevertheless expressed numerous grievances against local officials and felt themselves the target of systematic ethnic discrimination as Ossetians.

Ossetian residents of Kitaani village, administered by the Chumlakhi village council, recalled how Chumlakhi had fired its Ossetian employees, creating great hardship for their families, and effectively forced Ossetian youths to leave Georgia for North Ossetia in search of jobs. Relations in Georgia have improved, and Ossetian families were included in the land distribution, but many said they still felt like second-class citizens. They noted that the bus route that older children used to take from their village to the school in the district center, and that teachers used to get to the primary school in Kitaani, had been abolished. The village lacked a medical station as well as telephone connections with the district center. Although other villages received at least a few hours of electricity a day, their village had received no electricity in two years. Respondents also claimed their village was the only one that had not received government or humanitarian aid.

Although Ajara had been an autonomous republic during Soviet times and, with its predominantly Muslim population and conspicuously wealthy underground elite, had always been distinct from the rest of Georgia, it had not become involved in the separatist conflicts. Ruled by Aslan Abashidze, Ajara remained aloof from politics in the rest of Georgia, following a very different economic agenda. Yet despite the stereotype of local wealth, much of the population lived in poverty no less serious than elsewhere in the country. The authorities blamed Tbilisi for electricity shortages. A local respondent said, "All of Georgia has light; only we are living in a concentration camp."

Poverty and isolation in Ajara appeared compounded by a pervasive fear among the residents. Interviewers noted that respondents were frightened "as nowhere else in Georgia" and spoke fearfully of the strong and pervasive clan links of local authorities. They spoke of numerous cases of official extortion. One respondent described how he had opened a car parts shop, duly paid his taxes, and rented premises, when an old friend of the previous mayor decided to build a large supermarket where he had his shop, and evicted him. His neighbor, however, refused to move. As a result, his booth was destroyed, and he ended up paying the equivalent of $1,200 for the damage. Many respondents hinted about cases of extortion by the authorities but said very directly they were afraid to say more about it.

Changing Gender Roles

In the traditional Georgian family, girls had equal access to education, although it often served only to secure a better marriage, and career took second place to family responsibilities. Men were expected to provide well for their families, whereas women bore responsibility for the domestic domain. Women could rely on a host of state benefits and subsidies, including free provision of medical services, maternity leave, and subsidized child care. In today's Georgia, however, men were often unable to live up to their socially mandated role as the family breadwinner. Their sense of emasculation and failure often led to a host of physical ailments and sharply increasing mortality, alcoholism, physical abuse of wives and children, and divorce and abandonment of families.

In Soviet Georgia, women had clustered in the middle or lower echelons of certain professions: in education (as teachers or lecturers rather than school directors and faculty chairs), in medicine (as nurses, pediatricians, and general practitioners rather than surgeons or head doctors), and in social services generally. Certain industries were also feminized at the level of line workers (for example, food processing, textiles, and some light manufacturing) or administration (accountants, clerks, and secretaries). Although career usually came second to family, work and the "work collective" of colleagues and friends nevertheless played important roles in women's lives, giving them an income and a respected social identity outside the family.

Although women have been harder hit by unemployment than men, their secondary position in the labor market has paradoxically made them more flexible and adaptable. Where men have been paralyzed by the fact that their connections no longer function, some women have found it easier to take risks. Although men cannot do "female work," society pardons a woman for doing "men's work" to feed her children. Women have moved into the shuttle trade, traveling abroad and making independent decisions. The breadwinner of the family was now anyone—it could even be a child—who procured work and income, and holding this role gave one commensurate authority in the family.

Yet women were vulnerable in the new private sector: pregnant women and mothers found it harder to keep and retain jobs, and women had little recourse against sexual harassment. Women often had to leave small children home alone while, as one put it, she "runs like a dog from house to house, selling some sort of clothing or product just to make 2 lari a day."

The incidence of prostitution had risen, even among girls and new mothers with nursing infants at home. Some women found it less shameful to engage in prostitution in Greece or Turkey, in connection with the shuttle trade, sometimes sending money home to their families. In Marneuli some families were said to sell women and girls as brides to buyers in Uzbekistan; in 1989–92 the going price was 3,000 to 5,000 rubles.

Many female respondents felt that poverty was worse for them than before, because they were now completely "socially undefended." They complained that they no longer felt like women, because they had no time or resources to take care of themselves. In the same way, men unable to support their families or repay debts no longer felt like men, and some disappeared and lived by themselves. Many men had been injured in the civil conflicts, and widows or disabled men now headed many of the poorest families. Women who had previously worked only in the home were forced to take over primary responsibility for supporting the entire family. Some female respondents felt that they were the first to sacrifice their possessions when their family was in need. First they sold their own jewelry, down to their wedding ring, then their clothes, and then small household items such as linens and crystal, and only afterward did the men start selling the most expensive household durables such as furniture or vehicles.

Youth and the Elderly

Children suffered from malnutrition and the breakdown of health and education services. An increasing number of poor children had stopped going to school; many worked informally with their parents, while others worked independently as traders, goods handlers, or assistants, some doing heavy manual labor at young ages. Poor teenagers and young adults, especially those who were poorly educated, lacking training in foreign languages or computer literacy, faced difficulties entering the job market. Although many young people had dropped out of school to work, many who had completed higher education were unable to find work, especially since they lacked experience.

But young people are also adaptable. They now collected money from each other to buy a modest amount of food or drinks so they could socialize. While their elders deplored their own isolation from cultural life, young people had learned how to slip into the back entrances of theaters. Village youth experienced more difficulty, and the incidence of alcoholism among the young was rising. Older people tended not to judge them too harshly, for, as they put it, young people no longer had any prospects for the future.

The elderly were among the hardest hit. Those who lived alone, whose adult children were unemployed, or who bore primary responsibility for underage grandchildren lived from one pension payment to the next. Although respondents all claimed that there had been no cases of starvation, and that neighbors often fed the indigent elderly on a regular basis, large numbers of elderly now lived by begging. Brought up with a very different set of values, the elderly found it difficult to adapt to new practices. They found it confusing to deal with the three, and sometimes four, currencies in circulation: lari, dollars, rubles, and kupons (privatization vouchers). Many were passive and ignorant of their rights; others were too old, too ill, or too disabled to pursue their entitlements.

> A middle-aged respondent in Ajara laments, "In ten years there won't be one pensioner still alive, the majority of children will be uneducated because of the introduction of paid education, there will be selection of the fittest, and the least principled in the arena will win."

Community Relations

Poverty affected patterns of sociality, solidarity, and authority. Although physical conditions were worse in the villages, people felt their neighbors were more willing to lend a helping hand with small amounts of money and exchanges of food and services. In urban communities as well, the poor relied extensively on each other. People tended to appeal first to their neighbors, who were generally aware of their circumstances, and to close relatives (especially for larger sums); then they would go to friends, colleagues, and, only as a last resort, to their boss at work, who might give them an advance in an emergency. In many communities the poor and the rich moved in separate circles.

Social Isolation. Traditionally hospitable Georgians now lived in fear of being hosts or even guests. They had nothing to serve, and they were unwilling to be guests, because it was considered shameful to come to a funeral or wedding without a gift of money. For urban residents participation in cultural events had radically diminished, and people tended to live what one Batumi respondent termed "a hermit-like existence," avoiding visits and their related (monetary) obligations.

Increasingly, it was the newly rich who were becoming more powerful in the villages, whereas the authority of teachers and doctors, once privileged and respected, was declining. People noted an increasing distance from neighbors, friends, and relatives who had become rich. Many people observed increasing suspicion and envy, even among those close to them, as they tried to ascertain who had become richer, who poorer.

Family ties had been ruptured as families found themselves living in different republics, unable to communicate easily or cheaply. Within Georgia, poverty and overcrowding created stress and conflict. Families split, with adult children moving away and virtually abandoning their parents. Poverty also changed the significance and the shape of family relationships. An unmarried respondent complained that potential husbands were now mainly interested in whether she worked and how much she earned.

State and Society. Many Georgians mourned the passing of the old paternalistic state. They still expected the government to solve the problems of unemployment by "creating workplaces." Peasants felt their only hope lay in government assistance through credits, purchases of inputs, help with marketing, and attracting foreign partners.

Impoverishment had diminished trust. In rural communities, households complained of frequent thefts of livestock and harvest. A Signaghi respondent reported that now, before the harvest, farmers took turns watching the fields. Sometimes they found themselves confronting armed thieves. They had virtually no trust in the agents of the state, least of all the police. People described themselves as living in a police state, in which police paid for their positions and freely harassed citizens. Indeed, people often preferred to contact "criminal authorities" rather than even bring their problems to the notice of police, who often extorted payments from them.

The role of connections and bribes had also changed. The preexisting system of corruption had become more flagrant and ubiquitous. Poor people were outraged by the contrast between their own lives and those of officials. People in rural communities pointed out that local officials almost invariably ended up with the best and largest plots of land and the large businesses. An Ajaran, disputing the image advertised by the local leadership of Ajara as a "peninsula of well-being and prosperity" within Georgia, described the leadership as "moneybags," who "build fashionable hotels and tennis courts for high society, consort with local and foreign businessmen, and waste the people's money."

People felt betrayed after having waited for years for government apartments or telephones, only to learn that they had to pay outrageous prices for what they had been promised. An Armenian in Javakheti who wanted to move to Armenia or elsewhere in Georgia had to pay a bribe of $500 in order to "deregister" his household so that he could obtain a *propiska* in the new home. To change a car registration cost $1,500. Employment was obtained through connections, often accompanied by a bribe. The more lucrative the job, the larger the bribe: it cost $20,000 to become a customs official, for example. Bribery "inflation" can be said to be a distorted reflection of the transition to a market economy.

One bright spot was the state of the voluntary sector, which many international and local organizations characterized as the most vibrant in the South Caucasus. The Varketili association, a grassroots community organization, emerged in a high-rise district of 70,000 people on the outskirts of Tbilisi. The district lacks electricity, running water, postal service, and garbage collection, has few telephones, and rarely receives newspapers. The association formed in 1995, when a group of local intellectuals and journalists came to the head of a local cable television station to announce their intention to block the airport road in protest. Since its registration in June 1995, the Varketili organization has organized a number of community services, ranging from bus service to garbage collection.

Conclusions

The demise of the Soviet state left the field open for different competing elites: what Georgians and others refer to as "clans" or "mafias." Ethnic conflict and tension resulted in the destruction of cities, towns, and villages in Abkhazia, South Ossetia, and other parts of Georgia, as well as mass movements of displaced persons. President Eduard Shevardnadze and his government have largely succeeded in bringing stability to Georgia, but stability has not replaced the old, paternalistic Soviet structure, which forced at least a simulation of social responsibility.

Although Georgians remain strongly loyal to kin, neighbors, friends, and their immediate community, there is little sense of social responsibility to Georgian society as a whole. Respondents interpreted "market economy" and "capitalism" to mean the pursuit of one's self-interest without any regard for the impact of one's actions on those outside one's personal network.

Although Soviet Georgian society was always status oriented, status was a matter of connections and prestige achieved through education and work. The former elite have transformed their prestige into solid wealth, unrestrained by Soviet-era prejudices against business or "speculation." Loss of incomes from jobs, government benefits, and subsidies along with reduced access to health care, education, and previously subsidized social and cultural benefits have marginalized large portions of the urban and rural population. Those without connections are increasingly falling by the wayside.

As the gap between rich and poor widens, certain groups have emerged as particularly vulnerable to impoverishment. These include people without immediate families, such as abandoned and orphaned youths, and people without extended local networks, such as IDPs and rural-to-urban migrants. People who are unfit to compete in the labor market, especially in the emerging private sector, are also vulnerable: this includes the elderly, the chronically ill and disabled, mothers who have many children and no child care options, and recent school dropouts without work experience. Ethnic minorities also have disadvantages: many do not speak Georgian, and they may lack powerful protectors in government.

For poor Georgians the most difficult aspects of poverty include physical privation (lack of food, heat, decent shelter, and safe water) and social and cultural deprivation (presentable clothing, exclusion from social and cultural life). They attribute their plight to the lack of jobs, low and late salaries, inadequate benefits, loss of savings, indebtedness, and other contingent factors. Addressing these issues will be challenging, considering the larger economic context of a struggling economy, lack of government resources, and the fact that connections will remain important in Georgian society for some time to come.

Notes

1. World Bank (1999). The qualitative study is published in volume 2 of that study.

2. Although information for this section has come from several sources, Child and Environment, a Georgian NGO, was particularly helpful, and many of the interviews that contributed to this section were carried out by one of its members.

References

Jones, Stephen. 1996. "The Political Economy of Reform: Interest Groups in Georgian Society." Report to the World Bank. Processed.

Scott, Wolf, and George Tarkhan-Mouravi. 1995. *Human Development Report: Georgia*. Tbilisi: Lyceum Publishing House.

World Bank. 1996. "Land Reform and Private Farms in Georgia: 1996 Status." EC4NR Agriculture Policy Note 6. World Bank, Natural Resources Management Division, Country Department IV, Europe and Central Asia Region, Washington, D.C. (September 30).

World Bank. 1999. *Georgia Poverty and Income Distribution*. Washington, D.C.

.

---※---

PART FOUR

UKRAINE AND
MOLDOVA

Ukraine is the largest (603,700 square kilometers) and most populous (52 million) country discussed in this volume. During the Soviet era, agriculture, mining, and military production, based on Ukraine's good climatic conditions and rich "black earth," its coal and iron resources, and its well-developed infrastructure, were central to the economy. Eastern and western Ukraine differ along historic, linguistic, and religious axes. Parts of western Ukraine were annexed from Poland during World War II. The breakup of the Soviet Union ruptured numerous economic links and forced Ukraine, a large energy consumer, to start importing petroleum and natural gas at much higher prices. By 1993, hyperinflation of 10,000 percent a year had wiped out household savings. Production slumped, as did real wages (by 64 percent between 1990 and 1993). By 1996 almost 30 percent of the population lived below the poverty line. Poverty was most serious in the industrially depressed eastern regions and lowest in the temperate south.

Moldova has a population of about 4.3 million in an area of 33,843 square kilometers. Formerly known as Bessarabia, it was ceded by Romania to the Soviet Union in 1940. Ethnically and linguistically, Moldovans identify with Romania, but Russians, Ukrainians, the Turkic-speaking Gagauz, Bulgarians, and Jews are significant minorities. The country has experienced separatist aspirations among some minorities since independence. Problems with the Gagauz were resolved by the formation of an autonomous region in the southern part of the country; the conflict with the heavily industrialized, Russian-populated region of Transnistria continues. The Moldovan economy depends heavily on fruit, vegetable, wine, and tobacco production. It lost its most important market with the breakup of the Soviet Union, which also reduced access to subsidized petroleum, coal, and natural gas from Russia. Production sharply declined, and the country suffered one of the steepest drops in living standards among the countries of the former Soviet Union. About one-third of the population was considered poor in 1997, and this proportion has increased since this study was completed, making Moldova the poorest country in Europe today. The newly poor are largely rural and include the traditionally vulnerable as well as many who formerly enjoyed well-compensated professional positions.

Exchange rates

Ukraine: $1 = 186,000 karbovanets (March 1995 to October 1996)

Moldova: $1 = 4.6 lei (as of July 1997)

In Liviv, this retiree's monthly pension no longer pays for a loaf of bread.
Photo by Catherine Wanner

※

CHAPTER 9

"Children Have Become a Luxury": Everyday Dilemmas of Poverty in Ukraine

Catherine Wanner and Nora Dudwick

Ukraine is a large, highly industrialized country. Over half of its 50 million citizens live in urban areas. Before the disintegration of the Soviet Union, Ukraine's economy was largely based on heavy industry, machine building, weapons manufacturing, coal production, and metal-working; agricultural production was also quite strong. Since the late 1980s a breakdown of production, trade relations, and the delivery of basic social services has contributed to a severe decline in living standards. Many enterprises have closed, causing widespread unemployment. Wages have fallen and hyperinflation has eroded savings. An important factor that has allowed the Ukrainian population to cope with the resulting poverty is the strong networks of reciprocity that link relatives, close neighbors, friends, and colleagues. For urban families with relatives in the countryside, such networks ensure greater access to food. For people living in rural areas, friends or relatives in the cities can mean greater access to other goods and services.

The rapidly increasing poverty of the Ukrainian population is a recent phenomenon whose dimensions and implications are not yet fully known. The population's attitudes, expectations, and desires concerning poverty are equally unknown. To explore this issue, the researchers began with a simple working definition of poverty as the inability to provide for basic needs, such as adequate nutrition, minimal shelter, and access to basic health services.

Research Sites and Methods

Five sites were selected that exemplified the diversity of problems Ukrainians now face. Fifty interviews were conducted in the major metropolitan center in each region, and 50 in outlying rural areas. In Crimea most interviews were conducted in villages and small towns, to reflect Crimean Tatar resettlement patterns. The five sites were the following:

- *Kyiv*, Ukraine's largest city, has a population of 2.6 million and is the country's administrative, commercial, and cultural capital. Kyiv is located just 70 miles south of the Chernobyl nuclear plant in north central Ukraine.

- *Kharkiv*, the capital from 1919 to 1934, is the second-largest city in Ukraine, with a population of 1.6 million. Located in the upper Donets valley in the eastern part of the country, it remains an extremely important industrial and intellectual center. Its economy is linked to the iron mines of Kryvy Rih and to the coal mines of the Donets Basin. It borders on the Russian Federation.

- *The Donbas* comprises the city of Donetsk, with a population of 1.1 million, and its surrounding areas southeast of Kharkiv. This region contains one of the densest concentrations of heavy industry in the world. The economy is centered on coal, but heavy machinery, chemical and power plants, and iron and steel plants are also located in the Donbas. Inefficient coal mines, factories, and other state-run enterprises face the prospect of imminent closure.

- *The Crimean peninsula*, with its 2.3 million people, has enormous significance for Ukrainians, Russians, and Crimean Tatars. Multiple claims to this coveted peninsula have created a tense political situation. One of the focuses of this study was on poverty as experienced by the Crimean Tatars, an indigenous people who have recently resettled there.

- *Ivano-Frankivsk* is a smaller city of 215,000 people, located in a predominantly rural, Ukrainian-speaking region in western Ukraine. Ivano-Frankivsk was part of the Austro-Hungarian Empire before it was incorporated into Poland and eventually annexed to Soviet Ukraine in 1939. The region boasts some of the most fertile agricultural lands in Ukraine. Woodworking and furniture making are also prominent in this region.

This study was carried out between October 1995 and March 1996 by the authors together with social scientists from the Kyiv International Institute of Sociology, Kharkiv State University, and the Institute of Industrial Economics in Donetsk. Working in regionally based teams, the researchers conducted semistructured interviews with individuals from 500 poor households. This qualitative study aimed to complement the quantitative findings of Ukraina-95 (a household survey by the Ukrainian government of income and expenditure) and a labor sector study, and to contribute to the World Bank's Ukraine Poverty Assessment (World Bank 1996). Interviews were conducted in Ukrainian, Russian, and, occasionally, Tatar.

Dimensions of Poverty

Most interviewees identified Soviet President Mikhail Gorbachev's policy of *perestroika*, implemented in 1986, as the beginning of a general decline in their standard of living. The majority described their households as poor (*bednyi*) as opposed to destitute (*nishchii*). The destitute cited hunger as the worst aspect of their lives. After purchasing bread, these households had barely any money left. Many existed on bread, milk, and tea. Household and utility charges, medicine, clothing, and other necessities were entirely unaffordable. The destitute tended to be pensioners and young single people without a social support network.

Ukrainian society continues to embrace traditional gender roles. It is widely assumed that the man should be the provider and breadwinner of the family. Acknowledging poverty means admitting failure in this responsibility, and this was extremely difficult for many of the men interviewed. Husbands were frequently offended and embarrassed by their wives' admissions of dissatisfaction with the material conditions of their lives.

Rural residents defined poverty in terms of acute hunger, given that most people were already accustomed to longstanding rural shortages of medical, transportation, and educational services as well as persistent deficits of all kinds of consumer goods. Many rural families had very little cash, barely enough for bread. Those with a surplus of produce, meat, and dairy products were able to barter them for other goods and services, however.

Urban residents looked beyond food to consider housing, medical and educational services, and access to cultural events in characterizing poverty. Access to a garden plot and housing determined whether an impoverished urban family would be poor or destitute. Even if a family had access to a plot, if they could not store what they had grown, the necessary expense of purchasing food severely strained the family's budget. For urban households, monthly housing charges for heat, electricity, and gas constituted the second-largest expense after food.

Access to housing had become a critical resource. More rural residents were moving to the cities to find employment but faced a severe housing shortage, which thwarted their prospects for advancement. Pensioners in particular had begun to supplement their meager pensions by renting out rooms or selling their apartments to people seeking job opportunities in the cities.

One woman, in dire need of a Kyiv *propiska* (residency permit) to find work, bought a single room in a private house for $3,000. The owners sectioned off a room that has no running water, no toilet, and no gas and cannot be used as a primary residence.

The greatest discrepancies in living standards stemmed from the fact that some services and goods available in cities were absent in rural areas. Subsistence farming generally allowed rural households to consume more food, but transportation, health care, and educational opportunities in rural areas were minimal, and basic household conveniences, such as running water, indoor toilets, and telephones, were far less widespread.

Who Are the Poor?

Poverty defies easy categorization. This study found people who had lost their jobs or had not received a salary in months, yet had managed to find "unofficial" sources of income to support their families. Connections, social support networks, individual initiative, and talent helped them escape poverty. In such tumultuous economic times, even the nonpoor were subject to cycles of poverty and prosperity as inflation, irregular payment of salaries, and high taxes threatened self-sufficiency.

People who relied exclusively on government assistance because they were unable to work, such as children, elderly pensioners, the disabled, and the chronically ill, were the most likely to suffer poverty and to see their poverty continue and even deepen. Other respondents who experienced impoverishment due to a temporary inability to work, such as students, single mothers, and mothers with many children, could hope to see their standard of living improve over time.

Many people had been laid off or put on unpaid leave or received small or irregular salaries. Many collective farm workers, factory workers (particularly in the industrial east), engineers, and educators fell into this category. They remained unemployed or underemployed, although willing and able to work.

Migrants, including returning Crimean Tatars, refugees from the Caucasus and the Chernobyl-affected areas, those on the run from the mafia, and bankrupt businesspeople, were likely to suffer poverty. Their poverty was temporary, brought on by unforeseen hardship and aggravated by corrupt and ineffective government policies.

Alcoholics were another group with a high incidence of poverty. Vodka has enormous symbolic and practical importance in the culture and everyday lives of Ukrainians. In rural areas, homebrew (*samogon*) is so readily accepted as payment in a multitude of transactions that it is referred to as a "freely convertible currency." Nearly every family makes its own wine and spirits, and shortages of electricity leave many in the dark with nothing to do after sunset. Alcoholism posed a terrible drain on household resources for many respondents. The negative effects on health and family cohesion were well illustrated across Ukraine, as food prices soared but alcohol remained affordable.

Olga Vadimovna, 31, has two sons, 11 and 9. Her ex-husband is an alcoholic and provides no child support. When her older son was 6, she sent him to an *internat* (a government-run boarding school) because she could not afford to raise him. The younger son tells the interviewer, "I, too, want to go to the *internat*. There they eat four times a day. I want so much to eat. My mother has started to drink a lot lately. She washes or repairs things for people, gets some money, and drinks. There's not enough money for food."

The poorest members of Ukrainian society rarely had steady employment; instead they relied on government assistance and a host of informal mechanisms to survive. Food and housing costs were reported as the most significant expenses, but medical emergencies or chronic medical problems could force families into indebtedness and poverty.

Coping Strategies

Since the end of the Soviet system, Ukrainians have adopted a variety of informal strategies to put food on the table and secure adequate housing. Although the specifics differed between rural and urban areas, the strategies reported by respondents were in essence of two kinds: strategies to generate cash and goods, and strategies to reduce expenses.

Government Assistance

Government assistance in the form of pensions, subsidies, privileges, and discounts was critical for making ends meet among the poor interviewed for this study. Barring desperate need, however, the poor often found it was not worth applying for such assistance because of the paltry sums paid and because the application process was costly, time consuming, degrading, and humiliating. Mothers and pensioners were often the least able to stand in long lines, yet were usually the ones most in need of assistance.

Housing Subsidies. The government had recaptured some of the costs of providing basic services by increasing the housing and utilities charges (*kvart-plat*) due every month for rent, heating, electricity, gas, water, and garbage collection. Along with the new charges, a new subsidy had been created for the neediest households, but the applicant was disqualified unless previous charges are completely paid up. With each passing month and rate hike, more people faced housing debt.

Housing charges were assessed according to the number of inhabitants and the area occupied. If a household member leaves a residence, charges were still assessed unless they change their registration. Pensioners reported that they were commonly denied a subsidy if they had children. Often adult children were still registered at their parents' home but were not actually living there.

Nina Mikhailovna was denied a housing subsidy because of her joint income with her son. Her housing charges exceed her pension, and she resents depending on her son's meager salary after working 35 years and raising two sons as a single mother. "I can't ask my son to give me money for medicine and leave him hungry. I paid the government taxes throughout the 35 years that I worked! If the Soviet Union still existed, we wouldn't be living like this."

Other pensioners did not have the luxury of appealing to their children for financial support or help in applying for a subsidy.

Nina Ivanivna, a 65-year-old pensioner in Ivano-Frankivsk, relies on her pension as her sole source of income. Her son, consumed by his own difficulties, is unable to help her. When she applied for the housing subsidy, it took over a month to gather the necessary documents from the various government offices. The lines stretched to 300 people at the larger stations, with some people waiting outside overnight in temperatures well below freezing. Even with the subsidy, she pays more in housing charges than the $6 a month she has left for food—not even enough for bread. She has found a part-time job as a cleaning woman in a cafeteria for $4.25 a month, which helps, but she is considering another solution to her problems: suicide.

Pensions. Pensions were barely enough to supply one person with bread and milk every day. Housing and utility charges, especially in urban areas, consumed at least half if not all of the pension. All retired persons received pensions that were more or less equal, regardless of their profession or where or how long they had worked. Although pensions were generally paid regularly and without delay, the sums were so small that pensioners who did not receive substantial financial assistance from their children or other relatives were very likely to be impoverished.

Child Care Subsidies. Eleven different types of subsidy existed, leading to confusion. Some subsidies aimed specifically at families with three or more children. Many respondents felt entitled to criticize the mothers of large families. Some recommended refusing them assistance on the grounds that the parents were probably alcoholics and could not be trusted to use the assistance for their children. Others even recommended forced sterilization.

Natasha, a 31-year-old single mother of four, lives with her children in a dormitory room. When she became pregnant with her fourth child, she wanted to have an abortion. But with an abortion costing $30, she realized this would leave her with no money to feed the other three. All four children have the same father, who has promised for years to marry Natasha but never has. He provides no assistance.

With little support from her parents, who live in a faraway village, or from her neighbors or government assistance programs, Natasha relies most heavily on her best friend, Ira, and her son's school. Ira has no children of her own and readily helps Natasha financially and logistically with every aspect of raising her children. One month after Natasha's fourth child was born, her two-year-old fell ill with pneumonia. Ira was able to get the child admitted to a hospital and to recruit a doctor to treat her. Ira took full responsibility for the child, staying with her in the hospital and paying for all her medical needs.

The school provides significant assistance. In 1995 the school gave 20 kilograms of potatoes, 4 of onions, 4 of beets, and even some chocolate for New Year's. Her son receives free meals at school. Natasha hopes to return to work as soon as she is able to register her three youngest children for free child care.

Other Subsidies and "Privileges." Discounts for veterans of World War II, "veterans of labor," and pensioners are taken for granted. Government assistance on this level often provided some tangible relief to interviewees. All pensioners are entitled to unlimited free public transportation. Urban pensioners in reasonable health sometimes capitalized on this benefit by traveling to rural markets in the morning, returning to the city in the afternoon, and selling the food products they had just bought. Because of the free transportation and the willingness of urban residents to pay higher prices for food, these pensioners could frequently turn a quick profit. Rural pensioners with access to public transportation and some capital could also buy goods in the city to sell in rural areas, or bring surplus food products to sell in urban areas. The extensive travel by pensioners loaded down with sacks of goods significantly strained already-overcrowded transportation networks.

Children were regularly given free vaccinations and free periodic checkups through schools and local clinics.

Workers were sometimes given land to farm and one-time assistance to cover the cost of the birth of a child or a funeral, but most working respondents no longer counted on receiving salaries regularly, let alone any form of assistance from their employer.

Lack of Information. Nearly all respondents reported difficulties in finding out what forms of government assistance were available, who was eligible, and how to apply. Some respondents were so unfamiliar with government programs that they could not explain which subsidy they were receiving or why they received the amount they did. New programs, such as the housing subsidy, were announced primarily through television and newspaper ads. Yet virtually all of the respondents to this study had stopped subscribing to newspapers, and, to reduce electricity bills, many restricted the hours the television was on. As televisions broke down, they were no longer repaired. The serious information vacuum regarding government assistance programs is therefore likely to become worse among the poor.

Other Generative Strategies

Subsistence Farming. Subsistence farming was the single most important and widely practiced survival strategy among respondents. It was regarded as the only reliable way of obtaining food. Respondents cultivated plots to feed themselves over the summer and to supply fruits and vegetables to be preserved for the winter. Virtually all rural respondents farmed or raised livestock, chicken, or rabbits for personal consumption. The overwhelming majority of urban respondents either had a plot to farm or benefited from a plot that their relatives, usually a parent, farmed. Single mothers, mothers of large families, and students reported receiving packages of food from relatives in the countryside. Many urban respondents traveled to rural areas on weekends and during the prime growing and harvesting months to work their own land or to help relatives farm. Farming was the most difficult in Crimea, where water shortages frequently resulted in small harvests.

In rural areas the only reliable way to earn money was by selling produce and meat. The collective farms paid very low salaries, often with several months' delay, forcing their workers to supplement their incomes. After school or during the summer months, children worked on collective farms to generate additional income for the household. Adults followed the combines as they traveled the fields, collecting the vegetables that remained and bringing them home for the family's consumption.

Theft. With so few employment opportunities, some respondents had turned to street crime and theft. Most reported feeling a keen threat to their person and property and avoided going out after dark, preferring instead to pass up invitations or to sleep over at their host's apartment rather than walk poorly lit streets. During the day many opted to walk or take a taxi to avoid overcrowded public transportation and pickpockets. In urban areas there was a pervasive fear that one's apartment could be robbed at any time. Except in Crimea, however, not many respondents reported being victims of a crime. Rural respondents reported that their storage bins had been raided and livestock stolen. One person reported that his relative's seedlings had been stolen out of the ground hours after they had been planted. Several urban respondents noted that their summer houses had been robbed of food stocks. This rampant village crime shattered community cohesion.

Housing. Many elderly pensioners rented out rooms. Others opted to sell their apartment and buy a smaller one, usually located further from the center of town or with less convenient access to public transportation. Many elderly, however, refused to sell their apartments, feeling a moral obligation to leave them to their children or grandchildren, given the tight housing market. No respondents were able to start any kind of steady small business from home. Even offering child care services was not feasible when five or six people already lived in a single room.

Borrowing and Sharing. Family, neighbors, and friends are an important resource throughout Ukraine. Apart from some respondents in Ivano-

Frankivsk, however, almost no one reported receiving aid from relatives or friends abroad. When families emigrated, usually the entire multigenerational family would go, leaving only distant relatives behind. Dysfunctional consumer banking and postal services discouraged friends and relatives from sending money or gifts back to Ukraine.

The majority of Crimean Tatar respondents had large families and kinship networks and made a concerted effort to settle near each other.

Nusrat, Imine, her mother, and their four children arrived in Crimea from Central Asia with virtually no money and no immediate prospects of employment. However, they had been preceded by family members and relatives on both sides, who have been of enormous assistance since their arrival. In the five months that they have been in Crimea, Imine's uncle, who lives in the district center, has already traveled five times to their home to bring them food and goods. During the summer he gave them 20 chickens and animal feed, and he frequently brings them meat, milk, and cooking oil. Imine's brother has lived in this village for four years and works as a collective farm driver. He often brings them animal feed. He is considering going to Russia to try to find work there, and if he goes, he will take Imine's oldest son with him. Imine also has second and third cousins in the village, who help the family with gifts of food. Nusrat's sister, who lives in the same village, gave the family an oven. "Thanks to her, we can both warm the house and prepare food," Imine says.

The overwhelming majority of respondents regularly borrowed money from friends, relatives, or neighbors. Borrowing was a common practice, with little stigma attached to it. Most attempted to repay their debts as quickly as possible to avoid marring a relationship over money. Respondents reported vast informal exchanges of children's clothing, even between people living in different cities. Most large families outfitted their children entirely with hand-me-downs. When a household grew more vegetables or fruit than it could safely store, friends and neighbors benefited from their surplus. These periodic gifts and loans were a valued form of support.

Humanitarian Aid. Except in Crimea and the areas around Chernobyl, few respondents had received any humanitarian aid, and those who had received it expressed disappointment. At best, humanitarian aid came in the form of children's clothes, or packages of margarine or butter or condensed milk. Nearly all respondents had seen food products intended as humanitarian aid for sale in stores and kiosks. Many Crimean Tatar respondents had received humanitarian assistance, mainly from Turkey, from Tatars in Bulgaria, and from Germany. In general, the assistance was distributed by the Mejlis, the political organization representing the Crimean Tatars. Many respondents, however, suspected the Mejlis of distributing the bulk of the aid to their relatives and friends.

Reducing Expenses

Virtually all respondents had radically changed the way they ate and had eliminated purchases of clothing, medicine, household items, and recreational expenses. Since most income was spent on food and utilities, it was in these spheres that the greatest efforts were made to reduce expenses.

Diet. In spite of a culture that prides itself on hospitality and "setting a beautiful table" for guests, most respondents had sharply scaled back their eating habits and rarely invited guests over because they could not receive them in an appropriate manner. Poor families had ceased purchasing meat and fish altogether. In urban areas, potatoes and bread had become staples, supplemented by homegrown vegetables, usually consumed as soup. Families with children and pensioners tried to buy milk at least once a week. Other dairy products were usually unaffordable.

Utilities. For urban dwellers, finding a means to pay housing charges to retain electricity and telephone services was a primary concern. In rural areas, paying for electricity and heat over the long winter months was a problem for all respondents. The elderly in urban areas reported disconnecting televisions, radios, and refrigerators to reduce electric bills. These cutbacks came in addition to the frequent, government-ordered electricity shutdowns aimed at conserving fuel. Local housing authorities turned off the electricity with no advance warning. In several regions of eastern Ukraine such as Donetsk, it was forbidden to use electricity in public or office buildings after 5 p.m. Indeed, several interviewers for this study, especially in Kharkiv, had to type their reports by candlelight.

Heat was also in short supply. Heating levels were set by the state. Especially in eastern Ukrainian cities, respondents and interviewers kept their hats and coats on indoors because it was so cold. In rural areas, where most people live in single-family dwellings, the high cost of coal and gas heat had inspired very sparse consumption in an effort to save money. In coal-rich Donetsk oblast, salaries were sometimes paid in coal, which people then bartered for food and other goods.

Transportation. Increased cost and the general deterioration of the transportation system had led to fewer trains and buses, longer waits, and overcrowding. Transportation costs seriously encroached on salaries and were a factor that people balanced against potential salaries in evaluating whether a job was worth taking. Within cities, subway systems continued to provide good service. In Kyiv many respondents reported riding buses and trams regularly without buying a ticket. They felt entitled to do so because the service was poor (one rarely got a seat) and because tickets were not sold on the buses and were rarely collected. In other cities, such as Donetsk, conductors regularly patrolled the buses and trams checking for tickets. Few would risk a fine, and this had curtailed ridership.

Medicine. An illness in the family could devastate a household budget. Hospital costs and commercially manufactured medicines were well beyond the budgets of respondents. Most relied on herbs and other home remedies to cure minor illnesses such as the flu. Homeopathic folk remedies were the new centerpiece of self-administered medical care for the poor. Others simply ignored pain until a true medical emergency forced them to seek treatment or hospitalization.

Conclusions

Food and utility costs were the most significant expenses for impoverished Ukrainians. Respondents to this survey survived on a mixture of government assistance, subsistence farming, and gifts of food, money, and clothes from friends, relatives, and neighbors. Households without a strong social support network experienced more acute and prolonged poverty. They were forced to cut back on expenses by further reducing their diet or by selling their apartment, which deepened the risk that their children would continue to experience poverty as adults.

Transformations in the Labor Market

Krutit'sia (Russian for "to spin oneself") refers to the practice of incessant buying and selling, or hustling for a living, and evokes the tremendous effort needed to work at more than one job. This expression has practically supplanted the traditional verb for "to work." Yet many Ukrainians found it impossible to participate in the commerce that had invaded their streets because they lacked capital and connections. For some, selling something at a profit was considered "speculation" and a shameful form of employment.

The majority of respondents were poor because they were unemployed or working in low-paying state sector jobs. Very few were self-employed or employed at private firms, where incomes exceeded the poverty level. Some had been working, but their attempts were either unsuccessful or only temporarily raised the household's standard of living before they fell back into poverty.

Commerce

When a factory or mine closed or began to delay salaries, the option of selling goods informally on the street often appeared as the only real alternative to unemployment and poverty. Although very few respondents were involved in trade as a form of full-time employment, petty commerce was the main source of income for a significant part of the Ukrainian population. Hordes of traders gathered around every public transportation depot and in the flea markets that have sprung up in cities and towns across Ukraine, offering a plethora of goods.

The necessary prerequisites for this type of commerce included startup capital to buy goods, access to cheap goods, a means or a place to sell the goods, and payments to a gang or criminal organization for "protection" and the right to sell. The ability and willingness to sell informally on the street were key factors that determined who would fall into poverty and whether or not that poverty would be temporary. The difficulties of getting started and the social stigma attached to trading prevented many respondents from participating. Fear of indebtedness discouraged many. Given the unpredictability of inflation and exchange rates, they could not be certain that the reasonable sum they borrowed today would not be an astronomical debt tomorrow. Fear of entanglements with organized crime was also a pervasive consideration that gave many pause before embarking on a new career as a petty trader.

Brokers and Dealmakers. Ukraine's shared borders with countries whose economies are more robust provided employment for middlemen, brokers, and dealers. Quick trips abroad to buy goods to be sold on the streets of Ukraine had become a common activity, clogging airports around the country. The usual destinations were Turkey, China, the United Arab Emirates, and Poland. Although many Ukrainians managed to earn an adequate living by participating in some part of the process of informally importing goods (often illegally, without paying duties), respondents to this survey had not succeeded. Because they lacked capital, they went into debt. They were usually unable to repay those debts if they were caught at the border and forced to pay duty or bribes. Often they sold to a broker to avoid contact with criminal organizations and the associated payments, which quickly ate up profits. If one was unable to repay one's debts and any interest, the business would collapse. In many other instances, respondents imported inexpensive goods, such as candy and cigarettes, in such small quantities that they realized only small profits.

Mykola Petrovich's monthly salary of 7 million karbovanets as a freight loader is not even enough to feed his wife and three young children. To supplement his income, he travels from his home in a small village near Ivano-Frankivsk to Moldova, where he buys cigarettes to sell to a middleman in Ukraine. Usually an older retired woman sells the cigarettes on the street. Although Mykola Petrovich could sell the cigarettes directly for a higher profit, he prefers to keep his distance from the street thugs. The closer one is to the actual point of sale, the more likely the trader will have to pay for mafia or gang protection in order to sell.

Not everyone traveled abroad to find cheaper goods. Some bought goods locally.

Maria Petrivna, a 41-year-old woman in Ivano-Frankivsk, shares a one-room apartment with her husband, son, daughter, mother, and grandmother. The family became impoverished when her husband was hit by a drunk driver, lost his job, received no disability payments, and has since been unable to find work. It is impossible to feed six people on the family's monthly income of 11 million karbovanets, made up of her salary of 5 million karbovanets and two pensions.

To supplement the family's income, Maria buys goods wholesale through a friend with connections at a local factory and resells them to a middleman. She prefers to sell quickly, minimizing contact with the mafia and the likelihood that the goods will be stolen. From this she earns a negligible sum, not enough to keep her husband from having to work as a guest worker, another form of post-Soviet labor. The monumental task of getting a passport and a visa to enter another country, plus travel costs, is assumed by a broker, who breaks through the morass of bureaucracy to expedite the process. Of course, the broker demands prompt and ample repayment of his investment.

> Maria was disappointed when her husband returned from two and a half months of working in the fields in Greece. By the time he had paid the bribe to get the job and paid the broker for the trip, he was left with $200, hardly enough to feed their family even for two months.

Starting a Business. Attempts to start a business confronted numerous formidable obstacles: a shortage of startup capital and limited sources of borrowing; difficulty finding and paying for premises; high taxes; difficulty in knowing and anticipating changes in tax and property law; threats of extortion and robbery from criminal organizations; and erratic delivery of supplies. At any time, any one of these factors could force a new business into bankruptcy.

In these circumstances one needed powerful motivation and solid financial support to start a business. With no consumer banking sector to speak of, the support had to come from friends or relatives. Almost none of the respondents had networks that included individuals with sufficient income to assist them. Starting a new business was therefore not a realistic solution to their poverty. Fewer than 10 respondents out of 500 had tried to start a new business more substantial than trading on the street.

> Alla used to work in a day care center for children that was supported by a factory in Donetsk. Eventually the factory closed. Her neighbors, refugees from Abkhazia, asked her to prepare their daughter to enter school. She found the experience so rewarding that she has decided to open a day care center in her home, featuring specialized classes for three to five preschoolers. Ella anticipates that she can earn a satisfactory income and regain a rewarding career. The business will be unofficial to avoid tax inspectors, tax and legal regulations, and other outside interference.

Collective Farms and the Rural Labor Market

With few alternative sources of employment available in isolated rural areas without access to public transportation, workers pillaged collective farms to eke out a living, stripping them bare. Harvests were routinely plundered for personal consumption, supplies were unceremoniously taken for private use, and worker commitment was minimal, in part because salaries were a mere 2 million to 3 million karbovanets a month.

Seinor lives in a Crimean village known for its apple orchards. As at many other collective farms, the administration has hired a guard to protect the fruit harvest from increasing theft. Seinor describes how, during the summer of 1995, a fellow villager entered the orchard to steal apples. When the guard seized him, the villager pulled a grenade from his pocket and threatened to blow them both up if the guard did not let him gather the apples. "People have fallen into despair because they don't see the end of this crisis situation," Seinor says.

The rural labor market was heavily dependent on the state sector. Besides collective farms, respondents to this survey were employed in hospitals, at schools, and by the railroads. There were very few employment opportunities beyond farming, and precious few in the private sector. The possibilities for training or retraining for other skills were virtually nonexistent. A deteriorating infrastructure failed to encourage entrepreneurship. The transportation system was skeletal. Poor housing, medical, educational, and recreational facilities prompted many of the brightest and most ambitious—and most of the young—to head for the cities, making recruitment of trained personnel in rural areas a challenge.

Thieving from the State

Thefts from the workplace have increased. No longer afraid of being caught and reprimanded, many felt emboldened to steal as a form of passive resistance or active sabotage against the state. A pensioner from a village 40 kilometers from Donetsk said, "The government has ripped us off, so why shouldn't people steal a bit on the sly? We don't steal but we don't judge others who do. You have to survive!" Pinching materials from the state was widely practiced without shame throughout Ukraine.

Petia, a young man from a village south of Kyiv, stays at his job as an electrician on a construction brigade even though he is erratically paid only 6 million karbovanets a month, with no less than a two-month delay. He is able to supplement his salary by taking electrical parts and supplies from the brigade and selling them at the bazaar. His friend who works at a factory in Kyiv does the same and gives the goods to Petia to sell. For a while this was his family's only source of income.

New Trends in the Labor Market

A great number of people continued to report to work every day even though they had not received a salary in months. Many preferred to maintain a foothold with their current employer while they tried to earn money on the side. There were several reasons to stay in a job without pay. One was that new employment did not guarantee steady employment: should the new enterprise have difficulties, the last one hired was likely to be the first fired.

Another reason was that social networks were often centered around a work "collective" made up of trusted confidants, friends, and colleagues. The bonds of reciprocity developed over years of working together were not easily replicated in a new work environment. Employee benefits, such as a one-time cash advance for a birth or death in the family, allocations of garden plots, and the promise of privatization certificates, were incentives to accept unpaid leave rather than quit when salaries were not paid. Unless one's position had been officially terminated, one could not apply for unemployment benefits or free training.

Connections. Connections were essential in the search for a new job. The few jobs that paid a living wage were most often given to kin and close friends, to keep social networks strong. Trust between employer and employee was critical given the infamous system of "double accounting" to avoid taxes. In a tight job market, prior experience and a home telephone often became additional requirements for job candidates. This was not an issue in rural areas where almost no one had a telephone.

Discrimination. Three forms of discrimination in the current labor market discouraged people from looking for new employment or changing jobs: discrimination on the basis of age, sex, and disabilities. Job candidates were candidly told that, if they were over 40, they need not apply. Sometimes the threshold was as low as 35. It was assumed that older people would be slower to adapt to the new workplace. Older women suffered from age discrimination, but younger women suffered from sex discrimination. Employers frequently would not consider hiring a woman in her early twenties, because they feared that she would soon have a child and go on maternity leave for up to three years. If she already had a child, it was assumed that she would often be absent from work when the child became ill. Young women who did get hired often complained of sexual harassment. Male employers felt licensed to make demands on their female employees, because they knew the women's jobs were vital to their survival.

Ukraine has three levels of disability classification. The first represents severe disability, such as mental retardation or cerebral palsy, which precludes employment. The second and third levels are often acquired with age, such as deteriorating eyesight, or as the result of an accident. Because of entrenched biases, people with even slight disabilities faced very difficult prospects of securing employment without close family connections.

Employment Services

A large number of respondents had tried to register at Employment Services. Although hardly a charitable word was offered about these services, some respondents had received free training, courses in computer programming and accounting, and information about housing and child care subsidies. Some were able to collect unemployment subsidies. Employment Services offered only a very few, low-paying, manual labor jobs; the applicant had to pay a bribe to get one of the better jobs. Employment Services registered people who could provide documentation that they had been dismissed; poverty and bankruptcy were insufficient grounds. The application process was excessively complicated, and government workers treated applicants in a rude, degrading manner.

Vika, a construction engineer with 10 years work experience, obtained a list of job openings from Employment Services. She went to the potential employers to present her credentials, only to be told either that they were not hiring or that they had a job that could only be filled by a man. Not one of the leads turned out to be a real job. She gave up hope when she understood that she would have to pay a bribe to get the job and give a "present" as a sign of her gratitude after she landed the job. As she had no money for the first bribe, she recognized that she had no chance of finding anything other than low-paying manual labor.

Bika did receive a free computer course and unemployment payments of 700,000 karbovanets a month for six months. These payments stopped two months ago. As she cannot afford newspapers, a friend gives them to her, and she continues to comb the job advertisements. The main obstacles to her getting a job, she feels, are the collapse of the job market for engineers, lack of information about job opportunities, her own lack of computer experience, and her age. At 32, she has often been told that the employer is seeking "a young girl" and that she is too old for the job.

The charge was often made that Employment Services was something of a racket: the application process was made complicated to pressure those who wanted the best jobs to pay bribes. Young people complained that it was very hard to anticipate what professions or jobs to train for in a changing economy and which spheres of employment were the most promising over the long term.

Nikolai Andreevich, 38, was responsible for maintaining machinery at a factory in Kharkiv oblast. Seventy percent of the factory's orders were from Russia, and some of the raw materials were supplied by Russian factories. Without the numerous economic and trade links that characterized the Soviet form of production, the number of orders dropped sharply, and the factory began to pay salaries irregularly. As Nikolai Andreevich has a wife and two children to support, he decided to leave his job. But with manufacturing on the decline throughout Ukraine, his specialization and skills are "unnecessary."

Although his wife's job as a janitor at a day care center seems relatively stable, her $22-a-month salary is not enough for a family of four. Nikolai Andreevich began traveling to other cities in Ukraine, buying local goods and bringing them back to Kharkiv oblast to sell. Then he moved on to selling goods that someone else had imported from Turkey.

Selling in the market presents certain risks. There are inevitable confrontations with gangs or criminal organizations that control the market. Nikolai Andreevich explains, "You're standing somewhere and they come up to you and say, 'Bust outta here. No place for you.' I split, find myself another corner, and try to sell more quickly. Sometimes they threaten you because of your prices. They say, 'We'll break your face if you lower your prices.' Sometimes I was able to sell quickly and get out. But other times I saw these guys and understood that it's better not to deal with them and then I split right away. In short, it became unpleasant and dangerous. That's why I don't trade anymore."

When Nikolai Andreevich was interviewed in November 1995, trading was a thing of the past for him. His last job was in construction and lasted five months. Thanks to a friend of a friend, he was hired to be part of a construction brigade. Without a recommendation vouching for his honesty, reliability, and sobriety, he believes he would never have been hired. The choice of workers is so vast and the possibility of theft so great that employers will not risk hiring someone unknown to them. According to Nikolai Andreevich, the brigade worked from "dawn 'til dusk," and each man earned $100 a month.

He heard about Employment Services while watching television. He went there and was surprised to learn that he qualified for an unemployment subsidy. Employment Services sent him to an oblast center of "professional orientation," where he will learn new skills and become a welder for gas and electric enterprises, an option that he greets with optimism and enthusiasm. After he becomes trained in welding, Nikolai Andreevich hopes to go to Tiumen', Siberia, to work on the gas lines there. Welders are needed and the salary is good. If he doesn't leave his family and go to Siberia to make some money to get ahead, he sees an unending circle of deprivation for his family.

Conclusions

As the state sector contracts, employment opportunities are evaporating. Those who remain employed at state-run enterprises receive small salaries, often with delays of several months. Fledgling private enterprises remain highly vulnerable to collapse in the face of organized crime, indebtedness, taxes, and the difficulty of securing office space or manufacturing premises. The new labor market excludes whole categories of workers on the basis of age, sex, and disability. It is becoming an exclusive domain that can only be entered through the recommendation or invitation of close family and friends. Respondents felt that the prospect of finding meaningful and sustaining employment was moving further and further out of reach.

The Social Implications of Poverty

For most of the individuals and families in this study, impoverishment was a consequence of the general contraction of the Ukrainian economy. These abrupt and disorienting changes had affected relationships within families and between families and friends. They were profoundly altering the old social contract, by which the state guaranteed education, health, and safe streets in exchange for the hard work and loyalty of its citizens.

Changes in Family Structure

Given the difficulties of feeding a family, many would-be parents could no longer enjoy the "luxury" of children. Although having one or two children has long been a norm for urban families, many rural families have preferred large families of three, four, or even five children. In the past, parents of large families counted on government subsidies to help them raise their children.

Rosa, 58, a Crimean Tatar who moved to Crimea from Uzbekistan in 1989, finds it terribly painful that she and her husband can no longer help their grown children get on their feet. "Now our young women don't want to have many children. In Uzbekistan, they would give birth to six children, but now they say that two are enough. My oldest son has one child and they don't want to have any more. It's difficult to raise children. One no longer has the means."

For single mothers or women in unstable relationships, even a single child could restrict the hours or nature of employment open to them or the distance they could travel to a job. Single mothers had no way to oblige or even pressure fathers to provide assistance to their children. Family planning was often inaccessible for women who could not afford aspirin, much less a visit to the gynecologist and a regular supply of contraceptives.

Anya is a 23-year-old unemployed art historian. She lives in a dormitory room in Kyiv with her boyfriend, Sasha. Her parents have cut off all relations because he is Jewish. Anya and Sasha survive on his salary of 5 million karbovanets and very occasional private sewing orders. Now Anya faces a new and serious problem. She has not been able to afford contraceptives and fears she is pregnant. She cannot get a pregnancy test at the district clinic, because she lacks a *propiska* giving her the formal right to live in the dormitory, and she cannot afford to see a private gynecologist. She cannot afford an abortion, nor can she afford to raise a child. "I'm afraid that Sasha might leave me, and with a baby I won't be able to survive by myself. And what to do in this situation is just beyond me."

Curtailing Hospitality

Many respondents confided that a painful and humiliating aspect of poverty was that they could no longer offer hospitality, or could do so only very modestly. Hospitality—in the form of a rich offering of food, snacks, and sweets—on the occasion of visits, birthdays, holidays, New Year's, and especially at weddings and funerals, served several functions. It was a means of maintaining one's social standing, of bringing people together, and of renewing or cementing connections that might prove useful in the future.

Today, however, many people found that even serving tea and cookies strained the family budget. Because visiting required a small gift or at least a modest contribution to the meal, many people avoided social contact. The very poorest not only avoided inviting others but often refused invitations, since they could not afford to bring the requisite gift, and because they felt humiliated by the thought their host might think they had come just for a hot meal.

Commercialization of Education

In the Soviet era, students had enjoyed access to free schooling, after-school clubs, and the choice of technical, professional, or academic training. By the 1980s, however, it was already a widespread practice to pay bribes to be admitted to "prestigious" departments (such as foreign languages, medicine, and jurisprudence, which led to lucrative and privileged careers), especially in the best universities.

Parents were frequently required to pay for school renovations, school trips, special lessons, textbooks, and after-school clubs. Parents complained that teachers were absent for days at a time and then overloaded the children with lessons to make up for lost time. Children were often sick because of cold, unheated classrooms; many children were at home during interviews because nurseries and schools had closed for lack of heat or because of a flu epidemic. In one school several children had fainted during class from hunger. Now the school distributed tickets so that they would receive free meals.

One teacher observed, "Rich children don't have to perform well; they know that their parents' money will guarantee their success. The children already understand that what's most important isn't knowledge, but money. When the school organized a trip to Germany, it was only the children whose parents could pay half their fare who were able to go. . . . In many cases, directors falsify grades for rich students and simply sell them diplomas."

The state university was still ostensibly free, but students had to use connections and pay substantial bribes to enroll. Some felt that the introduction of formal fees for higher education would motivate both students and professors to work harder and help to defeat the system of bribes and corruption that regulated entry. Capable young people from poor families would be denied entry in either case. Especially in rural areas, where people had fewer ties to those in power in urban centers, the rise of private paid education was viewed as putting an end to their hopes for social mobility.

Health and Medical Care

Ukraine has seen the gradual de facto privatization of the public health care system and the growth of private, fee-for-service treatment. As with education, respondents for the most part felt that one received better treatment from private practitioners. The poor could not afford the prescribed remedies even with free medical examinations. As in education, a two-tier system was developing in health care in which the poor suffered disproportionately from poor-quality treatment, shortages of necessary medicine, and indifference on the part of medical practitioners. Most respondents had noted a deterioration in their health due to poor nutrition; environmental hazards, including radiation from Chernobyl; cold, unheated houses, schools, and workplaces; and stress.

Some doctors still gave free consultations, but most accepted a payment, and some would not treat without one. Gifts for checkups or diagnosis of minor ailments generally consisted of a box of imported chocolates or a bottle of imported liquor. More complicated treatments required cash payments in advance and gifts upon completion. One interviewer in Kharkiv began to wonder what doctors did with all the chocolate and liquor they received. Several doctors told her that they sold it right back to the kiosks where their patients had bought it.

Patients had to provide all medical supplies, including cotton, bandages, rubber gloves, needles, anesthetics, and antibiotics. For hospital stays, patients had to bring their own bed linens and food and arrange to have family members at the patient's bedside around the clock. Such measures forced poor people to resort to home remedies except in the direst emergencies. Emergency medical attention was still free, although hospitals increasingly demanded that patients pay for gasoline when an ambulance responded to their call. Thus many patients waited until their condition had become very serious before calling an ambulance. In such instances the ambulance team served as the family doctor.

In Crimea, Raya, 33, has become the main breadwinner for her six children. Her second husband entered the hospital two months ago with tuberculosis, and his firm has refused to pay compensation while he is there. The family survives on $47 a month from a pension and Raya's occasional earnings. Raya anticipates that her husband will remain in the hospital for three more months; then he must enter a sanatorium for another three months. Other medical expenses confront the family. Nine-year-old Vanya has one leg shorter than the other. He is entitled to receive massages every three months, but the village clinic demands a fee. The Lugovskii Hospital in Simferopol will provide massages for free, but Raya can no longer afford the cost of transportation. As a "child invalid," Vanya is also entitled to free two-month treatments at a sanatorium twice a year. Raya pays for the trip; the sanatorium provides medical treatment and feeds him well for two months. Raya's 16-year-old daughter suffers from epilepsy, but the medication that used to be free is now totally unaffordable. In December Raya's 13-year-old son became ill. The doctor wrote several prescriptions, but Raya had to resort to home remedies because she could not afford the prescribed medication.

People in rural areas felt especially poorly served. Rural respondents complained that the best doctors had long since left for the cities. Patients reported suffering as a result of incompetent treatment, lack of appropriate medication, and lack of transportation to medical facilities.

The Impact of Crime on Daily Life

Throughout Ukraine people expressed a fear of increased crime. Many urban respondents, especially old people and women, no longer left their homes after dark, and they worried when their children returned late from school or work. Perhaps because the media now reported much more crime than they had during the Soviet era, many respondents were frightened even though they had never personally experienced or witnessed criminal or threatening events. Respondents in Crimea felt that crime was completely out of control and that criminals were becoming ever more audacious.

Pavel, a 45-year-old Greek living with his Russian wife and two daughters in Simferopol, reports that thefts have occurred from the family's dacha. One of his daughters was physically attacked in their building's elevator, and a few days before the interview he found their neighbor reeling after a brutal attack by four men who had stolen his shopping bag, which contained several jars of preserved fruit. One morning, thieves broke into another neighbor's apartment and stole a radio. When they tried to break into the next apartment, a six-year-old child who was home alone managed to call the police, who caught them in the act.

In analyzing respondents' evaluation of the police, it must be recalled that, during the Soviet period, police had been responsible primarily for monitoring and controlling citizens in their lawful activities and for preserving order, rather than controlling crime. Soviet citizens obtained their residence permits (*propiska*) through the police. The police ascertained that citizens were employed and living where they were registered. They registered marriages and divorces in the internal passports that people still used as legal identification. Citizens also applied to the police for foreign passports and visas.

The gradual relaxation of state control had reduced some police functions. At the same time, however, it had reduced state control over the police. Citizens—especially the poor and the powerless—felt unprotected against the police. They had no recourse but compliance when police demanded bribes or threatened brutality. Stories circulated among neighbors and friends, creating and reinforcing a perception that city streets were unsafe and police unwilling to intervene. These stories kept people inside after dark, intensifying their sense of isolation and defenselessness.

Conclusions

The commercialization and privatization of medical and educational services have placed even basic services out of reach of the poor. Although most respondents accepted in principle the shift to a fee-for-service system, they feared that the services were no longer available to them or to their children. This served as a powerful disincentive to have children. The swift rise in crime affected those who, for lack of money, power, or connections, were most defenseless. Crime had bred pervasive fear and distrust. Most respondents believed that public transportation was dangerous because of pickpockets, that the streets and markets were dangerous because of street criminals and rackets, and that government authorities were influenced, if not controlled, by criminal organizations, and therefore unlikely to take a serious interest in the plight of the poor.

Regional Variation

Ukraine is a country of tremendous regional diversity. As a result of divergent historical influences and experiences, regional economic specializations and different cultures and languages have emerged. Two politically volatile areas, Crimea and the Donbas, merit particular attention. Acute poverty in Crimea, particularly among the Crimean Tatar population, has the potential to aggravate ethnic tension, and the Donbas is likely to experience massive, highly concentrated poverty in the near future. These two regions are also the most infiltrated with organized crime in all of Ukraine.

The Crimean Tatars

The Turkic-speaking, Islamic Tatars comprise an indigenous, ethnically and religiously distinct community in the Crimea. The mass return of Crimean Tatars from their forced deportation to Central Asia in the 1940s took place during a period of state collapse and economic crisis. The migrants' economic difficulties, coping strategies, and prospects for the future differ from those of their Ukrainian and Russian neighbors.

Deportation. In May 1944 the entire population of approximately 200,000 Crimean Tatars was deported for alleged collaboration with the occupying German forces. Armenians, Greeks, Bulgarians, and others were also deported. Most Tatars were sent by train to Uzbekistan or Kazakhstan. An estimated 42 percent died during the forced relocation, and others died shortly thereafter from epidemics. In November 1989 the Supreme Soviet declared these acts of deportation illegal, making it possible for deportees to return to Crimea. Repatriation reached a high point in 1990–91. As of April 1995, 239,515 Tatars had officially moved to Crimea; additional tens of thousands of Tatars are thought to be living there unregistered.

Resettlement. After World War II, people fleeing war damage in southern Russia and Ukraine occupied the houses in Crimea vacated by the Tatars. In 1954 Crimea was administratively transferred from Russia to Ukraine, and Ukrainians were encouraged to develop Crimean agriculture. Industrialization and militarization after 1963 were accompanied by an influx of Russians. Russians now comprise 65 percent of Crimea's population of 2.6 million, Ukrainians 25 percent, and Crimean Tatars about 8 percent. Over 30 percent of Crimea's population consists of retired military, KGB, and other government bureaucrats, constituting a conservative, pro-Russian bloc. At the time of this study, Crimea was also an object of contention because of the Black Sea Fleet and the local military-industrial sector, which represented 60 percent of the economy.

The Mejlis, the political organization representing the Crimean Tatar community, supported Ukraine's claims to Crimea. Crimean Tatars pointed out that it was not Ukraine that deported them, and that now Ukraine was the only government providing them any assistance. Many Crimean Tatars expressed a cautious desire for some kind of political autonomy in the future, and this frightened both the Russian and the Ukrainian inhabitants, who claimed that the Tatars "want to drive us out." The Mejlis advocated the return of the entire Tatar population to its historic homeland in order to create the critical mass necessary to claim autonomy. Some 250,000 Tatars were thought to remain in Uzbekistan and other republics.

Tatars in Uzbekistan. Despite the harsh postwar years of early exile, the majority of Tatar respondents achieved a relatively high level of prosperity and education: 14 percent had university degrees, and 40 percent had technical degrees (de Zwager 1995). Respondents who had returned after 1990 referred to a fear of ethnic violence in Central Asia, based on rising nationalism and the bloody conflict between Uzbeks and Meshketian Turks in the Ferghana Valley of Uzbekistan. As one interviewee put it, "Suddenly, everyone became fearful and nervous. And what should we do, stay by ourselves among the Uzbeks? They didn't actually force anyone to leave, but . . . a colleague might say, 'You don't like things here? Then go back to where you belong!' We felt that we were out of place."

Return to Crimea. After peaking in 1990–91, Tatar migration to Crimea slowed when it became more difficult to sell property in Uzbekistan to pay for the journey. The Tatar families who returned to Crimea contended with the same aspects of poverty as the rest of the population: a shrinking labor market, unemployment and underemployment, late payment of salaries, and spiraling inflation. But the Crimean Tatars saw migration as the main reason for their poverty; they also listed unemployment and inflation. Many Crimean Tatar respondents had become impoverished because they had converted their property in Uzbekistan into cash just as the introduction of monetary reform, a new transitional currency, and hyperinflation rendered the money practically valueless. Ukrainian families lost their savings; Crimean Tatar families lost their homes as well.

Shamil, 42, and his wife, Lilia, 39, live in a village near Simferopol with their four children and Lilia's mother (who came to visit but now cannot afford to return to Uzbekistan). Their household income, including child allowances, comes to less than $40 a month.

In Uzbekistan, they lived in a four-room apartment in the district capital, where Shamil was respected as a construction foreman; Lilia worked as a bookkeeper. Shamil recalls, "Beginning in 1988, a few separate Tatar families started the move, but I didn't hurry. In 1990 the mass migration began, and Tatars began to seize land in different districts of Crimea and put up temporary houses. My relatives seized a parcel of land for me and urged me to come, but I still didn't hurry. I continued to save money for construction. I thought I would just accumulate a bit more, and in one year be able to build a large home, and my family wouldn't experience too much difficulty.

"Things didn't happen as I had planned. In 1991, on the eve of the currency reform, I sold our apartment for $8,000 and began to collect our things to load a container. . . . After the reform, I couldn't even pay for the container I had ordered, although the buyer of my apartment was waiting for me to remove my things. I don't know how I offended Allah, but in one minute I became destitute—without money, without an apartment, and without building materials."

Land and Housing. Even after the Tatars began migrating to Crimea in large numbers, they faced numerous obstacles in obtaining housing and land. In 1987 the Crimean authorities distributed land from state farms to local residents who already had homes. As late as 1991, many Crimean Tatars simply seized land, which led to a number of confrontations with police and local mafias. In 1992 the government started distributing land to Crimean Tatars, in many cases on completely undeveloped territory without water, gas, electricity, or roads.

The majority of poor Crimean Tatars were extremely ill-housed. Many families lived in small, crudely built, difficult-to-heat temporary buildings (*vremianki*), in communities that lacked basic infrastructure. Others managed to sink a foundation for the large dwelling planned before inflation hit. Some of them simply covered the basement; others managed to finish one or two rooms and cover them with a temporary roof. For many of these families, obtaining electricity, fuel, and sometimes water was a huge headache.

Osman, 78, and his wife, Anna, 71, live with their unemployed son, his wife, and their child in two rooms covered by a temporary roof above a basement, which floods when it rains. In 1991 they sold a 13-room house in Uzbekistan, deposited the money in the bank, and lost the entire sum to inflation. They have illegally installed electrical wiring. For heat they rely on a wood stove, fed by wood that Osman cuts from trees 2 kilometers away. What disturbs them the most is the lack of sufficient water and a paved road in the settlement. A truck delivers drinking water, but they never have enough left over to water their garden, and this limits their harvest.

Registration. The Crimean Tatars experienced great difficulty in formally registering where they live. The absence of a *propiska* prevented many respondents from getting a job, retraining at Employment Services, and receiving pensions, discounts, subsidies, privatization certificates, and even a driver's license. Without a *propiska,* people could be evicted and fined.

Arsen and Zenife, both 38, live with two children in a poorly built, two-room *vremianka* made of clay, straw, and bricks. The unplastered walls leak. During the interview, the temperature is just above freezing, because, as Arsen explains, he and his wife are unemployed and cannot afford coal. Local authorities refused to give his family a *propiska,* which meant that Arsen was unable to receive benefits as an Afghan war veteran. He recalls, "For almost a year, the local authorities refused to register me or my family. They told me, get your own home and then you can get registered." Arsen appealed to the village council for help and asked them to give him a place in the dormitory. He was refused on the grounds that there was no space. "I was forced to resort to an extreme measure. I went to the village council with the threat to blow up everyone there with a gas canister." Three days later Arsen's family was registered.

Finding Work. Crimean Tatars found themselves at a serious disadvantage in the labor market. They lacked connections with those in important positions. Many were denied a *propiska.* Their educational levels were roughly the same as those of Ukrainians and Russians in the area, but Tatars experienced 51 percent unemployment compared with 24 percent for Ukrainians and Russians (de Zwager, 1995). Few respondents attributed their current unemployment directly to ethnic prejudice. Some respondents with a higher education were unable to find work in their field because they had moved from urban or town settings in Uzbekistan to Crimean villages. Women had a significantly higher incidence of unemployment, but they preferred to work close to home, even part-time. Tatars were more active in the private sector, marketing produce from their own garden plots in the nearest town, eastern Ukraine, and even Moscow.

Government Assistance. The Committee for the Return of Deported Peoples allocated land and distributes cash assistance for building materials to Crimean Tatars. It also funded a number of Tatar cultural activities, including publication of Tatar-language textbooks and literature, theater, and musical groups. Tatar pensions were 25 percent higher in compensation for their deportation. The Mejlis represented the interests of the Crimean Tatar community. On the local level, the Mejlis was represented by neighborhood committees, which distributed assistance and respond to complaints or appeals from the Crimean Tatar community. Almost all Crimean Tatar respondents had appealed for financial assistance or help with some bureaucratic problem.

Fatima, 42, married and with three children, describes her family as very poor. Recently, many of their possessions were destroyed in a fire, which they ascribe to a short circuit. Since 1993 she has been unable to find work as a hospital nurse. Finally, she appealed directly to the chairman of the local Mejlis: "I went to him and told him about our difficult circumstances. Right in front of me he phoned the head director of the district's main hospital," and asked for help. Within a week she had a job.

Despite complaints and cynicism at the local level about the Mejlis's performance of its social and charitable functions, to judge from respondents' comments, the community nevertheless accorded the Mejlis considerable legitimacy. Most Crimean Tatar respondents looked to the Mejlis as the one organization that came close to defending their interests.

Ethnic Relations. Many respondents recalled the hostility that had met them when they migrated to Crimea. They explained that this was to be expected, given the way in which Soviet authorities had rewritten history and depicted them as collaborators with the Nazis.

Amine, a schoolteacher, claims not to feel any discrimination, but notes, "At the same time, there is a particular category of people who relate to Tatars as if they were second-class citizens, and are still under the influence of prejudices they absorbed over many years, that Tatars are traitors. This is especially true among the older generation of Russian speakers. It has already entered into their blood. The first year at work, they were very careful, even suspicious, toward me—how could I, a Tatar, teach Russian language and literature? Normal human feelings finally won out, and they finally judged me just as a person."

Respondents recalled that now one rarely hears the kind of comments that were prevalent in 1991–92, such as "They've come in such great numbers that we don't have enough bread. They've occupied our fields."

Ali, 36, an unemployed electrician who bitterly regrets moving his family to Crimea, where three adults and three children live in two dormitory rooms on $50 a month, explains, "Tatars are people just like anyone else. Some people envy others, some owe others money, some become rich dishonestly, by cheating others. Relations with other people vary. It hasn't come to a big quarrel, but it could happen. A difficult life makes people mean and distrustful. But I am convinced that if something serious threatens the Tatars, they will quickly unite, like any other people."

The Slavic population viewed the Tatar families with some ambivalence. Most of the Slavic respondents in this survey said they had normal, neighborly relations with the Tatar migrants. Several of the older respondents hinted that the Tatars had deserved deportation and complained that they received preferential treatment from the government and from humanitarian organizations.

Olia, 26, a Ukrainian, feels "an imbalance" between the rights of the Tatar and Ukrainian populations in the village. As she sees it, the Tatars get help from everywhere. "We don't have equal rights. Where does all this humanitarian aid go? Only to the Tatars! I moved here—no one helps me. If I move, I will live in a mud hut, and not in a two-story house with a garage and a summer house."

The Crimean Tatars had returned to their homeland only to find themselves at the center of Russian-Ukrainian negotiations over the status and fate of the Black Sea Fleet, valuable parts of the military-industrial complex, and the ultimate status of this coveted peninsula. Many Ukrainians and Russians feared that the Crimean Tatars ultimately wanted to reclaim the homes from which they or their parents had been deported, and to establish their own government in Crimea. Power relations and alliances had been sharply altered by the plight of this ethnically distinct minority claiming indigenous rights.

Donbas: Cradle of the Proletariat

The Donbas region, dominated by the coal industry, was the site of some of the most intense labor struggles in the final years of Soviet rule. The miners demonstrated impressive levels of worker solidarity, labor organization, and militancy, forcing the Communist Party of the Soviet Union to capitulate to their demands on more than one occasion.

This explosive combination of recent political events and the prospect of massive economic restructuring gave Donbas miners a political importance that greatly exceeded their numbers. Impending economic and industrial change promised to create a highly disgruntled work force faced with regionally concentrated, prolonged unemployment and poverty. Privileges and prestige were fresh in the memories of miners as they grappled with shrinking salaries, vanishing benefits, and the ever-growing threat of unemployment. In addition to the sharp decline in their economic well-being, residents in the Donbas were encountering psychological dislocation caused by a widespread and public discrediting of the system and country that once heralded the Donbas as the pinnacle of Soviet accomplishment.

Miners still enjoyed a higher standard of living than many other residents of Donetsk oblast. The interviewers had no difficulty in locating needy households in Donetsk, but few miners were in this sample. Far more extensive unemployment and poverty can be expected as the mines close.

Crime. Donetsk is one of the prime centers of criminal activity. Respondents in Donetsk reported being affected by petty crimes for cash or goods: raids on food storage bins, pickpockets on public transportation, burglarized homes. Lawlessness, confusion, and angst are likely to grow as a result of massive economic restructuring. Young men can expect severe difficulties in securing gainful employment after the mines close; joining criminal organizations may provide an alternative to the old work collective. Criminal organizations and gangs offer an income, contacts, protection, and some kind of hope that the future will be more comfortable than the present.

Energy. Although many workers were paid in part or entirely in coal, this was usually sold or bartered for food. Rural residents reported that they balanced heating and health needs against nutrition and hunger when deciding how much of their coal to sell. Urban residents usually could not regulate the heat in their apartments. Respondents and interviewers alike reported that they often kept their hats and coats on indoors and bundled up in multiple layers before going to sleep to stay warm. Similarly, all electricity use, including lighting, was curtailed after 5 p.m. in Donetsk during the winter months of 1996.

Connections to Russia. Russia offers a number of possibilities for informal employment that could help reduce poverty. Unemployed workers travel to Russia to work temporarily, usually on construction brigades, or emigrate there to find better employment opportunities. Ailing though the Russian economy was, Ukrainians saw it as far stronger than their own.

Mine Closings. The many difficulties associated with poverty are likely to intensify in Donetsk oblast once the closing of mines creates regionally concentrated unemployment. The miners have already lost some of the vibrant solidarity they demonstrated in the final years of Soviet rule. The lack of any real progress in securing better work conditions has somewhat undermined the authority of the unions. Prolonged hardship, brought on by delayed and shrinking salaries, and the ever-growing prospect of unemployment have weakened self-confidence and self-respect, leaving the miners demoralized and exhausted.

One-mine towns run the risk of becoming ghost towns unless transportation improves. Respondents often suggested a public works program as a solution. People were accustomed to working for the state, and it was believed that only the state had the financial means and the commitment to undertake a program of job creation for miners. Most participants at the roundtable discussions convened for this survey criticized the idea of a one-time severance payment; it would merely fuel inflation. The option of relocating to other regions of Ukraine was hindered by an acute housing shortage. Social support networks are essential for finding a job, and there is no tradition of labor mobility in the region.

Emerging Institutions and Attitudes

Ukraine has undergone profound political, economic, and social changes since independence. The demise of old structures and institutions, which offered some forms of social protection, have left families legally and economically vulnerable. Although most people accept the inevitability of independence and the shift toward a free market, poor people lack the internal and material resources to cope with these changes.

Attitudes Toward Privatization and Commerce

Currency Reform. Many respondents attributed their current poverty to the 1991 monetary reform, which seemingly overnight had converted amounts sufficient to buy a car or an apartment, or at least to pay for a decent burial, to just enough money to buy a bottle of vodka. The introduction of a transitional Ukrainian currency and the ensuing hyperinflation had struck especially hard at the Crimean Tatars who had just sold homes in order to move back from Uzbekistan.

Banking. The spate of state-sanctioned investment firms and commercial banks that accepted deposits—only to vanish without a trace—had undermined public trust in private banking and the government's ability to regulate it. Responsible business practices will be necessary before public confidence is restored. Until then, grandmothers and mafia henchmen will continue to guard savings in a strictly cash-based economy.

Housing. Privatization of apartments has been slow. Potential owners have been unwilling or unable to take on the responsibility of paying for capital repairs, housing charges have gone up, and there is fear of a tax on assets. The legal system is too weak to protect individual investments and property, and most respondents found it unclear why they should pay to get something that they were already getting cheaply or for free.

Health and Education. Respondents accepted the idea of paying for services such as health care and education on the grounds that the only way to guarantee quality service is to pay for it. But they felt there should be an alternative for poor people unable to pay, such as scholarships, free schools, and free medical treatment. It was not acceptable that the quality of health care and education should improve for some while educational opportunities and medical treatment were closed to those unable to pay.

Employment. Older respondents still felt deeply ambivalent about commerce, which they viewed as "speculation," as opposed to production, which was "real work." Many respondents still defined employment as receiving a salary from the state; they clung to the state sector, which they still saw as providing more job security and benefits than the uncertain private sector.

Young women, even those without children, reported that potential employers sometimes rejected them out of fear that they would soon have children and go on maternity leave; older women were rejected as "unteachable" and less attractive as employees. Cultural perceptions of gender-appropriate jobs meant that whole categories of higher-paying construction and industrial work were closed to women.

Certain age and professional groups were more adversely affected in the new labor market. Men and women over 40 were often dismissed as job candidates because of their assumed "Soviet thinking." Certain workers and professionals who had been celebrated under the Soviet system, notably miners and engineers, faced a sharply shrinking labor market that no longer valued their skills.

The Challenges to Building Civil Society

Distrust. Many Ukrainians expressed a pervasive distrust and suspicion toward authority, from doctors and local administrators up to national leaders, based on what they considered to be overwhelming evidence of corruption and the unbridled pursuit of self-interest. When wages were not paid, when government assistance was not forthcoming, when people heard about but failed to receive humanitarian assistance, when students failed to gain admission to university, when jobseekers failed to find work, when discounted coal was unavailable, when police or doctors failed to respond to an emergency call, most people attributed the problem to their own lack of necessary connections or failure to pay the necessary bribes, or to the illegal appropriation of funds or goods by those in charge of distributing them.

Respondents distrusted voluntary activity because it smacked of the forced "voluntary work" to which they were subjected during the Soviet period. They also suspected fundraisers of raising money for themselves rather than for their organizations. They suspected those who aspired to leadership positions of trying to aggrandize power, fortune, and influence for narrow personal goals. As a result, the few existing local nongovernmental organizations experienced great difficulty in attracting volunteers and raising funds.

Government Corruption. Most respondents reasoned that not only the incompetence but also the dishonesty of their government had led them to their present disaster. Whenever the government failed to deliver on a promise or entitlement, people dismissed explanations about lack of funds and attributed the problem instead to deception. Many respondents were convinced that salaries, discounts, subsidies, and allocations to which they were entitled were paid months late, after they had lost value to inflation, because various "criminal structures" in the government had first used the money for investments and only later distributed it to the population.

Class Antagonisms. Poor respondents reported that the newly rich treated the poor with contempt and disdain. University students noted growing animosity and tension between rich and poor students, fueled by the privileges and insulation from failure that the rich students enjoyed while the poor competed fiercely for merit-based admittance. Differentials of wealth were translating into marital barriers and frontiers of friendship. Paradoxically, the poor sometimes expressed the same harsh judgments of poverty as the new rich. They, too, linked it to laziness, incompetence, and alcoholism. At the same time, they fully recognized the impact of Ukraine's economic crisis on their lives and on the lives of others. Respondents sharply criticized the new rich for what they perceived to be stolen or dishonestly accumulated wealth, compounded by a casual disregard and complete lack of compassion for the poor.

Gender-Specific Coping Mechanisms. For young men, proliferating armed groups were an alternative to the old work collective: they provided an income, contacts, protection, and some kind of hope that the future would be more comfortable than the present. For younger women (village girls and students were frequently mentioned in this connection), prostitution provided similar benefits: additional income, nicer clothes, and the dim possibility of exiting poverty. None of the respondents in this survey confessed to practicing these strategies, but many alluded to acquaintances who did.

Communication. Civil society depends in large part on a public sphere of informed debate. But the newfound freedom to publicly criticize those in power and discuss political and social issues has been checked by increasing difficulties in communication. The media has a shrinking audience. Many respondents no longer subscribed to newspapers, magazines, or journals; books were too expensive to purchase; and television and radio use was restricted to save electricity. Should a television or radio break, it was unlikely to be repaired or replaced. The vibrancy of cultural life in Ukraine and the use of the arts as a forum for expression are fading as it becomes unaffordable for growing numbers of Ukrainians to attend plays, concerts, or films.

Informal communications have also been reduced. Migration has ruptured families and friendships; expensive and unreliable postal services and telephone connections have drastically reduced interrepublic and international communications; the high cost of transportation and fear of street crime have reduced socializing; and the juggling of time-consuming jobs and subsistence farming has reduced visiting and the ability to share information by word of mouth.

Information Vacuum. One of the most pervasive complaints that interviewers encountered was the general lack of information on everything from job retraining possibilities to current world events. People did not know where to get information. Even if they got it, they had difficulty interpreting it or found that they could not rely on its veracity.

Lack of Accountability. Many respondents claimed they had experienced no violation of rights, but they would also describe the blatant discrimination they had experienced in government offices or in the workplace. Despite an overwhelming consensus that neither the government nor the private sector treated individuals fairly, most respondents felt they had no recourse when they were denied entitlements, treated unjustly, swindled of savings, or cheated of salaries.

Many of the serious problems experienced by poor Ukrainians can be alleviated only in the long term, if a strong, democratic state with a viable economy develops. Some of the more promising aspects of Ukrainian society that could facilitate development include the lack of extreme nationalism and ethnic tensions, outside of Crimea. The inertia of "old thinking" is balanced by resourcefulness, the work force is highly educated and skilled, and social networks are resilient. The people have accepted privatization and the principle of fee for service. There is a rich agricultural potential, with subsistence farming as an effective safety net, and there is widespread public concern over the environment.

References

de Zwager, Nicolaas. 1995. "Crimea: Baseline Socio Economic Survey with Emphasis on Returning Deportees." United Nations Development Programme (December). Processed.

World Bank. 1996. *Ukraine Poverty Assessment.* Washington, D.C.

A Crimean Tatar poses in
front of a local post office.
Photo by Elizabeth Gomart

✳

CHAPTER 10

After the Return:
The Struggle of the
Crimean Tatars to Reintegrate

Elizabeth Gomart

I n 1997, five years after the return of the majority of Crimean Tatars to Crimea,[1] most of Ukraine was feeling the aftershocks of the collapse of the Soviet Union. Crimea's main industry, tourism, was dwindling because of the lack of Soviet tourists and rumors of NATO exercises in the Black Sea. The central government in Kyiv was concerned, at least for stability reasons, about the plight of the Crimean Tatars. In contrast, local officials were dismissive of the needs of this ethnic group, claiming that other Ukrainians were in a similarly difficult position. In this highly politicized and hostile context, very little nonpartisan information was available about the situation of the Crimean Tatars. The Office of the United Nations High Commissioner for Refugees, concentrating its efforts on citizenship issues and other legal obstacles encountered by the returnees, funded the social assessment reported in this chapter in order to shed some light on the situation. The aim was to use the Crimean Tatars' own words to describe their priorities and their needs. The results were used to develop a United Nations Joint Appeal for funds from donors for the peninsula.

In keeping with the purpose of this volume, the findings presented here focus on the experience of social exclusion of the Crimean Tatar people.

An earlier version of this chapter was commissioned by the Office of the United Nations High Commissioner for Refugees and published by the UNHCR Bureau for Europe in April 1998 as "Social Assessment of the Formerly Deported Population in the Autonomous Republic of Crimea: A Participatory Rapid Appraisal," *European Series* 4 (1).

(Nationwide issues are covered in the previous chapter, on Ukraine.) Social exclusion is important to stability in the region, for within it lie the seeds of civil and ethnic conflict. From the Crimean Tatars' point of view, their communities are being excluded, even ghettoized. In the interviews conducted for this study they described myriad forms of exclusion from full participation in society in their homeland:

- Geographic, through regional limitations on resettlement and poorer living conditions in the "compact settlements" and hostels where they must live

- Social, with widespread ethnic discrimination and even antagonism

- Linguistic, as non-Ukrainian speakers in their own land, and cultural, with few Crimean Tatar schools and a dearth of Tatar language books, most of which had been burned by the Soviets after World War II

- Religious, with the destruction of mosques and the loss of knowledge of Islam during Soviet times

- Political and administrative, with exclusion from key city and administrative posts and obstacles to citizenship, as well as the perceived need to adopt a confrontational stance—expressed in mass demonstrations, road blockages, acts of self-settlement, and closing of railroads—to attract attention to their needs

- Economic, through job discrimination and limitations on resettlement in prosperous regions.

The study, which included interviews and community meetings, was conducted in nine sites throughout the Crimean peninsula, chosen to represent the diversity of socioeconomic, agroclimatic, and sociocultural contexts as well as country-specific conditions. The sites were Simferopol, Yalta, Kerch, the Leninskii district, the Belogorskii district, Evpatoria, Krasnoperekopsk, the Tchernomorskii region, and the Razdolnenskii district. The researchers were careful to include both Crimean Tatar and non-Tatar interviewers as well as both women and men. The fieldworkers were trained in participatory rapid appraisal tools and interview techniques over a period of seven days in Simferopol and the compact settlement of Kamenka. Fieldwork was conducted in August and September 1997. The fact that the interviews were conducted in the late summer and early fall probably led to a more optimistic view of the situation than would have been the case in the winter, when fuel shortages and housing issues would have been evident, or the spring, when food reserves would have been running low for many poor families.

Background

The Autonomous Republic of Crimea, part of the territory of Ukraine, occupies a peninsula jutting out into the Black Sea and the Sea of Azov. There are three main climatic zones: the southern mountainous region; the flat, dry northern steppe with some fertile black soil (*tchernoziom*) and irrigation in the east; and the Kerch peninsula in the east with its large mineral deposits, including offshore oil.

Demography and Ethnicity

The population of Crimea was approximately 2,193,000 in 1997. The ethnic makeup of the peninsula differed greatly from that of the rest of Ukraine, where Crimean Tatars were a mere 3 percent of the population in 1997. Since repatriation began in 1987, the Russian majority in Crimea had begun to decrease. Russians made up 61.6 percent of the Crimean population in that year, followed by Ukrainians (23.6 percent) and Crimean Tatars (9.6 percent; Open Society Institute 1996, p. 20). Only the Crimean Tatar population is growing, at a rate of 6 per thousand per year, compared with a national average of –5.8 per thousand. By the end of 1996, Crimean Tatars already made up 11.9 percent of the population, according to records in the archives of the State Committee on Nationalities (Goskomnats). The Crimean Tatars had settled overwhelmingly in rural areas; only 27 percent lived in cities. An estimated 16 percent of the registered Crimean Tatar population were children aged 16 and under; 51 percent of the population were capable of working, and 16 percent were pensioners.[2]

Historical Background

Many Russians and Ukrainians ask, "Why are the Crimean Tatars returning to Crimea when they had houses and jobs in Central Asia?" This question reflects a misunderstanding of the priorities and motives of the Crimean Tatars. The 250,000 Crimean Tatars who have returned to Crimea are motivated by a strong desire to return to their homeland after 45 years of exile in Russia and Central Asia. For many, "the return" was what people talked about, dreamed of, and planned for while in exile.

On the night of May 18, 1944, as World War II continued, an estimated 200,000 Crimean Tatars were forcibly deported from Crimea to Russia and the Central Asian republics for allegedly collaborating with the Germans. The deportation distinguished itself in its efficiency and scale from other deportations, such as that of the Korean population in the eastern Soviet Union and that of the Chechens.

A middle-aged woman recounted the ordeal as her mother had described it to her. In Crimea in 1944, the Soviet army sent all able-bodied Crimean Tatar men to serve on the front in Ukraine. Therefore, deportation consisted mostly of women, children, and the elderly. On the night of the deportation, my mother was awakened by a young Russian soldier banging on her door. She grabbed her children protectively. He said she'd better let go of them and gather some warm clothes, her documents, and some money. She put a bundle together, but in the bustle, her children got put into one truck and her bundle was thrown into another. She had to choose which to follow, and of course she chose her children. But the whole way to the train station she kept an eye on the other truck. When they got to the station, she wasn't even allowed to look for her bundle. They were packed into cattle cars and began a trip that lasted two months through the steppes of Russia. There was no air, no toilets, and no food or water. From time to time, they would unload the passengers and feed them a black, oily soup. Many got sick and died during the trip. When she arrived in Uzbekistan she was given a shovel and told to dig. Dig what? A hole, where she and her children would live. She dug the hole and huddled her children under one big coat.

Meanwhile, on the Ukrainian front, the men heard of the deportation of their families. There was a massive desertion. They heard that some family members had been sent to the Urals, others to Central Asia. My father jumped onto a freight train and made his way first to the Urals. He looked for his sister and mother, who he heard had been sent there, but could not find them. Then he came to find us in Uzbekistan. He ran into an acquaintance at a market who had seen us. After a few weeks, the men were rounded up and sent to prison for desertion. Six months later, after a general amnesty was declared, they returned. My father, who had been a big man, returned a mere skeleton weighing 60 kilograms. My mother nursed him back to health on the small amount of rationed food they were given.

Within four years of the deportation, according to Crimean Tatar sources, half of the estimated 200,000 deportees had perished from inadequate food and housing and a hostile climate.[3] Branded as "enemies of the people," the Crimean Tatars were not free to leave the immediate area. They were required to report weekly to the local administration and were barred from seeking higher education or holding management posts. Meanwhile, in Crimea, the Soviet authorities strove to eradicate evidence of Crimean Tatar culture: they resettled the area with Russians, destroyed Crimean Tatar religious sites—including mosques where birth certificates were kept—and cultural monuments, burned Crimean Tatar literature, and Russianized the names of towns and villages.

Conditions improved after Stalin's death. In 1957 Premier Nikita Khrushchev gave most of the Soviet Union's deported minorities the right to return to their homelands, but not the Crimean Tatars, the Volga Germans, or the Meshketian Turks. Political activism became commonplace in the Crimean Tatar community. In 1967 the Crimean Tatars were rehabilitated, but they were expressly barred from resettlement in Crimea. After surprisingly successful mass demonstrations, the Soviet government under Mikhail Gorbachev formed a commission in 1987 to study the Crimean Tatar issue. In 1989 the commission concluded that the Crimean Tatars should be given the right to return. This decision led to huge migration flows. Approximately 250,000 of the estimated 500,000 Crimean Tatars living in Central Asia had returned to Crimea by the time of the study, with a majority returning by 1993.

Resettlement and Internal Migration

The Crimean Tatars' experience in exile and return from exile set them apart from other exiled Crimean communities. The Crimean Tatars had been able to preserve their communities while living in Russia and Central Asia. In contrast, the other nationalities—Crimean Jews, Armenians, Greeks, and Bulgarians—were dispersed and assimilated in their place of deportation, and most did not seek to return to Crimea. Those who did choose to return were allowed to do so well before the breakup of the Soviet Union, and they had the benefit of access to social networks, jobs, and housing. The timing of the return of the Crimean Tatars also explains their poor situation compared with the situation of other ethnic groups deported from Crimea. Their history as ethnically homogeneous and politically active communities also helps explain their formation of strong networks in support of the return. Crimean Tatars claim to be (and were seeking the special status of) the indigenous people of Crimea. As Shevket Ramazov told the *Christian Science Monitor* in 1995, "We are not guests here. We are masters."[4]

Many Crimean Tatars sought to return to the villages of their ancestors, but this was not always possible. In a show of conciliation, the Crimean Tatar leadership forswore reclaiming Tatar homes even where predeportation ownership could be legally established. Thus the returning Crimean Tatars faced issues of affordability of housing, receptivity of local authorities (who controlled access to *propiskas,* or residence permits), and employment. Until recently, a formal ban on Crimean Tatars settling on the southern coast kept them out of the most lucrative tourist areas. Crimean Tatars wanting to settle in Yalta had to demonstrate ancestry in the region.

Whereas many Crimean Tatars had lived in urban areas in Central Asia and Russia during their exile, the returning population was concentrated in rural regions and in the poorer steppe zone, where residence permits were more easily approved. Crimean Tatars were 32 percent of the total population in the Belogorskii district, 26 percent in Sovietskii, 25 percent in Pervomaiskii, and 22 percent in Simferopolskii. Certain historically Crimean Tatar regions—the comparatively wealthy tourist cities and towns of Yalta, Alushta, and Sudak—had only very small Crimean Tatar populations in 1997.

The return slowed after 1991 because of the economic crisis and the static living conditions in the "compact settlements" (land without basic infrastructure provided by the government, often on the outskirts of towns, for building new communities) where most of the Crimean Tatars lived. The economic crisis was more severe in Crimea than in Uzbekistan, where most of the Crimean Tatars had been settled during their exile. Respondents reported that urban residents, the elderly, and second-generation Crimean Tatars born in Central Asia were likely to remain there. Urban housing was far more costly in Crimea, and adapting to village life was not always feasible. The trip to Crimea was difficult for the elderly, who were often reluctant to burden their already struggling families. Crimean Tatar youths had assimilated to life in Central Asia after two generations in Uzbekistan. Those most likely to return to Crimea were the first generation of able-bodied, foreign-born adults, brought up in the heyday of Crimean Tatar political activism.

A small number of returnees (estimated at under 2 percent) eventually went back to Central Asia. Interviews suggest that these emigrants were mostly dependents—elderly persons, single women, or families without a male worker—returning to live with relatives in Central Asia. Some able-bodied men and families also returned because they were discouraged about their prospects in Crimea. For most who returned to Central Asia, this was a temporary measure, until a house was finished or infrastructure could be set up in a compact settlement, or until the economic situation in Crimea improved.

Two distinct migratory trends affected the demographic distribution of Crimean Tatars within Crimea: a rural-urban current and a north-south current. The first was linked to the poor conditions in the villages in the central plains where Crimean Tatars were allowed to settle. Conditions in the countryside were difficult because of exceedingly low and often-unpaid wages and isolation from markets. In Central Asia two-thirds of the Crimean Tatars had lived in urban areas, whereas in Crimea two-thirds settled in rural areas in the steppe, creating a mismatch in terms of employment opportunities and living standards. It was very difficult for a rural resident to obtain a residence permit in town without a permanent address and formal employment. The north-south trend represents movement away from areas where Crimean Tatars were first allowed to settle, and toward their ancestral villages on the newly opened southern coast.

A repatriation program financed by the Soviet Union began in 1989 for 50,000 persons a year. After independence in 1991, Ukraine financed a resettlement program, but this program failed to meet its construction targets, and resettlement was reduced to a trickle. Construction of new housing and infrastructure was interrupted at the end of 1996. By 1997 Goskomnats programs were limited to rent subsidies for apartments and communal housing (*obshejitie*), ad hoc emergency health subsidies to vulnerable families, and reimbursement of transport costs (a third-class train ticket and leasing of one container).[5] The program was not perceived as meeting local needs.

Interethnic Relations

The seeds of civil and ethnic conflict remain in Crimea. From the Crimean Tatars' point of view, their communities continue to be excluded politically, administratively, legally, geographically, economically, socially, and culturally.

The Crimean Tatars remain underrepresented at the local and regional levels. In the Crimean Parliament, the Crimean Tatars' political organization, the Mejlis, obtained a quota of 14 seats in the 96-member body, but this may be lost under new election laws.[6] The Mejlis used confrontational methods including the closing of railroads, mass demonstrations, and acts of self-settlement. They explained that they were unable to obtain a fair distribution of resources through mainstream political institutions.

Many Ukrainians and Russians fear that the Crimean Tatars, as a growing percentage of the population, will someday reclaim their homes and establish their own government in Crimea. Indeed, some Crimean Tatar respondents cautioned that these claims for self-government and return of property might become more insistent with the continued decline in the economic situation and the perceived indifference of local officials. At a number of community meetings held within the context of the assessment, self-government was identified as the best means of resolving issues of housing, discrimination, unemployment, and lack of social and legal protection.

The Crimean Tatar leadership has succeeded in sidestepping these demands. As Mustafa Jemilev, the leader of the Mejlis, explained:

> We do not want handouts. If we had what was taken away from us [in 1944], we would be in fine shape. But this [restitution and compensation] won't happen and we realize this. What we want is a mechanism to defend our rights. We do not want to dictate to anyone, but neither do we want to be dictated to. (Open Society Institute, 1996, p. 55)

However, it was difficult to assess whether the decision to pursue legal issues was supported at the local level or, as some respondents claimed, whether the Mejlis was losing touch with the fundamental needs of the Crimean Tatar population: for infrastructure, housing, and higher incomes.

Few Crimean Tatars occupied management posts in administrative, executive, or implementing government bodies. Yet having allies within the system was very important for access to information and services. Municipal and regional departments tended to refer all issues related to formerly deported persons (FDPs) to the now-underfunded Goskomnats. The sites visited for this study did not have an integrated municipal plan that included the Crimean Tatar compact settlements, although they were part of the same municipality.

Because their housing was temporary and they lacked official employment, many Crimean Tatars lived without a *propiska*. Of those who were registered, 40 percent did not have Ukrainian citizenship.[7] Some Crimean Tatars claimed that they were treated as second-class citizens and harassed by the police for their lack of regularized status—even when they had proper documentation—because of their "Caucasian features."

Living conditions in the compact settlements and the hostels were substandard. In the compact settlements on the periphery of cities, families lived without basic infrastructure, with neither water, nor electricity, nor roads. Those who did have physical access to services were often unable to pay utility fees. They were isolated because the cost of transportation, even public transportation, had become prohibitive on their reduced incomes. Families were crammed into temporary housing. Hostels on the coast were not intended for year-round habitation. They lacked proper insulation against the cold and sufficient cooking and hygienic amenities. The isolation of Crimean Tatars in depressed areas and their exclusion from the lucrative southern coastal areas had engendered resentment. Some Crimean Tatar respondents predicted that conflict was likely to erupt on the southern coast because economic resources there, which promised higher returns than those available inland, were more tightly controlled.

An estimated 40 percent of Crimean Tatars were unemployed, and others worked in menial jobs despite having professional credentials or experience. Because of the timing of the return, their assets in cash or savings accounts were particularly vulnerable to hyperinflation and currency conversions.

There was widespread discrimination against the Crimean Tatars, who were called "traitors" and "blacks" and relegated to menial jobs. Many Russians and Ukrainians were disinterested in and even hostile to the group's plight. Interethnic relations were highly politicized and often fueled by misperceptions and incomplete information. There was very little interethnic socializing among adults and little exchange of information regarding living conditions in the compact settlements. Relations were strained in part as a result of years of Soviet propaganda. Even in 1997 official representatives dealing with migration and nationality issues still referred to the Crimean Tatars' "collaboration with the Nazis" to rationalize their exile to Central Asia. During the fieldwork for this study, at an informal dinner in Evpatoria, a number of Russian and Ukrainian city officials and entrepreneurs refused to raise their glasses to toast the "peaceful reintegration of the Crimean Tatars." Many Russian and Ukrainian respondents were resentful of the attention the formerly deported people were getting from international agencies. Many Crimean Tatars themselves had an incomplete view of the situation. Some, for example, hesitated to acknowledge that economic difficulties affected all Crimeans.

Cultural knowledge had been eroded by 70 years of Russianization and over 40 years in exile. Although most of the returnees spoke Crimean Tatar, very few could read literary works in the language. The national literature had been burned after deportation, and only a handful of literary classics were in print. The language did not reflect modern life and did not provide a contemporary vocabulary for scientific and technological advances. Knowledge of Islam had also been lost during Soviet times.

Defining Poverty

The dimensions and definitions of poverty among the Crimean Tatars had changed since Soviet times. Most of the former deportees did not consider themselves poor when they lived in Central Asia. They were able to afford housing and had enough money to cover basic purchases: food, clothing, utilities, education, and medical care. Leisure was a right of the worker, and most took vacations. City residents went to cultural events. Many had summer homes. In contrast, in Crimea the majority of Crimean Tatar house-holds said that they spent most of their income on food and very little on other basic needs. A poor family was one that did not have enough money even to eat.

The Crimean Tatars living in Crimea considered themselves poorer than either their Russian or their Ukrainian neighbors. Many lacked permanent housing and instead lived in crowded, unfinished, or temporary construc-tion; they had inferior access to infrastructure, transportation, and social services; many lacked formal employment or had to accept menial, low-paid jobs; and they had less effective local representatives than did other groups. As a group, Crimean Tatars were in a more precarious living situa-tion because of their lack of vertical connections to mainstream power struc-tures. But their social networks, although horizontal, could be characterized as more effective. However, social cohesion and neighborly support had decreased as the new arrivals had settled in and the crisis situation had become chronic.

Who Are the Poor?

According to respondents, there were no clear and consistent indicators of poverty. Whether a household was poor depended on its connections and support networks, on the availability of household garden plots for subsis-tence, on access to social services, and on the household's adaptability. Pen-sioners and invalids were traditionally perceived as more vulnerable, but some may have been employed or receiving salaries, or may have benefited from a strong family network, and thus may have been living far better than other, more isolated households. Single mothers were sometimes support-ed by relatives in the countryside, who provided child care and food, and they earned income from trading in fruits and vegetables in bulk.

According to respondents, poverty among the Crimean Tatars was due to the confluence of a number of factors. These included their late (post-1991) arrival in Crimea without housing; hyperinflation; the need to start afresh in a new location (as returnees, refugees, rural-urban migrants, or migrants to the southern coast); a mismatch of jobs of skills; and ethnic discrimina-tion. This contributed to household vulnerability: a high ratio of depend-ents (school-age children, invalids, elderly) to providers, and in particular a large number of single, divorced, or widowed mothers and pensioners with-out sons; small salaries and pensions; chronic medical expenditures; deplet-ed cash resources; isolation from markets; lack of land for subsistence farm-ing; and urban residence with no rural relatives nearby. Alcoholism, although less widespread among Crimean Tatars than among the Russian or Ukranian populations, was a drain on household resources because it led to unmet basic needs, forgone income opportunities, and depleted assets.

In the Belaya Skala hostel in Belogorsk town, a family of refugees from Tajikistan saw their circumstances stabilize slightly during 1997. After fleeing Tajikistan in 1994, where they were able to sell their home for train tickets and one 5-metric-ton container for their belongings, they arrived in Crimea with no savings or assets. Upon arrival in Belogorsk, they negotiated a room in a hotel for five people and were reimbursed for their travel costs. Once this money was spent, their standard of living deteriorated quickly. They lived on occasional income, on the edge of destitution. To make things worse, one of the three children became ill, straining the family budget. The mother has a degree in economics, but she was unable to find work because of her temporary residence permit. After two years she was hired as a housecleaner, earning 50 grivnas a month. She tried to work in the market, buying cheap produce in the morning and selling it for a few kopeks more per kilogram, but was unable to make a profit. Her husband earns an average of 50 grivnas a month at odd jobs, mostly construction. The son's student stipend is 7 grivnas a month. She estimates that the family's total income this month is 153 grivnas. Fifty percent of this is spent on food and close to 40 percent on medicines.

Many of the families who had arrived after 1992, especially refugees, reported going through a period of complete destitution once their small savings were depleted. The poor were limited to eating the cheapest food staples: potatoes, onions, and bread. In rural areas, poor families often had access to limited amounts of milk. Less poor families could afford some oil, sugar, and vegetables and fruits in season but bought little else. Purchases of clothing, basic health care, and education often required forgoing other basic needs.

Until 1992, Selite's family lived on a collective farm in Kurgan Tyube, Tajikistan. Although her mother, a Crimean Tatar, was married to a Tajik, relations with their neighbors and the management of the collective became strained. Selite was the first to leave. She stayed with relatives in the Dzhanskoi region and earned a bit of money working on construction, but never got a residence permit. Then she heard from the Mejlis in Simferopol that refugees from Kurgan Tyube had been sent to a hostel in Krasnoperekopsk, in the north of Crimea. She found the rest of her family had been living in the hostel, not knowing how to contact her. Selite is a professional dancer but took a job as a housecleaner at a salary of 70 grivnas a month. Her sister, a pharmacist, has also accepted a cleaning job.

The worst years were 1992–94. Selite's father fell ill and died. Her mother was also ill and had an operation. The family sold everything they could to cover the cost of the operation. In 1994 Selite married and continued living in the hostel with her husband. After a few months, her husband left her for a Russian woman who lives in a private home and owns a car. Soon after, Selite gave birth to a son, and she has had to quit her job and stay home to look after her child. Life became a little easier after her brother started buying cigarettes in bulk in Odessa and selling them in Krasnoperekopsk. The income for the two households is 300 grivnas a month for six persons. Selite spends the 20 grivnas she receives in child subsidies from the government on food for the toddler. From her perspective, they lived very poorly from 1992 until 1994, eating only bread. From 1994 until 1996 they were slightly less poor, eating bread and potatoes. The situation has improved because the family can now afford some sugar, oil, and fruits and vegetables in season.

Poor rural families routinely ate animal feed (*otrub*, the unprocessed bran left over after milling wheat flour) in the late spring when food supplies were exhausted. Some stole for survival. In a village in the Belogorskii region, only 26 kilometers from Simferopol, a group of respondents estimated that 20 to 25 out of the 300 Crimean Tatar households eat *otrub* in the springtime. In Vodopolnoe, in the Tchernomorskii region, families said that they and their neighbors fed *otrub* to their children because they ran out of wheat flour and other grains. One mother said she had received only 5 percent of her salary from the collective farm: 13 to 15 grivnas to live on the entire winter. Her family went without salt for two months because her husband forbade her to ask her neighbors for handouts and she could not afford to buy it.

Poor living conditions were more widespread in the compact settlements settled after 1991. More of the homes were incomplete and the settlements were sparsely populated. They had little infrastructure: no piped drinking water, electricity, roads, heating, drainage, or sewers. Many Crimean Tatars still lived in temporary housing: hostels or converted classrooms. Sometimes these were in the cities, but many people were isolated in the countryside without land, work, or transportation to generate an income.

Crimean Tatars interviewed felt that they had lost not only their savings to inflation, but also their investment in their homes. Housing was appreciating in the cities and on the southern coast, but depreciating in the areas where the majority of Crimean Tatars currently held assets. Rents were high relative to salaries and other income. Therefore poor families lived in hostels or in overcrowded apartments with relatives. Housing could be an asset, but very few Crimean Tatars owned apartments or homes in areas where they could be rented, because of the ban on resettlement on the southern coast and because of housing shortages in the cities.

Interview findings suggested that the social groups that were likely to be poor were refugees, pensioners, large families with young children, and single and divorced mothers.

A single mother living in Kerch with two young children and her mother estimates that her family of four had an income of 145 grivnas this month. Their main sources of income remain her mother's pension (55 grivnas), government child support (10.5 grivnas), the sale of assets (40 to 50 grivnas), and assistance from a family friend. Each month the friend gives them 20 to 30 grivnas in cash as well as food. In emergencies he has also provided cash for health expenses (450 grivnas). The mother is unemployed and has been struck from the roster of the unemployment office. She tried selling fruits and vegetables in the market but was unable to make a profit. The gas has been cut off because she cannot pay. Food constitutes the bulk of their expenses (100 to 120 grivnas a month). School-related expenses are the second-largest expense, followed by medicines for her elderly mother.

Workers in certain occupations had been hard hit by layoffs, unpaid leave, and irregular payment of salaries; these included collective farm workers, light industry factory workers, engineers, construction workers, medical workers, and school and kindergarten teachers. Crimean Tatars had been recruited as construction workers both in Crimea and in Central Asia by the Goskomnats-funded construction companies and "trusts." As a result, many families had moved to Crimea, relying on these companies to provide both salaries and housing. In recent years, however, they had been let down on both counts as the central government's funding for new construction had dried up.

Sever was recruited from his town in Uzbekistan in 1991 to work for a Crimean construction company. A large number of Crimean Tatars were recruited along with him and were promised housing. In 1995 Sever was fired, and the family of four now lives on his wife Rubia's salary. The Goskomnats has warned the residents that they now must pay for the rooms they occupy: 25 grivnas a month per bed. The family has decided to move out into a *vremianka* (a small temporary house) in the compact settlement of Stroganovka where his parents live. Sever estimates that without the income from sales of vegetables they produce, their children would not have had school supplies or new shoes for the new school year. The family's first priorities are to meet basic food needs and cover educational costs. Finishing their home, in which they invested 10,000 rubles in 1991, is not a realistic prospect without assistance.

Even the less poor had experienced spells of poverty because of unstable incomes over the last five years. The returnees suffered an initial drop in their standard of living when they moved to Crimea, because few had employment or permanent housing upon arrival. The second drop took place in 1992–93, when hyperinflation eliminated cash savings and the budgetary crisis reduced the value of salaries and pensions and initiated a series of layoffs and forced unpaid leave.

In the Leninskii region, on a Crimean Tatar collective farm, a Crimean Tatar couple says that the worst years were 1994–95, because they had not yet invested in their household plot. The husband arrived in 1990 and was followed by his wife and five children in 1991. Salaries were meager but reliable. They lived in a hostel and then in a rented apartment. They had enough money to buy coal. In 1993 the Goskomnats provided the bare bones of a structure; four years later the home still has concrete floors, no internal plaster or paint, and no glass in the window frames. The ceiling has not been finished.

Problems with late and unpaid salaries began in 1994. That winter, with no other sources of income, the household fell into poverty. They had spent their time and cash on finishing the house rather than buying cattle or exploiting the household plot. The house was unheated that winter because they could not afford coal or gas. The following year they tried to increase their household plot production, but the drought ruined the potato harvest. In 1996 the father was able to find seasonal work in construction, for which he was paid in kind (a calf). In September they received their last child allowances. In 1997 the calf is now a milk cow, contributing to the improved situation by providing milk, the only daily source of protein for the children. The family's diet consists of potatoes, bread, and dairy products. Cash remains very scarce. The mother sells potatoes when cash is needed for school supplies and shoes. In a recent health emergency they reduced their consumption of potatoes and milk and sold some in the market for cash to buy medicines.

Coping Strategies

Interviewees reported three main types of coping strategies: reductive strategies, productive strategies, and collaborative strategies. Reductive strategies included subsistence farming, reducing the quality and quantity of food consumption, and reducing cash expenditure by cutting back on fuel and utilities, not buying new clothes, forgoing medical treatment and opting for home remedies and folk healers, giving up cigarettes, and forgoing long-term basic needs (such as housing) to meet immediate needs (such as food). Productive strategies included selling produce, stealing goods and produce, self-employment, taking multiple salaried jobs, starting private enterprises, and renting land. Collaborative strategies relied on family and ethnic networks to access and pool resources, such as pooling the incomes of a number of relatives to build a common home, crowding many households into one home to reduce housing costs, and pooling labor for construction and income generation.

Demira, her husband, and their four children (aged 2, 15, 18, and 19) live in Zaretchnoe village in the Simferopolskii region. Her family has no stable income. Her husband was disabled in an accident but has not had the strength to obtain documentation to receive disability allowances. The children's allowances were last paid in the spring of 1997 to cover the first half of 1996. The family's main source of income is the household plot and two cows. Demira sells milk to bulk traders who come to her village three times a week. She earns 4.5 grivnas at each visit during the tourist season (on average 13.5 grivnas per week for eight weeks). The rest of the year there is little demand for milk. From September to May she goes to the market herself, incurring transportation and other market-related costs. Many times there are not enough customers and she cannot sell all the milk she has brought; other times the milk turns sour and cannot be sold.

At the end of the winter and in early spring, the family runs low on feed for the animals, and the cows stop producing milk. To make ends meet in the winter, Demira bakes bread at home to sell in the market. When the family runs low on money, they can exchange some of their milk products for other foods produced by their neighbors in the village. But everyone in the village is in similar straits and produces similar products. Sometimes the family can buy staples at the village store for credit. The store manager will sometimes accept eggs as payment for small necessities such as soap. Demira's elder son earns money at odd jobs during the fall and spring: cutting wood, carrying coal, working in construction. Her daughter is a trained seamstress, but she gets only four or five orders a year because few households in the village have the resources to buy new clothes.

Social Consequences of Poverty

Poverty had taken a toll on the Crimean Tatar community. There was less community spirit; more families were divided by divorce, separation, or abandonment; and there had been a rise in criminal activities. Respondents said that each household focused on house construction and household problems. Unlike in Central Asia, it was rare to see a group of neighbors volunteering to help each other build a home. Men and women were overworked. Men worked on construction in the evenings and weekends if there was any money for materials. In the compact settlements researchers saw men hurrying to finish the walls of houses before the winter, working by flashlight when night had already fallen. It was common for women to work both at a salaried job (teaching, for example) and in the market early in the morning or at the end of the workday so they could buy food staples. Neighbors had little opportunity to meet. There was no leisure time, and there were no recreational centers, shops, or social services in the compact settlements.

Resettlement and the ensuing poverty strained family integrity. There were considerable numbers of single and divorced mothers among the respondents. The women explained that the men's inability to provide for the family's needs had driven them to abandon their impoverished families. One husband had returned to live with his mother in Uzbekistan. Some husbands had left their family in Central Asia to look for opportunities in Crimea, started a second family, and were not heard of again. Cases where mothers had left their spouse and children for better prospects seemed more rare.

Theft, racketeering, and prostitution were on the rise. Lack of employment opportunities and recreational activities exposed the young people to the temptations of vandalism, alcoholism, and drug abuse. Crimean Tatar youths in Yalta said that most of their friends had used "soft" drugs such as marijuana. However, they knew of no one in the community who used "hard" drugs. Prostitution was also said to be widespread among Russian girls, but not among more traditional Crimean Tatar girls. In Yalta, key informants and youths estimated that 80 percent of Russian girls were to some degree involved in prostitution. Youths were drawn to criminal behavior because of the gap between the socioeconomic level of the visiting tourists and the low level of economic opportunity of the residents.

Ranking Priorities

One important exercise of the assessment was to elicit a discussion of community priorities using participatory rapid appraisal techniques. The results of the ranking could not always be taken at face value, however, because they could be manipulated by the participating groups. However, through triangulation with other methods such as interviews, researchers were able to understand the importance of these priority needs. According to individual and group interviews and community meetings, the main problems affecting returning populations and impeding peaceful integration were lack of infrastructure in the compact settlements, poor housing, lack of employment and other income-generating activities, lack of legal status (citizenship), lack of support for language and culture, and lack of social services (health and education facilities).

Infrastructure

At the community level, the top priority for residents of the compact settlements was the provision of basic infrastructure. The respondents repeatedly characterized infrastructure as a community priority, ranking it above individual needs such as work and increased income. The lack of basic amenities—water, electricity, and roads—created substandard living conditions for residents and impeded settlement and construction in some 200 compact settlements. These problems affected most of the estimated 25,000 families who lived in the settlements. As of 1997 only 20 percent of the compact settlements and residential neighborhoods had electricity, 30 percent had water, 15 percent had tarmac roads, only 4 percent had gas heating, and none had sewers. Those settlements that had been formalized after 1991 and those that remained unofficial had the least infrastructure, because that date corresponded to the end of the generous central government funding of resettlement.

Life could be very difficult in the compact settlements, especially in the winter. Lack of infrastructure deterred the return of more Crimean Tatars from Central Asia and the normalization of life. An icy wind gusted through the settlements in the barren steppe regions, where there were few trees to protect homes and people outdoors from the dust and the cold. The roads were transformed into muddy rivers, then covered by ice sheets, making them impassable. On the worst days, parents kept their children home from school and mothers stayed behind instead of going to earn a few grivnas in the market. Power outages in the few settlements with electricity became more common each day as the municipality attempted to ration energy resources. With the decline in incomes, many families were unable to buy coal to heat their homes. They relied instead on collected firewood or unreliable electricity.

Water problems worsened in winter because of frozen pipes, dry wells, and impassable roads. There was no piped water supply in a majority of the compact settlements, and so water was trucked in and rationed. In Ismail Bey and Sputnik, water was trucked in each week. Each household, regardless of size, received 100 liters. For lack of better containers, the water was often stored in old oil bins covered with cardboard sheets to keep out the dust. After residents had complained about poor water quality for months, tests by the government laboratory found fecal elements and ammonia.

Complaints about the lack of roads were widespread. Sidewalks and tarmac roads were the rule outside compact settlements settlements and in villages near towns, but not in isolated villages. In the mountainous southern coastal area, residents estimated that the lack of roads added 100 grivnas to the cost of transporting one truckload of sand from Yalta. Mothers complained that children from compact settlements got dirty on their way to school, and their shameful state was remarked upon by teachers and fellow students. In some cases, children stayed at home on rainy days because they lacked appropriate boots or a second pair of clean shoes to change into once they arrived at school.

In the past, some urban neighborhoods had been heated very inefficiently through a central district system. Since the energy crisis after the collapse of trade between the former Soviet republics, however, central heating had been discontinued in most neighborhoods, and residents had switched to coal, wood, or electricity. Coal was the preferred fuel for heating individual homes but was very expensive. Families had turned to firewood, the use of which has had a considerable environmental impact on the wooded areas of Crimea. In just seven years, the residents of Ismail Bey and Sputnik said, they had cut down 12 hectares of orchards for firewood.

Drainage and sewerage systems were never mentioned at the community or local government level as community needs. Yet, as already noted, none of the compact settlements was equipped with sewerage systems. As in other former Soviet republics, drainage and sewerage systems in Ukraine were rare outside of cities and towns and therefore may not have figured as a priority for communities who view their absence as normal. By Western engineering standards, in contrast, these systems would be considered requirements, especially where the water table is high and well water is used for drinking.

Housing

Upon their arrival, the returning Crimean Tatars faced an already tight housing and infrastructure situation. In 1995, one in seven Ukrainian families lacked separate or permanent housing and instead lived with relatives, in temporarily rented apartments, or in hostels. The budgetary crisis exacerbated the chronic housing shortage. For the estimated 50,000 Crimean Tatar families, 45,500 household plots had been given out as of January 1997, according to the Department for the Return and Shelter of Crimean Tatars. Still, 21,307 families lived in unfinished homes or *vremianki* (small temporary homes, usually with two rooms); 6,500 families lived with relatives, in hostels, or in rented flats; about 16,000 families were on waiting lists for municipal housing; 3,500 families were in homes built by the state; and 3,500 lived in homes for which Ukraine had received foreign grants.

Housing construction had all but ended at many of the sites visited, especially in rural areas and in the south where additional transport costs inflated the cost of materials by some 200 percent. A few families still resided in the shipping containers in which they had transported their belongings from Central Asia. Others lived in the basements of their unfinished homes. Comparatively well-off families resided in one or two rooms of incomplete homes and small temporary homes know as *vremianki*. To protect against the strong winds and humidity, residents covered the windows, roof, and doors with plastic. For many, construction had dragged on for more than five years. Some families saw no hope of finishing without an economic turnaround. Thus temporary housing had become long-term housing.

In Evpatoria approximately 75 families of workers of a construction firm live in the "refurbished" basements of five buildings. Conditions are very poor. As one descends into the basement, one is hit with the smell of mold mixed with that of cooking and the unmistakable stink of broken toilets. The ventilation in the toilets is blocked by garbage. The water and wastewater pipes line the ceiling of the corridor. Residents said that more than once a wastewater pipe had broken, flooding the corridor and the rooms where families cook, eat, and sleep. The families are crowded into small spaces. In one basement the average was 2.3 square meters per person. As the field worker noted, "That is 0.3 square meter more than a grave." There is an ad hoc lighting system, whereby flashlights are hooked up to the main system.

These dwellings were meant to be temporary until construction of homes for the workers was completed, but only 16 homes out of the 120 to 130 planned had been completed in the six years of operation. Foundations were built on all household plots and walls added to half of them. Workers do not have any property documents to show ownership of the household plot or the construction. Legally, the company is still the owner, although it is bankrupt and unlikely ever to finish the homes.

The construction firm has warned the residents of these basements that, starting in October 1997, the company will no longer be able to cover utility costs. The residents expect that the electricity—their sole source of energy for cooking, heating, and lighting—will be cut off. Because of breach of contract by the firm, the municipal residential management agency will have the right to repossess the dwellings.

Some families had only had time to build a *vremianka* before their money lost its value. A two-room *vremianka* could generally be completed for 2,000 grivnas through cost savings such as using half-bricks. After realizing in 1992 that these were now their permanent homes, some households tried to improve the structures by adding thicker walls or a porch. Living standards in *vremianki* varied greatly, depending on the ability of the family to expand and upgrade the structure.

In 1994 Ilias left Samarqand for Crimea. He lived with his son for a year until he got a household plot in Krasnokamenka, near Yalta, where he was born. In 1997 he was still working on a 30-square-meter *vremianka*. His resources consist of his retirement pension (54 grivnas), which he saved while living with his son, and sporadic material help from his children.

Another head of household reports, "In 1995 it became dangerous to live in Uzbekistan, and we were afraid to let our two children out in the street. Our neighbors would ask us what were we waiting for, since all the other Crimean Tatars had left. Though we lived well, with a car and savings in the bank, we decided to leave. When we arrived in Simferopol, our family moved in with my cousin, his wife, his mother, and his two children in their container. We asked to be put on a waiting list for a hostel or apartment, but the local government refused, saying that our family had been deported from Evpatoria and should expect nothing from the Simferopol administration. My cousin is trying to get a roof over his home so that he can move his family out of the container by winter. All our savings have been spent on food for the last two years. I have not been able to find any work or even get a permanent residence permit."

Some families continued to build through the crisis. Families who continued to build after 1992 were more realistic. Large houses were often left unfinished because the owner ran out of money. Building was a sign of savings, of a cash income more than sufficient to cover basic food needs and a family with multiple workers, few dependents, and time to build. Seasonal employment and odd jobs provided the flexibility for building. Higher incomes from a small or medium-size private business (not a microenterprise or self-employment) or, more commonly, seasonal contract work in Russia enabled some families to complete construction. The Crimean Tatars often pooled labor and income from multiple families (mostly relatives) to cover the cost of construction, each family planning to occupy one room. Sometimes men worked together on one house and then moved on to the next, sharing labor, time, and some resources.

In Sputnik, a household living in a relatively large home—one floor, four large rooms, with a finished façade but no internal comforts—is continuing to put money into construction. The head of the household explains that five couples (all relatives) pooled their receipts from the sale of their homes in Uzbekistan to build the home in Sputnik. Four of the couples are now living in the house. A married son is living with his wife's family, eight people in a two-room apartment, in Evpatoria. The income from these six couples continues to be pooled to finish the home. There are two regular salaries plus income from odd jobs. The wives also work in the market. The five-year-old child stayed in Uzbekistan with his grandmother because living conditions are too poor in the compact settlement.

An extended family in Kerch—three men, three women, and two children—is still building after nine years. The 56-square-meter home was begun in 1991 from the proceeds from sale of a home in Uzbekistan. The family ran out of money and could not buy materials for the roof, internal finishings, windows, or doors. From 1989 to 1991 the head of the household held a good position, which allowed him to buy and store construction materials, but he had no time to work on construction. After being "downsized" in 1991, he started working in earnest on the household plot and built a greenhouse. In 1992 he opened a small enterprise. He explains that about half his income is from his small business and the other half from odd jobs. He also grows vegetables in the greenhouse and on the household plot. The food they produce is a lot of help. His family, his brother, and his parents live on income from his business (300 grivnas a month). The income from the household plot goes to buy construction materials. Without his brother and father working on the household plot and construction with him, he would not have been able to build.

Employment

The economic crisis in Crimea had engendered financial insecurity at the household level. Salaries were insufficient to support a family adequately. According to Crimean Tatars interviewed, the returnees were locked out of better-paid skilled positions and were limited to physical labor because of the lack of relevance of the skills they had acquired in Central Asia, their lack of papers, and above all, discrimination. During the social assessment, researchers met with educated people with years of work experience who were employed as cleaners and watchmen. Just as for the rest of the population, salaried employment was unreliable. Contracts in the private sector were short-term, and work was often seasonal. Men commonly worked in construction, and women worked in tourist hostels during the summer. Sometimes salaries were paid only in part, in kind, or not at all. In all three collective farms the management was unable to pay salaries in full.

A trained economist with years of experience finally found a position for which she was qualified. The position was well remunerated (400 grivnas a month). After months of unemployment, she could not believe her luck. Rightly so. To her chagrin, the manager mentioned that salaries had not been paid for the last four months. Employees are welcome to take the equivalent of their salary in bricks, which the enterprise produces.

Official unemployment was low, with 2.4 percent of workers registered at the unemployment office, but the real unemployment rate was closer to 45 percent. Crimean Tatars interviewed claimed that unemployment affected them more than other groups. According to Crimean Tatar sources, state and private firms employed 60 percent of those capable of working. The rest were unemployed. Crimean Tatars were seldom offered jobs that matched their qualifications and experience. They were vastly underrepresented in the Ministry of the Interior, the procuracy, the courts, and the local administration. There were no Crimean Tatars in the security forces. Unemployment was also linked to the deurbanization of the Crimean Tatars. Too many city-trained specialists were living in villages. Crimea and Central Asia do not share industrial specializations; thus a valuable cotton production specialist from Central Asia had no future in Crimea.

Discrimination was perceived as the most important obstacle to employment. Examples abounded of employers retracting an offer once the Crimean Tatar applicant presented an old Soviet passport indicating nationality. Such cases were encountered in villages, in cities in the steppe regions, and along the coast. Workers either gave up and accepted lower-paying menial jobs or turned to self-employment.

In 1988 Zeide arrived in a small village in the Belogorskii region from Tashkent. She had over 10 years of experience working as a teacher in city schools. Upon her arrival she went to see the school director, who told her, "We are sorry, there are no vacant posts, and there won't be any." Shortly thereafter, the school hired a woman of Greek ethnicity, not formerly deported. When Zeide went to another village school nearby, the director asked incredulously, "How can a Crimean Tatar teach in Russian?"

Permanent employment required a permanent residence permit, which was difficult for residents of hostels and compact settlements to obtain. Some government agencies (including the tax agency) no longer hired noncitizens, and noncitizens already working in government agencies had been formally advised to seek other employment. Even though the deadline for obtaining citizenship had passed, however, no one had been fired at the time of the assessment.

Personal ties and nepotism were the predominant means of obtaining job placement. Thus those who had more of a history in a given area and more links (including ethnic allegiances) were more likely to obtain placement.

In 1988, after six months of struggling to obtain a residence permit and employment, a respondent decided to use his ties as a communist party member to resolve these issues. He went to the city council and met with the party representative, who called up the village council to resolve his residence permit. He also called up the local fish factory to provide him with a well-paying job, and the central city hospital to hire his wife, a doctor.

Self-Employment and Small Enterprises

Many households had shifted away from salaries, pensions, and other government benefits to private sector income, and some were successful entrepreneurs. The private sector provided a high level of income for sellers of local and imported goods, truck drivers, growers of produce, and producers of ethnic foods such as *tchibureki* and *bakhlava*. Micro- and small enterprises required very small amounts of startup capital and little to no equipment. In the best of cases, self-employment served as a building block for other, more ambitious activities.

> Lutfie, a refugee from the Kyrgyz Republic living in Zvezdotchka hostel in Yalta, says that she turned to self-employment after having been turned away for a job because of discrimination. Like the majority of residents of the hostel, she started frying *tchibureki* and doughnuts and selling them in the market. She then befriended some people who work in the market, who helped her get a spot selling vegetables and fruits.

The same characteristics that made the venture flexible—a low level of formality, low investment, and low liquidity—also made it vulnerable. Daily incomes were very small and could therefore be wiped out by increased costs or seasonal price fluctuations.

> Seiran bakes cakes and doughnuts, which he sells in the market in Yalta during the tourist season. In May his income from sales is about $300.[8] It increases to $700 in June and $900 in July and August. As the tourist season nears its end, however, his income declines to $700 in September and $250 in October.

Because the bulk of these enterprises focused on trade and marketing, they required access to markets and transportation. The majority of residents of isolated villages were not able to profit from their production because they lacked transportation.

> In Vodopolnoe only five families own cars. They are able to buy up local produce and make $500 a month during the summer by taking it to sell in Evpatoria. Those who have no cars do not bother going to the market, because the costs of bus fare and a spot in the market exceed the expected revenues.
>
> In Ay-Vasil, a compact settlement near Yalta, a young resident travels each day to the milk factory near Simferopol, where he buys milk to sell in the market in Yalta. His business is entirely dependent on his ability to transport cheap milk from the factory to the southern coast.
>
> Marlen provides transportation for construction materials. He does not own his truck but rents it for 200 grivnas a month. Today he had two customers. The first asked him to transport wood planks to a village 20 kilometers from Simferopol. Marlen was paid 50 grivnas for the trip,

realizing 32.5 grivnas after expenses. His second customer wanted to transport 10 metric tons of sand a distance of 10 kilometers. Marlen received 21 grivnas, but he spent 23 grivnas for an oil change, cigarettes, and lunch.

A single mother with two children wants her son to attend the better city schools. She spends three to five days each month traveling by bus to the villages, buying up produce to sell in the market, at 200 percent of her purchase price. Her expenses include bribes to the tax inspectors—she has no trade license—and the sanitation department, maintenance for the market, and her spot in the market, but no payment to the local mafia. She estimates she makes 10 to 15 grivnas a day, or up to $200 over the tourist season.

A combination of formal and informal costs made businesses unlikely to be profitable without entanglement with local officials. There was a high tax rate on small businesses (30 percent on profits and 52 percent on the salary fund) in addition to the official fees required for operating. A trade license cost 200 grivnas a year. It was difficult to rent a locale from the municipality in profitable places, and once the renter had refurbished the locale, it could be repossessed without compensation for the improvements. Mafia payments were 10 to 20 percent of profits in addition to other, less predictable payments to police, sanitation, and other officials. An entrepreneur needed a "roof" or protection agreement with a well-placed official. Some employees and business partners saw nothing wrong in stealing from inventories. Crimean Tatars who had spent their savings on housing lacked start-up and working capital. Many respondents said that they lacked ideas or understanding of management, accounting, tax, and legal issues. Finally, self-employment and trade had a low status. Yet self-employment was a main source of income for the many unemployed and unpaid workers in the transition.

The local sellers in Evpatoria benefit from the activism of their local Crimean Tatar representative on the city council. He has secured 30 to 40 free places in the market, saving them each 5 grivnas a day. This is an important sum, because they estimate that they make from 5 to 10 grivnas a day in winter and up to 25 grivnas in the summer. The representative recommended that they refuse to pay the 200 grivnas for the trading license or the fines of 3,000 to 5,000 grivnas for not having a license. While he takes on this issue with local officials, his constituents continue working in the market.

.

With adequate financing, some Crimean Tatar businesses have been able to grow, but at the cost of other long-term needs such as housing.

Hairie arrived in Crimea in 1990. The money she and her husband had realized from the sale of their home in Uzbekistan was not sufficient to buy a home in Kerch, so they rented an apartment and organized a cooperative in which they invested their money. Over seven years they have spent nearly $4,000 on repairs and construction of an extension to a centrally located shop. In 1994 they started producing doughnuts and *tchibureki* in the back of the shop. Today they also have five spots in the market. They would like to purchase equipment to process raw materials but do not have access to loans.

Privatized enterprises were required to retain the same production profile for two to five years and were not allowed to fire employees. These conditions slowed competitiveness and the development of new sectors. Advantages were given to full-time employees of enterprises engaged in the privatization process. Privatization of small enterprises was limited to Ukrainian citizens and permanent employees of enterprises undergoing privatization. Crimean Tatars were likely to be less well placed for privatization because more of them were employed part-time and excluded from management positions where they could make important decisions guiding privatization.

Citizenship

Recent returnees experienced a number of legal difficulties when trying to formalize their situation with a permanent residence permit or to obtain title to their home. They faced discrimination, harassment by officials and police, and other unpleasant encounters with local administrators and officials. Noncitizens were excluded from civil service employment; higher education was more expensive, and certain faculties, such as law, were closed to them; they could not privatize their household plots and enterprises or vote in national and regional elections. Travel abroad, and most importantly to Russia, was restricted to those with new Ukrainian passports.

Many interviewees had problems formalizing their residence, purchasing homes, and legalizing their residence in newly completed homes. Crimean Tatar sources estimated that as many as 100,000 Crimean Tatars resided in Crimea without residence permits, which required a formal home that had passed inspection. Many of the homes in the compact settlements were incomplete (without a finished façade) and would not pass such an inspection. The residence permit also required a formal address, not just a household plot number, and a minimum of 13.56 square feet per person. A room in communal housing was not considered a formal home, and residents there could only obtain a temporary residence permit. Without a residence permit one could be barred from formal employment and questioned and fined by the local police. Persons living in hostels and in the compact settlements were often without permanent residence permits and sometimes without any permit at all. Even when the requirements were met, obtaining a residence permit was not a straightforward process.

In August 1989, right after the decision of the TASS commission, Marlen came to Crimea to assess the situation. He then returned to Uzbekistan to borrow 17,000 rubles and came back with his sister's husband in October. They went to Bakhchisarai, the region where his father was born, to stay with his second cousin. The three of them lived together while they looked for a home to purchase. His cousin had not been granted a residence permit in Bakhchisarai. A number of times he had been dragged from his own home to the police station, where he was openly told that Crimean Tatars may not live in Bakhchisarai. The police repeatedly demanded that he pay fines. After two months his cousin's wife and two children arrived and they were again called to the police station. They were told to leave immediately.

After two years of constant harassment, the family was finally given residence permits. During that time the respondent continued looking for a home in the Bakhchisarai region. But potential sellers stated that they would not sell to a Crimean Tatar. The respondent decided to look instead for a home in Simferopol. He found two homes for his family and his relatives: an old home offered by an old Russian woman and a new, unfinished home. He bought the homes and went back to Uzbekistan because his wife would not be released from her job as a teacher until the end of the school semester. On January 10 he came back to Simferopol to find that the old woman had changed her mind. She gave him back the money, explaining that the police had come to see her and warned that the local authorities would not approve the purchase and would not grant a residence permit to the buyers. He went to the police, where he was told that it was still prohibited for Crimean Tatars to live in the city. He then met a friend on the street who recommended that he go talk to the management of the collective farm in a village in the Belogorskii region, a poor rural area. A bribe of 100 rubles would facilitate an agreement, the friend suggested. Indeed, the farm manager promptly helped him find a home and provided him with a residence permit.

Police harassment remained a salient issue for respondents eight years after the initial wave of immigration.

> One of the Crimean Tatar field workers working on the assessment was fined 17 grivnas in Yalta. His crime? Standing outside the hotel without his residence permit in his pocket. He had left it in his room. He asked the police officer to be given the chance to go get his papers. The officer refused and explained that the police have a daily quota to fill each day for rounding up "people with Caucasian features."

Language and Culture

Language is at the core of the Crimean Tatars' nationality, and nationality gave meaning to the current difficulties. As one respondent explained:

> Without our national language, we are not Crimean Tatars. If we are not Crimean Tatars, we are nothing. If this is not my homeland and I am not Crimean Tatar, then why am I putting up with [these poor living conditions in the compact settlement]?

Knowledge of language and culture suffered from the extended exile and lack of promotion by Soviet authorities. Most Crimean Tatar families said that they spoke Russian at home. There was a dearth of Crimean Tatar literature accessible to children and adults. The other deported minorities (Armenian, Bulgarian, German, and Greek) showed less concern as communities in maintaining their national language. During these interviews they also showed signs of a higher degree of assimilation than the Crimean Tatars: they lived in mixed settlements (mostly in cities), accepted mixed marriages, russified their names, and rarely expressed with the same intensity as the Crimean Tatars an interest in educating their children in the national language and culture.

The language issue had become politicized, pitting local officials against each other along ethnic lines. To support their demands for government support for national education, respondents cited Article 10 of the Ukrainian Constitution, adopted June 28, 1996, which states, "In Ukraine, the free development, use, and protection of Russian, and other languages of national minorities of Ukraine, is guaranteed," and the unratified Crimean constitution, which stated that the Autonomous Republic of Crimea had three official languages: Russian, Ukrainian, and Crimean Tatar.

Within the Crimean Tatar community, there was no consensus on how to address the issue of revitalizing the Crimean Tatar language and culture. The Mejlis, backed by some parents, requested that Crimean Tatar schools be opened. Many parents complained that the Crimean Tatar language was being taught as an optional course at the end of the schoolday to children of different ages and levels. The children were tired and hungry and unmotivated. In other schools the language was required for Crimean Tatars, but non-Tatar students took advanced classes in other important subjects during those same hours. Some parents were concerned that this put their children at a disadvantage academically. Parents expecting their children to go to university, were ambivalent about an all-Tatar education. They feared that their children would not be able to compete in exams for admission to higher education unless they attended Russian or Ukrainian schools. In addition, they suspected that Crimean Tatar schools might be inferior to other schools, just as national language schools had often not been as prestigious as Russian language schools in the Soviet education system.

For other respondents the schools were the sole environment where ethnic groups truly mixed. Although ethnic disputes among students did arise, parents valued the fact that their children had Russian and Ukrainian friends, something the parents themselves rarely had. They expected that through these friendships their children would build a network that would allow them to be truly integrated into Crimean society. According to some respondents, assimilation was inevitable: it would take place in Crimea as it had in Uzbekistan.

Social Services

Social services were not seen as a priority, but kindergartens and primary health clinics were consistently mentioned. The returnees placed new demands on existing social services. In the villages, the Russian and Ukrainian populations tended to be composed overwhelmingly of pensioners, often living alone, with few young families. In contrast, the Crimean Tatars were arriving with multigenerational families and with more children per couple than the Russians.

The main obstacle to access to social services was low income. The formal costs (transportation, medicines, supplies) and the informal costs (bribes and other presents to doctors to guarantee good treatment) had increased dramatically. Costs were an obstacle to those with low cash incomes and eroded savings and assets. In the Belogorskii district the head of the collective farm estimated that 20 children (out of 630) did not attend school regularly for lack of clothes. He estimated that a family needed to spend approximately 200 grivnas to prepare a child for the first day of school. Medical care was often unaffordable, especially in rural areas, with dire consequences.

In the Zvezdotchka hostel in Yalta, settled by Crimean Tatars, a child was badly burned when a kettle spilled over in a crowded room. The director of the collective farm refused to pay back salaries to allow his mother to take him to see a doctor. The child now has disfiguring scars.

The compact settlements located at the periphery of towns commonly used the social services in the city but were rarely linked by public transportation to these services. In villages, educational and health facilities were undersupplied. Very few medicines were provided at first-aid stations, limiting the local supply of services.

Conclusions

Even though the Crimean Tatars had been eager to return to the homeland, many still felt that they were treated as foreigners or, worse, second-class citizens on their own land. Their living conditions, which were below the norm for the country. were a main complaint. Whereas other Crimean citizens had been granted apartment rights during the transition and had benefited from sewerage, roads, water, and other basic services, the Crimean Tatars had been systematically left out because of lack of citizenship and the low level of investment in infrastructure in the compact settlements. Although Crimea had been for hundreds of years an ethnic mosaic with a plethora of minorities, relations between the larger ethnic groups succeeded in sidelining the Crimean Tatars not only geographically but also politically, socially, and economically. However, with their strong social networks and tradition of political activism, the Crimean Tatars remained a force to be reckoned with in the struggle for control over resources in the Crimean peninsula.

Notes

1. This chapter uses the term "Crimean Tatar" instead of "Tatar" because of the political implications of omitting the adjective. Crimean Tatars consider themselves distinct from other Tatars (for example, Tatars in Russia) and claim to be

the indigenous people of the Crimea. Omission of the adjective is seen as a denial of their claim to Crimea as their homeland.

2. Interview with Nariman Ibadulaev, representative of the City Council and member of the Plan-Budget Committee. Two of the categories are age groups and the third a status—"capable of work"—which excludes invalids and some others.

3. Open Society Institute (1996, p. 14). The author also notes, "Russian-dominated Crimean State Committee on Nationality Affairs and Deported People maintains about 45,000 persons died between 1944–48."

4. Brian Humphreys, "Unlike Chechens, the Crimean Tatars May Get Rights Without War," *Christian Science Monitor*, March 9, 1995.

5. Funded by the Ukrainian budget, Goskomnats was and remains the single funder of capital improvement projects benefiting the formerly deported persons in general and the Crimean Tatars in particular. City, district, and village budgets were not commonly used to meet these needs.

6. The Mejlis was structured with a 33-member executive board, the Kurultai. Each town, village, and compact settlement where Crimean Tatars resided had a local representative on the Mejlis. A representative also coordinated activities of local Mejlis at the district level. For more historical detail see Open Society (1996, pp. 46–51).

7. This was an unofficial estimate made by an official working at the passport agency in Simferopol. There were 245,624 Crimean Tatars with *propiskas* in Crimea, and 147,279 (60 percent) had citizenship. This estimate may be higher than the migration figures would suggest because many of the Crimean Tatars interviewed said that they had problems obtaining formal proof that they were residents as of November 13, 1991. People who sought to apply earlier did not have information about new regulations, which might have encouraged them to reapply.

8. Respondents sometimes expressed monetary amounts in dollars, reflecting the use of multiple currencies within the region.

References

Browne, Stephen. 1996. "Measuring Poverty." Note prepared for *Ukraine Human Development Report*. Kyiv: United Nations Development Programme. Processed.

Open Society Institute. 1996. "Crimean Tatars: Repatriation and Conflict Resolution." New York.

United Nations Development Programme. 1996. *Ukraine Human Development Report: Looking Beyond the Triple Transition*. Kyiv.

World Bank. 1996. "Poverty Assessment Report—Excerpts." Washington, D.C.

A pensioner in the Comrat district.
Photo from the World Bank Photo Library

 ✳

CHAPTER 11

Eating From One Pot: Survival Strategies in Moldova's Collapsing Rural Economy

Hermine G. De Soto and Nora Dudwick

A verdant country located between Ukraine and Romania, Moldova is the smallest of the Soviet successor states after Armenia. Located at a crossroads of Europe between the historical Roman, Polish, Russian, Austro-Hungarian, and Ottoman Empires, contemporary Moldova preserves many of these influences in an ethnically and linguistically rich culture. Today ethnic Moldovans make up two-thirds of the national population. They speak Romanian, and most, like the majority of Moldova's Slavic population, adhere to Orthodox Christianity. Moldova includes significant numbers of Russians, Ukrainians, Poles, Bulgarians, Jews, Gagauz (a Turkic-speaking minority), and Roma (gypsies). Following independence, a new law making Romanian the state language triggered ethnic and political tensions and led to separatist movements in the regions of Transnistria and Gagauzia.

Moldovans have experienced a sharp decline in their standard of living. As poor Moldovans struggle to feed their families and cover basic education and health costs, they have witnessed the appearance of a small, wealthy class of business entrepreneurs. In the countryside, collective farm workers have become steadily more impoverished, although some who have succeeded in fully withdrawing land from state ownership have managed to raise household incomes. These economic shifts have started to alter rela-

333

tions within and among families and communities, fragmenting former ties of solidarity and increasing socioeconomic differentiation.

Methodology

This study was carried out in October and November 1996 as part of a World Bank poverty assessment in Moldova (World Bank 1999).[1] It is based on qualitative research methodologies, including open-ended interviews and careful observation of 200 poor individuals and households, as well as key informant interviews with community leaders and international aid workers. The study was managed locally by Adsisto, a local nongovernmental organization established by the U.S.-based Volunteers in Overseas Cooperative Assistance. In rural areas, collective farm employees, independent farmers, and public sector employees were interviewed along with pensioners and the unemployed. In urban areas, intellectuals, skilled and unskilled workers, small entrepreneurs, office workers, state sector employees, and unemployed persons were interviewed. Interviews were conducted in the capital, Chisinau, and a sample of districts chosen to include the range of agricultural, climatic, ethnic, economic, and rural-urban differences. The sites included the Edenet and Balti districts in the north of the country, Ungheni and Nisporeni districts in the center, Comrat and Cahul districts in the south, and three poor districts in Chisinau: Centru, Ciocana, and Buiucani.

Defining Poverty

For most poor respondents, poverty was a very recent phenomenon. Most felt they used to live well; only a minority had always been poor. Today Moldovans compare salaries with the minimum food basket and conclude that "now we are all poor." Respondents said the worst aspects of poverty were hunger, poor health, lack of adequate clothing, and poor housing conditions.

Insecurity and Shame. Poverty has important social and psychological components. Respondents felt defenseless. They perceived that poverty was gradually destroying traditions that had once brought people together on a regular basis. They described their loss of hope for the future and the pervasive sense that they did not know and could not find out what was going on around them. For many poor people the words "independence," "democracy," and "transition" have come to signify a lack of social justice. People experienced their own poverty as deeply humiliating. Even those respondents who appeared extremely poor to interviewers often preferred to define themselves as "close to" but not completely poor. Under socialism, to the extent that poverty was acknowledged, it had been ascribed to individual failings. People were highly conscious of status and position, which could secure access to important goods and services. High status demanded, in turn, the ability of households or individuals to discharge their social obligations and to maintain the appearance of prosperity.

One respondent says, "Poverty is pain; it feels like a disease. It attacks a person not only materially but also morally. It eats away one's dignity and drives one into total despair. A person feels poverty every moment without even noticing it."

Generational Differences. Young people interviewed for this study saw poverty as the lack of decent clothing, humiliation in front of richer friends, inability to participate in a normal social life, and the inability to earn money. For young married couples, poverty signified the inability to separate from parents and start life on their own, or to enjoy a modicum of privacy and independence. For parents, anxiety revolved around feeding and clothing their children; the next worry was securing an adequate education for them.

Many young people welcomed the changes in the economy and society. They understood that the state would not help them and that they would have to fight to survive. They were more prone to characterize the poor as people who lacked initiative or entrepreneurial spirit and ability. The older poor and the disabled suffered uncertainty about the future.

A 48-year-old woman who imports goods to sell at the market sees it as follows: "When you are more or less healthy, you can still have some hope. I do not know for how many more years I will be able to travel abroad for merchandise. All these trips have damaged my health, and since I have no seniority at work, I cannot expect much from a pension. I am afraid to think about the future."

Who Became Rich and Who Became Poor? Middle-aged and elderly respondents contended that honest people became poor because they lacked the ability to cultivate, manipulate, and bribe influential people. These honest poor included intellectuals (especially teachers, researchers, professors, and writers), the old, and the disabled. Families with many children, pensioners, and people who lacked savings or assets when Moldova became independent had also joined the poor. The newly rich, in the eyes of respondents, consisted of the former political elite (who simply "exchanged their Party cards for parliamentarians' mandates"), bureaucrats, local officials, the "mafia," the beneficiaries of illegal privatization, rich gypsies, Russians, Romanians, and people who had used Soviet-era political and business connections to "grab material and start their own businesses." Poor respondents characterized these people as "dishonest," "swindlers," "speculators," and "thieves" and insisted that "politicians don't care about the suffering population." Yet some considered the rich to include people who were energetic and intelligent and had some capital when the reforms started. They had the potential to improve the country's economic situation and help the needy.

Conclusions

Moldovans interviewed for this study defined poverty in relation to the past, when the majority of respondents enjoyed secure employment and were able to live on their salaries and pensions. Despite generational differences, most disapproved of the increasing economic stratification and saw a causal link between wealth and corruption. Although impoverishment was widespread, poor people felt humiliated by their poverty and tried to minimize it in front of others.

The Material Dimensions of Poverty

Poverty now affected people who were always "vulnerable," such as unskilled workers or very large single-parent families, as well as educated persons who had once enjoyed prestigious and well-compensated positions. The poorest respondents agreed on the fundamental aspects of poverty: hunger, ill health, and bad living conditions.

Hunger

Poor urban families had little cash with which to buy food and lacked access to land. Even villagers said they did not eat as well as they used to; they sometimes ran out of food before summer. Many respondents said there were nights they went to bed hungry. Food played a very diminished role in social life. As one respondent put it, "Food in poor families is now solely for survival."

Poor people often expressed the sense that they had regressed to the poor peasant existence their parents and grandparents once led. Many respondents relied on *mamaliga*, a national dish consisting of corn flour boiled in water, rather than on purchased wheat bread. They viewed *mamaliga* as less nutritious than wheat bread and as a sign of their personal and national humiliation.

A woman in Chisinau tells the interviewer, "There was a time when I had two pigs and about twenty chickens, but now I have nothing. My money is hardly enough to buy bread every day."

Land plots and gardens formed the most important source of food for collective farm workers and some urban residents. As a collective farm worker insisted, "A family does not starve if at least one member works in the collective farm." In the past, families had enjoyed fresh fruits and vegetables and preserved them for the winter. Now poor households could no longer afford canning supplies.

Cutting Back. Villagers reported a summer diet of vegetables and fruits and a winter diet of potatoes, beans, *mamaliga*, pork fat, and sometimes wheat bread. Households with a cow and some chickens could consume milk and eggs. Rural respondents complained that they ran out of food stocks and often felt hungry and tired. Some started the winter without an adequate food reserve. This year the peasants on the collective farms had not been paid in grain, and the wheat harvest had been poor. A respondent complained, "Now there is no money to buy flour, and no flour to bake bread."

A worker at a collective farm paints a bleak picture: "Only God knows how we shall survive the winter. At night you wake up because of a stomachache and because of hunger. This year even *mamaliga* is a problem because of the drought and the bad corn harvest. When the grapes were ripe, we had *mamaliga* mixed with grapes to fill our stomachs. My family has milk only if the collective farm pays us in milk instead of cash, or if someone from the village gives milk to my son as a share of his salary as a shepherd. But this is rare. We can't afford to spend our monthly salary only on milk."

Families in Comrat and Cahul districts were forced to purchase wheat or switch to *mamaliga* because of delayed cash salaries, delayed in-kind payments of wheat, and high prices for having their flour milled. Potatoes formed part of the staple diet, but last year's potato harvest was poor, and the price had risen beyond the reach of cash-poor families.

Vulnerable Groups. Many pensioners asserted that they could manage if they received their pensions on time. A retired schoolteacher surviving in Chisinau on her monthly pension of 107 lei reported that, after paying utility costs, she had only 65 lei left for food and other expenses. Her breakfast and supper consisted of tea without sugar and one piece of bread. Many urban pensioners grew fruit and vegetables on small plots, but those who were very old or sick could not afford unsubsidized (and increasingly irregular) bus transportation to gardens located far from their homes; many lacked gardening tools, and when they did plant, they were unable to guard their crops.

Households prioritized the distribution of food among family members when there was not enough to go around. Respondents were quite consistent in saying that women fed their husbands first, then their children, and ate the leftovers only after the others had finished. A father of several small children described his family's meals as follows: "All the children eat from one pot. Each child eats as much as he or she can manage. My wife and I eat the leftovers. Sometimes there are no leftovers, and then we only eat a loaf of bread or *mamaliga* with onions." Despite the efforts of most parents to make sure their children were fed, many children went to school hungry. Teachers reported that, by the third or fourth hour of class, they began to notice which children had come to school without breakfast.

Housing

For rural Moldovans, building and owning a house is an important measure of family well-being. Today, families could no longer afford paint or materials for repair, and many houses remained uncompleted. Complaints centered on leaking roofs, moldy and smoke-blackened walls, rotten floors, broken water pipes and taps, and windows with broken glass. Families coped by covering leaking roofs with transparent oil cloth and broken windows with cardboard. In urban areas many respondents lived in privatized apartments, rented rooms, or worker hostels. Overcrowding was a problem for people who had started families in a hostel and never received a state apartment. One respondent in this situation had lived with her husband and two children in a single room for the last 23 years. Many poor households lacked basic furniture. Large families might have one bed and one couch and keep their food in the neighbor's refrigerator. In several homes children shared a single bed or slept on the tile stove, or on the floor.

Utilities

In urban and rural areas alike, many houses had no gas or water connections. In Balti district, people with gas connections complained that they had not received gas in two years. Municipally supplied hot water was a thing of the past.

A pensioner comments, "The mayor promised that he was going to give us gas and hot water, but since the whole town has been privatized, we don't have anything. I cook on a single electric plate."

Heating and Cooking. Coal used to be a common fuel, but many families could not afford 900 to 1,000 lei for 2 tons of coal to heat their home for the winter. In Nisporeni district, respondents claimed their coal had been mixed with gravel and barely heated their homes. Pensioners, although entitled to free or discounted coal, often lacked the 30 to 40 lei needed to transport their 500-kilogram entitlement. Some households had installed wood-burning stoves, but their unventilated rooms filled with smoke. In any case, wood was costly: in Comrat and Cahul, a cubic meter cost 40 lei. People conserved fuel by moving into one or two rooms in winter. Some who lived near forests cut their own wood. In rural areas people collected small branches to burn along with sunflower stems, corncobs, corn stalks, dried grape vines, nut shells, or dung mixed with straw (*kizyak*), an effective but foul-smelling alternative. Poor urban families gathered wood after the town hall had cleaned the parks. Others gathered cardboard from the town markets.

A young mother of four keeps her three school-age children out of school so they can help scavenge cardboard. She explains, "We simply have to survive. If we had nothing to burn, we would die. My children can't go to school because, without them, I wouldn't be able to gather enough cardboard every day."

Despite the high price of electricity, many families resorted to electric heaters and hot plates for cooking. Families unable to pay their bills had their service cut. Some people hired an electrician to connect them directly to a power source, bypassing the meter. By paying the electrician 10 lei a month, they received free electricity.

Water and Waste. Throughout the country, access to potable water was a problem. Apartment dwellers complained that their pipes were rusty. The local housing offices demanded payments for every service and would not undertake capital repairs. Especially in southern regions such as Comrat, apartments had water for only a few hours a day; tenants got water at other times from wells, lugging heavy containers. In the city of Balti many people relied on well water, but residents believed it to be contaminated. In villages water was supplied exclusively from wells, and the villagers had to wait hours in line to get it. In villages such as Crihana Veche, in Cahul, the wells are a few kilometers outside the village, and villagers paid for water to be delivered to their homes. Respondents linked contaminated wells to outbreaks of hepatitis and cholera, and parents blamed the lack of water for washing (and a warm room for bathing children) for epidemics of scabies and lice. A family in Rotunda, a village in Edenet district, reported that they had been unable to wash themselves for three weeks. They did not have soap, shampoo, or even enough fuel to heat water.

Respondents complained about waste disposal. In urban areas garbage piled up in apartment chutes, where it attracted rats. In villages and small towns, people dumped it in nearby ravines, on roads, or even near their homes, where it formed unsightly heaps that attracted stray cats and dogs. People expressed concern that garbage was polluting the water supply.

Conclusions

The material dimensions of poverty affected all aspects of life. Access to cash to buy food, or land and the resources to cultivate it, made the difference between adequate nutrition and hunger. Even in rural areas adults and children suffered from poor nutrition and literal hunger. Housing conditions had deteriorated; people could no longer protect themselves from cold, damp weather or be assured of enough fuel to heat their houses or prepare hot meals. The struggle to find food and fuel was matched by the constant fear of falling ill.

Health, Education, and Social Assistance

Health

Poor families interviewed for the study feared bad health. It threatened their ability to keep their jobs and drained their limited resources. In Moldova, although the state officially continued to provide free or low-fee medical services, serious shortages of hospital equipment and medicine, low salaries for medical personnel, and a long tradition of doctors and nurses demanding and accepting small "gifts" for special attention had created a de facto system of private medicine.

A blind woman from the city of Tiraspol says, "For a poor person, everything is terrible—illness, humiliation, shame. We are cripples. We are afraid of everything. We depend on everyone. No one needs us—we are like garbage that everyone wants to get rid of."

People who were hospitalized had to provide everything necessary for their stay: bed linens, blankets, food, medicine, syringes, even blood for surgery. Patients had to bribe doctors and nurses with food or cash just to look in on them. Often they had to borrow the money. Rural families sometimes sold food surpluses, even farm animals, to cover emergency expenses.

Poor families were often unable to treat chronic or serious illness. Even when they had started treatment, they sometimes found they could not afford to complete it. Many diabetics could no longer afford their daily insulin.

In many cases people preferred to call upon folk healers, mostly older women, because they charged more affordable fees. They called on their patients at home and accepted in-kind payments. One woman from Crihana Veche complained of an illness that was causing hearing loss, a swollen chest, and such weakness that she could not even stand. She now paid a folk healer to "exorcise" her. Respondents reported that some folk healers did real harm, for example, performing incomplete abortions.

Dentistry. Poor nutrition had worsened dental problems, yet visits to the dentist had become less affordable. Parents delayed their own treatment as long as possible.

In a village in Edenet district, two dentists have opened a clinic. They have offered to treat children, the elderly, and the disabled free of charge, if the mayoralty will pay their monthly wages. But the mayoralty claims it does not have the money, and so the dentists charge all their patients.

Abortions. During the Soviet era, abortions often served as the principal means of birth control. According to a doctor interviewed, the number had increased, especially among young women between 18 and 20.

> Unable to afford an apartment, Tatiana moved into a hostel where a neighbor had been evicted because her newborn's crying disturbed the other residents. When Tatiana became pregnant, she elected to have an abortion rather than risk eviction herself.

Childbirth. Pregnancy inaugurated an endless series of expenses and debts. Decreased access to prenatal and postnatal care had had a marked impact on the health of babies. Pregnant farm women often worked up to the seventh month of pregnancy at such physically demanding jobs as hoeing, picking fruit, and loading vegetables. Some miscarried. Many women refused to deliver in a hospital, to avoid paying fees of hundreds of lei.

Child Health. Children's health reflected the poor conditions in which many lived. Parents in Chisinau noted the increase in chronic bronchitis and stomach problems, which they linked to the fact that their children often skipped meals or went to bed hungry. Children in rural and urban areas still received basic health examinations and vaccinations in school free of charge, however.

Education

The educational system no longer paid adequate, on-time salaries, maintained infrastructure, or purchased new equipment. Private schools, tutors, and institutions of higher education had moved in to compensate for the disastrous fall in quality. Few parents in the sample could afford to pay fees of 1,500 lei for these private schools, but even in the public schools, activities that once were free now cost money. Teachers and parents were particularly distressed by the deterioration in a system in which they had once taken pride, and which had provided an avenue of social mobility even for children from remote rural villages. The outflow of qualified and experienced teachers contributed to the deterioration.

Increasing numbers of children were missing school because of demand for their labor (especially in rural areas), inability to buy essential school supplies and clothing, and the breakdown of intervillage transportation. The number of bright, motivated school graduates who could continue their education had sharply decreased: they could not afford the tutoring fees or bribes. Students from villages had the additional burden of paying for board and lodging away from home.

Deteriorating Infrastructure. Neither municipalities nor collective farms took responsibility for maintaining, repairing, or heating school buildings, and many parents kept their children at home during the winter. The villages of Pirlita and Milesti had considered transferring the summer break to winter. The school in Avdarma closed down for two months during the winter. Few schools could offer children a snack or a hot meal, and pupils had to pay for even modest snacks. In many communities parents maintained the schools through their labor or through frequent monetary donations, or both. Parents also provided fuel.

Materials and Supplies. Teaching materials had become more expensive and less available. Few textbooks with the new Latin orthography had been printed. In Cahul and Comrat many schools relied largely on the old textbooks. Poor families had difficulties finding enough money to buy their children notebooks, pens, and paper. Outfitting a first grader with clothes and supplies could come to 200 to 250 lei, more than a month's salary.

Rising Absenteeism. Students in Moldova are expected to complete nine years of basic education. Teachers said that up to 15 percent of pupils regularly absented themselves from school; some parents failed to enroll young children, and some older children left school before completing their nine years. Parents took children out of school to help with farmwork, especially during the busy agricultural months of spring and fall. Children helped prepare fields for planting, looked after younger siblings while parents worked, and helped with the harvest. Some left school to work full-time as herders to provide cash or in-kind income for their families. In some areas children as young as 10 worked on farms as wage laborers.

Children also stayed at home because they lacked warm clothes or footwear. The amounts in current school funds were too small to cope with the growing need. Sometimes siblings shared a single warm outfit and alternated going out. Others refused to attend school because they were afraid other children would make fun of their clothing.

The new system of private classes in public schools singled out a few "elite" children and demotivated the rest. In some poor households children had nowhere to do their homework; they did not even have their own beds. These were often the children who fell behind or left school early. They were also more likely to be labeled "backward" and further stigmatized. In some cases medical commissions labeled such children from particularly poor households "mentally handicapped" and assigned them to special boarding schools. Some parents kept their children at home rather than surrender them to these schools.

Children missed school because intervillage buses no longer ran regularly. In Antonovka village the bus was frequently out of commission, sometimes because of fuel shortages. Elsewhere the roads turned into mud during the winter. In Mihailovca and Marculesti, in Balti district, the collective farm provided no transportation.

Although many parents made considerable sacrifices to keep their children in school and buy the necessary school supplies, others no longer saw much value in education.

Ghenadie is a collective farm worker whose eldest son just finished ninth grade and whose next-eldest son already works as a shepherd. As far as this father is concerned, working and contributing money to the family have become more urgent tasks.

Teaching. Teaching used to be a prestigious profession for men and women. Now, however, teachers received delayed monthly salaries of 100 to 150 lei. Those in the countryside supplemented their salaries by extensive subsistence gardening. Teachers were not entitled to full land shares under the agricultural privatization laws, however, but instead received half shares at best. In the cities teachers complained that the loss of staff had forced them to work several shifts and teach subjects outside their specialty.

Teachers had left their positions in large numbers. In the village of Rotunda only one male teacher remained at the school. Most village teachers reported that they would leave their positions if better-paying opportunities were available elsewhere, and young teachers entering the market were often unwilling to work in the villages. Some teachers made extra money by tutoring. The new emphasis on Romanian meant that language teachers were in demand. In Ungheni some teachers sold textbooks to earn extra money.

Bribery. Some teachers pressured their pupils to pay for extra coaching. After exams some teachers expected gifts ranging from produce to jewelry. Many parents hired tutors to ensure their children's success in university entrance exams. The interviewers heard many accounts of village youths with excellent grades who had tried to enter university but had returned to their villages because their parents could not pay the large bribes professors demanded to guarantee their admission.

Higher Education. Many children had lost hope, interest, motivation, and ambition. They saw teachers and other educated people falling into poverty, while the new businessmen became rich. Gifted children from poor families knew their parents could not help them, while those from prosperous or rich families exerted themselves less because their parents could virtually buy their diplomas. Sometimes village students could not even afford the basic expenses for education in the town center.

The daughter of a village respondent dropped out of the lyceum in Cahul, where she had hoped to prepare for medical school: her parents could not even cover her basic food, lodging, and clothes. A student from Pirlita who had hoped to study accountancy at a vocational school in Chisinau also gave up because her family could not afford the school fees, transportation costs, or living expenses. One girl from Pirlita passed the entrance exam to the medical college in Ungheni and receives a monthly stipend of 35 lei, which covers rent at 20 lei a month. Her parents provide her with food.

Exchange Programs. Some students from modest backgrounds benefited from the exchange program between Moldova and Romania. Some families started their grade-school children there; university students also attended. Moldovan students received small stipends but claimed they received a better education than in Moldova. Young people found Bucharest a much livelier city than Chisinau, with more cultural offerings and activities. Russian-speaking students used to go to Moscow or St. Petersburg; these universities were now inaccessible to most of them.

Social Assistance

Pensioners now made up a sizable part of the Moldovan population. For those who had lost their savings, anxiety about their funeral costs matched their distress at the day-to-day discomforts of hunger and poor health. Many people still appealed to the authorities for assistance during periods of difficulty. Some appeals might result in sums up to 100 lei, although it was considered pointless to apply too often.

Late Payments. Pensions averaged about 70 to 80 lei a month; despite their small size, many pensioners claimed they could manage on them if they only received them in time. Many felt it would be helpful if their monthly electricity payments were simply deducted from their pensions. Although many government pensions and allowances still existed on the books, most no longer functioned, and state assistance was administered in an inconsistent manner. Distribution of and access to state and humanitarian assistance differed a great deal between city and village. In Balti pensioners received their pension with delays of one or two weeks, whereas in nearby villages, such as Prazhila or Antonovka, villagers had not received their pensions in 10 months.

Qualifying for Assistance. Not everyone could afford the procedures to qualify for disability payments; the medical examination alone was 170 lei, and families outside Chisinau also had to pay for transportation. Assistance was administered inconsistently. Victims of the Chernobyl disaster and veterans received pensions, loans equivalent to several hundred dollars for house construction, and a 50 percent discount on apartment fees, land and house taxes, electricity bills, urban transportation, and medications. Some received only 25 percent off, and most pharmacies refused to honor the discount. Some villages and collective farms allowed the disabled to buy small amounts of food at a 50 percent discount.

Bankrupt Local Governments. Mayoralties often refused to make payments. The mayors themselves claimed their offices had not received financial support for years, and they regretted their inability to help the population. In the villages of Blesteni and Gordinesti in Edenet district, the mayoralty distributed coupons, which families could redeem for food at local shops.

Family and Child Benefits. There were still discounts and allowances for large families and children, although the amounts had been reduced and payments were made late.

Galina had a baby in June 1996, but by the end of the year she had still not received any maternity allowances. Her workplace should be paying her 500 lei for the four months before and after childbirth, but each time she inquires, she is told that they have no money.

Primary schoolchildren often received free breakfasts and a snack at school. The kindergarten subsidy was disappearing, but some villages allowed poor families to send their children to kindergarten free of charge. Poor rural parents often took their preschool children into the fields with them; urban parents preferred to leave them with older siblings or grand-parents.

Humanitarian Assistance. Some enterprises sponsored poor or orphaned children, providing food or warm clothing. The district offices of education offered small sums to the very poorest families. The Salvation Army now operated in Balti and Chisinau, where they fed 100 people a day in a free kitchen. Visiting members of the new evangelical religions provided assistance to indigent families in the form of secondhand clothing, food, and medicine. A number of respondents in Chisinau reported considerable assistance in the form of good-quality used clothing and food staples from the Salvation Army, a Moldovan-American society called Anacom, the Catholic Church, and a Jewish-American organization. Disabled respondents had received very small amounts (15 to 40 lei) from the Invalids' Association.

Attitudes. In the past, large rural families had received gifts of food products when children were born. They perceived these forms of assistance as a demonstration of the state's respect for its citizens rather than as a form of charity. Now large families felt ashamed to ask for help. Many pension recipients felt cheated, and others were angry at the senseless bureaucratic obstacles. Respondents were convinced that much of the aid was being siphoned off or sold for profit. They felt that officials were refusing to share information and making excuses to deny assistance. When used clothes appeared on the market, people assumed they had arrived in the form of humanitarian aid.

Conclusions

Given the precipitous decline in the purchasing power of pensions and other forms of assistance, social assistance played a smaller role in household economies than before. People felt that timely, predictable payment would be a great improvement. Many reported receiving various kinds of ration cards but resented the fact that, when they used them, they ended up paying higher-than-market prices. Some received assistance from humanitarian and religious organizations, but they suspected that much of it had been diverted to the private use of politicians. Overall the majority of social assistance recipients received little help, and this left them cynical and embittered toward local and national government.

Agriculture

Subsistence farming had become the mainstay of rural households, whether they worked on restructured collective farms, on privatized "peasant farms," or on their own household plots. Over a million rural households had title to household plots distributed during the first phase of land reform.

Land Reform

Restructuring of collective and state farms had begun after independence but proceeded slowly. Farmers faced many obstacles, including time-consuming and arcane procedures for withdrawing land shares from collectives; hindrances posed by farm managers and local officials; and fears about the risks of independent farming (World Bank 1996a, 1996b). After the distribution of 0.30-hectare household plots in 1992, a second phase began, which involved distribution of land and other assets through paper shares or certificates of entitlement. Privatization was suspended in 1994, but the Constitutional Court of Moldova declared limitations on exit unconstitutional, and the process again accelerated with more government support.

As of mid-1996, 983,000 households had rights to a land share. Most households had received certificates of entitlement, but only 10 percent had been assigned a specific plot of land. By October 1996 there were 90,000 independent private farmers, farming alone or in groups, on 5 percent of the total arable land. At the time of the study, organizations working with agricultural reform in Moldova estimated that the number of private farmers might be over 200,000. The remaining farm population continued to work on restructured collective farms or on farm associations and cooperatives that have split off from them.

Most collective farms had made little change in their organization. Now they paid "dividends" as well as salaries to collective farm workers for the use of their land shares. Farm managers treated "members" as wage workers rather than as participants with a say in decisionmaking, and they prevented households from withdrawing land and nonland assets. The true associations of peasant farms allowed independent farmers to acquire their "value-shares" in the form of a tractor, combine, or other heavy equipment or nonland assets.

Collective Farms. Working conditions on collective farms had deteriorated since independence: farm equipment was falling apart and farms could not buy spare parts. In many collectives people continued to work in specialized teams of several dozen farm workers, on vineyard, vegetable, field crop, tractor, and other "brigades." Plowing, sowing, cultivating, and harvesting were mechanized, but farm workers pruned, harvested fruit and grapes, and hoed manually.

Radu, a farmer in Cahul, works on a specialized collective farm team responsible for the vineyards. The brigade concentrates on the same task for the whole year, although it may help others during harvest time. Radu's team has to walk to the field every day. This is fine in good weather, but in rain or snow "you're tired before you've even gotten to work." Each team member hoes 4 hectares of vineyard and 1 of cornfield. Radu submitted a request to withdraw his land, but "the official tore it into pieces." The collective farm leaders use the farm's assets as their own, but when the farmers ask to use the vehicles, the farm lenders claim they do not have enough gas.

Farm workers throughout Moldova expressed deep dissatisfaction with these working conditions and with their pay. They should have received monthly salaries of 30 to 100 lei. Instead, land and house taxes and electricity fees were subtracted from this amount, and they took home only 50 to 200 lei a year in cash, along with milk, meat, wheat, sunflower seeds, sugar, wine, and other products. Some farm workers complained that their in-kind payments were based on higher-than-market rates.

Respondents on a collective farm in Balti district say they work 12 to 17 hours a day during the busy seasons, resting only on Sunday. In addition, some work on a norm (a plot that the family works in exchange for a portion of the profits, which they receive once or twice a year, after the crop has been sold) of sugar beets or tobacco. A family will receive 30 lei plus 5 kilograms of sugar for each ton of cleaned sugar beets that they load on a truck. In most cases, whole families work on the norm, taking even their small children with them.

In Gordinesti, Rotunda, and Blesteni in Edenet district, families were assigned a land share when their collective farms were changed into "joint-stock companies," and they now "rented" these land shares to the collective farms. Like farm workers elsewhere, they felt their in-kind payments were much too low. They were also angry that they had to buy wheat. None received cash, but few understood the reasons. Yet most were reluctant to withdraw their land: they worried about lack of access to transportation and equipment, and they feared their expenses would exceed their profits since they could not afford inputs. They comforted themselves with the fact that they brought home something every day to feed their families.

In Comrat, farm workers received land shares of 1.5 to 2 hectares, depending on their years of employment. Workers reported that working methods and the way profits were distributed had remained unchanged. Payment was made in kind, depending on the number of days worked. Members could also receive agricultural goods at below-market rates. Although pensioners with 25 years of work experience were supposed to receive a share of the profits, pensioners who had not achieved seniority received nothing at all.

Workers cultivating profitable crops expected higher earnings, paid as cash. A Gordinesti worker expected to receive 1,400 lei for picking 1.2 tons of tobacco leaves. The farm was to sell the tobacco for 4 lei per kilogram, 30 percent of which had been promised to the workers. In Balti some young farm workers agreed to receive their salary in the form of building materials for repairing their homes. In Mihailovca, an extremely poor and relatively isolated village in the same district, apples were very profitable. Some farm workers insisted on being paid in apples, and in some cases the collective farm provided transport from the fields and allowed them to use farm buildings to store the apples.

Worker-Management Relations. Relations between farm workers and farm managers followed a pattern established during the Soviet era, when decisions were made centrally, implemented by farm managers, and simply presented to farm workers. Lack of funds and growing farm indebtedness had turned management and farm workers against each other. Farm workers claimed that the farm management used pretexts such as the drought, bankruptcy, unforeseen expenditures, and the farm's indebtedness to cheat them of their earnings. Farm workers had little knowledge of the actual finances of the farm, since management never shared information on earnings or expenditures.

The administrators of the collective farms and joint-stock companies claimed that, when they had funds, the banks forced them to pay back old loans rather than distribute salaries. These debts included the profit tax and the value added tax, as well as payments to the social funds. Many of these farms conducted transactions through barter. A farm near Balti worked out an agreement with some farms in Belarus and commercial agents from the Baltic countries, where they traded apples for spare parts and fertilizers.

Farms were obliged to sell their wheat to state enterprises at a fixed price, but they did not receive full payment.

Leaving the Collective. Attitudes toward land reform differed. Farm workers felt exposed to risks, and some people were deeply disturbed by the increasing gap between rich and poor in the formerly egalitarian village communities. One said, "If the collectives were dissolved and land distributed to individuals, five or six people would buy most of the land, while the rest of the people would end up working for them, as in the past when we worked for the Romanian boyars." People with more resources, strength, or confidence claimed that only the lazy and the envious opposed privatization.

The degree of privatization differed both from region to region and within regions and districts. In Comrat only a few farming households had applied to withdraw their land shares. The majority expressed the fear that poorer soil and frequent droughts in the south would require additional inputs—fertilizer, intensive irrigation, and access to farm machinery—all of them inaccessible. Even the collective farms were plagued by lack of spare parts and lack of cash to replace them. In Sadova, Balti district, tractors had been breaking down. The collective farm manager finally cannibalized parts from three tractors to make one functioning tractor. With such problems, workers on collective farms hesitated to privatize. Many saw independence as a burden rather than an opportunity.

In Pirlita village in Ungheni district, and in Milesti village in Nisporeni district, quite a few households had exited from the collective farms: 93 out of 1,600 households in Pirlita; 200 out of 1,100 households in Milesti. Many of these farmers reported that they had been forced to assemble many documents, acquire signatures from officials (who often delayed), and get approval from leaders at the village, the district, and the national level. Others worried about taxes. Many had to travel to the district center and on to Chisinau as many as five times to find the official who was to sign a given document.

Some farm managers prevented workers from withdrawing their land shares by threatening to withhold farm equipment. One respondent said he had submitted a request to the mayoralty to withdraw his land quota, but withdrew it when the head of the collective farm warned him that the collective would not give him any assistance. In many cases farm managers prevented the distribution of or access to farm assets. According to regulations, tractor drivers on collective farms were not allowed to rent out their services to private farms without permission of the mayoralty, to whom farmers were to submit a formal request and pay in advance. Several respondents alleged that their requests were refused in order to force them back into the collective and prevent others from trying to withdraw.

Most people remained ignorant about relevant legislation and regulations. They rarely protested their meager in-kind salaries from the collective farms for fear that the farm manager would respond, "If you don't like it, take your land and leave the collective. Then see what you will do!" Some workers feared that the Communists would return to power and that they would be deported to Siberia as the kulaks (rich peasants) had been several decades earlier. They also believed that if they withdrew from the collective, they would be totally isolated from their workmates and would owe taxes to the state.

Many local people did not receive land shares. This included people who worked for state organizations as well as many young people who had moved back to their parents' village in recent years. In Edenet this included people from the village of Gordinesti, who had worked as miners in the Cupcini mines before they closed down. They had banded together to write to Parliament but had not received an answer.

Pensioners and Land Reform. Pensioners made up a sizable portion of the rural population and of the former collective farm enterprises.[2] Because their long years of service entitled them to large asset ("non-land") shares, and because they were more likely to lease than farm their own land, pensioners became objects of struggle and competition. As the mayor of one village explained, "There was and still is a fight for pensioners; everyone wants them to join their own group—they have the biggest asset shares, and they can be manipulated and deceived more easily since their land is worked by someone else." In many of the new cooperative farming enterprises, pensioners made up the bulk of the members, although many were not active workers.

Their desirability resulted in leaders of the large farming associations accusing each other of attracting pensioners by a variety of unsavory means, including spreading disinformation and rumors. On several farms respondents said that the chairman of the former collective had told pensioners that they would lose their pensions if they withdrew their land. In a nearby village, this threat effectively prevented a number of pensioners from applying to leave. In another village a farmer told interviewers, "In 1997, everybody would have left the association, but the manager promised to prepare ownership titles for all of them. He lies to people that if they leave the association, they will not receive pensions. He wants to keep them with him and then form a limited liability company."

In one village a young specialist had received his land parcel and applied to get his retired father's parcel as well. His father, however, was convinced that it was the collective farm that paid his pension and that he would lose it if he left. It took the specialist a year to persuade his father that pensions were completely outside the control of the farm.

A key issue for pensioners was health. Often pensioners preferred to remain in the joint-stock company or join one of the large successor organizations because of their own limited ability to engage in hard physical labor. A pensioner in one village told interviewers she could claim four land shares but was afraid to do so: her husband and one son were disabled, and her elderly parents were too old and frail to help her. Those who had no access to vehicles pointed out that the joint-stock company often transported them to the fields, whereas if they were on their own, they would have to walk to plots that might be quite distant from their homes.

Many pensioners were deeply skeptical about the reforms. Several were unsure about what, if anything, they would receive at the end of the growing season. They felt that, in order to farm independently, one should be able to obtain one's rightful share of property assets, but as one pensioner explained, "The experts, who understood in what direction the reform process was moving, stole the equipment, so that there was nothing left to be distributed." Other pensioners expressed fear of farming without access to machinery and inputs.

A pensioner who had inherited a separate parcel from his wife when she died told interviewers that he would remain in the joint-stock company. He was afraid he could not pay the taxes; he was too old to work the land alone and would have had to hire people to help with the farm work and marketing, tasks he found overwhelming. In other cases pensioners had watched their own children withdraw from the collective, encounter serious problems obtaining inputs, and find themselves unable to market what they produced.

Pensioners who did leave the collective were often motivated by their desire to subsist on their land with some help from their adult children, and then ensure that their children inherited the land. Some had moved from collective farming to private farming through a series of steps. Disappointed with the shrinking salaries from collective farm work, several pensioners reported leaving the collective to join a farming association led by a relative. Disenchantment with this association then spurred them to start farming in a smaller group with only a few close relatives. Members of one such family compared their collective farm salaries—300 kilograms of corn, 150 kilograms of wheat, 100 kilograms of sunflower seeds, and small amounts of sugar, cabbage, and onions—with their yield as independent farmers: 300 kilograms of sunflower seeds, 9 or 10 tons of corn, and 1 ton of grapes. This family, however, was able to rely on some help from their seven daughters, one of whom lived with them while the other six lived in Chisinau.

In 1987 Viorel, a pensioner, joined nine other pensioners to take advantage of a land lease policy in his collective. They rented 10 hectares and planted watermelons, harvesting 330 tons, which they immediately sold to middlemen from Chisinau. After 1990, however, marketing became difficult and they gave up this project. But in 1993 the family withdrew both their land quotas. Maya, Viorel's recently widowed sister, independently farms an adjacent plot of land. The families help each other, renting the services of their cousin, a tractor owner and driver, and relying on help from their adult daughters during periods of peak labor demand. Occasionally they engage day laborers in return for in-kind payments. Both families plant mainly corn, because it demands the least work. Both families manage to subsist on their earnings and pensions, but Viorel explains, "At our age and with our health, we do not need anything. But our children, if they wish, will be able to work the land better—it was for them that we withdrew our land quotas."

Of those who had withdrawn from the collective, many had still not received asset shares, including all of the pensioners interviewed in one village. Elsewhere pensioners complained of receiving their assets as a portion of a unit of property—in some cases as "part of" a cow. One such pensioner reported selling his portion of the cow for 200 lei to the person who had the actual responsibility for raising it. Another had received part of a tractor, the right to which he was pressured to exchange for the new owner's promise to make one free delivery of goods from the farm to his home.

Most pensioners, whether or not they remained in the collective, had household plots where they grew vegetables and cultivated fruit trees; some also had vineyards. Most used the grain they received (or grew themselves on their household plots) to raise livestock and poultry. Many were able to buy nonfood items by selling dairy products, lambs, or mature livestock, especially to pay for farming expenses. Some pensioners remained in the collective for strategic purposes, because they were paid in fodder (and could pilfer additional fodder) to feed their household livestock. Others collected "rent" for their shares while working as seasonal day laborers on other farms.

Farm Reorganization

The American Project. The "American Project," funded by the U.S. Agency for International Development (USAID) and originally piloted in Nisporeni district, was carried out in 70 farms throughout the country. The project attracted interest and controversy for its unique approach, which clearly favored the maintenance of large farms and stressed the critical role of "natural leaders" in facilitating this process. For their part, participating villagers hoped to receive American technology and assistance through the project. One of the villages in this study had recently become part of the program. The following case study (adapted from Dudwick 1997) illustrates how the project was implemented on one collective farm.

In the spring of 1996 the Ministry of Privatization, together with George Soros' Center for Private Business Reform (CPBR), funded by USAID, piloted the breakup of the Mayak Collective Farm. An aim of this pilot project was to work out the methodology for ensuring the fair and transparent distribution of collective farm land and property within the framework of existing Moldovan laws and regulations.

In the view of the CPBR, most collective farm workers still hesitated to exit from collective farms out of a combination of fear, ideology, and passivity; only 10 to 12 percent were "real" farmers with sufficient independent initiative, knowledge, and interest to make a go of independent farming. The restructuring program was based on the premise that most farm workers needed a "leader"—a person with or without official power in the village but who was widely respected and trusted—to convince them to disband while providing them a structure in which they felt protected enough to take the risk.

The CPBR privatization process began when a former collective farm agreed to participate in the program; the CPBR stipulated that the farm must not already be bankrupt. Program employees were to ensure that the entire community was informed about the privatization process and all that it entailed. After several informational meetings, villagers were anonymously polled as to whom they considered potential farming association leaders. Ultimately, any villager could place himself or herself on the list of leadership candidates. Finally, these candidates each undertook to persuade the collective farm workers to give them their land shares as "proxies." A special committee would then decide how to allocate the land to the various leaders, who participated in this process as representatives of the persons whose land shares they held.

The program did not require people to join with a leader in order to get their own land, but it did actively encourage them to do so, and many villagers in the study did not understand that joining a group was optional.

Villagers learned about the informational meetings through posters displayed in the village. But a number of respondents, including pensioners, told interviewers they had never heard of the leadership poll and had not been approached. According to others, the survey had not been administered anonymously. One recalled, "Mr. B. [the leader of the collective] came with some Americans; they walked through the village and distributed questionnaires. These questionnaires were not in envelopes, and everyone could read what others had written." Some—including the agricultural specialists—believed that individuals would have to pay to have their land surveyed. They were not aware that the program paid for surveying.

Many villagers, especially the pensioners, did not understand the organizational difference between the current collective and the new enterprise to be managed by the leader or leaders to be selected. Many simply envisaged the continuation of the same collective form of organization. According to a village official, "People in our village think they will be together in the same collective and that they have no other option than to give their land to Mr. B." This official argued that most villagers did not understand that, in the new farming association, the leader would have no obligation to retain them as workers and could fire them and hire workers from other villages. If they had known this, he told us, they would have exited the collective independently, but the competing candidates had deliberately obscured this point.

Many villagers thought that, under the program, they could not leave the collective and receive their asset shares. One said that "Workers were not really presented with the choice of farming independently but were told they must choose a leader." Some were angry at this and did not understand why they were under this pressure.

In the end the overwhelming majority picked the director of the collective farm, Mr. B., to be the new leader. One other person obtained about 70 proxies and will form a much smaller farming association. Some villagers were still debating what course of action to follow. Some had heard rumors that, because of high taxes, people in the neighboring village had returned their land to the collective farm. Others cited rumors that the program was actually a disguised attempt by the Americans to buy up their land and "leave them with nothing," and that the "leader" who won would sell their land to the Americans.

From the perspective of the farm experts and leaders, however, villagers "will always see a collective farm director in Mr. B., no matter what the new organization is called." In the view of one technical expert, the villagers were used to the collective and would only work when they wanted to, with the knowledge that they could still rely on their salaries without taking on the responsibility of independent farming.

Mr. B. hoped to sign one-year lease agreements with members of his company initially, and 5- or 10-year leases thereafter. People who wished to leave his company could take their land from the outskirts of the farm. As he viewed it, members would consist of two groups: one group of pensioners, the disabled, and rural social services employees, who would lease their land but not work on it, and a second group, who would perform agricultural work.

Why did the collective farm workers choose the collective farm director to lead the new farming association? One of them explained it as follows: "People were scared. They did not want to destroy the collective. They do not understand what 'leader' means. They thought the collective would be destroyed if B. were not elected." Another observed that "B. is both parliament and government in our village. Nothing is resolved without him." A candidate who had withdrawn from the competition commented, "I don't have the relations B. has. People like him [collective farm directors] always have the necessary relations both in the district and the Ministry [of Agriculture]. Do you really think that anybody else would get the same support?" Yet another summarized the confusion felt by many: "Now we have an 'association' in the village, and not a collective farm. People do not care what it is named. They do not know what an association means. They do not want to change or organize something else."

Several dozen interviews from this village suggested that, despite the efforts of the local program representatives, many villagers, especially pensioners, did not understand the implications of the restructuring. To some extent, it appeared that the former collective farm manager was complicit in minimizing the significance of the reform, including the fact that he could and likely would fire many workers. Given the great power and authority of former collective farm directors, which extends to their network of ties to authorities at the district and sometimes even the national level, they have a great natural advantage as potential "leaders." Hence the emphasis of the program on assisting reform by encouraging farm workers to turn over or lease their land to these "natural leaders" may make farm workers vulnerable to pressure to lease their land for long terms or, when land becomes fully commoditized, to sell it prematurely. Thus, in the interests of maintaining large, ostensibly more viable farms, the CPBR may further a process by which ordinary collective farm workers are disenfranchised before having had a chance to try independent farming, or even to secure a small farm by which they can guarantee themselves subsistence, if not a profit.

The Zavoieni Peasant Farmers Association. Although villagers in Crihana Veche in Cahul district remained on the collective farm, farm workers in the nearby village of Manta successfully withdrew their land despite the resistance of the collective farm management. At the time this study was conducted, almost 50 percent of the land had been withdrawn. One association of peasant farms (consisting of 234 members) and two separate family farms existed alongside the collective farm.

In 1995, 400 collective farm members submitted withdrawal applications to the village mayoralty. The farm administration tried to discourage applicants, forecasting famine. The applicants decided to elect a leader, who would be in charge of getting the applications processed. They selected an agronomist to organize the plowing, sowing, seed buying, and other collective tasks in return for a payment of 1 leu per member (234 lei total) per month and a share of the farm's income. The farm association would be structured on the basis of individually owned farms. The collective farm leadership created numerous difficulties, and members of the Agrarian Democratic Party (an offshoot of the Communist Party), the head of the collective farm, and the chairman of the district executive committee tried to halt the privatization.

The association drew up a business plan, which budgeted 5,000 lei for use of equipment, plowing, and sowing. Part of this sum was to be gathered from members, and the rest paid out of earnings. The 234 member households ended up with a total of 203 hectares of arable land, 116 hectares of vineyards, 15 hectares of orchards, and 20 hectares of pasture. The land was distributed by lottery, with each member receiving land in each category, sometimes in lots separated by 8 to 10 kilometers. Members could use their value-shares to acquire livestock as well as other nonland assets. Most of the farm buildings were in such a state of disrepair they could hardly be used; members collected money among themselves to repair four tractors (4,100 lei), to buy seed, and to pay for hiring equipment. They harvested manually, because the combines were old and inefficient.

The members experienced a number of problems: they could not afford enough diesel fuel to finish their plowing; the collective farm's winery owed them 30,000 lei but proposed to pay them in wine in lieu of cash; indifferent or lazy members still claimed a share of the harvest. Overall, however, the group was pleased with the results of its efforts. Average yields per member of 740 kilograms of wheat and 110 to 140 kilograms of sunflower seeds far exceeded the 300 kilograms of wheat and 40 kilograms of sunflower seeds received by households on the collective farm. Out of the earnings from sales, members paid taxes, transportation, and electricity. They hoped to obtain a low-interest loan to purchase technical equipment, pesticide, fertilizer, and seeds to improve future harvests.

This experience shows that farm workers are not completely defenseless when it comes to establishing themselves as independent farmers, yet they confront an array of hostile individuals and authorities who appear determined to thwart change and sabotage their efforts if they succeed in withdrawing their land. The households least able to withstand this kind of opposition, who feel dependent on the goodwill of farm management, often prefer not to antagonize the authorities.

Private Farming. Many farmers who had managed to withdraw land shares from collective farms received parcels far from their homes, with poor soil. Some complained that their land—a mix of vineyards, orchards, and arable land—required too many different kinds of tools, equipment, and expertise for a single land owner to manage. The high price of inputs has been daunting, and some farmers regretted their move. In Comrat the few households that succeeded in exiting the collective lacked cash to pay for seeds, fuel, and rental of heavy equipment. Services for plowing land could amount to as much as 200 to 300 lei per hectare; taxes could come to 110 lei per hectare. Pensioners were exempt from this tax; others simply refused to pay.

Independent farming has pushed some new farmers into debt. One independent farmer who cultivated 2 hectares of beans and 3 hectares of corn offered her crop and a cow as collateral for a short-term loan at the local bank, at an interest rate of 28 percent. The drought resulted in a poor crop: 500 kilograms of corn and 10 kilograms of beans. She was forced to sell her cow and borrow money from relatives to repay the principal on her loan. She still owes 850 lei in interest and 900 lei for her land tax.

Farm families with off-farm income had more chance of success.

One couple in the Ungheni district withdrew their 2.6 hectares of land in 1993. Ghenadie, 46, periodically goes to Russia to earn cash. Although their land is located 8 kilometers from their house, he and Lena depend on their old car to get them there, at least when the weather is dry and the unasphalted road has not turned to mud. They purchase seeds but use animal manure for fertilizer. Last year they paid 260 lei in land taxes, 300 lei in road repair fees to the local government, 548 lei in plowing fees to the collective farm, 192 lei in cultivating fees, 260 lei in sowing fees, and 40 lei to transport manure to the fields. They harvested 1.5 tons of corn to feed their two cows and their poultry, to consume themselves, and to sell. They sell milk for 1.50 lei per liter, and onions for 0.40 lei per kilogram. They grow alfalfa as forage. The child allowances for the family's six children have been deducted from their land taxes. On the whole, they are satisfied with independent farming. Their harvest far exceeded the yields of local collective farm workers.

In the village of Marandeni, Balti district, about 20 households had exited from the collective farm. The director of the collective forbade the tractor drivers to assist them, on pain of dismissal, and so the farmers had to rent tractors from neighboring villages at a higher cost. They were concerned about the lack of markets. The state bought first from the collective farms at a higher price, and private owners were forced to sell for much lower prices. Despite these hindrances, the farmers received much better yields than those in the collective.

Changing Attitudes. The most conservative farm workers expressed negative attitudes toward land privatization. Others had changed their thinking about independent farms: "The more you put in, the more you get out. One cannot blame the drought for all the problems." Farmers felt the following measures could ease their burdens: access to farm machinery; a five-year moratorium on state taxes and repeal of export taxes; access to longer-term, low-interest loans to invest in advanced technologies for food processing; information about soil cultivation, chemical use, and crop rotation; instruction in new methods, technological advances, how to farm more efficiently, and how to protect their legal rights; information and advice about export regulations and procedures for local and foreign markets; distribution of land to all interested potential farmers; reduced interest rates on loans for purchase of machinery with low fuel consumption; a single purchase price for crops from collective and private farms; and a state policy that actively supports and assists private farmers.

Subsistence Farming

Many rural households depended on the 0.3-hectare plot they had received in the 1992 distribution. Married couples who lived with their parents received their own plot. Families used the plots mainly for subsistence, selling or bartering their surpluses. Sometimes the collective farm provided tractors for plowing, cultivating, sowing, and harvesting. Most rural households also had gardens near their houses, which they worked manually. These gardens often produced better crops than more distant plots. In many cases these plots were redistributed each year. Peasants in Balti district complained that they tended to receive poor-quality plots, where the soil has been exhausted by years of sunflower cultivation. They could not plant fruit trees or vineyards and had no incentive to make long-term investments. A number of plots were flooded during recent heavy rains, and crops were destroyed. Other households complained that their crops had been stolen.

Many elderly and disabled farmers were unable to walk to distant fields, transport water, or perform other heavy labor. A female pensioner from Congaz village had not cultivated her plot for three years. She had given it to relatives, who occasionally "throw [her] some potatoes." Pensioners often gave their land to their children in return for a share of the harvest.

Animal Husbandry. Rural households supplemented their income from the collective farm by raising their own animals. In Balti district people raised turkeys and chickens, selling them on the market, or cows and hogs, some of which were purchased by local merchants with trade relations in Bulgaria and Turkey. Raising hogs was relatively profitable if one could afford the initial 125 lei per pig. In Milesti village, Nisporeni district, several families combined their cows into a single herd and took turns guarding them. Livestock breeding provided seasonal income to youths who herded cows for a number of families. Some people paid in cash, others in food. There was work for watchmen in the fields of the collective farm, and beekeeping provided some households a stable source of income.

In Comrat, families with a cow were considered relatively well off. They used milk and cheese for family consumption and marketed the surplus several times a week in town, earning 15 to 20 lei each time. The Gagauz government taxed animals at 10 lei a head and pastureland at 40 lei a month to control overgrazing and rapid deterioration during droughts. The poorest families could not even afford animals. In Cahul a cow cost 1,000 lei; forage was an additional expense. Some families complained about the lack of veterinary services. Poultry and rabbits were particularly vulnerable to disease.

Marketing. Marketing garden crops was an important way of generating income. In the north, apple selling can be profitable. Starting in November, people from Balti traveled by train to Odessa, each taking 150 to 200 apples packed in cardboard boxes or sacks; they sold the apples wholesale or in the market over several days. Villagers would sometimes hire a bus and take produce to Ukraine or Russia, paying bribes of up to $100 to customs officials. Middlemen from Moscow or St. Petersburg drove their trucks to the villages. In villages where collective farm workers lacked cash to buy even soap, they exchanged agricultural produce with middlemen. The farmers complained about the rates: 8 kilograms of wheat for a bar of soap, 200 kilograms for a pair of children's boots.

Stealing. Illegal gathering of others' crops was an important survival strategy in most regions. People stole corn from nearby collective farms to sell at the market or to neighbors raising poultry. Unemployed youths, town residents, or people without land would sometimes ride their bicycles at night to apple orchards, give the guards a bottle of spirits, and spend several hours gathering apples. They risked beatings, fines, and confiscation of their bicycles. Near Gordinesti, several families regularly stole apples in fall and winter, and vegetables in summer.

Urban Gardening. Beginning in 1987, state enterprises established "partnerships" whereby employees could each receive 0.06 hectare of land near the city. Few respondents in the sample had managed to privatize their plots. In Balti and Chisinau, however, these plots played an important role in subsistence. Families often raised enough vegetables to get them through the winter. One Balti respondent had raised 150 kilograms of potatoes, 20 kilograms of carrots, 35 kilograms of onions, 10 kilograms of beets, and a pail of beans, and had managed to pickle 50 kilograms of cucumbers and tomatoes. Some people built small shelters where they lived during the summer to prevent crop theft. Others feared being beaten by thieves but lacked sufficient money to pay a guard and still make a profit.

Some people grew vegetables on their building lots. Others cultivated unclaimed patches of urban land, growing vegetables and herbs using animal manure and their own manual labor. A few had fruit trees. On the outskirts of Chisinau, people had larger lots where they could grow cash crops. A lecturer from the Agricultural Institute borrowed 1,500 lei to build a 250-square-meter greenhouse on his parents' land; he invested a further 300 lei for seeds, chemicals, and pesticides and earned 3,500 lei selling the seedlings and tomatoes. Urban families often bought animals, which they kept with their elderly parents in the country. One respondent living in a high-rise on the outskirts of the city raised six cows and three heifers in the woods near his apartment, where he built a small shed. He sold dairy products and manure.

Conclusions

Farm managers and local officials had considerable power to prevent households from privatizing. They threatened to withdraw access to heavy equipment by seizing, destroying, or failing to act on applications; they tried to convince households that inadequate resources and knowledge would guarantee failure. The families who withstood these pressures were often those with greater access to information, strategic ties to those with political or economic power, or specialized skills. For many members of the restructured collective farms, household plots provided their basic subsistence. For some this experience provided a transition to independent farming; for others, it supplemented their income.

Changing Livelihood Strategies

Since independence, many enterprises have closed or sent their workers home on extended leave without pay; salaries have shrunk drastically. Benefits, subsidies, pensions, and allowances, if received at all, are late or in small amounts. Yet although some people have found it difficult to adapt, others have managed to survive and even prosper during the transition. This study focuses on those who have been less able to adapt because they lack skills, opportunities, or access to people and resources, or because of illness, disability, or family responsibilities.

Formal Employment

Formal employment includes public sector employment in industry, agriculture, and the services sector, and private sector employment in the emerging private factories, firms, and enterprises. Although most rural respondents worked full-time in agriculture, some still worked for the state as teachers and medical personnel. Many urban respondents clung to state sector jobs, often holding several at once.

Many respondents saw getting and keeping a permanent job as key to survival. For some it was the only source of cash to supplement subsistence gardening and barter. Many feared total unemployment. Those near retirement age felt psychologically protected by having a job. They knew it was unlikely they would find other work, and they wanted to accrue seniority for pensions.

Although state-funded construction had stopped, people remained on job-linked waiting lists for housing. Many people lived in crowded worker hostels, holding jobs without a salary, sustained by the hope of procuring an apartment after many years of waiting. Some took a job in order to obtain space in a hostel.

Olga, a dressmaker, took on a job as a laboratory assistant so that she and her husband could move into a 12-square-meter room in the Medical Institute's hostel. There they share a toilet, shower, and kitchen with five other families.

Many large enterprises now worked at a reduced capacity. The former Lenin Munitions Plant in Balti once employed 8,000 workers; now it employed 2,000 and produced consumer items. Salaries had been cut from 200 to 300 rubles a month, a comfortable amount during Soviet times, to a meager 100 to 150 lei, paid with a delay of several months. Often employees were paid in goods. The workers could not predict their salaries from month to month.

A worker at the Bucuria Candy Factory reports that her salary depends on the number of orders received: "When we have orders, I make 300 to 400 lei a month; sometimes I get nothing at all for several months in a row. I intended to search for another job, but I was promised an apartment next year. Now I live in a two-room apartment with my three children, my mother, and my husband, who is paralyzed. Where can I go?"

Finding Work. A few Soviet-era industrial enterprises had recently found new markets and started hiring. Some had even invited their former workers to return. Finding formal employment was particularly difficult for young people without job experience, for the ill or disabled, and for women with young children. People could not register at the employment office if they had privatized their land. In Comrat few people were aware of the employment service's existence, and even fewer made use of it. It could take six months to accumulate the necessary documents to register, compensation of 18 lei a month was paid with a delay of three to four months, and few jobs were offered. People frequently obtained their jobs through bribes.

Unemployed Youth. Many rural respondents were concerned about the lack of prospects for young people. Although some had left to seek work in cities within Moldova or abroad, others worked part-time in agriculture and remained idle during the long winter months. Educated youths found themselves entering the labor market at a time when the few jobs available were being given to those with more work experience.

Roman recently graduated as an engineer and registered at the employment office. He has been receiving 25 lei a month in unemployment payments but has not had a single job offer. He was told that far more experienced engineers than he remain unemployed.

Well-educated and enterprising youths sometimes found work after retraining. The daughter of one respondent took a course in waitressing; this helped her find a well-paid job. Others had finished courses in accounting and were being hired by new businesses. Young people who spoke English or other languages found well-paid work with the foreign organizations and private businesses in Chisinau.

Illness and Disability. The ill and the disabled were unable to compete in the new job market. An employee of a candy factory reported that employees had to pass a medical examination twice a year; anyone found ill was fired. Those with permanent disabilities had worked in special factories during the Soviet era and took pride in their ability to work and earn a salary. Others were able to hold down ordinary jobs, which they were now terrified of losing.

A disabled teacher reports, "Despite my low salary of 160 lei a month, I am not looking for another job; everyone is letting employees go. I don't dare think of leaving this school. Who needs me with my crutches?"

Working Women with Children. Women with small children had trouble finding work because employers knew they would often be absent.

Elena, a young economist with a brilliant record from the Academy of Economic Studies, was constantly passed over for jobs because she has two small children; her male colleagues have found jobs in private firms for salaries of 500 to 600 lei a month.

Sometimes women left their jobs because of their small children.

Veronica, a single mother of three, found a part-time evening job through the unemployment office, washing dishes at a restaurant for

80 lei a month. She worked in the evenings after her ninth-grade son returned home to look after his younger siblings, but she quit when she realized the children were often alone until 11 p.m. Her employment possibilities are limited: she cannot start a daytime job because she cannot afford clothing and fees for her children to attend kindergarten.

Women no longer enjoyed up to three years of maternity leave.

Svetlana, a milkmaid on a collective farm, went on leave to give birth to her fourth child. The collective farm started shedding workers, and she lost her job. Svetlana protested her firing and was rehired. She was placed on the brigade in charge of the vegetable fields, but she is fearful that any small mistake will provide grounds for her boss to fire her.

Informal Employment

Most respondents tried to combine several strategies: formal employment with time off to pursue other ends; subsistence agriculture; income-generating activities such as trade; small-scale production and sales; and services. For some families informal employment had developed into full-scale, profitable enterprises, but most respondents had succeeded at best in just making ends meet.

Buying and Selling. Trading in consumer items and food across the new international borders had become a lucrative source of income for a few, a helpful supplement for many, and a financial catastrophe for some. People drew on kinship and other personal ties to find work or establish trading relations throughout the former Soviet Union and in Romania, Hungary, Greece, Turkey, and Western Europe. People studied customs regulations to learn how best to exploit them.

Because Romania does not tax Moldovans who bring goods through the country en route to other countries, Romanian merchants hired Moldovans to declare the goods. Once in Romania the goods were sold on the spot.

Marcu, a Moldovan, teams up with a Romanian partner, with whom he travels to Turkey. There they buy goods to resell in Romania. This earns him $200 a month.

In both rural and urban areas, serious farmers and gardeners bartered or traded surplus produce. People who lived near national frontiers, as in the district of Cahul, often took produce to Romania; others traveled to Ukraine. Women frequently traveled to Moscow to sell herbs and vegetables. People profited from the price differential, for example, buying agricultural products in Chisinau to resell in Transnistria, using the pretext of relatives there to avoid the customs taxes that this separatist region has imposed. Likewise, people who had relatives in Ukraine bought goods to take to their relatives, who then bartered them locally. Some traders brought secondhand clothes from abroad and sold them in villages. In Comrat many villagers wore such clothing.

Ira used to work as a secretary in the Ministry of Agriculture. The salary was low and was paid with delays. On the advice of her sister, she borrowed the equivalent of $1,000 from relatives and started importing goods from Poland. A typical trip involves the equivalent of $160 for bus transport, $20 in customs fees, 240 lei a month to rent a space in the market, and 100 lei a month for warehouse space. In the market itself, police protect the sellers from rackets. The best seasons are spring and fall, just before school starts. In a good month Ira makes 400 to 500 lei; in a bad month, she breaks even.

Small-Scale Retail Vending. Some people acquired goods wholesale, selling everything from sweets, pastries, soap, and shampoo to underwear and even alcoholic drinks. Some unemployed teachers and engineers had started to bake pastries at home, to be sold by their husbands in the market.

After losing her factory job, Irina tried to start a modest bookselling business. It took seven months to complete the necessary documents. After a few months without success, she began to sell chewing gum, cigarette lighters, and cigarettes. The police began to harass her, but she solved this problem by giving them a carton. Streetchildren often harass her, begging for cigarettes and gum. She is frightened that they will overturn her counter and steal her money. Irina sells on the street from May until October, unless it is raining.

In villages, people with a small amount of capital had opened small booths where they sold sweets, cigarettes, liquor, soap, and shampoo. Their profits were small since few villagers were able to buy.

Petty Enterprises. A host of small enterprises had sprung up to serve the newly wealthy in both town and countryside. Men and women with skills in painting and renovating houses often worked privately.

Dimitru quit his job and now repairs apartments, painting walls and doors and putting up wallpaper. With two other men, he makes 1,000 lei for each apartment they fix up. Over the summer his team renovated three apartments.

People often used their connections or access to resources to start their own businesses.

Two brothers in Chisinau cleaned out their basement, installed a stronger door, and set up a carpentry shop. One of them is a student who works part-time at a lumber factory, where he can buy lumber.

Skills sometimes became businesses: growing seedlings to sell, sewing dresses on order, breeding dogs, or performing at weddings and other ceremonial functions. In summer and autumn, elderly people picked berries, medicinal herbs, mushrooms, and nuts. One family of Chisinau pensioners earned 2,000 lei in one season this way.

Renting out Rooms. Renting out an apartment, a few rooms, or even just a bed was an important source of income in urban settings. People often sold their bigger apartments and bought smaller ones, supporting themselves on the difference. People doubled up so that they could rent their apartments or rooms to others. A pensioner who had been selling clothing, dishes, and books just to survive found a student willing to pay 50 lei a month for a room.

Illicit Activities

Prostitution. A few respondents suggested that young women, including some of their acquaintances, who had returned from abroad after long absences with large amounts of cash, had been working as prostitutes. Many newspapers now carried job offers for "nice girls who are not self-conscious" and invitations for weekends or longer vacations, with a list of young women and their photographs. Streetwalkers worked openly in front of many hotels, and some women stopped cars on the outskirts of cities to offer their services.

Bribes. Poor people were usually not in a position to demand or receive bribes of any size, although they sometimes received small gifts for expediting services or solving a problem. This group included people remaining in public sector employment, where they periodically received a bottle of champagne, a box of chocolate, or a package of coffee.

Begging. Elderly beggars were increasingly visible in towns and cities. In Cahul a pensioner spent the summer begging in front of the market, using the money to buy bread. In winter she planned to go to a sanatorium or pension and ask if she could eat the leftover food after meals had been served. Child beggars, sometimes accompanied by their mothers, were also seen in Chisinau, often occupying regular places in front of food shops or bread stores.

A widow of 74 lost her home in the catastrophic flooding of 1991. She had long since buried her only son and had no living relatives to help her. A farm worker her whole life, she came to Chisinau to beg, to supplement her 60-lei monthly pension. She asks for very small amounts in the produce market so that she can buy some rolls. She lives in cellars during the summer, returning to the countryside in the winter, where she asks people to house her for a night.

Theft. Theft is an ambiguous concept in Moldova, given the long history of "appropriating" goods from state-owned enterprises for personal use or resale. This practice has continued, with some respondents declaring that they considered it a legitimate practice, since these enterprises had not paid their salaries in many months. People also stole crops from collective farm fields to resell.

Labor Migration

Labor migration has become a significant way to make money. People in rural areas frequently left in late autumn and winter, when there was less agricultural work to do. A number of new companies offered to arrange documents and ease relations with customs officials, police, and racketeers. On several occasions, however, applicants found, after they had paid their fee of 12 to 20 lei and filled out the forms, that the office had disappeared.

In Russia, the most important single destination, men worked in heavy construction, as builders and masons on private homes of the newly rich, in agricultural brigades in orchards or in vineyards, or as drivers and tractor operators. In Comrat a local private enterprise hired people to work as foresters for the companies from which they imported wood. Payment was made to the employees' close relatives in Comrat. People with special skills could emigrate permanently to countries in the West where they had relatives.

Both men and women traveled to Russia, Ukraine, or Hungary to work in agriculture. People living in border communities often found casual work. In districts such as Cahul, people would take leave from the collective farm to go to Romania to pick cherries for a few weeks. Greece had become a significant destination for young women, who worked as maids and nannies for $400 to $600 a month. Others wished to go but lacked the $600 needed to pay for a passport, visa, and transportation.

Some went abroad in groups, ranging from a pair of friends or relatives to a whole team. People often suffered from the many rackets operating in Russia. Many reported that their documents and money had been stolen. Sometimes they were forced to remain in Moscow, wasting money on hotels, until the documents could be replaced. In most cases the work was unofficial, without working agreements, contracts, or visas. Work elsewhere in Europe was less dangerous and quite lucrative.

Changing Attitudes and Risks

Older respondents still considered buying and selling to be a form of "speculation." Some respondents were initially ashamed of being seen selling goods on the street. Young people had fewer misgivings.

Connections. Many individuals and households in the sample were virtually forced to work in the shadow economy, where they were vulnerable to organized crime and the police.

Nina, who makes funeral and wedding wreaths, obtained her license through her mother, who had connections in the licensing department; the license has now expired, and Nina does not know who can help "expedite" her application.

Many market or street vendors worked without licenses, suffering constant harassment by police. In many cases they paid a bribe and were then left in peace.

Alexandr, an unemployed locksmith in Chisinau, sells wine for his neighbor for 15 to 20 lei a week, without a license. He believes that his neighbor hired him so that, if trouble arises, it will fall on him, not the neighbor. But Alexandr is prepared: if a policeman comes to his home, he plans to buy him a bottle of cognac and slip him a bribe.

Working in the large city markets, small traders were harassed by gang members and cheated by customers. Nineteen-year-old Petre was cheated when a customer paid him with a bank-sealed wad of 400 lei in which only the top and bottom consisted of banknotes. His mother had to borrow 395 lei to pay back his employer. Other cases were reported of sellers whose goods were stolen or who were cheated and then brutally beaten by "friends" of their employers.

Borrowing and Lending. Although people regularly borrowed small sums from neighbors, friends, and relatives, they relied on relatives for larger sums. Some obtained bank loans at high interest rates, others borrowed from wealthy acquaintances, and still others used moneylenders, often with catastrophic consequences. Professional moneylenders had a reputation for being extremely ruthless. Failure to repay large loans from kin could rupture family relationships.

Conclusions

The labor market in Moldova is in a state of transition. Although most people coped with nonpayment of salaries and pensions by looking for other sources of income, some were paralyzed by the fact that skills they had mastered after years of study were not in demand; still others had turned to alcohol or crime. Success depended on having close kinship or friendship relations to people with power; having entered the transition with money that was not devalued during currency reform; having assets such as large apartments or working vehicles; and having skills. Enterprising people without these resources often found themselves unable or unwilling to deal with the complications and expense of obtaining registrations, licenses, and protection, and therefore very vulnerable to harassment.

Social Integration and Disintegration

The effects of poverty on social relations were apparent both in families and in the larger community. Although many people relied heavily on their closest relations for assistance, many families were disintegrating under the combined pressures of unemployment, alcoholism, shifting gender expectations, and extended work-related separations. In many cases, relatives could no longer fulfill basic social obligations. The increase in theft and violent crime and the growth of youth gangs had frightened many people off the streets and decreased trust, especially in urban communities. The old ideology of egalitarianism was disintegrating, dividing communities into distinct layers of rich and poor. Some people had withdrawn into isolation, jealous and suspicious of their neighbors, nostalgic for the past, and frightened of the future. With increased economic stratification, open borders, new patterns of migration, ethnic homogenization, and the pervasive impoverishment of state and family budgets, the social landscape and accustomed patterns of social interaction have altered.

The Family

Moldovans rely heavily on their closest family relations, but poverty has weakened kin relations, preventing relatives from keeping in touch or sending help. Sometimes people lacked the financial and emotional resources to help.

Stefan, a pensioner, has an unemployed son searching for a job and a daughter-in-law who is employed in a collective farm in Nisporeni district. Stefan takes care of his two grandchildren, doing electrical repair work for his neighbor in exchange for a pot of porridge to feed them.

Varvara, from Nisporeni, is 84. She has one daughter in Russia but has not heard from her in 10 years. Her other daughter lives in the same village but is an alcoholic who cannot take care of her own household, much less her aging mother.

Men used to be the family breadwinner, and they felt displaced when their wives earned more than they did. Women often blamed their husbands for the family's financial situation and criticized them for their lack of success in finding work. These tensions contributed to family stress and disintegration.

Maria, living in Chisinau, feels that her unemployed husband has become indifferent to his family. She complains that he sleeps or drinks the entire day, sometimes bringing his other alcoholic friends home with him. She has become the family breadwinner. When she returns home from work, her husband often picks a fight and then beats her. He has also begun to sell household items, even furniture.

The prolonged absence of husbands and, in some cases, wives, challenged the division of labor and power in the family. When husbands left, their fathers sometimes stepped in as household heads, but often women took over the traditional male responsibilities.

Community Relations

Weddings and funerals have always been important social events for both urban and rural Moldovans. By offering hospitality to relatives, neighbors, colleagues, and friends, families maintained their honor, earned respect, and fulfilled necessary social obligations. Today, however, ceremonies that once included whole neighborhoods or the entire village took place within a small circle of close relatives.

Ion, from Ungheni, declined several wedding invitations last fall, but refusing to attend the wedding of his sister's daughter would have been dishonorable. He borrowed 35 lei for the wedding gift.

Regular socializing has radically diminished. People were afraid to impose on their hosts and afraid that, if they went visiting, they would have to receive guests in turn. Visiting used to cement relationships and facilitate information sharing; the decline of such socializing left people feeling isolated. Social institutions were no longer funded by municipalities, and people could no longer afford to go. In many villages, clubs and movie theaters were open only a few times a year. Pensioners who used to seek solace in the local church could not afford to buy candles yet found it shameful to go without lighting a candle.

Children and Youth. Children had become a liability for poor families. The birth rate was falling, the abortion rate was rising, and rumors abounded concerning poor mothers who had sold their newborns. Abandoned children and runaways slept in cellars, sewage pipes, and train stations. Schools often closed in winter, and there were no jobs for dropouts. Boredom and poverty combined to create a sharp rise in youth gangs and criminality. In Chisinau and Balti, people spoke frankly about acquaintances who took drugs. Respondents feared going out in the evening because the streets were filled with "aggressive and intoxicated youths."

Crime. Violent crime had risen sharply. In cities such as Balti, drug-related crimes had increased. In towns that had eliminated street lighting to cut

374 | When Things Fall Apart

electricity costs, people felt that burglaries had become more common. Women noted increasing numbers of sexual assaults. Villagers were aware of increased theft but powerless against it. Items ranging from tools to poultry were taken from houses, yards, or farm buildings. The rise in crime left poor people feeling extremely defenseless.

Increasing Social Differentiation. The majority of rural and urban workers expressed great resentment at the newly rich. Rumors, jealousy, and resentment were easily stirred as people compared the situation of their own families with those of people who had managed to retain their jobs or find new ones. People were fearful of the future. If they kept their money in their sock, they feared it would lose its value; if they spent it, they might not earn any more the following day. Poor people felt greater solidarity with other poor as the distance between them and their more prosperous kin, friends, and neighbors increased.

Ethnic and Regional Variation

Separatist movements arose after independence in the Gagauz region in the south (centered around Comrat) and in Transnistria. The Gagauz, a Turkic people who practice Orthodox Christianity, make up about 70 percent of the population in Comrat. Their conflict with the Moldovan central government was resolved with the creation of the Gagauz Eri autonomous unit. In Transnistria, which has considerable industrial capacity and a pro-Russian political orientation, ethnic-related political confrontation turned into a serious armed conflict, starting a flow of refugees into Chisinau and other cities and creating an economic crisis for much of Transnistria's population. The situation was so volatile at the time of the study that Transnistria was excluded from it.

Migration Patterns. Many people from minority groups left Moldova following independence in part as a result of the country's new nationalism and in part because economic conditions in Russia were better. Approximately 190,000 people emigrated to Ukraine and Russia, 38,000 to Israel, 10,000 to the United States, and 5,000 to Germany. At the same time over 150,000 immigrants, mostly ethnic Moldovans, arrived from Russia, Ukraine, and other former Soviet republics. Many ethnic Moldovans fled from Transnistria to other regions of Moldova. Overall, Moldova is now more homogeneous, although it retains a significant Russian-speaking, Slavic population (35 percent of the total). Many Moldovans have relatives in Ukraine, Romania, and Russia, and they use these ties extensively in commercial transactions.

Linguistic Issues. In 1989 Moldova passed a law giving primacy to Romanian as the state language. Lack of Romanian-language proficiency has become an economic impediment to many Russian speakers. A respondent who had graduated from an institute of higher education in Tiraspol found her diploma was not acceptable elsewhere in Moldova. Romanian speakers in Gagauzia's Comrat district complained that higher education in local institutes was conducted primarily in Russian, forcing them to study elsewhere. In Romanian-speaking regions, Russian speakers made the same complaint.

Regional Variation. Patterns of poverty appeared to derive more from regional variations than from particular patterns of ethnic exclusion. The strongest regional differences were observed along the north-south axis. Living standards appeared to be lower and opportunities scarcer in the south, which is more agricultural and more conservative in its orientation. Many respondents in the south felt that the Moldovan government was dominated by people from the northern part of the country, who neglected the south. Many villagers were very poorly informed about the process and procedures of privatization and experienced many obstructions. In the Comrat district in the south, many respondents were also fearful about the risk of independent farming in an area so prone to drought. In neighboring Cahul, farm workers in Crihana Veche felt forced to stay on the collective farm, but those working nearby in the village of Manta pushed aggressively to form the Zavoieni farming association (described above). Similar differences were evident within the central districts of Nisporeni and Ungheni, where some farm workers had managed to form an independent farmers' association, yet others remained within the collective farm.

This study found important differences between villages in the same region, often based on the presence or absence of direct road and rail links to towns and cities. In the north such a pattern could be seen in the Balti and Edenet districts. Mihailovca village, located off the main transportation routes, lacked its own school, town hall, and market. Its inhabitants expressed a much greater sense of dependence on local officials and were much more vulnerable to intimidation.

Conclusions

Poverty in Moldova appeared to be linked to regional variations and available opportunities rather than to particular patterns of ethnic exclusion. In addition to the north-south agroclimatic differences, there were significant intraregional variations in infrastructure development, available resources, trading patterns, and integration with Chisinau. People often attributed their perceived disadvantages to their ethnicity and employed ethnic stereotypes to boost their own group identity.

Summary

For the majority of respondents, impoverishment has been recent and rapid, and few people have fully grasped the causes, consequences, and implications for the future. Many factors have contributed to household poverty: unemployment, a dramatic fall in the real value of salaries, pensions, and other forms of social assistance; loss of lifetime savings; and the introduction of fees for health care and education. Factors of importance in rural areas include the rupture of trade relations within the former Soviet Union; new regulations and fees for cross-border trade; land reform and competition to assert rights over land and assets; and several years of bad weather and poor harvests.

Moldova's citizens are beginning to understand that they can no longer rely on the state to guarantee their well-being. A majority of respondents resented those leaders who had used their connections in the old system to secure their own prosperity in the new one. Many people viewed the growing differentiation between the newly poor and the newly rich with great antagonism; only younger respondents felt that the transition offered them positive economic possibilities. For the poorest, especially those without the skills or resources to compete effectively in the new economy, such as the elderly, the disabled, and single parents without marketable skills but many dependents, life has become a struggle to survive.

Notes

1. The full-length qualitative poverty study is published in volume 2 of that report.
2. This section is adapted from Dudwick (1997).

References

Dudwick, Nora. 1997. "Land Reform in Moldova" World Bank, ECSSD, Washington, D.C. Processed.

World Bank. 1996a. "With Farmer's Eyes: A Grassroots Perspective on Land Privatization in Moldova." EC4NR Agriculture Policy Note 7. World Bank, Natural Resources Management Division, Country Department IV, Europe and Central Asia Region, Washington, D.C. (October 17).

———. 1996b. "Land Reform and Private Farming in Moldova." EC4NR Agriculture Policy Note 9. World Bank, Natural Resources Management Division, Country Department IV, Europe and Central Asia Region, Washington, D.C. (January 29).

———. 1999. *Moldova: Poverty Assessment. A World Bank Country Study.* Washington, D.C.

---　✳　---

PART FIVE

LATVIA

Latvia, one of the smaller former Soviet republics (64,589 square kilometers), with a population of 2.5 million, has a 500-kilometer coastline on the Baltic Sea and borders Belarus, Estonia, Lithuania, and the Russian Federation. A province of the Russian Empire in the 19th century, Latvia enjoyed independence between 1918 and 1940. Deportations, executions, emigration, territorial change, and evacuation resulted in huge population losses during World War II. A harsh program of russification under Soviet rule, along with deportations and large-scale Slavic immigration, reduced the share of ethnic Latvians in the republic from a prewar 75 percent to 52 percent in 1989 and facilitated rapid urbanization and industrialization. This allowed the country to attain a high level of consumption per capita relative to other Soviet republics. By 1997 only 55.3 percent of the population were ethnic Latvians, 32.5 percent were Russian, and 12.2 percent were other nationalities. Major port cities (including Riga, with a third of the population), together with the woodlands that cover 44 percent of the country, are important resources for this otherwise resource-poor nation. By 1998 the poverty rate was about 11 percent, with rural poverty at 28 percent. Given its history, location, and the incentive of potential membership in the European Union, Latvia has pursued the reforms urged by the international financial institutions, and better-educated urban groups have benefited from the resulting economic growth. Nevertheless, a banking crisis in 1995 wiped out many families' savings. Although Latvia is a small country, the income gap between urban and rural areas has steadily widened. Riga and other major ports have attracted most investment, while the dismantling of agricultural and industrial enterprises has created high regional unemployment, particularly in the southeastern region of Latgale.

Exchange rate

Latvia: $1 = 0.59 lat (April 1998)

A blind musician plays for money at the main
retail market in Riga.
Photo by Nora Dudwick

　※

CHAPTER 12

Prosperity and Despair: Riga and the Other Latvia

Institute of Philosophy and Sociology, Riga, with Nora Dudwick

L atvia is a small, largely urbanized country, with over two-thirds of its population settled in urban (town and city) areas. It achieved one of the highest standards of living in the Soviet Union, where, along with Estonia and Lithuania, it was frequently referred to as "our Europe" or the "Soviet abroad."

After independence Latvian industries lost their sources of raw materials as well as their Soviet market. The collective farms were privatized, but farmers were unprepared to compete with Western agriculture. Since 1997 the macroeconomic situation has slowly improved, although the agricultural sector has continued to decline (United Nations Development Programme 1997). The restructuring of the economy has been accompanied by the closure or failure of many large enterprises, along with mass layoffs. Poverty has become widespread.

The study reported in this chapter, co-financed by the World Bank and the United Nations Development Programme (UNDP), was undertaken during the first half of 1998 to complement a number of other World Bank and UNDP studies and projects under way, including the Latvia Welfare Reform Project and the World Bank Poverty Assessment (World Bank 1999). Researchers from the Latvian Academy of Sciences managed the study and produced the final report, with substantive and editorial input from the World Bank author.

Interviews were conducted with 400 households, 20 local experts (including staff of government offices, teachers, and medical personnel), and several international experts (including representatives from U.N. agencies, bilateral donors, and international nongovernmental organizations). A purposive sample of households was drawn from the capital city of Riga, from other large cities, and from towns and rural districts or villages categorized as high, medium, and low according to human development indicators. Historical and geographical dimensions were also taken into account. Thus communities from all Latvia's major historical regions, including Riga and its district, Vidzeme in the northeast, Latgale in the east, and Kurzeme in the west, were included in the study.

The Dimensions of Poverty

As in other former Soviet countries, mass poverty is a relatively new phenomenon in Latvia. Only at the end of the 1980s did people start to speak publicly about poverty and the problems of survival. How Latvians thought about poverty reflected recent experiences and ideological changes. Should individuals take responsibility for their own economic situation? What role should the state play in economic life?

Conceptualizing Poverty

Poverty as a widespread phenomenon and as a topic of research and public debate was not a major issue during Soviet times. Although much of today's poverty was the result of a society-wide economic transition, many respondents retained from the Soviet era a sense of shame at being poor. In those days being poor was the equivalent of being a virtual social outcast, the result of uniquely personal failures. Many respondents preferred to describe themselves as "needy" or "on the verge of poverty." They accused national and local government officials of incompetence and indifference and expressed their own sense of guilt, shame, and humiliation.

Most respondents described their own situation in relative terms: they tended to compare their own position with that of those around them, often comforting themselves that they were no worse off than others.

Although her family has undergone a rapid decline in well-being during recent years, Galina, an unemployed 49-year-old in the city of Liepâja, claims that her situation is not so bad. She does not consider her family "poor." Where they live, she points out, there are many who are poorer, such as the old women who beg for money and food in the market. Galina feels sorry that she cannot help them by giving them food or money. She explains that she is unemployed and they understand.

Able-bodied respondents preferred to identify themselves as *maloobespechenniye* (Russian for "poorly provided for"). The exceptions were families whose standard of living had declined abruptly because of business failure or large, unforeseen medical expenses. Pensioners viewed their situation much more grimly, observing their severe decline in living standards and their lack of prospects for improving their situation.

An 81-year-old female pensioner in Lielvarde says, "Previously, pensioners could help their children and still keep something for themselves, but now you can just lie down and die. . . . The unbearable thing about this situation is the constant feeling of being dependent on somebody or something—on rude young people, on the willingness or unwillingness of bureaucrats, on people from whom you have to borrow money."

In comparing themselves with others, Latvians evoked widely held stereotypes: urban residents had more difficulties because they could not provide their own food; villages were desolate, isolated, and devastated by unemployment and widespread alcohol abuse; large families and unemployed people had the most difficulties; retired people living alone were in the most difficult situation. The few respondents who compared themselves with the wealthy spoke in hostile terms, emphasizing the social injustice and the unfair distribution of resources that had taken place after independence.

A widowed nurse in Livani, 36 years old and mother of four, reflects on her situation: "When I compare myself with others, I feel poor, because I cannot give to my child what he needs. When working people have to worry about whether they have enough money to feed their children and they can hardly make ends meet, it isn't normal. It isn't fair that top government officials can add large sums to their salaries, whereas we. . . . The comparison is dramatic."

People compared their current living standards with the past and spoke nostalgically of the time when they could raise even large families without worrying about necessities. Most distinguished between extreme poverty—not being able to afford food—and the inability to afford important items such as school supplies for their children.

A 50-year-old cleaning woman in Rezekne district recalls a more prosperous time: "In the past we even wanted to buy a car and were saving money for it. We could raise a calf, sell it, and buy a sofa with the money; now it is no use to raise livestock for the market. Forage alone costs more than what you finally get for the calf."

A 35-year-old father of four small children observes, "The worst thing in this situation is the feeling that you are a pauper, that you have to go somewhere and beg."

Explaining Poverty

The main reasons given for poverty were the collapse of the old economic system—which resulted in unemployment, low salaries paid late and only partially, the wiping out of savings by hyperinflation (with high prices for agricultural inputs and technical services but low market prices for produce), and the loss of family benefits—and the fact that a new system had not yet developed to take its place. Government reforms failed to reach the poor, government officials were seen as incompetent and indifferent to people's suffering, there were constant changes in policies, and the legal environment was full of contradictions. Many poor respondents did not have the money to take advantage of the reform process by privatizing land or houses. Others sold their privatization vouchers just to cover the cost of daily essentials. Sometimes the individual was blamed for being overly dependent on the state. In many cases the causes were complex and interrelated: a person might lose a job because of enterprise closure, become depressed over the situation, start drinking, and become even less capable of finding work to improve his or her situation.

Many of Latvia's poor were working, but their real salaries had dropped precipitously as prices rose. When they received salaries, they were more often than not months late, paid only in part or in kind. Members of a school staff reported they had not received wages in months.

A 42-year-old nurse who earns 70 lats a month describes her work situation: "The amount of work has significantly increased while salaries remain the same or are even smaller. Besides, we are in constant fear of losing our jobs, and therefore intrigues flourish. Medical personnel try to slander each other in order to maintain their own good relations with the authorities. Often I have to smile when I am angry or feel injustice. My work in the emergency room is really difficult, and I am exhausted at the end of a workday. Nearly all my salary goes for rent, and nothing is left for me or my children."

Respondents emphasized the devastating consequences of unemployment. The long-term unemployed often became apathetic, depressed, and prone to alcohol abuse. Several respondents had family members who had committed suicide after prolonged periods of unemployment. One respondent described the anomaly of being capable and ready to work but unable to manage: "Your hands and feet are whole and all right, but you are unable to earn a living."

Tatiana, an unemployed woman in Malta village, remarks on the idleness she observes around her: "Young people of about 30 or 40 walk around the village in groups of four or five. They do no work. Could one see anything like that before? Women sit at home in nearly every apartment—you can go and see it wherever you like. They keep visiting one another and chatting. Where has it been like that before? You hurried home from work and had hardly any time for doing household chores."

Rural families found it difficult to make money because of low prices for produce and the high cost of inputs and technical services. The Soviet market for cash crops had collapsed. Collective farms that used to purchase and market local produce now only bought "from their friends." Restaurant and shop owners had little interest in buying locally from small producers, preferring to buy cheaper imported produce.

Respondents expressed considerable distrust in government and in government officials, whom some respondents blamed for their poverty. Some felt that the former members of the Communist Party had been the main beneficiaries of the transition.

A 72-year-old retired woman expresses her contempt for the bureaucrats: "They have been plundering everything and eating so much that they cannot carry their own stomachs. . . . During the Soviet period, at least people had a place where they could complain. Now the state does not wish to take any responsibility, and people are exhausted from their economic and social problems."

Respondents expressed a sense of powerlessness. They acknowledged that socialism had cultivated dependence and that people lacked initiative. Many respondents distinguished between those who were trying to extricate themselves from poverty and those who abused alcohol and failed to seek employment or take care of their children.

The Impact of Poverty on Social Relations

In Latvia as elsewhere, people were accustomed to relying on social networks to cope with short-term and long-term difficulties. However, poverty had reduced people's abilities to maintain these networks.

Poverty affected men and women in different ways. Men were more able to find casual jobs requiring physical strength or operating heavy farm equipment; women had more opportunities to work in the services sector. Women tended to experience more discrimination on the basis of age, or because they had small children at home. Respondents felt that poverty had very different psychological consequences for men and women. In a society where men were still considered the primary breadwinner, unemployment weighed very heavily on men. Although depression was common among both men and women, men were more likely to increase their alcohol consumption and to resort to suicide.

Many families simply disintegrated under the stress. The continuous anxiety to make ends meet and the sense of unequal effort worsened many marital relationships to the point of separation or divorce. In other cases, however, the difficult economic situation kept families together and even drew them closer: women with young children stayed with their husbands because they understood they would have had difficulty alone. Respondents reported many examples of unemployment-related alcoholism that had caused the disintegration of marriages and the severe neglect of children. Relations were strained when parents were unable to meet their children's material and status needs.

People curtailed their socializing, and this led to further depression and isolation. Holiday celebrations were limited to the immediate family, eroding the extended family and neighborhood networks. Interviewers noted that people without family support networks—childless couples and individuals, in particular—had many more day-to-day difficulties. For people from other parts of the former Soviet Union, particularly Russia or Ukraine, opportunities to stay in touch with relatives were much more limited.

"During the past two years we have not celebrated any holidays with others. We cannot afford to invite anyone to our house, and we feel uncomfortable visiting others without bringing a present. Before, we used to celebrate all our birthdays by inviting guests, usually 10 friends and relatives. We also visited people often, because we could afford to buy flowers as well as small gifts. The lack of contact leaves one depressed and creates a constant feeling of unhappiness and a sense of low self-esteem."

Although poverty generally had a negative impact on relationships, close friends played a significant supportive role, providing information or help in locating employment and material assistance. Neighbors were also a critical support. Many borrowed and lent small amounts of money from each other for daily necessities. Some of the poor ate with neighbors at the end of the month, when they ran out of money. Neighbors looked after each other's children or helped each other in the field during harvest season. In one case neighbors in a rural apartment building combined their households in order to survive.

Poor households in the sample experienced exclusion in various forms: physical exclusion as they moved to the outskirts of town; intellectual and material exclusion as their choice of schools was restricted and prospects for good employment were reduced; and social and cultural exclusion as they withdrew from the life of their society. As people became more isolated, they inadvertently cut themselves off from assistance that could have helped them reenter society.

Social Stratification

Many poor respondents deplored what they saw as a general trend in their society, namely, an increasing differentiation between rich and poor: those with possibilities and those without.

A mother of five in Liepāja says, "The people who make decisions and have high salaries do not understand those who do not have work and money. They send their children to good schools. They take their child to school by car, and they meet their child by car. In some schools there are children who have seen the world only through the window of a car."

Respondents observed that the economic changes had resulted in new forms of spatial stratification as people moved out of large, well-appointed apartments in prestigious areas in town and city centers to smaller apartments or small private houses in order to conserve on costly utilities. In some cases municipalities contributed to this process by rehousing destitute and problem families in special buildings or neighborhoods of their own. Parents were distressed at the impact on their children, who were publicly singled out as "poor" at school because they received free lunches (often served separately), dressed poorly, or had to use photocopied class materials. Poor parents feared that this stratification would continue because of the high informal and formal costs of education.

Ethnicity and Poverty

The study did not demonstrate a correlation between ethnicity and degree of poverty, but it did suggest that people who lacked Latvian language competency, regardless of their citizenship status, faced an additional obstacle to retaining their job or finding a new one. Poor people who had immigrated to Latvia from other parts of the former Soviet Union often had less extensive social networks; many of their relatives lived abroad, and it had become expensive to travel or maintain telephone contact. Inability to speak Latvian also affected Latvians from mixed families where Russian was spoken at home.

Regional Variations in Poverty

The experience of poverty was affected by location and by the social context of the immediate neighborhood, the community, and the region. The Soviet regime had built huge factories in Daugavpils (Latgale region), Jelgava (Zemgale region), Liepâja (Kurzeme region), and Valmiera (Vidzeme region) and had encouraged workers from Russia and other Soviet republics to settle in these cities. The closure of these factories had produced concentrations of unemployed whose social support networks and Latvian language skills were limited.

Latgale region had an official unemployment rate of 24 percent, compared with 3 percent in Riga. Ruled for many years by Poland, Latgale has a strong Catholic identity and an ethnically diverse population, with large numbers of ethnic Russians, Poles, Belarussians, and others. It is considerably poorer than other parts of Latvia. Life expectancy, educational attainment, level of employment, and average incomes in the rural districts around Jekabpils, Daugavpils, Rezekne, and Gulbene are below the national average, and mortality rates among the working-age population are higher. The fact that a large proportion of the long-term unemployed do not receive unemployment benefits has contributed to deepening poverty. Viesite district is sparsely populated, with large swamps, extensive forests, and many scattered, isolated homesteads. According to 1997 city statistics, Viesite ranked lowest among Latvian cities in terms of employment and demographic trends. A number of enterprises had closed. The majority of the rural population survived on private or leased land and some forestry work.

Riga and Ventspils are relatively more prosperous urban areas where residents have more opportunity to find work. Complaints focused on the difficulty of finding well-paid jobs or work in one's specialty. In smaller towns and villages, unemployed respondents were eager for any work. Respondents in Bauska district, south of Riga and bordering Lithuania, were marginally better off: none had experienced real hunger, they had retained their homes, and they were able to supplement salaries and incomes with a variety of small-scale entrepreneurial activities.

In Liepâja district, the village of Bunka was built around a collective farm, but little infrastructure remained after the farm was liquidated. Respondents depended on subsistence agriculture; alcoholism and depression were widespread. Neighboring Rucava had a more developed infrastructure, and its population was more closely linked with neighboring regions and countries. Many farmers grew cranberries, a profitable crop; others cut reed in Lake Pape and exported it to Denmark. An ornithological park was being developed around the lake to attract tourists.

In Kuldiga district, considered average in terms of economic development, Renda was one of the more developed municipalities, linked by road to Riga, whereas Kabile had poorer infrastructure, with mostly dirt roads. Renda municipality offered more assistance to residents than did Kabile.

The interviews suggested that urban poverty was both more visible and more anonymous. Neighbors did not know each other's living conditions, and few people interested themselves in the nameless beggars or in the people searching through garbage containers. In the countryside poverty was less noticeable. Although there was greater poverty in rural areas, the high price of rent, heat, and electricity was a greater problem in large cities such as Riga, Jelgava, Liepâja, and Daugavpils. Rural respondents relied more on subsistence agriculture and other forms of self-employment.

Material Living Conditions

For many people the cost of monthly communal services equaled or sur-
passed their salaries, and many had accrued significant debts. To keep up
with payments, families increasingly cut back on food, medicine, and
school fees. Some unsuccessful households were evicted and resettled in
substandard housing; others left their apartments voluntarily. Neither
municipalities nor most private landlords were willing to put money into
capital repairs. Apartments were cold and largely uninsulated. Poor-quality
pipes and joints resulted in frequent plumbing problems and interruptions
in water supply. Some respondents had sold much of their furniture. If they
had appliances, they were usually on the verge of breaking down. Television
was the only link to information and to cultural life remaining for many
poor households.

Housing

The households in the sample occupied a range of different types of housing. Apartments ranged from those in municipally owned buildings, with
indoor plumbing, electricity, hot and cold water, and central heating, to
shabby tenements that lacked central heating or gas. Smaller buildings
owned by private landlords and small privately owned houses, usually heated with wood, often lacked indoor plumbing. Residents of apartments still
served by central heating and hot water were faced with monthly bills of 40
to 60 lats, which often exceeded their monthly incomes. In some of the
newer apartment buildings in Jelgava, respondents were unable to regulate
their central heating. In a Livani apartment building the local government
had disconnected the hot water and central heating. This lowered the rent.

Milda, a 51-year-old Latvian woman in Daugavpils, explains that "The
main problem is the high cost of rent and other services. It amounts to
45 to 50 lats a month, but the official salary is only 42.50 lats. One
salary is not enough to pay for the apartment."

Some rural homes had been heated by communal boiler houses belong-
ing to the local collective farm. At the time of the research, virtually everyone had a wood-burning stove. Heating with wood was considerably
cheaper than using electricity. Some respondents obtained wood from relatives who had forests on their land. One had boards, twigs, boxes, old

furniture, and other materials lying in her courtyard to be used for fuel. Still others cut wood illegally from the forests, risking fines if they were caught.

Many houses had outdoor toilets or latrines, and residents had to get their water from a well. Some people were able to pump water in their houses, but others had to carry water. In some cases even cold water had become a problem. In the villages of Pale district, only apartments had indoor running water. Wells were often several hundred meters from the houses. Some residents siphoned water into their homes; in winter, they carried it in cans. The respondents coped with the lack of hot water by washing at the public sauna, "like our fathers' fathers did," going to visit relatives with showers, or heating water at home.

Not all families (particularly in rural areas) had telephones. Those who did were angry at the rising costs and poor service. In municipalities in Pale district, villagers reported that local telephone calls were free. Calls to Riga or other cities could raise a monthly telephone bill to 10 lats. The telephone company cut off service after one month of nonpayment; several Riga respondents reported that their service had been terminated.

Paying for Utilities

The cost of heat and hot water was reckoned according to the number of registered occupants and the apartment's square footage. In Ventspils, in an apartment building with all amenities, a family of 10 occupying a four-room apartment paid 200 lats a month. Families with children often ran up large debts, whereas pensioners were more likely to cut back on heat or food to avoid going into debt.

Tekla, a pensioner of 71 living in Daugavpils, always tries to pay her apartment rent on time, for she hates to be in debt. She was brought up with this attitude and has tried to adhere to it her whole life. A mother of five children in Bauska district spends her resources differently: "I am unemployed and have five children. Do you think we can live without food? I cannot pay anything for the apartment."

People economized in various ways. A Riga interviewer noted that most poor households he visited used only a few lightbulbs in their apartments. Households sometimes heated the entire apartment with the gas oven. (Latvijas Gaz planned to install meters in the near future.) One family reported that their children stayed later at school rather than study at home by candlelight. Rent was cheaper in private houses, and the homes were heated by wood. Most households closed down several rooms during the winter or kept the house relatively cold. Meals were prepared on the wood stove or on a gas stove, using canisters of propane gas. Poor families limited their telephone calls, shared a single telephone line, or cut off their telephone service as a way of economizing. A pensioner in Vescaule municipality let neighbors use her telephone; in return, each household took turns paying the basic rate for a month, and everyone covered their own intercity calls.

Although some poor households allowed debts to accrue, others struggled to pay at least a portion of their housing bill each month as evidence of good faith. Some respondents were threatened with eviction. Others were able to work off their debts. In Pale several residents of Aloja municipality reduced their housing debt by making payments in firewood, which the local council used or passed on to needy families. Households were compelled to live with debt, sometimes even losing track of their debts.

Some respondents had left centrally located, well-served apartments for smaller apartments in the outskirts. Others had been forced to leave apartments they had occupied for many years.

Vera, a 36-year-old teacher, her son, 16, and her daughter, 10, used to live in a two-room apartment with all amenities in Riga. Since Vera is the only wage earner in the family, her salary of 70 to 80 lats cannot cover the 50 lats monthly bill for the apartment together with other living expenses. She began paying 20 lats a month, and within a few years her debt had reached 500 lats. The housing manager refused her requests for an extension and insisted that she vacate the apartment or be evicted. At the end of 1997 the family moved to an apartment consisting of one and a half rooms in a small wood frame house without a bathroom. The apartment is heated with wood and lacks hot water. Because the rooms are small, the family has had to give up some of their furniture.

Some respondents managed to repay housing debts by selling their furniture or other assets. Others got reconnected illegally or used a large magnet to slow down the electric and gas meters, thus saving a few lats a month.

Housing Debt and Eviction

Under a new law, people could be evicted from rented premises when their debts for rent and utilities exceeded 300 lats. In principle, evictees were to be offered cheaper housing. The municipality provided social assistance in the form of housing where residents shared kitchens and bathrooms. But these "social houses" had become dumping grounds for dysfunctional families and individuals.

The Director of the Social Assistance Center in Daugavpils described one such social house:

> A former hostel, the social house has 280 places for single people and the same number for families. The Social Assistance Center houses people who have been unable to keep up with housing payments or to maintain their families, as well as ex-prisoners who lived in Daugavpils before imprisonment. The house lacks both hot water and gas. People have access to electric cooking facilities in shared kitchens, and to showers located on the first floor. Because of the volatile mix of people, the house is guarded around the clock by a regular member of the police, and doors are locked between 11 p.m. and 6 a.m.

About 9,000 Riga families faced possible eviction in the winter of 1998 for nonpayment of housing expenses, according to a Riga City Council member. The courts ordered the eviction of about 1,500 families, many with children, and each month the Riga city courts reviewed another 40 to 60 cases involving housing arrears (*ETA Baltic Economic News*, August 25, 1998). Some respondents found themselves homeless, forced to camp out with friends or live in buildings never intended for human habitation.

> Eduards, now 49 and living in Daugavpils, became unemployed when the municipal transport depot closed in 1993. In 1996 he was evicted from his apartment of 16 years for nonpayment of rent. He now lives in the attic of a building. He has made a makeshift room for himself from cardboard boxes and pieces of boards. Neighbors are aware that he lives there and sometimes give him food.

Patterns of Ownership

Few respondents had privatized their apartments in municipal housing. Some had sold their privatization vouchers because they needed the money for food or medicine; others owed debts for rent and utilities, and apartments could not be privatized until these debts were paid off. Sometimes the residents could not afford the 50-lat fee. Privatization certificates were distributed on the basis of years of occupancy and assessed value; citizens received 15 more certificates than noncitizens. Not everyone received enough to privatize their apartments. Some were obliged to privatize because the municipality had chosen to sell the entire building.

Monika, a 78-year-old woman living in Kurzeme, describes her experience with housing privatization: "All private owners of houses and land had to resurvey and reregister these assets after independence, at considerable expense. I have a feeling that we gave someone a gift. Nothing changed, but I had to spend a lot of money. In order to pay, I had to sell my privatization vouchers."

Victor, 43, and his family live in a Kurzeme apartment building built in an empty field. In spring and autumn the building is surrounded by mud, and water seeps in. The local municipality forced everyone to privatize their apartments because someone had made an offer to buy the building. In order to protect their rights to remain there, the occupants were pressured to use their certificates to privatize.

Residents of privatized buildings hoped that their new landlords would undertake major repairs that had been neglected for 50 years, but pensioners did not have the resources. Living conditions remained poor, but rents could be as low as a few lats a month.

Asja, a retired teacher in Ape, regained half of the house that once belonged to her mother. She lives in one room, without any amenities, since she was not able to pay the 45 lats a month for heat in her previous apartment. She is unhappy that she had to leave that apartment, where she had lived for 35 years. Her new property needs major repairs, but she has no money to pay for them. Some tenants pay a single lat in rent; others pay in kind with a liter of cream, for example. Overall, Asja feels the return of her property has only brought her worries.

Neighborhoods and Communities

Access to transportation varied greatly by region. In some regions transportation had become less accessible to poor people. Service had deteriorated and ticket prices had increased. In Pale villagers complained that only one bus a day linked Pale municipality to the district town of Limbazi. There were rural areas with no public transportation, where the residents lived cut off from schools, medical care, and community events. In Pale residents living on the outskirts of villages, in the forest, said that the unasphalted roads were impassable after rains. "In a big blizzard I am cut off from the world and can only leave the house driving a tank," said one. In a village near the Estonian border, respondents noted that there was no local transportation at all, although long-distance bus service had improved and the fares were reasonable. In another village, residents said that even though transportation had come to a near standstill after independence, in recent years it had been even better than under the Soviets, with regular service provided by numerous Swedish buses.

In some urban districts, respondents emphasized their feeling of complete insecurity. Whereas during Soviet times they had felt comfortable walking around at night, now they were fearful even during the day. In Riga, near the center, and in the Latgale district, vandals had broken windows, forced open mailboxes, covered walls with graffiti, stolen light bulbs from the halls, and destroyed the greenery surrounding apartment buildings. Fights frequently took place near the apartments, and teenage gangs were engaged in mutual reprisals. Respondents reported rapes, car thefts, apartment burglaries, beatings, and personal attacks. No one mentioned the police—only one rape victim had called the police, and she never followed up in person.

Perceptions of crime and safety differed between rural and urban areas and within cities. In the city of Rezekne only 2 of the 18 respondents said they felt safe, and they lived in the center, where streets were well lit and police cars cruised in the evening. Some noted that high-crime areas included those around bars and nightclubs. In the Aluksne region, near the Estonian border, respondents felt that crime was related to young people getting drunk. In a village near the Russian border, a respondent characterized the crime situation as serious. In the Livani region respondents noted that theft of farm animals, bicycles, and mopeds had increased despite the evident attempts of the police to do their job.

Ozoli village in Renda municipality was originally developed to serve workers in the peat industry. Since the closing of the factory, many apartments stand empty. This village is now considered one of the worst places to live. People think of Ozoli as a "criminal place." Valdis, 28, has a large family. The local municipality offered him an apartment in Ozoli. Valdis and his family do not communicate with their neighbors, nor do his children play in the yard, although it is impossible to completely isolate them from their social surroundings. There is no shop nearby, but there are many places where vodka can be purchased at any time.

In towns where most people lived in apartments, building exteriors and stairwells were badly run down, poorly maintained, and vandalized. In rural areas such as Varnava, now part of Viesite region, buildings that had housed the local library, the post office, the collective farm office, and the auditorium were in a state of collapse, contributing to the deterioration of the village as a whole. The apartment buildings that had housed the collective farm workers exhibited increasing disrepair. A certain trend toward differentiation could be observed: high monthly payments and the large penalty fees that accompanied indebtedness were forcing poor people to move into cheaper accommodations on the outskirts of town. In addition, the municipalities housed the homeless in buildings that were in very bad condition or even condemned.

Raisa, 50, a Russian without Latvian citizenship, is an alcoholic who searches for food in garbage containers. She resides in a one-room apartment in Liepâja, near the military harbor. Only about five families still live in the building, which lacks central heating, gas, and even water. Most of the apartments have been demolished, and many lack windows and doors. Residents get their water from a neighboring building. Raisa's apartment is sparsely furnished. Her electricity was disconnected, but a friend reconnected her. She prepares meals on a small electric stove but does not switch on her light in the evening because then everybody could see inside.

Survival Strategies

The collapse of enterprises had left people competing for the few remaining jobs, without the resources or the confidence to move elsewhere in search of employment. In rural areas the dissolution of collective farm enterprises had left behind dense settlements with little access to alternative employment. Urban and rural respondents tried to piece together incomes from a variety of poorly paid salaried jobs in small private companies, shops, restaurants, farms, and rural enterprises; through temporary or seasonal jobs; and through small-scale entrepreneurial activities. They were usually unregistered, and their employers did not pay social taxes. Thus the workers were not entitled to unemployment benefits or pensions.

Self-Employment in Urban Areas

Even though women complained of numerous disadvantages in finding employment, the growing services sector appeared more open to women than to men. In Rezekne there were shops on every street corner. Salespeople earned 40 to 50 lats a month and often worked evenings and weekends. They knew that if they protested, they could easily be replaced.

A 33-year-old shop manager in Atasiene in the Vidzeme region, divorced and with two children, observes that the worst sign of the times is that there is no time to look after the children, or one's health, or to rest. The shop is open seven days a week.

A number of respondents earned money by engaging in small-scale trade. A mother of eight reported that no employer would take her on. She had begun selling cosmetics, then switched to used clothing, which was in high demand in the countryside. She sold door to door but hoped to open her own shop. A disabled respondent used his free train pass to travel to Riga to purchase books in a wholesale shop for his wife to resell in a market stall.

Anda, 42, a biologist by training, works as an accountant for a Swedish cosmetics firm, which employs women as direct salespeople. Her husband, Raitis, 43, is a construction worker. They have three children. Anda distributes cosmetics to supplement her income. She offers the goods to friends, acquaintances, her daughter's teachers, in hairdressing salons, and wherever customers can be found. She earns 5 or 6 lats a month and buys cosmetics for herself at wholesale prices.

Respondents often tried to use their training or experience to find casual work. Educated people gave private lessons. Nurses gave injections and massages to neighbors after work. Kaspars, a musician, earned 10 lats playing at parties. Janis, an unemployed geologist, put his training to use searching for natural water springs or constructing wells. Many female respondents knitted clothes to sell at the local market; others baked on order. Those selling products in large quantities—hand-painted holiday cards and other handicrafts, for example—had to take care to avoid the local police. Able-bodied men looked for skilled construction work as plumbers, welders, or electricians. Renovations were a reasonable source of income at 25 lats per room. They found such work through word of mouth and acquaintances. Skilled workers were vulnerable to extortion by rackets, since many small enterprises were unregistered and did not pay taxes. Local criminals tried to extort protection money. Women worked as cleaners for businesses or wealthy households, sometimes assisted by their oldest children. Others took care of children or looked after pensioners. One respondent in Liepâja earned 45 lats a month taking care of single pensioners.

Some people moved to the countryside to farm, leaving their children in town with relatives to finish school. Others sought work abroad, particularly in Western Europe. A 30-year-old respondent from Zemgale considered himself lucky to find work as a driver in Germany, where he earned 500 lats in just over two months. Although working abroad was lucrative, it also carried risks. Illegal workers had little protection against unsafe working conditions, unscrupulous employers, and unpredictable bankruptcies.

A family of intellectuals in a small town maintains close contact with the husband's family on a farm. Although the wife has regular income as a schoolteacher, they survive thanks to the milk, meat, and vegetables from her in-laws. During the growing season her husband and his brother and sister from Riga help farm.

A common practice was to search for bottles in garbage bins and take them to places that purchased glass for recycling.

Jelena, 72, lives alone in Riga with her dog. After paying 48 lats for communal services and rent, only 10 to 12 lats remain of her monthly pension. Her application for social assistance was rejected because she is not a Latvian citizen, only a permanent resident. Jelena often experiences real hunger. When she walks her dog in the morning, she looks in garbage containers to find bottles. She makes a few lats a month this way. Later in the day, alcoholics and homeless people start looking for bottles. They consider the garbage containers to be their personal property, and they do not tolerate competitors.

Rural Strategies

Few respondents who owned land had the resources to develop it, since they were just as poor as those who rented land. For the poorest respondents there was not a significant difference between cash and subsistence farming.

Biruta and her husband, pensioners living in Lielvarde, have worked hard over the years to build their own house. They used to grow tulips and take them to Leningrad to sell. They have also grown strawberries for the market, but now they find there are not enough buyers to make the endeavor worthwhile.

Laura, 26, and Uldis, 29, and their four children live in the countryside and occupy a two-room apartment in Kurzeme. Uldis works as an electrician in town. They have 3 hectares of land not far from the house, where they grow vegetables and fodder for their animals. They raise hogs, rabbits, geese, and hens, all for their own subsistence, because they cannot find buyers. Cultivating the land, they complain, demands large investments. One must provide for fuel, pay someone to plow and till the land, and buy seeds. Laura estimates that cultivating their 3 hectares requires at least 150 lats a year. They have already started saving for next spring's expenses. The land keeps them where they are; otherwise they would move into town.

Many respondents farmed for a combination of cash and subsistence. They calculated the relative advantage of selling produce or retaining it for their own use. A respondent in Ventspils region found it more profitable to sell her apples and berries, as well as what she collected in the forest, than to preserve it for her own use. A teacher in Bauska raised rabbits to sell, in addition to growing vegetables and picking berries and mushrooms. Even people who lived in apartment buildings often raised animals. People combined numerous small jobs with subsistence farming.

Yuris and Indra keep animals and cultivate 2 hectares of land with equipment Yuris has managed to put together from different parts. He borrowed money from a former employer to buy a used car for 450 lats. He drives his disabled child to a special kindergarten and drives his neighbor to work; his neighbor pays him the equivalent of bus fare.

Respondents bought only the most essential items, usually at a market, where groceries were cheaper. Residents of Riga sometimes had access to land through parents or relatives and cultivated it on weekends, although profits were offset by the cost of gasoline.

Inga, 40, and Aleksandrs, 38, live with their four children in a three-room apartment in suburban Riga without any conveniences. Inga works part-time as a teacher, but Aleksandrs is unemployed after trying to earn money abroad. They have a plot of 100 square meters where they grow vegetables and flowers, and this year a friend offered them 1.5 hectares of land 28 kilometers from their home, where they can raise food for their own subsistence: potatoes, carrots, beets, and cabbage. In exchange, they help their friend with her garden in autumn. They have 8 hens, which provide the family with eggs, and they have bought an additional 18 chickens, 14 for eggs and 4 that they will raise for meat. They have a small shed for the chickens, which the children take care of. Inga does most of the work on the land.

Many respondents, whether they lived in the cities, small towns, or rural areas, reported earning extra income picking berries, mushrooms, and various medicinal plants in the summer, which they sold, sometimes in Riga. One family reported earning 300 lats in a single summer. Many forests were privately owned, but the proprietor's rights were not clearly stated.

Many collective farm workers had become unemployed when the farms dissolved. Lacking their own land, some worked for local farmers performing a variety of tasks: cutting wood, helping with farm animals, repairing buildings, slaughtering livestock, or harvesting crops. Payment ranged from 1.50 to 3 lats a day plus a midday meal. Farm workers might also be paid in food or alcohol, depending on the location. In Pale, for example, a respondent reported a daily rate of 0.50 lat an hour or a measure of potatoes, plus the midday meal. Farmers regularly took on farm hands in summer. Schoolchildren also worked during the summer. In Pale children worked in a factory stacking peat briquettes. Four children from one large family earned 70 lats total. They had found the job easily because it was considered so difficult and poorly paid that the factory always had vacancies.

During the summer Liene, 24, a student in Liepâja, manages to earn about 70 lats and potatoes for the winter, plus free room and board, working for a local farmer. She milks the cow, collects the hay, weeds, and does other tasks.

Farmers complained that they were not always able to find diligent workers for their farms when they needed them.

A farmer in Rucava says, "It is not advantageous to hire workers because I have to pay social tax for them, and people have become lazy in the countryside. In summer it is not easy to find workers. The collective farms spoiled people—they want to get paid and do nothing. They complain but are reluctant to start something themselves. They would rather accept humanitarian aid than work."

Near Varnava people found seasonal employment in the local tree nursery, where they earned up to 50 lats a month. In forested regions men earned money cutting lumber for local sawmills. This was short-term, sporadic work for which they received 1 or 2 lats a day. Although forestry provided potential employment for men, it took resources to find work.

The chairman of a municipality in Cesu district describes the forestry industry there: "There are six sawmills in this municipality. Men work in the sawmills, in two shifts, or in the forests. The average age of workers is 17 to 22 years. These young people are not protected against industrial accidents. They are paid in cash, and their employers do not pay the social tax. They never completed basic education but consider it unnecessary to continue learning because they can make 100 lats a month."

Victor, in Kuldiga district, finds odd jobs cleaning up forest areas where trees have been felled. He was unable to afford the 90 lats for training in the use of a chain saw.

A respondent from Daugavpils, without work for five years, earns money doing casual jobs. He lives near a development of private homes. In the spring he helps by splitting wood, transporting manure, repairing greenhouses, and doing other odd jobs. He is paid with a meal and a bottle of schnapps. Occasionally his customers pay him 1 to 3 lats. Others pay in food. Sometimes there is a chance to make a little extra cash by glazing a new roof for a greenhouse or digging up a garden.

Coping Strategies

A great deal of assistance, in the form of money, agricultural products, other goods, different services, and favors, flowed between relatives, and especially nuclear family members: husband and wife, grandparents, parents, and children, or adult siblings. Assistance was in the form of gifts or exchanges, without expectation of precise repayment. A large part of this flow consisted of farm produce that rural inhabitants supplied to their town or city relatives, often in exchange for labor. In many neighborhoods where people had lived in one place for many years, neighbors also helped out with babysitting, or with agricultural tasks such as weeding and gathering hay.

Janis, 30, and Valentina, 38, and their two children live in a village. Their most regular guests are Valentina's parents, who live in Riga and work at the market. Each month they give Janis and Valentina a sum of money that exceeds Janis's monthly income. Thus the family's budget amounts to 130 lats a month.

Pensioners were frequently a mainstay of their children. In families with unemployed adults, an elderly parent's pension sometimes provided a major portion of the household income. Some pensioners supported adult children who were alcoholics, or economized on their own spending to save money for grandchildren's school expenses. Families sometimes split up in response to labor market demands. A father might move to Riga, where the economy was livelier and work more accessible. Couples moved to rural areas to find work in farming or forestry, leaving children with grandparents in the city to continue their education.

Many households sold the possessions they had acquired during their years of employment in the Soviet era. Others sold their privatization certificates. Some respondents sold blood to local hospitals or pawned gold jewelry for cash. Many respondents bought their clothing in secondhand stores or in humanitarian-run shops. Others bought clothes in Lithuania, where they said everything was half what it cost in Latvia. Families with many children devoted most of their resources to purchasing food, while going into debt for their rent. Pensioners prioritized by paying the rent first, then spending the rest on medicines and groceries. They bought the cheapest groceries from the market; they disconnected their refrigerators; they no longer watched television, to save on electricity and avoid the monthly payment; they did not buy clothing or shoes.

Elizabete, 74, and Viktors, 70, have no close family members to help them. They try to economize to get by. Velta, 81, reports that she spends 5 lats a month on food and the rest on housing costs (30 lats during heating season). She watches 30 minutes of news each evening but goes to visit neighbors if she wants to see movies on television.

Some families supplemented their meager incomes through theft. They took items from their workplace that they could use, barter, or sell. Someone who worked at a bakery would bring home flour, milk, and eggs to barter with neighbors for other products or services. In Vescaule pagast (*pagast* is Latvian for "municipality"), a single mother of five acknowledged that her children had been committing petty thefts from cellars and gardens to get food.

Some female respondents cohabited with men who provided them with goods, or performed jobs that entailed sexual services. The single mother of an eight-year-old child lived with a butcher for her own survival and to feed the child. He provided her with meat and sausages. She also worked as an erotic masseuse in Riga for a regular salary. People thought of prostitution as "semilegal." Knowing it was illegal, those who engaged in it were reluctant to report violence or other forms of abuse by their clients.

Some old people registered younger people as residents in their apartment or house so there would be someone to help them with household chores and gardening. The young registrants were then entitled to inherit the home after the owner's death.

Searching for Employment

Respondents searched for jobs by responding to newspaper advertisements, registering with the National Employment Service (NES) and following up on job referrals, and even paying private employment agencies. Many respondents felt that the only reliable way to find employment, even a cleaning job, was through personal connections. In rural areas, where social relationships were more public, the role of jobs as a "benefit" to be distributed was even more apparent.

Respondents highlighted being female, age, and disability as particular obstacles to finding work. Women reported being refused jobs because they were too old (over 35, or even 30 in some cases) or had young children. A staff member of the Daugavpils Social Assistance Center cited a job advertisement placed by the telephone company for a "young, pretty worker, well-built, with long legs."

Dace, 42, living in Liepāja, was refused the opportunity to attend a bookkeeping course for the unemployed because preference was given to younger women. A year ago the Metalurgs factory advertised for women who could work as managers. It was well-paid work for which she was qualified. Dace applied, and the factory was on the verge of hiring her until they saw in her internal passport that she has five children. Dace knows that mothers have a very hard time finding work.

It was especially difficult for men and women close to retirement age to find work.

The father of a large family in Malta municipality became unemployed two years before reaching pensionable age. He laments, "I had long years of service behind me. If I had been working for those two years I would have had a large pension, but I remained unemployed."

Jekaterina, 54, worked 35 years as a kindergarten teacher. Last year there was a staff reduction and she was let go. She was very upset at losing her job because she had hoped to work there until retirement. She applied to work in a hospital as a hospital orderly. The head of personnel told her they have a waiting list of young, strong people and that she is simply too old.

Those with medical problems or disabilities had a much harder time finding employment.

Since 1992, Vjaceslavs, 38, has been classified as "second group disabled" on the basis of having epilepsy. After colleagues became aware of his disability, his employer sent him to a doctor for an examination and then fired him. Since then he has not been able to find work, since no one wants to employ someone suffering from epilepsy. He now receives a disability pension of 42 lats a month.

Some respondents believed that unemployment in Latvia affected citizens and noncitizens equally. Others claimed they had been refused employment as non-Latvians. According to a representative of the Organization for Security and Cooperation in Europe, there were few non-Latvians in the public sector, and the law prohibited them from working as pharmacists or lawyers, in security services, or for the airlines. Russians dominated the business sector by about a four-to-one margin. Some Russian respondents were planning to leave the country, since they could no longer work in their field. In industrial districts such as Livani, Latvian respondents claimed that Russians had an advantage because they had maintained their contacts "from the factory times."

Lack of proficiency in Latvian limited the chances of non-Latvian speakers to find work, but many non-Latvians did speak Latvian, and conversely, even some Latvians did not speak adequate Latvian. The language examination was not as difficult as people feared: the basic grade required knowledge of only 1,000 words. Many respondents admitted they had tried to purchase the certificates or have a Latvian-speaking friend take the examination for them.

Galina, 49, is Russian, a noncitizen living in Liepâja. Her insufficient knowledge of Latvian kept her from getting a job as a nurse, which requires a second-level proficiency. She started to read Latvian newspapers and listen to Latvian news on television. She took two courses, the first for 10 lats, and the second for 15 lats. She nonetheless failed the exam and started taking private lessons. Eventually she passed the second level. The State Employment Service sent her to a job interview at a hospital, which needed someone to prepare medicines. During the interview, conducted in Latvian, Galina answered incorrectly and was informed that her knowledge of the language was not sufficient for the job. The whole exchange happened so quickly that Galina still does not know what her mistake was.

Many respondents said that the unemployed lacked the funds to keep themselves attractive for the labor market. In the rare event that someone decided to hire a stranger, even a farmhand, the employer would prefer the person to look neat, attractive, and strong. The unemployed were often unable to maintain their appearance because they had no money to invest in medical and dental care or clothing, or even decent food.

A single mother of three, seeking employment through the want ads, says, "As soon as they look at me, old, hungry, toothless, and three children listed in my passport. . . . I am not yet 40, but already I have no teeth."

Unemployed respondents were pessimistic about moving where there were more jobs. They were often responsible for parents who lived in poverty; if they moved, their parents would be left quite alone. Sometimes villages were no longer connected by regular bus or train transport to nearby towns.

Gundars, a father of six, obtained work in a sawmill 50 kilometers from his home in Kuldiga district. Although the pay was reasonable at 50 lats a month, he ended up quitting when he found that transportation, plus the cost of meals on the job, was eating up too much of his salary.

It was not uncommon for firms and shops to hire someone for a week's trial, without pay, and then fire them only to hire someone else under the same conditions. Sometimes employers fired employees after longer periods without paying their back wages. Most people did not realize that without a contract they had no protection. Employees did not try to seek justice through official channels.

Felicija, a retired Belarussian, 56 and living in Daugavpils, found a job through friends, washing dishes at a private cafe. She receives 30 lats a month and gets paid regularly "in an envelope," but does not have a contract. She understands her employer could fire her the next day if she displeases him.

Most respondents pieced together income from poorly paid jobs in the private sector, temporary or seasonal work, unregistered home enterprises, social assistance, and sale of assets. Poor people accepted poorly paid public works jobs to offset housing costs. Even those with full-time jobs felt vulnerable. Most of them lacked contracts; they knew they could be fired at a moment's notice, pressured to work extra hours, or denied benefits. They were also aware that, since their employers often failed to register them or pay social tax, they would not receive pensions or unemployment compensation.

Social Protection

Social assistance, even in small amounts, was often a critical component of monthly household incomes. Pensions were generally paid regularly and on time; in rural areas they were often the only reliable source of income. Government assistance and social transfers were provided by the National Employment Service, the national government (state-funded pensions and benefits), and the municipalities (subsidies and one-time-only payments).

The National Employment Service

There are offices of the NES in all regions of Latvia. Respondents registered with the NES to receive unemployment benefits, employment offers, or direct employment in public works; to qualify for training courses and grants; and to ensure that they would receive their pensions. Many respondents expressed a very negative attitude toward the NES: they distrusted its staff and considered it one more state institution that was unable to provide real assistance. Respondents had very little information about their rights, about recent changes in labor legislation, or about existing opportunities.

Lolita, 54, and Ivans, 57, live 9 kilometers from a village in an old forestry house. They used to work at a collective farm, where they made a reasonable living. The collective farm was liquidated in 1992, and they had to vacate their house because the former owner had reclaimed it. They now survive on what they grow in their own garden, various temporary jobs Ivans finds, and what Lolita can gather from the forest and sell. They live on potatoes; last winter they had no bread at all. Neither has applied to the NES; they live 40 kilometers from the municipal center of the region, and Lolita has been told there are no jobs for people her age.

To qualify for unemployment benefits and pensions, a person must have worked 9 of the previous 12 months, and the employer must have paid the social tax. Many people worked after losing their formal employment, but unofficial work did not entitle them to benefits. According to the director of the Malta district NES office, 60.5 percent of people who had registered as unemployed could not receive benefits or qualify for employment in public works because their most recent employer did not pay their social tax.

Volodja, 48, and his wife Larisa, 47, a nurse, live in Riga with their two children. Larisa explains that they used to be well off. The main breadwinner, Volodja, can no longer work. He was diagnosed with stomach cancer in June 1997. After the operation Volodja was categorized as "second group" disabled (a Soviet-era classification, which categorized disability according to three levels of severity). When he applied for the disability pension, he learned that his employer had not paid the social tax for the last five years. Larisa asked the employer to pay retroactively, but to no avail. Volodja receives only a social pension of 25 lats a month.

A number of respondents, particularly in Russian-speaking areas such as Daugavpils, complained that they had not been able to register with the NES because they did not know Latvian. Indeed, by law, registrants who had not graduated from a Latvian-language school were required to provide a certificate of proficiency in Latvian. The Council of Ministers ruled that this requirement should be dropped as of May 15, 1998.

Respondents expressed skepticism about finding work through the NES because work was generally found through contacts. The NES had few jobs to offer, and those it did offer usually involved poorly paid work not in line with the applicant's education and qualifications. Female respondents complained that the NES had very few job vacancies for women.

A few unemployed respondents were reluctant to embark on retraining; those who were willing reported serious difficulties. According to NES staff in Liepâja, one-third of those registered as unemployed—about 1,000 to 1,500 people—requested training courses, but only 347 received training in 1997. About half of them found employment. Similar problems were reported in other regions. In Viesite only 36 people had completed courses in the past five years.

Nationally Funded Social Transfers

Respondents noted that pensions and child benefits were paid regularly and on time. Some found, however, that their pensions had not accumulated as expected because employers had failed to pay taxes for them. Although families complained about the low amount of child benefits, they were the only form of assistance that arrived without interruption, for citizens and noncitizens alike. For families in which one or both parents were unemployed, child benefits made up a substantial portion of household income. Pensioners voiced considerable bitterness over their small pensions. They also expressed anger that pensions were practically the same for those who had worked hard their whole lives as for "drunkards" who had never worked at all. Having looked forward to a secure old age, they instead found themselves "standing at a broken trough."

Municipal Social Assistance Services

Municipalities offered a range of programs, including one-time payments for unforeseen expenses, free school lunches, and rent and heat subsidies. During the previous few years support from the state, which supplied part of the social budget, had shrunk. Municipalities differed considerably in the amount available for social assistance, the kinds of programs they funded, and the way they defined eligibility.

To qualify for social assistance services, applicants filled out a declaration of their monthly income. They were eligible if their monthly income per capita was less than 75 percent of the "crisis minimum." In some municipalities a family income under 45 lats a month was considered impoverished; in wealthier communities such as Ventspils, 60 lats was the cutoff. In some municipalities social assistance staff called on the disabled to determine their needs for assistance. Elsewhere, applicants came frequently to the social assistance offices.

Vita, 22, lives in Jurmala. She is second group disabled. She describes
applying for her low-income status as sheer agony. She had to stand in
line on the stairs because there was nowhere to sit. As a disabled person, she felt she was not up to this task.

Neighboring municipalities offered different amounts and kinds of assistance. Renda pagast in Kuldiga district paid 10 lats to each pupil at the
beginning of the school year and covered half the cost of school lunches for
families on their rolls; Kabile pagast paid 5 to 10 lats per pupil but only
sometimes paid for lunches. Both provided one-time payments for essential
surgery. Renda pagast paid maternity allowances and contributed toward
the rent and heating for families with children under three; in Kabile pagast
a mother's maternity allowance of 25 lats was applied to her rent debt, not
paid in cash. Pale residents reported that the local social assistance office
gave food assistance to poor families in the form of vouchers, which could
not be exchanged for alcohol or cigarettes, so that people would not "drink
the money away."

Whereas respondents knew their rights to state-funded benefits, they
reported great uncertainty regarding their rights to municipal assistance
because of the great autonomy that these municipal offices enjoyed. A number of urban respondents did not even know where the social assistance
office was located. In a few municipalities respondents received information
on available assistance from the social assistance staff. Because procedures
were often unclear and appeared arbitrary, people reacted with suspicion and
distrust; rumors about misallocation of funds or inappropriate grants were
rife. Applicants in Riga experienced rudeness and condescension. In Livani
respondents felt that local officials were doing their best to distribute assistance fairly and that local staff treated them with respect. Likewise, respondents in Ventspils found the staff there to be "understanding" and "polite."

Many respondents found asking for help from government institutions
to be demeaning and perceived it as a form of begging. As one respondent
explained, "As long as we are not going hungry, I will not ask for assistance."
Even respondents who appeared badly in need of assistance explained they
had not applied because they felt others were even worse off than they. Usually these respondents were people with a higher education, or families
where both parents worked but received very low salaries.

A Riga respondent says, "If you go and ask for help in those social
offices, they say, 'If you have [grown] children, let them take care of

you.' A neighbor who lives with her unemployed son was shouted at by the staff that her situation was her own fault, since she had not managed to bring up a good son."

Standards and procedures differed among municipalities and often depended on the individual judgment of staff. As a result, applicants often felt that the difference between successful and unsuccessful applicants was a matter of individual persistence or the ability to gain the attention of municipal authorities. Unsuccessful applicants were bitter that people with alcohol problems were more likely to receive assistance, whereas those with more pride gave up after one refusal. No applicant admitted to receiving assistance based on personal ties, as opposed to neediness.

Olga, 44, is an unemployed single mother of five children from Daugavpils. She has four children under 18, and another son, 20, is a student living at home. They live in a three-room apartment. Olga applied for assistance from the social assistance service, but the amount she was awarded was too small. She applied to the mayor of Daugavpils and wrote to the Latvian parliament, explaining her situation. She feels it was her persistence and her appeal to the higher authorities that helped her gain more social assistance. Now she is paid the entire monthly bill for communal services and an additional 40 lats a month for other expenses.

Some respondents said that social workers had rejected their requests for assistance because of their attitude toward families with many children. Some pensioners complained that social assistance workers had refused to consider their case if a family member was registered as living with them. Social assistance staff often failed to take into account whether this person actually lived there or gave their elderly relative assistance.

Leonija, 55, now lives with her oldest daughter, 34, who has five children ranging in age from 2 to 12. Once a hard worker, her son-in-law had begun drinking heavily and finally committed suicide. Last year, when Leonija applied to the municipality for assistance, she was told, "It is necessary to plan for children. But some people just make children and then ask for help. What should we do about it?" Leonija says that she will no longer humiliate herself by begging for help, recalling that "Communist times were bad, but I did not have problems raising my children."

Ilze, 40, unemployed and divorced, is raising three sons, 11, 12, and 17. She receives 40 lats a month in child support, and her eldest son earns 100 lats a month working nights at a sawmill. When she applied to the municipality, the social worker asked her angrily, "Why did you have so many children?"

Milda's daughter rents a room in a neighboring town where she has found work. But because her daughter is registered in Milda's apartment, Milda, 61, is ineligible for housing subsidies.

Municipalities provided limited employment in public works, cleaning, maintaining, and repairing public areas and facilities. The payments were usually applied directly to rent and utilities arrears. In Liepâja people could work off their debts at the rate of 3 lats a day; from October 1997 through March 1998, 875 people performed public works. Some respondents expressed considerable embarrassment that acquaintances who did not know that they had "fallen so low" might see them doing this work.

Dace, 40, Janis, 42, and their five children, 5 to 18, have lived in their three-room apartment in Kurzeme for 14 years. They have accrued a debt of 795 lats. Dace is now working this sum off. She is limited to 58 days, which will only reduce the debt by 175 lats. The work is often dirty and unpleasant, but she would be glad for more.

The municipal social assistance service provided support for families with children. Since the economic crisis, many families had collapsed. The government did not have laws compelling deserting parents to pay child support. Children of unemployed parents or of a single-parent household were entitled to basic benefits; the death of a parent entitled children to special benefits. Foster parents received allowances for child care. Ironically, respondents pointed out, it was the need for assistance that often forced parents to give up their children to foster care.

Mara, a mother of six living in Liepâja, reports that her municipality is assisting her to arrange for a neighbor to become the guardian of one of her children. As a foster parent, the neighbor will receive payments to which Mara herself is not entitled. She is hoping her neighbor will use the payments to buy all the necessary items for her child to start the school year.

For many poor families, free school lunches were very important. Whether free lunches were offered to a given family depended on the budget of the municipality and on the attitude of individual social service employees toward that family. In some municipalities soup was free, but the parents were required to pay for the main dish. In rural areas some families had to contribute produce to the school. Some parents put in days of work at the school. A working mother in Aloja district complained that working 12 days per child would be impossible for her. Some parents would have liked to have free lunches for their children, but they felt ashamed to be "begging." This attitude was common among people in the larger cities who had some higher education but badly paid jobs. Some parents in Riga complained that children who received free lunches were served at a separate table, received poorer-quality food, and felt humiliated when the other children claimed they were eating "from other peoples' money."

Inga, an agricultural economist living in Riga, was unemployed for two years before she found her present job teaching math. She has four children. When she requested free lunches for her school-aged children, she was required to work for 100 hours cleaning the street in front of the school where she now teaches.

Nongovernmental Organizations

Relatively few respondents had received assistance from NGOs. Those who had tended to live in large towns or cities and were already receiving assistance from the municipality. In many cases the municipality took on the task of distributing humanitarian aid. Some respondents expressed suspicion that municipality staff had skimmed off the best part of the shipment for themselves and their friends. None of the respondents made such claims regarding the NGOs themselves. Overall, people had very positive attitudes toward NGOs and foreign organizations; they did not expect regular or long-term assistance from them. Fewer people had received assistance from religious organizations. People who did not belong to any congregation did not ask religious organizations for assistance, nor did regular members report asking their church for assistance. Respondents did receive help from a local Catholic parish and from an Orthodox-run soup kitchen in Riga.

Health Care and Nutrition

Poverty and poor health were often interconnected. In some cases a serious accident or illness pushed a family over the edge into poverty. All respondents reported some health problems. Since most medical care must be paid for, respondents tended to delay visiting a doctor, preferring to treat themselves if possible or seek advice from friends. This was particularly the case with chronic illnesses. When discussing medical care and health, our respondents raised the following concerns: the cost of health care, the poor quality of public medical services, the lack of preventive care, the inability to maintain good nutrition, the health implications of alcoholism and smoking, and the impact of poverty on mental health.

Access to Health Care

Respondents visited a doctor for a preventive examination only when it was required for employment. Some doctors dropped requests for payment when the patient was a small child or when the family was visibly very needy. In other cases they were sympathetic but still demanded their 5 lats. Some pensioners felt that in Soviet times doctors sought to cure patients. Now they tried to ensure that the patient returned frequently.

Although people were entitled to a variety of discounts for medical treatment, many were unaware of their rights. According to an interview with a health expert from the Swedish International Development Cooperation Agency in Riga, Latvians were entitled to a tax exemption if they had particularly high medical fees. Poor people got no benefit from this exemption, however, because they do not pay taxes.

A respondent remembered painfully the humiliation she felt when asking for assistance after the complicated birth of her last child. Her husband was out of work. When she was discharged from the hospital she owed more than 20 lats, which was all the savings the family had. The hospital told them that by law they were entitled to a refund from the municipality, and they were given a receipt. A few days later, the respondent went to the municipality, but the employee on duty threw her receipt at her, refusing to handle it on the grounds that "you have paid it yourself."

Few of the families had purchased health insurance, and then only for family members who were due to have an operation or needed long-term treatment. Reasons given for not purchasing insurance were the high cost and the chaos they saw in the health system. Health insurance covered payment for medical services in most cases. When respondents thought they might have to go to the hospital, they bought insurance and waited the requisite 10 days before seeking treatment. Not everyone could afford insurance; it was especially costly for large families. Price increases in health insurance in 1998 led some pensioners to cancel their insurance.

Many respondents were unable to obtain free treatment for ostensibly free procedures such as cancer treatment or surgery. Whether or not treatment was free, most respondents made additional payments to doctors, nurses, and other medical personnel ranging from gifts of chocolate and cognac to hundreds of lats in cash, a significant hardship for unemployed families. When someone was hospitalized, it was necessary to pay hospital personnel to ensure they received attention.

In 1997 Volodja, 48 and living in Riga, was diagnosed with stomach cancer. The head of a hospital department, a well-known surgeon, agreed to operate for 300 lats; officially, cancer treatment and surgery in Latvia are free. Volodja's wife Larisa paid the fee from their savings. During his month in intensive care, Larisa spent another 200 lats on gifts for doctors and unofficial payments to nurses and orderlies. Larisa claims that everything had to be paid for, or else no one would come near her husband. The treatment depleted the family's savings.

Although in some cases disabled people received free or discounted medical help and medicines, the privation of recent years had affected their health. Opportunities to receive physiotherapy or spend time at a sanatorium had diminished because of lack of funds.

Ausma and her husband Guntis live with their four children in a village in Cesis district, about 100 kilometers from Riga. Guntis does casual labor while his wife takes care of the house and children. Their five-year-old son is seriously disabled and requires expensive medicine. The doctors repeatedly forget that the child is entitled to free medication, and it is embarrassing to keep reminding them. Sometimes the medicine is not available at the local pharmacy, and Ausma must go to Riga for it. According to the legislation, however, she is only entitled to free medicine at the regional pharmacies.

Most respondents concurred that the quality of medical services had improved since independence, at least in urban areas. Doctors were more qualified, and foreign medical literature, equipment, instruments, and medication were more available. At the same time, however, medical services were more expensive, indeed out of reach for many low-income families. In some rural areas medical services had deteriorated. Hospitals had closed in a number of small towns, such as Ape and Ligatne, where people had grown to trust the local doctors. Respondents criticized the qualifications of small-town medical personnel and their poor facilities. Some rural residents trusted the paramedics at the local clinics, who understood local conditions and often gave medicine and advice for free or at low cost, but they were not competent to treat serious illnesses. Increasingly, rural people resorted to folk healers, with mixed success.

Health Problems

All respondents had problems with dental care. Many could not pay for preventive treatment. In some cases that led to real suffering and loss of teeth. One 42-year-old mother of 15-year-old twins put off visiting the dentist, who charged 5 to 10 lats for a visit. That meant going without food for a week just to repair one tooth. Older respondents needed dentures, which cost as much as 100 lats. Female respondents were acutely aware of the condition of their teeth. Young women who were missing teeth tried to cover their mouths when laughing. In some cases pregnancies had worsened the condition of their teeth. Several women recounted that potential employers had pointed out their teeth as a reason not to hire them. Poor appearance prevented women from finding work, but if they did not work, they could not afford to repair their teeth.

Most families tried to limit the number of children they had. Some respondents felt it was important to set aside money for contraceptives, but there was little information on the most suitable kinds, especially for rural women. Pregnant women usually took advantage of both prenatal and postnatal leave and received all the provided benefits. Most of the women who had given birth during recent years had received free prenatal examinations by a gynecologist. Urban women were generally pleased to be able to choose their doctor and satisfied with the examinations. Rural women had to travel considerably farther for their prenatal examinations. They found the travel tiring and expensive. Urban women were generally satisfied with the maternity hospitals, although they said that if they could pay more, they would receive better service and individual attention.

In rural areas women went to the closest regional town to give birth, because the small rural hospitals were either closed or badly equipped, and the doctors were less qualified. Women brought all the necessary supplies with them, including cheesecloth, cotton, and even dishes for their meals.

Both parents and medical professionals thought the health of children from poor families was deteriorating. Medical professionals saw increased medical problems among elementary school children, ranging from spinal deformation to bad teeth, mainly as a result of poor nutrition. They were convinced that the children were smaller than they should be for their ages. A pediatrician in the Cesis region noted that 70 percent of infants there had been born with some health problem, and 30 percent had developmental disorders, in some cases related to parental alcoholism or smoking. In such families pregnant women registered late for prenatal care and did not consult a doctor in cases of complications. Infants in these families often suffered from infections because of poor care. Respondents also noted that diseases that had disappeared during the Soviet era had now reappeared.

The typical diet had changed a great deal in recent years. Consumption of meat, the traditional mainstay, had decreased, along with bread and bread products. For many respondents the main food items were potatoes and other vegetables. Cheap fish also featured in the diet. Winter was a difficult period, when supplies ran short. In urban areas, or among people without land or relatives who could supply them, respondents tried to buy the cheapest possible food. One respondent bought discounted bread and fried it in pork fat, as "a cheap way to feel full." Few could afford to buy fruit, even at the markets. Although few respondents complained of outright hunger, many said that they often ate less than they would have liked. Many tried to maintain their family's health by providing the children with nutritious food. Some parents, especially those who were aware that their diet was poor, bought vitamins for their children. Otherwise they relied on fresh and preserved fruit from their own gardens, ate a lot of garlic and onions, drank herb teas, and ate honey.

Respondents frequently reported feelings of depression, ranging from mild apathy to an obsession with suicide. People complained about the enforced idleness of unemployment: "I am a healthy person who stares out the window and doesn't know what to do out of idleness." Most attributed severe depression to the unremitting economic pressure, constant insomnia, and worry. A few respondents reported suicides by men in their own families or among close acquaintances.

Rita, 34, and her son, 5, live in a good four-room apartment. Rita is university educated but has been unemployed since May 1997. For the last few years, Rita has suffered from depression. Everything gets on her nerves, nothing tastes good, she cannot sleep, and she has become indifferent to social life and politics. She always feels tired and angry, because she cannot see a way out of her present situation. She has thought of suicide, but concern for her child keeps her alive.

Antonina, 52, works as a cleaner for a soap company in Riga. Her husband Grigorijs, 56, was an unemployed mechanic. Both are Russian. They have a daughter, 23, a son, 14, and a granddaughter, 4. Antonina is the only provider in the family. During the interview she describes how Grigorijs had been looking for work for a year and was deeply upset at his failure. Lately he had begun returning drunk, which triggered family arguments. Sometime after this interview, the interviewer learned that, a week after the interview, Antonina had found Grigorijs in the kitchen, where he had hanged himself.

Alcoholism was one of the most striking leitmotifs of the household interviews. It came up in the context of unemployment (as cause and consequence), road and work-related accidents, the death of a breadwinner, indigence and homelessness, and dysfunctional families and neglected children. Alcoholism affected women as well as men and was said to characterize whole villages where employment possibilities had vanished.

Latvians have long been heavy consumers of alcohol. A 1997 World Health Organization report based on 1990 statistics gathered in 50 countries showed that Latvia had the highest number of deaths of any country from alcohol-related toxicity and trauma; only Russia had higher figures for alcohol-related psychosis. In a recent six-year period, 25,000 people died from alcohol-related causes (Birzulis 1998).

Alcohol production and legal consumption started decreasing in 1985 as a result of Soviet President Mikhail Gorbachev's anti-alcohol campaign. At the time of the research there were noticeable class preferences: the middle class tended toward wine, the working class preferred hard alcohol (*krutka*, or "moonshine"), and the drinking culture among young people tended toward beer and hard alcohol. Sales hours were unrestricted, and there was no minimum age except in the new supermarkets. Alcohol was sold in grocery stores and kiosks, and homemade alcohol was widely available for sale, around the clock. Illegal manufacture of homemade alcohol was a major source of income for some. Low-quality alcohol was being smuggled into Latvia, and alcohol prices remained relatively low. The old "sobering-up stations" no longer functioned.

Many interviews suggested that people who may have used alcohol to a limited extent now found employers much less tolerant. Whether they were fired for consuming alcohol at work or had lost jobs during mass redundancies, respondents reported that difficulties in finding new employment and the whole nexus of financial and family stress led to increased alcohol use. This made them even less employable. It reduced their ability to earn money, even in the informal sector, and led to housing debt and eventual eviction, homelessness, and ever-deeper alcoholism. Serious alcoholics were sometimes unable to work even for brief periods. In Rezekne, where the social assistance services offered free meals to children of the unemployed in exchange for 10 days of work arranged by the local government, parents were often unable to meet even such modest requirements because of heavy alcohol use.

A number of female respondents had lost spouses to alcohol-related car accidents; a former policeman in Kabile pagast observed that alcohol contributed to many road accidents. Although both men and women abused alcohol, respondents of both sexes felt that women were psychologically more resilient during periods of economic stress, since their identity depended more on domestic and child-related tasks. Men crumbled more easily and responded to economic difficulties by retreating into alcoholism and suicidal depression. Perhaps a third of the respondents mentioned alcohol-related problems in their household and felt that alcoholism had increased dramatically. They never spoke about their own alcohol use as a cause of poverty but instead focused on related reasons such as job loss. The predominance of alcoholism in the sample was even more striking given the slight bias among interviewers, social assistance staff, and other referrals toward selecting the "deserving poor."

Education

During the 50 years of socialism, two parallel school systems—Latvian and Russian—had existed side by side. Every Latvian graduate mastered spoken and written Russian, but not all Russian graduates mastered Latvian. In 1991 schooling was changed to 12 years regardless of the language of instruction. Children under seven attended kindergarten, education was compulsory through ninth grade or age 15, and there were three options for secondary education: general (three years), vocational, or specialized (three to five years).

At the time of the research, the use of Latvian, the state language, was a crucial issue for the educational system. Language instruction was a particular worry for parents who did not speak Latvian. In the Daugavpils region many Russian-speaking families sent their children to schools where Latvian was the language of instruction. Latvian-speaking families complained that the Latvian children lost time while teachers explained things to the Russian children. In kindergartens with few Latvians, the whole group would start speaking Russian.

Respondents were eager to speak about youth and education, and the theme of education was usually discussed by all members of a household. Educated respondents saw education as a value in itself as well as an essential means to getting a good job and earning money. Such parents were prepared to sell family assets in order to provide a higher education for their children. Other families, especially where the children were neglected and often did not go to school at all, did not see education as necessary.

Svetlana, 38, is an unemployed Russian living in Daugavpils. Her son Misha is formally enrolled at school, but he frequently skips classes and takes part in petty thefts. Svetlana reports that Misha's teachers used to lecture her, but they gave up when they saw nothing was being achieved. Svetlana herself doubts the value of education: "Why does he need school anyway? It is just money wasted on books. He can read and write well." Noting that one of her friends, an unemployed alcoholic, has a higher education, she concludes, "If you're too smart, you won't get a job."

School-Related Costs

For many poor families school-related costs were a major part of the family budget. In Pale a respondent reported paying 80 lats to send her son off to school in September. Money was needed for shoes and clothing, school equipment such as book bags, and bus, tram, or trolley transportation. For parents with several school-age children, such expenses mounted up.

Alla goes to Daugavpils Primary School No. 1, where she gets fed three times a day. The school has boarding facilities, and her mother would be happy to have Alla spend her nights there, since the school is located on the city's outskirts and she has to take two trams to get there. The high schools nearby do not provide free meals or other expenses. Alla's school does not demand any school fees, but at the end of the year they expect parents to donate 3 lats to cover school repairs, and excursions cost 0.30 to 0.50 lat. Alla has been to the children's theater and the circus several times this school year.

Although education remained officially free in state educational institutions, many schools demanded "voluntary" donations for the "school fund." The school director decided how to use this money, for example, to supplement teachers' salaries, to pay for school redecoration, to photocopy teaching materials, or to buy a computer for the school.

In several of the smallest municipalities, schools were provided with textbooks. In the better Riga schools, parents had to purchase all textbooks and exercise books. Parents complained that teachers wanted pupils to purchase the very latest textbooks, at a cost of 2 to 3 lats each. The textbooks used by older children were not necessarily passed on to younger siblings. Some parents who could not afford to buy the textbooks made photocopies for their children.

Access and Quality

Many families expressed concern about reduced opportunities for a good education now that schools were requesting fees to cover operating costs, for "optional" classes in a foreign language, or to participate in sports or school excursions. Poor parents feared that tuition for higher education would be introduced. This would prevent their children from studying at a university or other institution of higher education.

Guntis, 23, studying at a Riga trade school, is unable to combine work with classes, and his parents cannot afford to help him buy the necessary tools and equipment. Iveta, who has several children, will choose the best student among them to study at the vocational high school; the others must stay to work on the farm in Aloja municipality.

Arturs, 34, has a higher education and is the father of 11-year-old twins. He sends his children to the best schools in Riga. He is very proud that his children passed the entrance exams for an elite middle school. He admits that these schools are expensive but declines to reveal the sums involved. "You should not talk much about your poverty in these schools," he says, "or they will advise you to send your children to cheaper schools."

Truancy

Some children had dropped out of the educational system. School directors, inspectors of children's rights, and other school authorities suggested that although school expenses can present a formidable burden, nonattendance was more common among children in families where one or both parents were alcoholics and had no more than an elementary school education, often in schools for those with serious learning disabilities. Some children did not attend school because their families were not registered in the municipality where they lived. The children might have moved in with relatives, or the family might have been evicted from their home for nonpayment of rent and forced to move into premises not considered habitable. When local authorities became aware of truancy, they tried to have the children admitted into special boarding schools, or *internats*, where they would also receive clothing, decent food, and responsible attention.

Truants and dropouts fell into several categories: children of single-parent families with financial difficulties who were concerned about education; children of poorly educated parents who had learning difficulties; children kept at home because they were chronically sick; children of alcoholics; children and grandchildren who moved to new municipalities where they were not registered; and children born in rural areas who had never been registered and who remained entirely outside the system. Another important group were those who had reached the age of 15 and were no longer obliged to attend school. This included children with learning and discipline problems, who had repeated grades so often that they were older than their peers. Usually these teenagers already had problems at home.

In Daugavpils a school was opened for Russian-speaking teenagers who have dropped out of school. The authorities do not have sufficient funds to open a similar school for Latvian speakers. For one poor Latvian family in Daugavpils there are no other options. Private teachers would be too expensive. The mother hopes her son will live and work in the countryside, since "You don't need to be too smart there!"

Many problem teenagers left school before acquiring a basic education or professional training. Under existing labor legislation they could not be employed or apply for unemployment benefits. As some older respondents noted, a whole generation could be lost to criminal and gang activities, alcoholism, and prostitution. The Ministry of Education was discussing the idea of extending the age of compulsory education.

Conclusions

Although poverty in Latvia cuts across all boundaries, the study identified household types whose situation put them at greater risk of becoming and remaining poor. In such households, all the members were at greater risk of prolonged poverty. They included large families with three or more children; single-parent families; households or families with unemployed persons, especially those nearing pension age; households with one or more seriously ill, disabled, or alcoholic member; households without close family networks; and rural households in general. The experience of poverty was affected by where people lived, both the immediate neighborhood and the larger community. Thus in Daugavpils, Jelgava, Liepâja, and Valmiera, where huge factories had been built during the Soviet period, closure of these enterprises resulted in concentrated unemployment among a highly specialized labor force. The Latgale region, with official unemployment eight times that in Riga, was characterized by extensive joblessness. Life expectancy, education levels, level of employment, and average incomes in the rural districts around Jekabpils, Daugavpils, Rezekne, and Gulbene were lower than the national average, while mortality rates, particularly from parasitic infections, respiratory illnesses, and accidents in the working-age population, were higher. In rural areas, liquidation of the former agricultural collectives left a decayed infrastructure and vandalized facilities. As an official from the Daugavpils Social Assistance Center bitterly observed, "Don't let anyone tell me that prosperity in Latvia is developing; maybe a deputy or someone who makes large investments says that. We feel that there are two states in Latvia: Riga and the rest of the country."

Overall, the findings of this study demonstrate that poverty is a multidimensional phenomenon—much more than an inability to afford goods and services. In Latvia, poverty affected the ability of people to participate effectively in economic, political, social, and cultural life. Our respondents experienced exclusion in many forms: physical exclusion, when they sold and left long-inhabited apartments in pleasant parts of town to move to cheaper homes in urban peripheries; intellectual and material exclusion, as poor children faced a narrower choice of schools and reduced prospects for good employment; and social and cultural exclusion, as the poor withdrew from social and cultural life. As people became progressively more isolated, they cut themselves off from information and assistance that could help them overcome their problems and reenter society. Households at risk of long-term poverty faced general exclusion from society, unless the many dimensions of poverty could be tackled together.

References

Aasland. A., K. Knudsen, D. Kutsar, and I. Trapenciere, eds. 1997. *The Baltic Countries Revisited: Living Conditions and Comparative Challenges: The NORBALT Living Conditions Project*. FAFO Report 188. Oslo: FAFO.

Birzulis, Philip. 1998. "Staggering under the Influence of Alcohol." *Baltic Times* (February 19-25).

United Nations Development Programme. 1997. *Latvia: Human Development Report*. Riga.

World Bank. 1999. *Latvia Poverty Assessment*. Washington, D.C.

Young and old alike wait in line for daily
announcements about social assistance
and pension payments that are already
six months in arrears.
Photo by Kathleen Kuehnast

✳

Conclusion:
Toward a Better
Understanding of the
Multiple Dimensions of Poverty in
Transition Societies

T he studies reported in this volume used qualitative methods to identify, describe, and analyze various dimensions of poverty in eight countries of the former Soviet Union. Since 1993, when the first study was carried out, conditions have changed substantially, and countries are developing along different trajectories. Their shared Soviet history remains important for understanding how poverty has developed, but their differing economic endowments, policies, and unique sociopolitical contexts play a more important role in explaining poverty today than was the case several years ago. In particular, significant differences have surfaced between those countries that have experienced real economic growth and those, such as Georgia, Moldova, and the Kyrgyz Republic, that have not managed to carve out a new and sustainable economy.

An increasing concern is that poverty is not necessarily declining, even in countries where GDP has grown. Indeed, given the striking inequalities that have developed since 1991, it will take many years of strong, consistent growth to meaningfully reduce poverty, and even longer to address the pockets of extreme poverty and exclusion in many of these post-Soviet societies. For the very poorest, access to quality education, health care, and other essential services has seriously diminished and has already begun to erode the potential of an entire generation of children and youth who will soon enter the labor market. Some regions where subsidies have been drastically cut find their poor suffering from extreme isolation. Few are able to risk uprooting their households for uncertain opportunities elsewhere. Women, minorities, the disabled, and other groups once protected by policies of full employment and the availability of social supports now face much harsher competition in the constrained job environment.

For all of these countries, reform of institutions, from the civil service to the judiciary, is a priority. There is ample evidence that effective governance is central to laying the foundation for economic growth and poverty reduction. A critical aspect of reform, however, is addressing the institutional barriers that impede efforts to reduce poverty. Among the many questions that still need attention are the following: How can countries reduce the overt and less visible forms of discrimination that limit poor people's access to good education, health care, social assistance, or legal advice? In what ways can the poor influence their local elected officials to address their priorities? In societies where access to resources of all kinds is extensively regulated by informal connections and transactions, how can the poor access these influential networks?

Because widespread poverty is such a new phenomenon for most of the countries covered in this volume, governments have not yet developed sophisticated tools for monitoring poverty in its many complex manifestations. To the extent such tools exist, they usually consist of strictly quantitative instruments such as household expenditure surveys. Qualitative assessments of the kind presented in this volume have mostly been supported by external donors and international NGOs. More recently, however, the social scientists who typically use these qualitative research tools are being brought into the investigative process. In the last few years many local research institutes and NGOs have received training in qualitative methods, but government structures are as yet not necessarily equipped for or interested in integrating these methods. As a result, policymakers' access to these informative data remains limited. For those countries serious about addressing poverty, introducing qualitative and quantitative mechanisms for monitoring living standards is an important priority, and institutionalizing the findings into policy formulation even more so.

In the future, studies of poverty need to carefully examine mechanisms of social exclusion and the resulting plight of specific social groups and isolated regions. These issues call for highly focused studies that take into account the multidimensional nature of poverty and reveal how informal networks operate, how hidden discrimination and prejudice contribute to exclusion, and how sociocultural factors and changing values affect policy. It goes without saying that studying poverty is not enough. Integrating the understanding provided by these analyses into policies and ensuring that institutional changes work in favor of the poor present an enormous challenge for all these countries.

Research Teams

The fieldwork for the 12 studies presented in this volume was managed and carried out by local research teams that were familiar with local traditions and issues. The team members were familiar not only with local traditions and practices, but also the daily problems and concerns of the interviewees. In addition, the teams were ethnically and linguistically diverse—to ensure that respondents were interviewed in their preferred language.

Armenia (*Chapter 6*)
Iulia Antonyan, Vahagn Barseghian, Artak Dabaghian, Mekhitar Gabrielyan, Mihran Galstyan, Araik Gulyan, Zaruhi Hambartsumyan, Harutyun Marutyan, Rafik Nahapetyan, Anna Khachatryan, Gayane Khachatryan, Hranush Kharatyan, Hairapet Margaryan, Shushan Manucharyan, Nikol Margaryan, Susanna Melikyan, Hamlet Petrosyan, Svetlana Poghosyan, Repsime Pikichian, Hamlet Sarkisyan, Gayane Shagoyan, Aghasi Tatevosyan, Hovhannes Vartanyan, Bella Zakaryan

Armenia (*Chapter 7*)
Hranush Kharatyan, Araik Gulyan, Harutyun Marutyan, Hamlet Petrosyan, Repsime Pikichian, Hamlet Sarkisyan, Gayane Shagoyan, Linda Gamova

Armenia (*Education and Health Sectors, Chapter 7, Appendix A*)
Araik Gulyan, Harutyun Marutyan, Hamlet Petrosyan, Svetlana Poghosyan, Repsime Pikichian, Hamlet Sarkisyan, Gayane Shagoyan, Svetlana Topchyan, Anahit Gasparyan, Eva Avakyan, Aghasi Tatevosyan, Migran Galstyan, Ruzanna Stepanyan, Nune Mangasaryan

Armenia (*Paros Social Asssitance Program, Chapter 7, Appendix B*)
Hranush Kharatyan, Araik Gulyan, Harutyun Marutyan, Hamlet Petrosyan, Svetlana Poghosyan, Repsime Pikichian, Hamlet Sarkisyan, Gayane Shagoyan

Crimea (*Chapter 10*)
Project managed by Timur Dagji. Gulnar Velieva, Nariman Zenedinov, Elvira Seotova, Hairi Dagji, Akim Kadirov, Akhtem Zaytulpaev, Seyar Tchilingirov, Elena Burtseva

Georgia (*Chapter 8*)
Project managed by Guram Svanidze and his deputy, Aleksandr Nalbandov. Amara Abashidze, T. Abuladze, Vera Adelkhanova, Gvantsa Ananiashvili, Tamuna Bikashvili, N. Bikoeva, Gocha Divada, Y. Dzitstsoiti, Diana Driayeva, D. Dzhavakhishvili, Marina Gegelashvili, Nino Gvakharia, A. Imedashvili, Marina Imerlishvili, Gezam Ismailova, Vahagn Khachvankian, Tinatin Lekishvili, Nana Kokielova, T. Lekishvili, Nino Makhashvili, Fati Megrelishvili, Georgii Meskhidze, Aelita Mikhailova, Maya Mindiashvili, Mariam Mumladze, Inga Kochieva, Kostya Kochiev, Khatuna Nachkebia, Koba Noniashvili, Yurii Pogosyan, Nato Sardzhveladze, Nino Tsiklauri, Tamara Tsilosani, A. Tskhovrebov, Nino Tukhashvili, and Aleksei Yermolov

Kyrgyz Republic (*Chapter 3*)
Rakhat Achilova, Gulnara Bakieva, Daniyar Dubanaev, Mariam Edilova, Sagyn Imailova, Medet Sultanbaev

Latvia (*Chapter 12*)
Ilze Trapenciere, Maruta Pranka, Tania Lace, Mara Zirnite, Ritma Rungule, Dace Bormane, Oleg Kopeikin, Rita Samusa, Ineta Pikshe, Dmitri Trubetskoj, Evija Eglite, Lita Hofmane, Liene Puishe, Lolita Baramskova, Aigars Ikarts, Anita Birmbauma, S. Revele, L. Liepkalne, Ruta Andersone, Andris Andersons, Janina Krutskikh, Kristine Grigale

Moldova (*Chapter 11*)
Team coordinated by Nina Cainarean; project managed by Vasile Munteanu.Oleg Bivol, Valeriu Burca, Nina Cainarean, Igor Cobilteanu, Victor Manolii, Maria Mamaliga, Sergiu Martinenco, Mihai Mereacre, Gheorghe Munteanu, Sergiu Munteanu, Tatiana Munteanu, Svetlana Ojog, Felicia Parasca, Lucia Pogor, Olga Savenco, Gheorghe Tofan, Irina Tretiacova, and Elena Triboi

Tajikistan (*Chapter 4*)
Maksuda Sanginova, Rasul Khudoidov, Davlatomo Yusufbekova, Shavkia Pachadjanova, Abdugafor Khaidorov, Muhabbat Kamilov, Dustmurod Khasonov, Kamol Atoev, Djema Yusupdjanova, Firuz Saidov

Ukraine (*Chapter 9*)
Project managed by Vladimir Paniotto (KIIS). Natalia Kharchenko, Elena Popov, Alexandr Podorozhnii. Regional team leaders: Valentina Pavlenko (Kharkiv), Tamara Polskaia (Crimea), Igor Iaroshenko, Elena Martiakova, and Alexandr Podorozhnii

Uzbekistan (*Chapter 5*)
Project managed by Arustan Joldasov and Aysholpan Dauletbaeva. Sanim Joldasova, Nigar Julamanova, Khasan Nazarov, Sadriddin Edgorov, Ulugbek Duvlaiev

Index